*Oracle Press*™

Predictive Analytics Using Oracle Data Miner

About the Author

Brendan Tierney, Oracle ACE director, is an independent consultant (Oralytics) and lectures on data mining and advanced databases at the Dublin Institute of Technology in Ireland. In addition to being Oracle ACE director, he has extensive experience working in the areas of data mining, data warehousing, data architecture, and database design. Brendan has worked on projects in Ireland, the United Kingdom, Belgium, and the United States, and has been working with the Oracle Database and tools since 1992. Brendan is the editor of the *UKOUG Oracle Scene* magazine and deputy chair of the *OUG Ireland BI SIG*. Brendan is a regular speaker at conferences across Europe and the United States, including Oracle Open World. In addition, Brendan has written technical articles for *OTN, Oracle Scene, IOUG SELECT Journal*, and *ODTUG Technical Journal*.

You can follow Brendan on this blog and on Twitter:

Blog: www.oralytics.com/
Twitter: @brendantierney

About the Technical Editor

Paul McElroy lives and works in Dublin, Ireland. He has 19 years' experience in the financial services sector, specializing in the provision of full lifecycle information technology (IT) services for mainly bespoke software solutions in the areas of debt management, treasury management, fund management, and claims management. He currently works as the IT business services manager for a leading Irish government organization that specializes in debt and treasury management and leads a team of 30 people from various IT lifecycle disciplines including project management, business analysis, solution delivery (Oracle and Microsoft), software testing, and quality assurance. Paul is Prince2-certified. His primary degree is a BSc in information systems from Trinity College in Dublin. Paul also holds an MBA from University College Dublin's Smurfit Business School. He has developed skills in the strategy and practice of employing leading-edge technology solutions in support of business process automation and related activities. He also provides an analytical support base to senior business managers in regard to design, redesign, and optimization of key business processes.

Oracle Press™

Predictive Analytics Using Oracle Data Miner: Develop & Use Data Mining Models in Oracle Data Miner, SQL & PL/SQL

Brendan Tierney

New York   Chicago   San Francisco
Athens   London   Madrid   Mexico City
Milan   New Delhi   Singapore   Sydney   Toronto

Library of Congress Cataloging-in-Publication Data

Tierney, Brendan, 1970- author.
  Predictive analytics using Oracle data miner : develop & use data mining models in Oracle Data Miner, SQL & PL/SQL / Brendan Tierney.
      pages   cm
  ISBN 978-0-07-182167-4 (paperback)
  1. Data mining.   2. Forecasting—Statistical methods   3. Oracle (Computer file)   I. Title.
  QA76.9.D343T54   2014
  006.3'12—dc23
                                                                            2014018977

McGraw-Hill Education books are available at special quantity discounts to use as premiums and sales promotions, or for use in corporate training programs. To contact a representative, please visit the Contact Us pages at www.mhprofessional.com.

Predictive Analytics Using Oracle Data Miner: Develop & Use Data Mining Models in Oracle Data Miner, SQL & PL/SQL

1 2 3 4 5 6 7 8 9 0   QFR QFR   10 9 8 7 6 5 4

ISBN   978-0-07-182167-4
MHID   0-07-182167-8

Sponsoring Editor Paul Carlstroem	**Technical Editor** Paul McElroy	**Production Supervisor** James Kussow
Editorial Supervisor Patty Mon	**Copy Editor** Andy Saff	**Composition** Cenveo Publisher Services
Project Manager Hardik Popli, Cenveo® Publisher Services	**Proofreader** Paul Tyler	**Illustration** Cenveo Publisher Services
Acquisitions Coordinator Amanda Russell	**Indexer** James Minkin	**Art Director, Cover** Jeff Weeks

Contents at a Glance

PART IV
Migration and Implementations

Contents

PART I
Oracle Data Miner Fundamentals

PART IV
Migration and Implementations

Acknowledgments

Many thanks go to Paul Carlstroem, Amanda Russell, and the production team at McGraw-Hill Education who made this book possible. There were many people involved in the production of this book, and while I may not know all your names, I thank you for your work.

Special thanks to Charlie Berger (product manager for Oracle Data Mining and Oracle Advanced Analytics), Mark Kelly, Mark Hornick, Marat Spivak, Denny Wong, and all the members of the Oracle Data Mining team at Oracle who have supported my work over the years.

Thanks also to Paul McElroy, who did a great job of carefully performing the technical edit of this book. Your work ensures that what I say in the book makes sense, the examples work, and all the code examples work too.

The biggest personal thanks I owe to Grace, Daniel, and Eleanor, who through their constant encouragement and support made this book possible, by giving me the time and space to work on it, and the necessary encouraging words when they were most needed. This book would not have happened without you.

Introduction

Oracle data mining implements a variety of data mining algorithms inside the Oracle relational database. These implementations are integrated into the Oracle Database kernel, and operate natively on data stored in the relational database tables. This eliminates the need for extraction or transfer of data into stand-alone mining/analytic servers, thus greatly improving performance, efficiency, and speed.

With the significant increase of interest in data mining, predictive analytics, data science, and Big Data, Oracle has seen a steady increase in interest in advanced analytics. *Predictive Analytics Using Oracle Data Miner* focuses on Oracle Data Miner (ODM), which is part of the Advanced Analytics Option. With this book, you will perform the following tasks:

- Installing and setting up Oracle Data Mining on your Oracle 11.2*g* and 12*c* Databases

- Setting up and configuring the Oracle Data Miner Repository

- Creating your initial project and workflow

- Using the Oracle Data Miner workflow to create a variety of data mining models using association rules, classification, clustering, regression, and anomaly detection

- Understanding the in-database PL/SQL, SQL, and Data Dictionary views that are available to you

- Knowing how to use the PL/SQL packages to create new data mining models, allowing your database developers to automate the process

- Being able to explore the models produced by ODM to evaluate their efficiency and to select a model to use on your new data

- Knowing how to use PL/SQL and SQL to apply a data mining model to new data in real time or in batch mode

- Understanding how your Oracle database administrator (DBA) can migrate your data mining models from one schema to another or from one database to another

- Knowing how your BI analysts and BI developers can integrate your data mining models in their dashboards and other BI analytics

- Understanding how your DBA can use the Parallel Query option to run your ODM models on large volumes of data

- Being able to use the new 12c in-database Predictive Queries to build and use transient data mining models

This book contains 20 chapters.

Chapter 1: Oracle Data Miner

In this chapter, you'll get the background to Oracle Data Miner, its various parts, its history, and the main benefits of using this in-database data mining feature. Oracle Data Miner and Oracle data mining are part of the Oracle Advanced Analytics Option, along with Oracle R Enterprise.

Chapter 2: The Predictive Model Lifecycle

Lots of people have performed data mining projects before you, and just as in any other IT environment, there are some lifecycles to help you perform your project in an efficient manner. For predictive analytics, there are a few different lifecycles. This chapter briefly explains these lifecycles as well as the main predictive analytics lifecycle of the CRISP-DM.

Chapter 3: How to Install, Set Up, and Get Started

With most tools, there are some steps that need to be performed to get up and running with a tool or product. Similarly, for the Oracle Data Miner tool, there are a few steps that you need to perform to install an ODM Repository and configure your schemas to use the repository.

Chapter 4: ODM Menus, Projects, and Workflows

In this chapter, you learn about the various menus that are part of the Oracle Data Miner tool and how to go about creating your ODM projects and ODM workflows. The chapter also gives examples of how you can export and import your workflows from other schemas. A summary is given of the ODM nodes that are available under the Components Workflow Editor.

Chapter 5: Exploring Your Data

When you start any data mining project, one of the initial tasks includes exploring the data to see whether you can start to build up a picture of what is happening in your data. In this chapter, you look as some examples of how to do this using the various graphical and statistical features that are available in the Oracle Data Miner tool.

Chapter 6: Data Preparation

The Oracle Data Miner tool comes with a number of built-in nodes for preparing your data for data mining. These include aggregating data, filtering columns, filtering attributes, using advanced algorithms to select appropriate attributes, joining a number of data nodes, sampling your data, and more. Examples are given on how to use each of these nodes.

Chapter 7: Association Rule Analysis

Association rule analysis is commonly used to analyze transactions to see whether there are linkages between certain products. In this chapter, examples illustrate how to use the Oracle Data Miner workflow to create an association rule analysis model and how to explore the results to identify the frequent itemsets that will be of most interest to you.

Chapter 8: Classification

Classification can be used in a wide variety of data mining projects. Examples are given showing you how to develop a workflow using the various classification models, evaluate these models, and manipulate the model generation. Examples illustrate each step of the process and show how to apply the classification models to new data.

Chapter 9: Clustering

In this chapter, examples are given showing how to create a cluster model using the workflow-based tool. These examples demonstrate how you can explore the generated clusters to try to attach some business meaning to them. The examples also show how to apply a cluster model to new data.

Chapter 10: Regression

Using the Oracle Data Miner workflow tool, you can create a regression model and apply it to new data without writing a line of code. This chapter takes you through the steps involved in creating a workflow for your regression model.

Chapter 11: Anomaly Detection

Anomaly detection involves a two-stage process using a single-class Support Vector Machine. The examples given in this chapter guide you through the different steps involved in creating the anomaly detection workflow.

Chapter 12: The ODM Data Dictionary, SQL, and PL/SQL Packages

The Oracle Database comes with a variety of features for data mining. In this chapter, you look at the different Data Dictionary views that are available, see how these can be used, and discover the kind of information you can find in them. SQL comes with 15 scoring functions. These functions allow you to apply an ODM model on data in a real-time mode. Finally, there are a number of PL/SQL packages. A summary of these packages is given and there are plenty of examples of their usage in the various chapters in this part of the book.

Chapter 13: Data Preparation

The data preparation phase of any data mining project can consume a significant amount of time. During this phase, the database developer is required to use his or her extensive skills in PL/SQL and SQL to prepare the data. This chapter shows examples of some of the main data preparation tasks and demonstrates how you can perform them using the PL/SQL and SQL functions. These tasks include handling missing data, aggregating data, sampling data, generating histograms, and binning, using the in-database automatic data transformations and also using the `DBMS_DATA_MINING_TRANSFORM` PL/SQL package. The final part of the chapter looks at how you can embed some of these transformations into your ODM model.

Chapter 14: Association Rule Analysis

Association rule analysis is a very popular data mining technique that is used to find associations of items that are grouped together. Typical scenarios include Market Basket Analysis, financial product analysis, telecommunications, and more. This chapter looks at how you can build an association rules model and then query the model to find the itemsets that have been identified by the association rules model.

Chapter 15: Classification

Classification is perhaps the most common data mining technique that is in use. In this chapter, examples are given to show everyone from the data scientist to the database developer how to build and apply a classification model using the PL/SQL and SQL functions.

Chapter 16: Clustering

Clustering can be used in many application domains, and in this chapter examples demonstrate how to build a clustering model using the in-database clustering algorithms. The examples given in this chapter illustrate the steps required to build and apply a cluster model using the PL/SQL and SQL functions.

Chapter 17: Regression

Using the in-database PL/SQL and SQL functions, you learn how to build a regression model and then apply it to new data. As with all the data mining techniques, the models can be applied in batch mode and real-time modes, and examples are given to illustrate all the steps involved for regression.

Chapter 18: Anomaly Detection

Anomaly detection enables you to find anomalous case records in your data sets. In this chapter, you discover the steps needed to build and apply an anomaly detection model using the PL/SQL and SQL functions.

Chapter 19: How to Migrate Your ODM Models

Typically you will develop your ODM models in your development or test environments. At some point, you will want to move the ODM models to your production environments. This chapter takes you through the steps required to migrate your ODM workflows and your ODM models. Examples are given on how to use the built-in features of the ODM graphical user interface (GUI) tool and how to use the PL/SQL procedures to export your models and then to import them into your new database.

Chapter 20: Implementation-Related Topics

This chapter covers some additional topics that may be of use to you. These topics cover some of the typical implementation issues that you will encounter and suggest how you can use Oracle Data Mining to address them. The topics include how to add ODM models to your OBIEE dashboards, how to run your ODM models in parallel, and how to use the new Oracle 12c feature called Predictive Queries.

Intended Audience

This book is suitable for the following readers:

- Data analysts looking to use the in-database data mining features

- Data scientists who are looking to use the workflow data mining tool, SQL, and PL/SQL

- Database developers who will be implementing the in-database data mining models in their applications using SQL and PL/SQL

- Database administrators who will be administrating the schema and databases

- BI developers who want to embed the data mining models in their dashboards

- Technical managers or consultants who want to learn how to perform in-database data mining

Although the book covers the main in-database data mining features and the algorithms that they implement, the book does not cover the theory behind these data mining techniques and algorithms. If you do want to learn what happens under the hood of these algorithms, then there are lots of books and courses available where you can learn these details.

I hope you enjoy this book!

PART I

Oracle Data Miner Fundamentals

CHAPTER
1

Oracle Data Miner

U nderstanding your data and gaining an insight into the behavior of your data (and hence your customers) have been goals that companies have been chasing for some time now. Myriad technology solutions are available to help you achieve this understanding and insight, but just as you accomplish those goals, some new challenge emerges to force you to look at new alternatives. One alternative that can help you achieve this deep insight into the behavior of your data is technology that makes use of some of the advanced machine learning algorithms. These are commonly referred to as data mining algorithms.

The data mining algorithms can be considered a process of searching data to discover patterns and trends that may have some competitive element to it. The following is one of the most commonly used definitions of *data mining*:

> *Data mining is the non-trivial extraction of previously unknown and potentially useful information from data.*

Data mining can be used in addition to the traditional data analytics and statistical approaches to discover patterns in the data that could not be discovered using traditional approaches. The patterns that are discovered need to be evaluated to access their usefulness, as the results from data mining are not always useful.

One particular aspect of a data mining or a data science project that differentiates itself from other analytical or statistical approaches is that a very clear project problem definition is given. This allows the data mining or data science project to be directed by the problem definition to determine what needs to be achieved, and hence the desired outcome can be clearly defined. This approach can then be used to identify what tools and techniques are most appropriate to achieve these goals.

Data mining algorithms are implementations of advanced statistical and machine learning algorithms that can be used in certain problems on certain types of data to identify patterns that exist in the data. The data miner or data scientist can then examine these patterns to determine what they mean and relate them back to the business and the problem definition.

As the volume of data that companies capture and store in their database or the use of other data storage techniques increases, the need for these data mining techniques increases. This is particularly the case as companies begin to use data from their Big Data sources and as data increasingly becomes available from new data sources, such as the data that will become available with the Internet of Things (IOTs). Data mining will play a significant and central role with the management, integration, and delivery of decisions through the company.

Data mining is not a new technology. It has been around for many decades now, but started to become widespread in some industries, such as telecommunications, insurance, and finance, during the 1990s and 2000s. Data mining does not need to have a large volume of data before it can start delivering useful results. Many companies have been able to achieve a competitive advantage by using a data set consisting of a few thousand records.

In-Database Data Mining with Oracle Data Mining

In most typical data mining applications, the data in the database must be extracted from the database, transported to the data mining application server, loaded into the data mining application, and prepared for data mining; the data mining model is then produced and evaluated. This process occurs whenever you want to build a data mining model or to refresh an existing one. As you can imagine, the steps of extracting, transporting, and loading into the data mining application can take a considerable amount of time. As the data volumes in companies are growing at an ever-increasing rate, particularly when we consider the data that is available via Big Data sources, the time required to extract and move your data will become longer and longer. In addition to all of these steps, whenever you want to use the data mining models in a real-time scenario, such as giving a car insurance quote, the Risk Scoring data mining model will need to perform a set of steps similar to those just outlined. This will make the applications run seemingly at a snail's pace. As the volume of data increases, the number of customers increases, and so on, the Risk Scoring data mining model will take longer and longer to run.

But what if you could eliminate most of these steps that involve the movement of data? What if you could do all of this in the database? After all, that is where the data will be!

With in-database data mining, the data mining algorithms are built into the database. You no longer need another application and another server to run the data mining applications. This is what Oracle has done with Oracle Data Mining (ODM). It has taken a suite of data mining algorithms and built them into the kernel of the Oracle Database. A common phrase associated with this is as follows:

> ...*move the algorithms to the data, not the data to the algorithms.*

With in-database data mining, there is no need to extract the data, move the data to the data mining application, and load the data into the data mining application. The data is already there in the database, so there is zero data movement. By eliminating the data movement, you can save a significant amount of computer processing time, as well as the human effort required to set it up and to manage the process. This can result in your data mining projects running in a fraction of the time that the alternative approach requires. Many companies are reporting such success stories. Some examples of these companies are listed in the section "Customer Success Stories" later in this chapter; several of these companies have actually reduced their data mining projects from weeks to minutes. Figure 1-1 illustrates the Oracle in-database advanced analytics proposition.

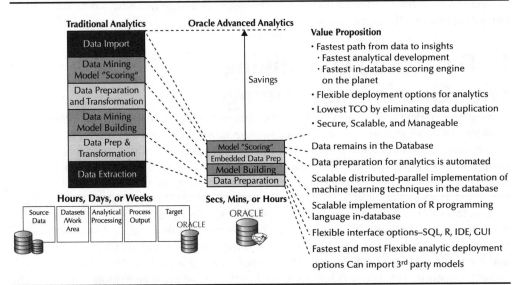

FIGURE 1-1.   *The Oracle in-database advanced analytics proposition*

Data mining within Oracle Database offers many advantages:

■ **No Data Movement**   Most data mining products require that data be exported from a database, converted to a format required by the data mining tool, then loaded into the data mining tool before any database mining can be performed. With Oracle Data Mining, no data movement, data conversion, or loading of the data into another application is needed. This simplifies the entire data mining process, making it less complex and consuming significantly less time. In addition to giving the data scientist more time to work on the defined problem, it also allows the data scientists to work with a larger data set. As companies expand into the Big Data world, having very little or even no data movement can facilitate these projects being completed in a quicker time frame.

■ **Security**   The extensive security features of Oracle Database protect your data. This ensures that you can easily comply with all your data security and audit requirements at company, industry, and regulatory levels. Using and running the data mining algorithms within the Oracle Database require specific database privileges. This allows for full control over who is allowed to perform what activities on your data.

- **Data Preparation and Administration**   Most data must be cleansed, filtered, normalized, sampled, and transformed in various ways before it can be mined. Up to 80 percent of the effort in a data mining project is often devoted to data preparation. Oracle developers have the key skills required to perform these tasks and can utilize the various in-database functionality to prepare the data for data mining, therefore eliminating the need for any external applications for data preparation. This also ensures that your company can easily comply with any data security and traceability requirements.

- **Ease of Data Refresh**   The data mining processes within the Oracle Database already have ready access to data required and can easily produce a refreshed data set with minimum effort. This can allow the real-time scoring of data as it is being captured and can allow for highly efficient updating of your Oracle Data Mining models.

- **Oracle Database Analytics**   The Oracle Database comes with many features for statistical analysis, including many specific data analytics methods that are common in business intelligence and data warehousing. As these features are all embedded in the Oracle Database, the Oracle Data Mining functions can easily utilize these features.

- **Oracle Technology Stack**   You can take advantage of all aspects of Oracle's technology stack to integrate data mining within a larger framework for business intelligence, scientific inquiry, and Big Data analytics.

- **Application Programming Interfaces**   The PL/SQL application programming interface (API) and SQL language operators provide direct access to Oracle Data Mining functionality in Oracle Database.

Oracle Advanced Analytics Option

The Oracle Advanced Analytics option comprises Oracle Data Mining and Oracle R Enterprise. The Oracle Advanced Analytics option is available as an extra license cost option with the Oracle Database Enterprise Edition. By combining the powerful in-database advanced data mining algorithms and the power and flexibility of R, Oracle has provided a set of tools that allows everyone, from the data scientist to the Oracle developer and the database administrator (DBA), to perform advanced analytics on their data to gain a deeper insight into their data as well as to achieve a competitive advantage over their competitors.

The following sections give an overview of the components of the Advanced Analytics option. In a later section, the architecture and the various elements of Oracle Data Mining will be explored.

NOTE
The Oracle Database Advanced Analytics option came into existence when Oracle released Oracle R Enterprise. Oracle Data Mining and Oracle R Enterprise comprise the Oracle Advanced Analytics option.

Oracle Data Mining

Oracle Data Mining contains a suite of advanced data mining algorithms that are embedded in the database that allows you to perform advanced analytics on your data. The data mining algorithms are integrated into the Oracle Database kernel and operate natively on data stored in the tables in the database. This integration removes the need for extraction or transfer of data into stand-alone mining/analytic servers, as is typical with most data mining applications. This can significantly reduce the time frame of data mining projects by requiring nearly no data movement.

In addition to the suite of data mining algorithms, which are listed in Table 1-1, Oracle has a variety of interfaces to enable you to use these algorithms. These interfaces include PL/SQL packages that you can use to build and apply models to new data,

Data Mining Technique	Data Mining Algorithms
Anomaly Detection	One Class Support Vector Machine
Association Rule Analysis	Apriori
Attribute Importance	Minimum Description Length
Classification	Decision Tree Generalized Linear Model Naïve Bayes Support Vector Machine
Clustering	Expectation Maximization K-Means Orthogonal Partitioning Clustering
Feature Extraction	Non-Negative Matrix Factorization Singular Value Decomposition Principal Component Analysis
Regression	Generalized Linear Model Support Vector Machine

TABLE 1-1. *Oracle Data Mining algorithms available in Oracle 12c*

a variety of SQL functions for real-time scoring of data, and the Oracle Data Miner tool that provides a graphical workflow interface for creating your data mining projects.

TIP
Oracle used to provide a set of Java APIs to the in-database data mining algorithms, but these are no longer supported.

TIP
Oracle Data Mining is the term used to describe the in-database data mining algorithms, functions, and procedures. Oracle Data Miner is the graphical workflow tool that comes as part of SQL Developer.

Oracle R Enterprise (ORE)

Oracle R Enterprise (ORE) was introduced in 2011 and enables the open source R statistical programming language and environment to be run on the database server and within the database (see Figure 1-2). Oracle R Enterprise integrates R with the Oracle Database. When Oracle R Enterprise was released, it, along with Oracle Data Mining, was repackaged to form the Oracle Advanced Analytics option.

While analysts interactively analyze data and develop R scripts, the data they will be using will reside in the database. With ORE data scientists can still write their R scripts and analyze the data, but now the data can remain within the Oracle Database. No data has to be downloaded to the data scientists' computers, thus saving a significant amount of time and allowing data scientists to concentrate on solving the business problem at hand. By allowing the R scripts to run in the database, these scripts can utilize the ability of the database to manage the processing of many millions of records in an efficient manner and they can utilize

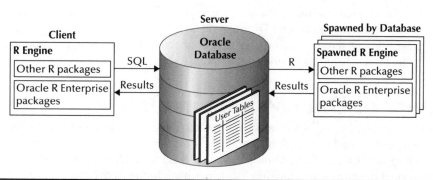

FIGURE 1-2.   *Architecture of Oracle R Enterprise*

other database performance options, including the Parallel option. This capability overcomes many of the limitations of running R on the data scientists' computers. Oracle R Enterprise consists of the following components:

- **Transparency Layer**   The transparency layer is a collection of packages that map R data types to Oracle Database objects and generate SQL transparently in response to R expressions on mapped data types. The transparency layer allows R users to interact directly with database-resident data using R language constructs. This enables R users to work with data too large to fit into the memory of a user's desktop system.

- **Statistics Engine**   This is a collection of statistical functions and procedures corresponding to commonly used statistical libraries. The statistics engine packages execute in Oracle Database.

- **Statistics Extensions**   This supports the R engine execution through the database on the database server. These SQL extensions enable R scripts to be run inside the database.

In addition to Oracle R Enterprise (ORE), Oracle also provides the following:

- **Oracle R Distribution**   This Oracle-supported distribution of open source R is provided as a free download from Oracle and also comes preinstalled on the Oracle Big Data Appliance. Oracle also provides some additional libraries to enhance the performance of certain functions. These libraries include Intel's Math Kernel Library, AMD's Core Math Library, and the Solaris Sun Performance Library.

- **ROracle**   This is an open source R package, maintained by Oracle and enhanced to use the Oracle Call Interface (OCI) libraries to handle database connections, that provides a high-performance, native C-language interface to the Oracle Database.

- **Oracle R Connector for Hadoop**   Oracle provides R users high-performance native access to the Hadoop Distributed File System (HDFS) and MapReduce programming framework. The Oracle R Connector for Hadoop is a component of the Oracle Big Data Connectors software suite.

History of Data Mining in Oracle

Oracle Data Mining has been available in the Oracle Database since Oracle 9*i* R1, but it wasn't until Oracle 9*i* R2 that Oracle Data Mining became an important feature. Originally Oracle Data Mining was called Darwin. Darwin was a data mining product developed by Thinking Machines back in the mid-1990s. Table 1-2

Version	Date	Description
Darwin	Mid-1990s	This product was first developed by Thinking Machines.
Darwin (Oracle)	1999	Oracle purchased Darwin from Thinking Machines in 1999 and continued to distribute Darwin.
		Work began to integrate the data mining algorithms into the next release of the database. At the same time, the Darwin team was renamed Oracle Data Mining. Also during this time, the Oracle Data Mining team developed Oracle Personalization, which was a web-based recommendation product.
Oracle 9*i* R2	May 2002	Although some data mining functionality was released with Oracle 9*i* R1, the main ODM release was with the R2 release of the database, with more algorithms, support for PMML, and automated binning. The API for using ODM consisted of a set of Java APIs and required the installation of an ODM server in the database.
Oracle 10.1*g*	February 2004	This release enhanced the existing algorithms and improved data processing. The `DBMS_DATA_MINING` `PL/SQL` package was introduced as an interface to the algorithms. A new Oracle Data Mining Client (DM4J) based on Oracle JDeveloper components enabled graphical specification of ODM objects and a graphic user interface for interacting with key Java objects and processes in the ODM server.
Oracle 10.2*g*	July 2005	The Decision Tree and One-Class SVM algorithms are added. A revised Java Data Mining (JDM) JSR-73–compliant Java API is provided. The `DMBS_PREDICTIVE_ANALYTICS` PL/SQL package is added. Oracle Spreadsheet Add-In for Predictive Analytics enabled Microsoft Excel users to mine their Oracle Database or Excel data using the automated methodologies provided by `DBMS_PREDICTIVE_ANALYTICS`; the Add-In is distributed on Oracle Technology Network. SQL functions are added that include `PREDICTION` and `PREDICTION_PROBABILITY`, among others.
		The first ODM graphical user interface (GUI) is provided for preparing data, building models, and applying to new data. This was a wizard type of application.

TABLE 1-2. *How Oracle Data Mining Has Evolved Over Time* (continued)

Version	Date	Description
Oracle 11.1*g*	September 2007	This release provided additional improvements in the algorithms with better automated and embedded data transformations. It also added multivariate linear regression and multivariate logistic regression. The Profile procedure was added to the DBMS_PREDICTIVE_ANALYTICS PL/SQL package. Additional SQL functions were added, including PREDICTION_BOUNDS, cost matrix in PREDICTION, and more details in GET_MODEL_DETAILS procedures.
Oracle 11.2*g*	September 2009	Support was added for the importing of external data mining models (linear and binary logistic regression) using PMML. The Java API was deprecated in this release. Support for native transactional data was added for Association Rules. The release also provided some additional small enhancements to the algorithms and the DBMS_DATA_MINING package.
SQL Developer 3	March 2011	SQL Developer 3 came with the first release of the Oracle Data Miner GUI that had the workflow functionality. This gave the user a graphical interface for querying and exploring the data, applying data transformations, building models, and applying models. The graphical workflow environment provided a simple interface for the SQL and PL/SQL data mining functions and procedures.
Oracle 12*c*	June 2013	This release added new and improved Clustering algorithms, new Principal Component Analysis algorithm, GLM models that now supported feature selection and creation, simplified text mining, and more SQL functions that enabled users to view model prediction details. Also added was Predictive Queries (also known as Dynamic Scoring), which allows scoring data dynamically without a predefined model.

TABLE 1-2. *How Oracle Data Mining Has Evolved Over Time*

summarizes the main developments and releases of Darwin and subsequently Oracle Data Mining.

With each subsequent release of the Oracle Database and SQL Developer, Oracle has added greater Oracle Data Mining functionality. Check out the "new features" documentation for each release to see what new features have been added.

Oracle Data Mining Components

Oracle Data Mining is an option in the database. It is fully integrated into the kernel of the database. This means that all the data mining algorithms are built into the database engine, and this allows these algorithms to be easily used in applications by using the SQL and PL/SQL functions and procedures. Any data mining objects created for data mining become first-class objects in the database and can be treated similarly to any other SQL function and other database options. Before you can use Oracle Data Mining, a repository needs to be built that manages all Oracle Data Mining objects and their usage.

Oracle Data Mining Architecture

Although Oracle Data Mining and all its algorithms come prebuilt into the database, you will need to create the Oracle Data Mining Repository before you can start using Oracle Data Miner. SQL scripts come as part of SQL Developer, which allows your database administrator (DBA) to create the ODM Repository in the database. An alternative approach is to allow functionality embedded in the SQL Developer tool to manage the creation of the ODM Repository. The architecture of Oracle Data Mining is illustrated in Figure 1-3.

The enterprise edition of the Oracle Database includes the following database features that support Oracle Data Miner:

- **Oracle Data Mining** A component of the Oracle Advanced Analytics option to Oracle Database Enterprise Edition; Oracle Data Mining provides the model building, testing, and scoring capabilities for Data Miner.

- **Oracle XML DB** This database provides services to manage the Data Miner Repository metadata, such as the details of the workflow specifications.

- **Oracle Scheduler** This component provides the engine for scheduling the Data Miner workflows.

- **Oracle Text** This feature provides services necessary to support Text Mining.

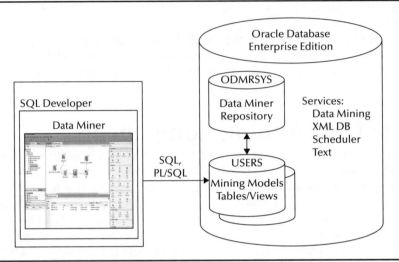

FIGURE 1-3.   *Oracle Data Mining architecture*

Oracle Data Miner GUI Tool

The Oracle Data Miner tool is a component of SQL Developer. The Oracle Data Miner tool is a GUI workflow–based tool that allows everyone from data scientists, data analysts, developers, and DBAs to build quickly and simply data mining workflows for their data and data mining business problem. The Oracle Data Miner workflow tool was first introduced in SQL Developer 3, and with all subsequent releases additional functionality has been added.

The Oracle Data Miner tool (see Figure 1-4) allows you to build workflows by defined nodes that enable you to accomplish the following:

- Explore your data using statistics and various graphical methods

- Build various data transformations that include sampling, various data reduction techniques, create new features, apply complex filtering techniques, and create custom transformations on your data

- Build data mining models using the variety of in-database data mining algorithms

- Apply your data mining models to new data to produce a scored data set that can be acted upon by your business users

- Create and use transient data mining models using Predictive Queries

- Create and apply complex Text Analytics models on your semistructured and unstructured data

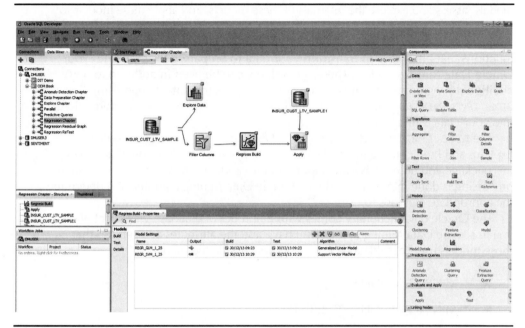

FIGURE 1-4.   *The Oracle Data Miner tool in SQL Developer*

When the time comes to productionize your workflows, full support is provided by the generation of all the required SQL scripts that are needed to run the workflow. These can be easily scheduled in the database to run on a regular basis.

TIP
The second part of this book contains chapters illustrating how you can build workflows for each of the main data mining techniques.

Oracle Data Mining Using SQL and PL/SQL

Data Mining models are database schema objects that perform data mining by applying a model created using one of the in-database data mining algorithms. A number of PL/SQL packages and SQL functions are provided to allow you to define, create, apply, and assess data mining models in the database.

The main PL/SQL package for Oracle Data Mining is called DBMS_DATA_MINING. This package contains all the procedures you will need to create your data mining models, assess and explore the internals of these models, and apply these models to new data.

The DBMS_DATA_MINING_TRANSFORM PL/SQL package contains various functions that allow you to transform your data to prepare it for input into your Oracle Data Mining models. These procedures can be used in addition to any additional programming that is necessary to prepare the data. When using the DBMS_DATA_MINING_TRANSFORM procedures, you can embed their transformations into your Data Mining models.

The DBMS_PREDICTIVE_ANALYTICS PL/SQL package allows you to Profile, Explain, and Predict using the in-database Data Mining functions, but when using this package you do not have any input into the predictive analytics process. All the processing is done internally inside the Oracle Data Mining algorithms to determine the appropriate methods to use.

The Oracle data dictionary comes with a number of database views that allow you to see the Data Mining models you have and the attributes and settings that those models use. These data dictionary views include the following:

- *_MINING_MODELS

- *_MINING_MODEL_ATTRIBUTES

- *_MINING_MODEL_PROPERTIES

where * can be replaced by

- ALL_ This view contains the Oracle Data Mining information that is accessible to the user.

- DBA_ This view displays the Oracle Data Mining information that is accessible to DBA users.

- USER_ This view contains the Oracle Data Mining information that is accessible to the current user.

Oracle has at least 15 SQL functions that that allow you to score data using a data mining model. There are two primary SQL functions that you will use most commonly. These are PREDICTION and PREDICTION_PROBABILITY. The other SQL functions allow you to determine the outcomes of applying a Clustering data mining model; establish predicted features; and define various prediction values such as costs, value bounds, and prediction rules/details.

TIP
Part III of this book will cover the details of how you can use these data dictionary views, PL/SQL packages, and SQL functions. Examples will be given to illustrate how these can be used for different data mining techniques.

Oracle Statistical Functions

All versions of the Oracle Database come with a comprehensive collection of statistical functions built into the database. These statistical functions come standard with the Oracle Database and do not require any additional licences. The database features more than 110 SQL and PL/SQL statistical functions that can be grouped under a variety of headings, as illustrated in Table 1-3.

Ranking Functions

rank, dense_rank, cume_dist, percent_rank, ntile

Window Aggregate Functions
 (moving & cumulative)

Avg, sum, min, max, count, variance, stddev, first_value, last_value

LAG/LEAD Functions

Direct interrow reference using offsets

Reporting Aggregate Functions

Sum, avg, min, max, variance, stddev, count, ratio_to_report

Statistical Aggregates

Correlation, linear regression family, covariance

Linear Regression

Fitting of an ordinary-least-squares regression line to a set of number pairs
Frequently combined with the COVAR_POP, COVAR_SAMP, and CORR functions

Descriptive Statistics

DBMS_STAT_FUNCS: summarizes numerical columns of a table and returns count, min, max, range, mean, median, stats_mode, variance, standard deviation, quantile values, +/- n sigma values, top/bottom 5 values

Correlations

Pearson's correlation coefficients, Spearman's and Kendall's (both nonparametric)

Cross Tabs

Enhanced with % statistics: chi squared, phi coefficient, Cramer's V, contingency coefficient, Cohen's kappa

Hypothesis Testing

Student t-test, F-test, Binomial test, Wilcoxon Signed Ranks test, Chi-square, Mann Whitney test, Kolmogorov-Smirnov test, one-way ANOVA

Distribution Fitting

Kolmogorov-Smirnov test, Anderson-Darling test, Chi-squared test, Normal, Uniform, Weibull, Exponential

---

TABLE 1-3. *Summary of Free Statistical Functions in Oracle*

Some advanced statistical functions were introduced in more recent versions of the database. These functions enable you to perform various statistical analysis using windowing or moving window calculations; these advanced functions include `Pivot`, `Rankings`, `Lead/Lag`, and more. These are particularly useful in data warehousing and some advanced analytics projects.

TIP
If the statistical function you want to use is not included in the Oracle Database but it exists in R, then you can use the R statistical function on your data in the database.

Applications Powered by Oracle Data Mining

Over the past few years, Oracle has been integrating into some of its applications the functionality available in the Oracle Advanced Analytics option. For example, Oracle has integrated Oracle Data Mining into the applications by building data mining models and making these available as features of these applications. The Oracle Data Mining functionality allows the applications to predict turnover, perform what-if analysis, real-time fraud and security analytics, customer churn and segmentation, anomaly detection, customer loyalty analysis, among many other tasks. The following are some of the Oracle applications that have Oracle Advanced Analytics and Oracle Data Mining built into them:

- Oracle Fusion HCM Workforce Predictions

- Oracle Fusion CRM Sales Prediction Engine

- Oracle Spend Classification

- Oracle Sales Prospector

- Oracle Adaptive Access Manager

- Oracle Airline Data Model

- Oracle Communications Data Model

- Oracle Retail Data Model

- Oracle Security Governor for Healthcare

- Oracle Social Network Analysis

Watch out for more applications that will have Oracle Advanced Analytics added to their functionality in the future.

How Are Customers Using Oracle Advanced Analytics

The Oracle Advanced Analytics option has a considerable amount of advanced functionality built into it. This functionality includes the in-database Oracle Data Mining features and the advanced features of Oracle R Enterprise. The typical data mining functionality available in these products can be grouped together, and the following are some examples of the typical application areas for data mining:

- Identify most important factor (Attribute Importance)
- Predict customer behavior (Classification)
- Predict or estimate a value (Regression)
- Find profiles of targeted people or items (Decision Trees)
- Segment a population (Clustering)
- Find fraudulent or "rare events" (Anomaly Detection)
- Determine co-occurring items in a "basket" (Associations)

These typical data mining areas and problems can be applied in a number of industries to gain a deeper insight into their customers, their environments, their processes, and so on. The following are some typical use cases:

- Targeting the right customer with the right offer
- Discovering hidden customer segments
- Finding the most profitable selling opportunities
- Anticipating and preventing customer churn
- Exploiting the full 360 degree customer opportunity
- Providing security and detecting suspicious activity
- Understanding sentiments in customer conversations
- Reducing medical errors and improving quality of health
- Understanding influencers in social networks

Customer Success Stories

Being able to see and understand how other companies have used Oracle Advanced Analytics can help you determine how you can use this option in your company. Oracle Advanced Analytics has a wide customer base spanning many industries and types of projects. Some Oracle Advanced Analytics customers have shared the details of their projects at various conferences and in various publications. The following table lists some of these customers and how they have used Oracle Advanced Analytics.

Customer	How They Used Oracle Advanced Analytics
Turkcell	Turkcell is the largest telecommunications (telco) company in Turkey. It is using Oracle Advanced Analytics and Oracle Data Mining to analyze customer call records with the aim of identifying potential fraudulent calls to their prepaid customers.
Dunnhumby	Dunnhumby is one of the world's largest customer analytics companies. It provides customer insight for some of the largest retail companies in the world. Dunnhumby is using Oracle Data Miner to build many customer loyalty models. The company has succeeded in reducing the total time required on a monthly basis to process data, build models using Oracle Data Miner, and score its customers from weeks to minutes.
Stubhub	Stubhub is a fan-to-fan ticket marketplace. It is using Oracle Advanced Analytics to gain a better insight into the company's customers and their online behavior. By using Oracle Advanced Analytics and the in-database capabilities, Stubhub can produce its advanced analytics in a much shorter time frame.
Oracle Racing	How did Oracle win the America's Cup? The winning team used Oracle Advanced Analytics and Oracle Data Mining to analyze the racing performance of the team's yacht using over 2,500 variables. During each training session and race, data was constantly being collected from sensors located all over the yacht. The data was constantly being collected and fed back to the team's analytics database. The data was analyzed and the outputs were used to make adjustments and improvements to the configuration of the yacht.

Customer	How They Used Oracle Advanced Analytics
Argonne National Laboratory	Argonne National Laboratory uses Oracle Data Mining to model and predict protein crystallization propensity from protein sequences. The lab's scientists were able to use Oracle Data Mining to identify the set of attributes that correlated with the protein's propensity to crystallize and used the SVM algorithm in Oracle Data Mining to build the model.
StuartMaue	StuartMaue receives over 4,000 submissions per month for payment. This equates to over $200 million worth of legal invoices per month. StuartMaue wanted to automate and improve the review, categorization, and investigation of possibly noncompliant legal submissions. This was a very labor-intensive process that involved trying to spot potential fraudulent or erroneous submissions. Oracle Data Mining was used to mine the structured and unstructured data in the firm's Oracle Database. By automating the process, StuartMaue was able to scale to large volumes, saving time and money.
Xerox	Xerox is using Oracle Data Mining to analyze its customer data. The company has been able to save a significant amount of processing time by using Oracle Data Miner in its Oracle Databases, as it no longer has to move its data out of the database to another data mining application. Using the Oracle Data Mining in-database capabilities has saved Xerox both time and money.

NOTE
Many more companies have used Oracle Advanced Analytics, but the details of their projects are not publicly available. Watch out for more customer case studies at conferences such as Oracle OpenWorld, in publications such as Oracle Magazine, *and on the Oracle website.*

CHAPTER
2

The Predictive
Modeling Lifecycle

Over the years, the software industry has developed a number of different software development lifecycles. These were developed to standardize the process of developing software, defining the different phases and tasks to be completed in each phase. We all know the benefits of these lifecycles. Likewise, for Data Mining projects, various groups have come together to create a lifecycle that is suitable to this specific type of work. In this chapter, the main data mining lifecycles are presented, in particular the CRISP-DM lifecycle.

Predictive Modeling Lifecycles

Although the CRoss Industry Standard Process for Data Mining, more commonly known as CRISP-DM, has been around for a long time now, it is still considered the main lifecycle to use for data mining projects. There are various surveys conducted on an annual basis that support this. But these surveys also highlight that organizations are also using some other lifecycles or are using their own that are based on another or a combination of other lifecycles. The two main other lifecycles that you will come across are the Knowledge Discovery in Data process and the SEMMA process. The following sections summarize these two lifecycles.

Knowledge Discovery in Data (KDD) Process

The Knowledge Discovery in Data (KDD) process was first published by Usama Fayyad, Gregory Piatetsky-Shapiro, and Padhraic Smyth in 1996 in their paper titled *From Data Mining to Knowledge Discovery in Databases*. The KDD process is one of the most commonly cited and published data mining processes. The KDD process consists of five stages with the ability to step back to a previous stage if needed, as illustrated in Figure 2-1. One of the assumptions about using the KDD process is

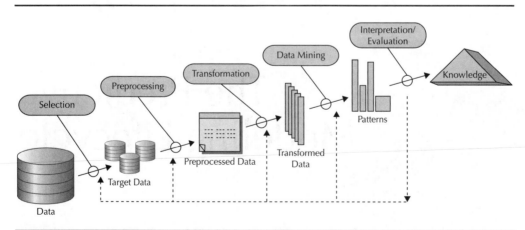

FIGURE 2-1. *The Knowledge Discovery in Data (KDD) process*

that project goals and underlying business requirements have already been defined. The KDD process can be used to work through the remaining part of the project. The KDD process consists of the following five stages:

- **Selection**   This stage consists of creating a target data set from your available data sources. During this step, there is a focus on attribute subset selection and data sampling to reduce the number of records to be used during the remaining stages.

- **Preprocessing**   This stage consists of cleaning and preprocessing the data set to be used for data mining. Some of the tasks involved in this stage include the identification and removal of noise, identifying and deciding how to manage missing data, cleaning up inconsistencies in the data, and so on.

- **Transformation**   This stage consists of identifying and implementing any data transformations that are required. This may involve the use of various binning and aggregation methods to be used in transforming the data and reducing dimensionality of the data.

- **Data Mining**   This stage consists of selecting the appropriate data mining algorithms to the business problem and selected data set. These data mining algorithms then search for patterns that may exist in the data. Appropriate parameter settings will need to be determined to ensure the optimal operation of the algorithms.

- **Interpretation/Evaluation**   This stage consists of reviewing the results and the outputs from the data mining algorithms to see whether suitable and usable patterns have been discovered. Various visualization and statistical tests will be created as part of the evaluation stage.

SEMMA

The SEMMA data mining process comes from the SAS Institute and covers the main processes of conducting a data mining process. The SEMMA process can be applied to any data mining project and consists of the steps Sample, Explore, Modify, Model, and Assess, as shown in Figure 2-2. The steps are described as follows:

- **Sample**   This step consists on sampling your data sources by extracting the important information so that the sample size can be manipulated quickly. Various sampling techniques can be deployed to ensure that appropriate data is extracted. By working with a representative but smaller sample of the data, you can conduct data mining on a subset of the data instead of having to work with all the data.

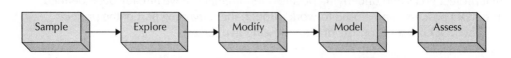

FIGURE 2-2. *SEMMA data mining process*

- **Explore** The Explore step consists of exploring your data, performing some simple statistical analysis, creating graphs, and interpreting the results to gain a better insight into what simple behavior is going on with your data. You might use these insights to help focus the data mining task or to identify additional techniques that can be deployed on the data.

- **Modify** This step consists of the modification of the data by creating, selecting, and transforming the attributes and/or variables that are necessary for the data mining algorithms. You may look to remove outliers from your data set, define suitable binning for your attributes, define new attributes based on specific business rules, or identify attributes that can be removed from the data set.

- **Model** The Model step consists of modeling the data by using or combining one or more data mining algorithms to predict a desired outcome. Data mining techniques can include regression, classification, clustering, anomaly detection, association rules, and a variety of other statistical modeling techniques. Only the appropriate data mining techniques and algorithms should be used for your particular data mining scenario.

- **Assess** This step consists of assessing the results of the data mining algorithms by evaluating the usefulness and reliability of the findings and estimating how well the algorithms perform. Each of the data mining algorithms will have a variety of statistical measures that allow you to determine which model performs best for your data in a particular scenario.

You will see that there is a lot in common between the SEMMA data mining process and the other data mining processes or lifecycles described in this chapter.

CRISP-DM

CRISP-DM is the most widely used data mining lifecycle. This is based on regular surveys over the past 10+ years by various groups including KDNuggets, Rexter Analytics, and others. Some call it the de facto standard lifecycle for data mining. Many other lifecycles that have data mining as part of their lifecycle follow a similar approach to the CRISP-DM lifecycle. The CRISP-DM lifecycle is designed to be independent of any software, vendor, or technique.

CRISP-DM was originally developed by a consortium of organizations consisting of leading data mining vendors, end-users, consultancy companies, and researchers. The original CRISP-DM project was partly sponsored by the European Commission under the ESPRIT program. For many years, there was a dedicated website for CRISP-DM, but in recent years this website is no longer available and occasionally you might get redirected to the SPSS website by IBM, which was one of the original contributors to the project.

The CRISP-DM lifecycle consists of six stages, as illustrated in Figure 2-3. Although the arrows indicate a particular direction, it is not uncommon to have to go back to a previous stage if required to gather more information or to rerun certain processes.

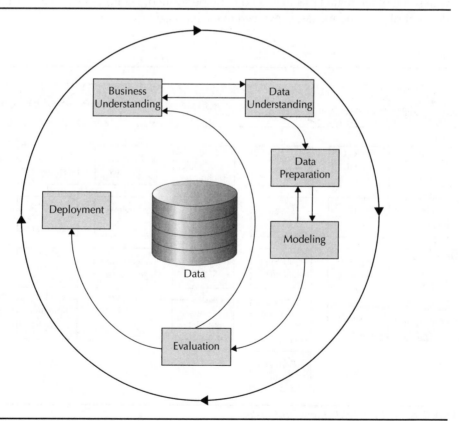

FIGURE 2-3. *CRISP-DM lifecycle*

The outer circle in Figure 2-3 illustrates the cyclical nature of data mining projects. This is perhaps one of the important aspects of these projects that is not commonly discussed. After you have developed and deployed your data mining models, you should continually review your data, your data mining scenario, the business changes that will impact on the data mining scenario, changes in the data behavior, and the suitability of the data mining techniques used. All of this needs to be reviewed and updated on a regular basis. How often you will need to do this? This is a very difficult question to answer. It really depends on how quickly the data evolves. For example, in some scenarios you will have to do this on a weekly, monthly, quarterly, yearly, or even daily basis.

During this cyclical reviewing of your data mining project, you will typically keep on refining your data mining goals. This will lead you into initiating many new data mining projects.

The following sections describe each phase of the CRISP-DM lifecycle along with some of the main tasks that need to be performed. Figure 2-4 summarizes the different phases and the tasks involved in each phase.

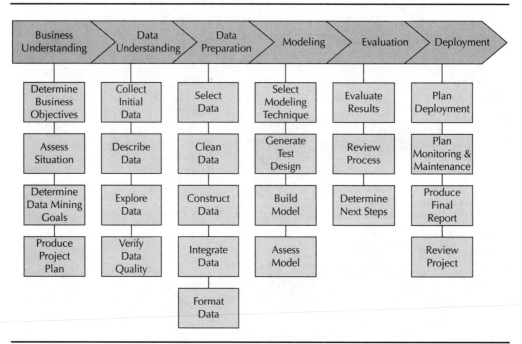

FIGURE 2-4. *CRISP-DM stages and tasks*

Business Understanding

During the Business Understanding phase, you try to focus on the objectives of the data mining project and the requirements from a business perspective. These are used to refine the goals of data mining problem, giving clear reasons for the data mining project. With this focus in mind, you can create a project plan to meet your objectives.

The main tasks of the Business Understanding phase are as follows:

- **Determine the Business Objectives**   The first objective for the data scientist or the data miner is to understand fully, from a business perspective, what the business user really wants to achieve. Too often, business users have only a general idea of what they would like to achieve or misunderstand what can be achieved through data mining. It is the job of the data miner to work with the business user to refine the user's problem areas so that a clear set of data mining projects are defined.

- **Assess the Situation**   With the set of clearly defined data mining projects, the data miner then assesses the business to see whether these data mining projects are actionable. In most cases, the business or data mining project will need refining so that it can fit within the constraints of the business. In other situations, a project might not be possible due to the required data being unavailable. What software is to be used for managing the data and for performing the data mining tasks? If this software does not exist in the organization, then a product selection project will need to be initiated.

- **Determine the Data Mining Goals**   A clear goal can be defined for each data mining project. This should clearly state not just the objective of the project, but also what the business user wants to achieve from the project. For example, you might want to reduce customer churn by 5 percent, or you might want to increase revenue from certain products by 12 percent.

- **Produce the Project Plan**   Based on the information that has been gathered in the previous tasks, a project plan can be created that details all the tasks that need to be completed, what resources are needed to complete each task, and how much time you estimate will be required to complete each task. The project plan will include all identified dependencies and a risk assessment.

Data Understanding

The Data Understanding phase involves gathering an initial data sample from the various source systems that contain the important and relevant data for the data mining project. This data will be examined using a variety of statistical and graphical techniques to gain an understanding of the data. During this investigation, you should discover some initial insights, and using these you can start to build up a picture of what your data is representing.

There are arrows that point from the Business Understanding to the Data Understanding and from the Data Understanding to the Business Understanding. These arrows indicate that this is an iterative process of learning. As you explore the data, you will start to develop questions about some of your discoveries. You will need to go back to the business users to get these questions answered. This will give more clarity to the business problem for your data mining project and in turn will give you a better understanding of your data.

The mains tasks of the Data Understanding phase are as follows:

■ **Collect Initial Data**   As your data will exist in a variety of locations and will come with varying data volumes, this task will involve the extraction of the data from these data sources. If the data volumes are very large, then you may want to use some sampling techniques to extract an appropriate subset or sample of the data. Using this sample will allow you to perform the later tasks in a timely manner. A data dictionary type report can be generated that lists all the data, their properties, their location, the methods used to acquire them, and details of any resolutions to problems you might have encountered.

■ **Describe the Data**   This task involves expanding the report produced during the previous task to include the format of the data; the quantity of data, including the number of records; the identifying attributes; and other information that is easily identifiable from the data.

■ **Explore the Data**   For this task, you examine the data at the attribute and record level using querying, visualization, and reporting techniques. Most data mining tools come with a variety of statistical techniques that can be used automatically on the data to identify specific information about each attribute and record. These can include distributions of the attribute values, relationships between pairs or among small numbers of attributes, results of simple aggregations, properties of subpopulations, and other simple statistical analyses.

■ **Verify the Data Quality**   It is important to determine the quality of the data you are going to use. During the Explore the Data task, you may have discovered certain characteristics of particular attributes of particular portions of the data set. You may need to go back to the business users to seek clarification of why you may have certain data values that are not typical in your data set or to understand some of the business rules that determine the values in the attributes.

NOTE
It is typically reported that the Business Understanding and Data Understanding stages can take up to 70 to 80 percent of the total project time.

TIP
If you have a mature BI environment in your organization, then most of the tasks involved in the Business Understanding and Data Understanding stages will already have been completed. All you have to do is perform the necessary steps and gather the information required for your specific data mining projects.

Data Preparation

The Data Preparation phase covers all the data manipulation tasks that are necessary to prepare the data so that you can create the data set that will be used during the Modeling phase to create the data mining models. The typical tasks involved in preparing the data include integrating, cleaning, translating, transforming, and binning the data; creating the target attribute; and so on.

The main tasks of the Data Preparation phase are as follows:

- **Select the Required Data**   During this task, you decide what data is necessary for your data mining project. In addition, you need to set up the extraction mechanisms necessary to get the data from your various source systems.

- **Clean the Data**   When you have a copy of the data within your work area, you can clean the data. For example, this cleaning can involve the removal of incomplete records, identifying missing data, and substituting suitable default values. Any data-specific issues should have been identified during the Data Understanding phase, and it is during this task that you will attempt to clean the data to get it ready for the analysis.

- **Construct Required Data**   At times you will need to create or construct new attributes to be part of your data set. This can be done to extract embedded values that might exist in other attributes. Perhaps the use of the values in an attribute might not be appropriate for data privacy reasons or for analysis. An example of this would be when including the date of birth or age of a person might not be suitable. In this kind of scenario, you might create a new attribute that will contain a binned value for peoples' age that groups people into certain age ranges. For a classification type problem, you will need to construct an attribute that will contain a target value that is based on some business rule and that will need specific code written to generate the value.

■ **Integrate the Data** Your data will come from a variety of data sources and from a variety of tables within each of these data sources. As the number and types of data sources are constantly increasing as more data becomes available as part of the Big Data environment, a number of programming languages and integrating methods will need to be utilized to integrate the data. Once the data is integrated, you will then have one data store and structure for your data.

■ **Format the Data** In the previous tasks, you put a lot of work into preparing the data for analysis and data mining. In this task, Format the Data, you concentrate on producing specific versions of the data sets that are required as input to the data mining algorithms. Certain data mining techniques and their implementation in various data mining tools will require the data to be in a specific format and layout. During this task, you will prepare the data for input to the data mining algorithms.

TIP
Some knowledge of the data modeling and data mining techniques that will be used in the Modeling phase is needed. Each of these techniques may require the data to be prepared in a certain manner for input to the algorithms.

Modeling

The Modeling phase involves taking the data set that was prepared in the previous phase and using it as input to a number of modeling techniques. Several such techniques will be used to help meet the goals of the data mining project, and perhaps a number of data modeling techniques need to be used together to meet the desired outcome. For each of the data mining or modeling techniques to be used, each will have its own specific parameter setting that will need to be refined to meet the goals of the data mining project.

The main tasks of the Modeling phase are as follows:

■ **Select the Modeling Technique** Although some initial identification of appropriate data mining techniques may have already been performed so that the data can be created correctly, during this task each of the data mining techniques is examined with the specific aim of identifying the appropriate algorithm, appropriate algorithm settings, and so on. If multiple data mining techniques and algorithms are to be used, then this task needs to be performed separately for each, with a documented understanding of how these can work together.

- **Generate Test Cases**   A test plan is needed to assess the outputs of each data mining model to determine its quality and validity. This plan involves the identification of appropriate model build output statistics, ensuring that the training and testing data sets are created with appropriate distributions of case records.

- **Build the Model(s)**   This task involves taking the data set, the data mining techniques, the specific algorithms and their settings and using your data mining tool to generate the data mining model. This is where the machine learning algorithms are applied to discover the hidden patterns in your data.

- **Assess the Model(s)**   This task involves assessing the outputs from the Build the Model task. To do so, the data miner uses the test cases, the model outputs, and the statistical measures to determine the success of the data mining algorithms in discovering patterns in the data. He or she also takes into account the overall business objectives of the project and uses these as part of the assessment of the models. The data miner also discusses the outputs with a variety of people involved in the project and in particular discusses the outputs with the domain expert to see whether any additional insight can be found from the model outputs.

Evaluation

The Evaluation phase of the project involves the assessment of the data mining models that were created during the previous phase. This involves reassessing how well each of the models addresses the goals of the data mining project to ensure that the best or most appropriate data mining model is selected.

The main tasks of the Evaluation phase are as follows:

- **Evaluate the Results**   The evaluation of the models performed in the previous phase focused on the accuracy and generality of the model(s) produced. In this task, the data miner assesses the degree to which the model(s) best meet the original business objectives of the project and identifies any issues or deficiencies.

- **Review Process**   During this task, you can perform a review of the entire project, including the outputs and results generated up to this point. You look to see whether the data mining model(s) appear to be satisfactory and to satisfy business needs. This task can be considered part of the quality review of the project and can be used to determine whether any important factors or tasks have been overlooked. If any have been, then you can address them before moving to the Deployment phase.

■ **Determine the Next Steps**   Depending on the results of the previous tasks, you perform an assessment, and the project team decides what the next steps should be and how to proceed. The team can decide whether all the models and assessments meet the business objectives to deploy the data mining model(s). If the team decides that more work is required to finish the project, the planning of further iterations or the setup of new data mining projects is considered.

Deployment

In the Deployment phase, you determine how you are going to deploy the selected data mining model or models in your environment. Deployment can be performed in a variety of ways, from using the models to generate mailing campaigns right through to having the data mining models fully integrated into your production applications.

Unfortunately, a lot of the literature does not really cover the deployment of your data mining models, covering only up to the Modeling and/or Evaluation phases of the CRISP-DM lifecycle. You will find that there are many sections in various chapters of this book that cover how you can integrate your Oracle Data Mining models in your production applications.

The main tasks of the Deployment phase are as follows:

■ **Plan the Deployment**   This involves examining how you are going to deploy the data mining models, as part of your back-end or front-end applications or as part of your reporting and Business Intelligence infrastructure.

■ **Plan the Monitoring and Maintenance**   Ongoing monitoring and maintenance of your data mining models are very important. You have built your data mining models based on the data you had available. Over time you will gather more data. Your data mining models will need to be updated to include this new data and the different evolving business scenarios that this data represents. Depending on your business and how it evolves, you may need to update your data mining models every week, month, quarter, or year. Each business scenario is different. Constant monitoring of the models will tell you when a model performance starts to drop and will require a remodeling.

■ **Produce the Final Report**   All projects require good documentation and reports of what work was performed at each stage of the project. It can be typical of data mining projects that gaps occur between different phases. For example, there may be some months between deploying the data mining model(s) and the need to rebuild the models. The project personnel may have moved to other projects or new people will be hired. Good documentation will assist the project team (new or old) in getting up to speed on what previous work was completed on the project.

■ **Review the Project**   As with all projects, it is good practice to perform a review of the project. During this review, you can look at what worked well during the project and what didn't work so well. For example, you can gather and list lessons learned, so that for the next data mining projects you can build on the experiences of previous work. Another important part of the project review is to see whether the use of data mining achieved the required goal. Back in the Business Understanding phase, you would have set out specific goals you wanted to achieve. For example, you may have wanted to reduce customer churn by 5 percent or to increase revenue on certain products by 12 percent. During the review project task, you can measure to see whether you achieved these goals.

Summary

Using a good data mining lifecycle allows you to learn from the work of others. The CRISP-DM lifecycle has been around for a long time now, and many organizations are using this lifecycle for their data mining projects. The benefits of using a lifecycle are well known, but for data mining projects the use of such a lifecycle is critical due to the typical start-stop nature and the either short or long duration of these projects. For data mining projects, some gaps typically occur during the various phases of the projects, during which your staff may be reallocated to other projects. Sometimes you may be able to get these staff back to work on the project. Following a good lifecycle and fully documenting each of the tasks will help to ensure that all staff (whether they helped start the project or joined at later stages) can easily transfer between projects with the minimum time required to get up to speed on the work already completed.

CHAPTER
3

How to Install, Set Up, and Get Started

B efore you can start using the Oracle Data Miner tool or using the in-database features, there are a few installation and setup steps to perform. The first of these steps requires you to have Enterprise Edition of an Oracle 12c or Oracle 11 R2 database installed. The focus of this chapter is to walk you through the remaining steps to get you fully set up with Oracle Data Miner.

In addition to these core steps, you may want to set up your data mining schema to use the sample schemas.

Prerequisites

- You have installed Oracle 12c Enterprise Edition or Oracle 11 R2 Enterprise Edition.

- You have installed the sample schemas in the database.

- You have downloaded and installed the latest version of SQL Developer (version 4 or later).

- You have the SYS password or you have your DBA available for the steps that require this password.

Enabling the Oracle Advanced Analytics Option

Oracle Data Miner is a component of the Advanced Analytics option in the Enterprise Edition of the database. This option is installed and enabled by default when the database is installed. In addition to needing the Oracle Advanced Analytics option, you will also need to have the Oracle Text option installed and enabled in the database. If the Advanced Analytics option and Oracle Text were disabled after the installation of the database, you will need to ask your DBA to enable them.

To enable the Advanced Analytics option, you can use the chopt command. The chopt command allows you to enable and disable the following database options:

Database Option	Description
dm	Oracle Data Mining RDBMS Files. This enables the Advanced Analytics option.
olap	Oracle OLAP
partitioning	Oracle Partitioning
rat	Oracle Real Application Testing

Before you change the option, you will need to stop the database service and restart the service after the following command has been run on the command line:

```
chopt enable dm
```

Creating a Data Mining Tablespace

Although this step is not really mandatory, it can be very useful to have a separate area in your database where you can create all your data mining objects and where you can keep all your data mining models. By having a separate data mining tablespace in each of your Oracle databases, you can easily transfer your Oracle Data Mining models from database to database.

The following command can be used to add the DATAMINING tablespace:

```
CREATE TABLESPACE datamining
DATAFILE '/u01/app/oracle/oradata/cdb12c/pdb12c/datamining.dbf'
SIZE 500M AUTOEXTEND ON;
```

Depending on your installation and platform, you will need to change the DATAFILE location to where you keep those files in your environment.

CAUTION
If you do not know where you should keep datafiles in your environment or if you do not have the necessary access, you may need to consult with your DBA and get assistance regarding where to store your datafiles.

Creating an ODM Schema

Before you can start using either the Oracle Data Miner tool in SQL Developer or the Oracle Data Mining in-database functions, you need to create a schema. This schema will contain all your Data Mining work. Just like the previous step, when you created a Data Mining tablespace, you will need the SYS password for the database. If you do not have access to this password, you can ask your DBA to perform the following steps using SQL Developer or SQL*Plus.

You can use SQL Developer or SQL*Plus to create your Data Mining schema. To use SQL Developer to create the Data Mining schema, you must create a connection for the SYS schema. See the next section for details of how to create a SQL Developer Connection. When you have the connection created for the SYS schema, you can double-click on the connection to open the connection to the database. A SQL Worksheet for SYS opens when you have made your connection. Under the SYS connection is an expanded tree of objects for the schema. To create your Data Mining schema, scroll down this list of objects until you come to the Other Users option. Right-click the Other Users option and select the Create User option from the menu. The following example gives the parameter values necessary to create a schema called DMUSER. We will use this schema throughout this book to illustrate how to use Oracle Data Miner. In the Create User window, enter the following schema name, password, and tablespace information. Then click on the Roles tab and tick the Granted box for the CONNECT and RESOURCE roles given in the following example. Finally, click on the Quotas tab and set it to Unlimited.

Schema Name:	DMUSER
Password:	DMUSER
Default Tablespace:	DATAMINING
Temporary Tablespace:	TEMP
Roles:	CONNECT, RESOURCE
Quotas	Unlimited for tablespace DATAMINING

A second option is to use SQL*Plus to create the user. Your DBA might use this option when you need to set up Data Mining schemas in different development, test, and production environments. The following commands can be used to create the DMUSER user:

```
CREATE USER dmuser IDENTIFIED BY dmuser
DEFAULT TABLESPACE datamining
TEMPORARY TABLESPACE temp
QUOTA UNLIMITED ON datamining;
GRANT CONNECT, RESOURCE to dmuser;
```

See the later sections "Setting Up Additional Users to Access ODM" and "ODM Schema System Privileges."

Creating a Connection for Your DM User in SQL Developer

To create a connection for your new DMUSER schema in SQL Developer, you must select the green plus symbol in the Connections tab on the left-hand side of SQL Developer. This opens the Create New Connection window. In this window, you can enter the DMUSER connection details. The following are the details necessary to create the DMUSER schema that you created in the previous section, and Figure 3-1 shows the Create User window.

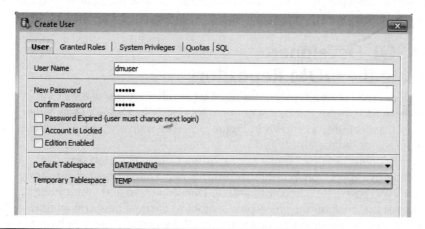

FIGURE 3-1.   *Creating the DMUSER connection in SQL Developer*

Setting	Description
Connection Name	This is a label in which you can enter something meaningful.
Username	Enter **DMUSER**, the name of your ODM schema.
Password	Enter **DMUSER**, the password for your ODM schema.
Hostname	Enter the name of the server that contains the database. If it is your local machine, you can enter **localhost**.
Port	Enter **1521**.
Service Name	You should select Service Name instead of SID. Enter the service name for your pluggable database, such as **pdb12c**.

When you have entered the connection details, you can click on the Test button to check that the connection can be established. Any errors will be displayed, or if all the details are correct you will see a message on the left-hand side of this screen saying "Status: Success." When you have a successful connection, you can click on the Connect button to open the connection. The new connection is added and saved to your list in the Connections tab, and a SQL Worksheet opens for your DMUSER schema.

Creating the Oracle Data Mining Repository

Before you can start using Oracle Data Mining, you need to create an Oracle Data Mining Repository in the database. The simplest way to do this is to use the built-in functionality in Oracle Data Miner (which is part of SQL Developer). The alternative method is to use the scripts that come with SQL Developer to create the repository.

You need to have the SYS password to use either of these methods or you can ask your DBA to perform these steps for you.

Using SQL Developer to Create the ODM Repository

SQL Developer maintains a separate listing of what schemas you use for Oracle Data Miner. To attach your DMUSER schema to this list, select View | Data Miner | Data Miner Connections, as shown in Figure 3-2. Alternatively, you can select Tools | Data Miner | Make Visible.

A new tab opens beside or under your existing Connections tab. You can reposition this tab to your preferred location. This new Data Miner tab lists any connections you have associated with Oracle Data Miner. To add your DMUSER schema to this list, click on the green plus symbol to create a new connection. Figure 3-3 shows the window that opens listing all the connections you have already created under the SQL Developer Connections list. Select the DMUSER schema from the drop-down list.

The DMUSER schema is now added to your Oracle Data Miner Connections list. When you double-click on the DMUSER schema, SQL Developer checks the database to see whether the Oracle Data Miner Repository exists in the database. If the repository does not exist, a message displays asking whether you would like to install the repository. Click the Yes button to proceed with the install. Next a Connection window appears that prompts you to enter the password for SYS. If you have this password, you can enter it; if not, you will need to ask your DBA to enter it for you. After entering the password, click on the OK button. In the new window,

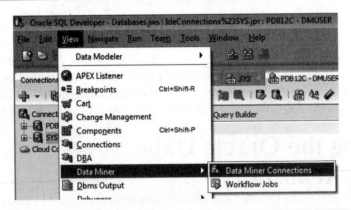

FIGURE 3-2. *Selecting Oracle Data Miner connections using the View menu*

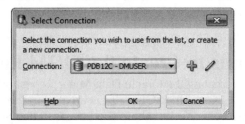

FIGURE 3-3.   *Oracle Data Miner Select Connection window*

you are asked for the Default and Temporary tablespace names for the repository account/schema ODMRSYS. In this book's examples, a new tablespace named DATAMINING has been created that will contain the user's data mining work. Enter this tablespace name for the Default tablespace and then click the OK button to proceed. The next window charts the progress of the repository's creation. Make sure that the Install Demo Data is checked. You can then click the Start button to start the install. SQL Developer then proceeds to create the repository in your Oracle Database, and the progress bar is updated as the repository is created, as shown in Figure 3-4.

The repository install can take anywhere from approximately one minute for a local database and up to ten minutes for a remote database. When the repository install is completed, you see a window with the message "Task Completed Successfully." You can close this window and start using ODM.

As part of the repository install, the DMUSER is granted all the Oracle system privileges necessary to create and use Oracle Data Mining objects. Additionally, the DMUSER schemas are granted access to the sample schemas, all necessary views are created on the sample schemas, and two tables containing some demo data are created in the DMUSER schema. These tables containing the demo data are called

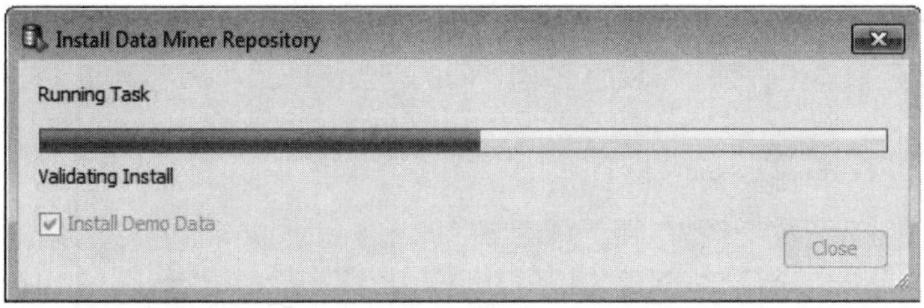

FIGURE 3-4.   *Install Data Miner Repository progress window*

INSUR_CUST_LTV_SAMPLE and ODMR_CARS_DATA. These views to the sample schemas and the new demo data table are used throughout this book.

Using SQL Scripts to Create the ODM Repository

An alternative method of creating the Oracle Data Miner Repository is to run the SQL script installodmr.sql. This SQL script is located in the dataminer subdirectory for SQL Developer. Go to where you have installed SQL Developer and work your way down the directories until you find the installodmr.sql SQL script located in dataminer directory for SQL Developer, that is, \sqldeveloper\ dataminer\scripts. To execute the script, you need to log in to SQL*Plus (or SQL Developer) as the SYS user.

 @installodmr.sql <default tablespace> <temp tablespace>

   Example: @installodmr.sql DATAMINING TEMP

This SQL script creates only the repository. It does not create any of the sample data, grant your Data Mining schema access to the sample schemas, or create the demo table in your schema. The scripts necessary to create these items are explained in the following section.

Setting Up Additional Users to Access ODM

Typically you need more than one schema for your Data Mining work. A number of people will work on a given Data Mining project, and you can allocate each user a different schema, where the users can work on their different models. You could create these new users in SQL Developer using the steps outlined in the previous sections. As each schema connection is assigned as an Oracle Data Miner connection, you are prompted to give the schema the required system privileges, as shown in Figure 3-5. If you click the Yes button, SQL Developer runs the necessary scripts for the schema.

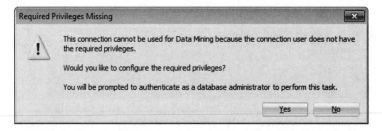

FIGURE 3-5. *Assigning a new schema the system privileges to use ODM*

As before, you will need to have the SYS password, and you can monitor the progress of the script as it completes its steps. In addition to giving the new schema the required system privileges, the script sets up the schema with access to the sample schemas and demo data.

When you have to set up a number of users in your database to use ODM, these steps can become somewhat repetitive. Your DBA will probably want to script this process, particularly as he or she will have to create a number of ODM schemas in the Development, Test, and Production environments.

The first step is to create a new schema and allocate it to the Data Mining tablespace. Connect to the database as SYS, issue the CREATE USER command, and grant the user the typical roles, as follows:

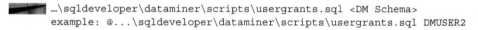

```
create user DMUSER2 identified by DMUSER2
default tablespace DATAMINING
temporary tablespace TEMP
quota unlimited on DATAMINING;

grant CONNECT, RESOURCE to DMUSER2;
```

The ODM repository is already created. Only one ODM repository is required per (12c pluggable) database. For each new schema you want to use for Oracle Data Mining, the DBA needs to grant the necessary privileges to use the ODM repository. The usergrants.sql script in the SQL Developer dataminer directory contains all the commands necessary to grant these privileges. The following example shows you how to create the DMUSER2 schema.

```
...\sqldeveloper\dataminer\scripts\usergrants.sql <DM Schema>
example: @...\sqldeveloper\dataminer\scripts\usergrants.sql DMUSER2
```

TIP
The schema name needs to be in uppercase.

TIP
You should run these scripts as SYS.

If you want your new schema to have the Oracle Data Miner demo data and links to the sample schema, you need to run the following script:

```
...\sqldeveloper\dataminer\scripts\instdemodata.sql <DM Schema>
example: @...\sqldeveloper\dataminer\scripts\instdemodata.sql DMUSER2
```

All of these ODM scripts, including some sample code, scripts that create and drop the repository, and more, can be found in the following SQL developer directory:

```
\sqldeveloper\dataminer\scripts
```

ODM Schema System Privileges

At a minimum, each Oracle Data Mining schema must have the CREATE MINING MODEL system privilege. This privilege enables the user to perform any operation on the models that he or she creates. In addition to this privilege, the following is a list of the minimum set of system privileges that a schema needs:

- CREATE MINING MODEL

- CREATE SESSION

- CREATE TABLE

- CREATE VIEW

- EXECUTE ON CTXSYS.CTX_DDL

In previous sections, the granting of some of these privileges is taken care of by the GRANT statement. The additional privilege of CREATE MINING MODEL allows the schema to create, view, and use a model in its own schema. The EXECUTE ON CTXSYS.CTX_DDL privilege gives the schema access to the PL/SQL package CTX_DLL. This package is used for processing text. It contains functions and procedures that create and manage the preferences, section groups, and stoplists required for Text indexes.

The system privileges for Oracle Data Mining are as follows:

System Privilege	Description
CREATE MINING MODEL	This allows for the creation and use of models in your own schema
CREATE ANY MINING MODEL	Allows for the creation of models in any schema
ALTER ANY MINING MODEL	This allows for changes to the model name or cost matrix of any mining model in any schema
DROP ANY MINING MODEL	You can drop any model in any schema
SELECT ANY MINING MODEL	This allows you to select, view, and apply any model in any schema
COMMENT ANY MINING MODEL	This allows for comments to be added to any model in any schema
AUDIT_AMIN role	This can be used to generate an audit trail for any model in any schema

Setting Up and Using the Pre-built Database Appliance

If you do not have access to an Oracle 12*c* or 11.2*g* database that you can use, you can download and install one of the VirtualBox Pre-built appliances that Oracle has available on Oracle Technology Network (OTN). Full instructions are available on how to install each VirtualBox Pre-built appliance.

Oracle has a number of pre-built appliances that it updates regularly to have the latest versions of the software. The appliances are supplied for testing purposes and are not suitable for production-type use, but they are a great way for trying out the different products that Oracle makes available in the pre-built appliances. You can download an appliance that is built having all the software installed and configured for you to test. Some of these appliances come with tutorials, sample data, sample applications, and videos to help you learn how to use the products. This training material is very similar to what you will find for the sample products in the Oracle Learning Library.

For Oracle Data Miner, you need to download the Database App Development VM appliance. To set up your virtual machine to use Oracle Data Miner, double-click the SQL Developer icon. When SQL Developer opens, follow the instructions provided in the previous sections for setting up the schemas and the repository.

After completing all the setup and configuration, you should be ready to start your Oracle Data Miner learning experience.

Summary

In this chapter, you worked through the steps that are required to set up your database, install the Oracle Data Miner repository in the database, create a schema to use for your Data Mining work, configure the system privileges that are necessary for each schema, and set up access to the sample data (which will be used in each chapter). These are all important steps that you need to complete, with the help of your DBA, before you can use Oracle Data Mining functionality in the Oracle Data Miner tool that is part of SQL Developer or the Oracle Data Mining SQL and PL/SQL in-database functions.

PART
II

Using the Oracle Data Miner Tool

CHAPTER
4

ODM Menus, Projects, and Workflows

The Oracle Data Miner (ODM) tool is part of SQL Developer, and there are a small number of menu options for ODM. In this chapter, we look at the menu options that are available, how to create a project and workflow, how you can change or customize the layout, and what data mining nodes are available in the Component Palette. This chapter also shows how you can export your Oracle Data Miner workflows. These exported workflows can be used as a backup of your work and they can also be imported into another schema, thus allowing you to share your workflows with other members of your project team.

The ODM Menus

When you start to use Oracle Data Miner for the first time, you need to make the different elements of the tool visible. To do this, you need to select Tools | Data Miner | Make Visible (see Figure 4-1).

When this menu option is selected, it opens the Data Miner Connections tab and the Workflow Jobs tab on the left-hand side of the screen. The Data Miner Connections tab lists all your database connections that you have set up to use the Oracle Data Mining functionality. The Workflow Jobs tab is used to monitor the progress of the Oracle Data Miner workflows that you run from within the ODM tool.

If you happen to close either of the Data Miner Connections or the Workflow Jobs tabs, you can use the Make Visible menu option to make them reappear or you can use the View menu option. Under the View menu option there is a submenu, Data Miner. From this submenu, you can select Data Miner Connections or Workflow Jobs.

There is a comprehensive set of help documentation for Oracle Data Miner. This documentation can be accessed by selecting Help | Data Mining, as shown in Figure 4-2.

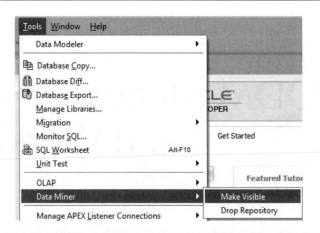

FIGURE 4-1. *Make Oracle Data Miner visible*

FIGURE 4-2.   *Accessing the Oracle Data Miner help*

The other Oracle Data Miner menu options are available when you have opened an Oracle Data Miner connection and opened or created a workflow. These menu options are described in the section "The ODM Workflow Menu" later in this chapter.

Creating a Project

Before you can start using Oracle Data Miner, you need to set up a project and a workflow. You create these under your schema connection in the Data Miner Connections tab. Creating a project allows you to group all the workflows associated with the project under one umbrella.

To create a new Data Mining project, you should right-click your schema in the Data Miner Connections tab and select New Project from the menu. You can then enter the name of your project and a comment indicating the purpose of the project, as shown in Figure 4-3. You can then click the OK button to create the project.

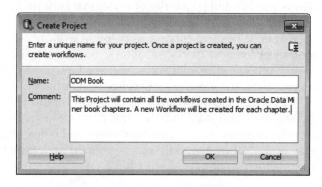

FIGURE 4-3.   *Creating a project for your workflows*

FIGURE 4-4. *Oracle Data Miner project menu options*

The project is then created as an object under your schema in the Data Miner Connections tab. If you right-click the project name, you can see the menu options that are available for a project, as shown in Figure 4-4.

The main project menu options that you will be interested in are New Workflow and Import Workflow. These are described in the section "Creating a Workflow." The other menu options allow you to create a new project, delete a project and all associated objects in the database, edit the properties (which is the project description), and rename a project.

Creating, Exporting, and Importing a Workflow

A workflow is one of the most important parts in Oracle Data Miner. The workflow allows you to build up a series of nodes that perform all the required processing on your data. You cannot use Oracle Data Miner until you have created a workflow for your work. When you create a workflow, a worksheet opens in the middle of the tool. This Workflow Worksheet allows you to create the various nodes, linking them to each other, and enables you to create a flow of work that needs to be performed on your data. The workflow works from left to right.

It is good practice to create a separate workflow for each piece of Data Mining work you want to build. This practice helps you avoid having multiple workflows appearing on your worksheet and helps reduce any confusion that may occur. All your workflows are grouped under the project you created in the previous section.

Creating a Workflow

To create a workflow, you must have a project already created (see the earlier section "Creating a Project"). The workflow can be created by right-clicking on the project name, which is located under your Data Miner connections. A menu appears, and the first item on this menu is Create Workflow. Select this option from the menu. The Create Workflow window opens. You can enter the name for your workflow. In the example illustrated in Figure 4-5, a workflow called Explore Chapter is created. You will use this workflow to explore your data in Chapter 5.

The new workflow now appears under the project. When the workflow is created, a few additional areas appear on your screen: Workflow Worksheet, the Components Workflow Editor tab, and the Properties tab. The Components Workflow Editor consists of all the nodes for Oracle Data Miner. The Properties tab lists the various properties and features of each node on the worksheet. You will use the Components Workflow Editor and the Properties tabs extensively in your Oracle Data Miner projects and throughout this book.

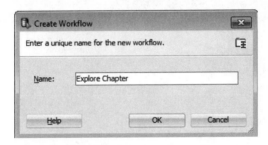

FIGURE 4-5.   *Creating a workflow for Chapter 5*

TIP
Try to use different names for the project and workflow.

Exporting a Workflow

Oracle Data Miner stores the objects relating to a workflow in the database and in the Oracle Data Mining Repository. It is good practice to back up your workflows so that you can have record of how your Data Mining work has evolved over time. Oracle Data Miner has a feature that allows you to export your workflow. The Export process creates an XML file on your file system. This XML file contains details of all the nodes and settings in your workflow, as well as details of what nodes are connected to each other. The exported workflow can be imported back into your schema or a different schema, on the same or a different database.

To export your workflow, you should right-click on the workflow name under your schema in the Data Miner Connections tab. Select Export Workflow from the menu. The example shown in Figure 4-6 exports the workflow that is created in Chapter 8.

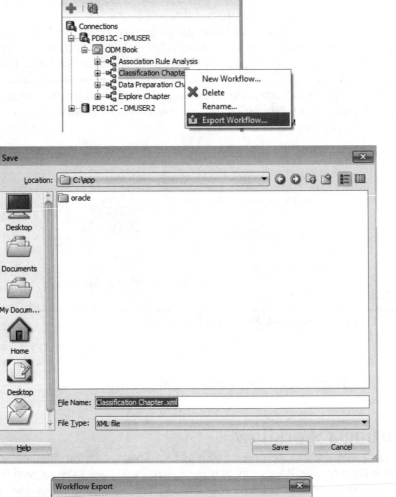

FIGURE 4-6.   *Steps for exporting the workflow discussed in Chapter 8*

A Save File dialog box opens. You can select the location where you would like to save the workflow. The name of the workflow is used as the default name of the XML file. You can change the location and filename. When the file has been saved, a window appears with the message "Workflow Exported Successfully."

Importing a Workflow

You can import an exported ODM workflow into any schema in the database. That can be into the database in which the original workflow was created or into another database. Before you import your ODM workflow, you need to make a number of checks. These checks include that you have the Oracle Data Mining Repository created in the database, that the schema into which you are going to import the workflow has all the necessary Oracle Data Mining system privileges, and that the data specified in the data source nodes exists in the schema or that you have access to the data.

To import a workflow into a schema, you need to open the schema in the Data Miner Connections tab. You need to create a project if you don't have one already. To import the workflow, right-click on the project name and select Import Workflow from the menu, as shown in Figure 4-7.

An Open File window opens, and you can navigate to the location when the exported workflow XML file is located. Select the workflow XML file you want to import into your schema, then click the OK button. The example illustrated in Figure 4-8 shows the importing of the Classification workflow that you exported in

FIGURE 4-7. *Importing a workflow into a new ODM schema and project*

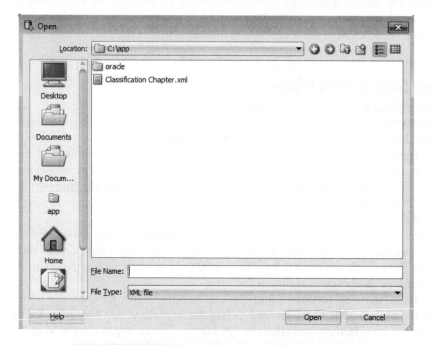

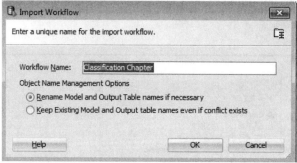

FIGURE 4-8. *Import Workflow dialog box*

the previous section. This example shows the user importing the workflow into the
DMUSER2 schema.

After selecting the workflow file that you want to import, the next window asks
you about how to manage the naming of the workflow objects as they are being
imported into the schema. The first option in the Import Workflow window is Rename
Model and Output Table Names If Necessary. If you select this option when a

workflow or objects already exist in your ODM schema, the import process provides an alternative name. The second option is Keep Existing Model and Output Table Names Even If Conflict Exists. With this option, you need to step through the imported workflow to ensure that the correct data sources are being used and that any output tables will not conflict with any of the other objects in your other workflows.

When the workflow has been imported, the worksheet for the workflow opens displaying the workflow. To ensure that everything works correctly, you need to run the workflow to check for any errors and to create the models and other objects that the workflow produces.

A possible issue that might arise after you have imported your workflow is the identification of the schema for the source data. The account from which the workflow was exported can be encoded in the exported workflow; for example, the exported workflow may have been exported from the account DMUSER and contain the data source node with data MINING_DATA_BUILD. If you import the schema into a different account (that is, an account that is not DMUSER) and try to run the workflow, the data source node fails because the workflow is looking for USER .MINING_DATA_BUILD_V.

To solve this problem, if it occurs, right-click the data node (MINING_DATA_ BUILD_V in this example) and select Define Data Wizard. A message appears indicating that DMUSER.MINING_DATA_BUILD_V does not exist in the available tables/views. Click OK and then select MINING_DATA_BUILD_V in the current account.

Adjusting the Layout

When you use SQL Developer and the Oracle Data Miner tool, you will notice that they open the various tabs in certain locations. One of the features of SQL Developer is that you can move these tab regions around the SQL Developer window to create a customized layout. When you open a workflow in the Oracle Data Miner tool for the first time, you see that the Components Workflow Editor opens on the right-hand side of the SQL Developer window. Just under the Components Workflow Editor the Properties tab region also opens. Apart from the Workflow Worksheet, these are the two most common tabs that you will be using when creating your Oracle Data Miner workflow.

Figure 4-9 shows a suggested layout of the tab regions when using Oracle Data Miner. The Components Workflow Editor, when all the parts are expanded, can take up most of the window height. To allow enough space for this expansion, you can move the Properties tab region to be located just below the Workflow Worksheet. To perform this move, click on the header region of the Properties tab. This region will now have a red border. This indicates that the region is movable. While holding down the left mouse button, move the region to the left-hand side. Move the mouse to the lower part of the worksheet until you see the red box appearing at the bottom

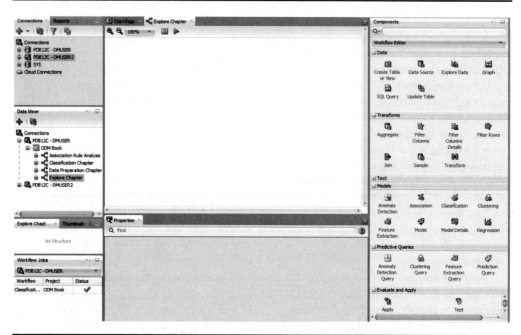

FIGURE 4-9. *Suggested layout of Oracle Data Miner and SQL Developer*

half of the worksheet. When you have the red box located where you want it, you can release the mouse button. The Properties tab region now appears as illustrated in Figure 4-9.

If the tab regions end up not being in the position you want, you can easily move them again until you get a setup that works for you.

The ODM Workflow Menu

The ODM Workflow screen is where you will do most of your work building up your Data Mining workflows. Each node that you create on the workflow will have its own menu that will allow you to edit its properties, view data, run the node, and view the results once the node has successfully run. These node menus are discussed throughout the book in the chapters and sections that look at the functionality of each node. To view the menu for each node, you need to right-click on the node in the workflow.

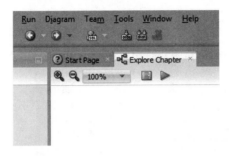

FIGURE 4-10.   *ODM worksheet menu options*

Along the top of the ODM worksheet are a number of menu options illustrated by different icons, as shown in Figure 4-10. The icon menu options on the Workflow Worksheet allow you to zoom in, zoom out, change the percentage size of the diagram, show the event log to view any message (including errors), and select the Run workflow button.

In addition to these menu items, a new menu option appears on the main menu for SQL Developer. This new menu option, Diagram, appears between the Run and Team buttons on the main menu. The Diagram menu option allows you to organize the workflow by aligning the nodes, repositioning them, and creating an image file of the workflow. The available formats for the image file are SVG, SVGZ, JPEG, and PNG. You can use this feature to create images of your workflows that can be included in design documents, presentations, and more.

The Components Workflow Editor

The Components Workflow Editor, shown in Figure 4-11, contains all the nodes that you can create in your Workflow Worksheet. The nodes can let you define what data you are going to use, perform various data updates and transformations, detail what algorithms to use and their setting, apply a model to new data, and prepare data for text mining.

The Components Workflow Editor is divided into a number of sections. Each of these sections corresponds to a stage of the Data Mining process or to a particular group of nodes that related to a specific task (such as Text and Predictive Queries). Table 4-1 briefly describes the nodes in each section. Subsequent chapters provide detailed descriptions of these nodes.

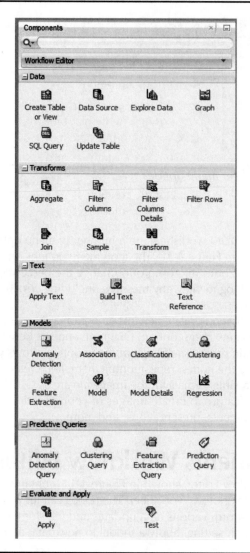

FIGURE 4-11. *ODM Components Workflow Editor*

Sections and Nodes	Description
Data	
Create Table or View	Allows you to create a table or view based on the outputs from a previous node.
Data Source	Defines a data source. This can be a table or view in your current schema or a table or view that you have access to in another schema.
Explore Data	Generates some statistics and graphs for a defined data source.
Graph	Allows for the creation of graphs based on a data source. The available types of graphs include Line, Scatter, Bar, Histogram, and Box.
SQL Query	Writes some customized SQL, PL/SQL, or R (in-database ORE) code to extract new information from your data.
Update Table	Performs an update on a table based on outputs from a previous node.
Transforms	
Aggregate	Performs an aggregation on your data source.
Filter Columns	Filters the columns from your data source. You can also use this node to perform filtering based on certain conditions and attribute importance.
Filter Columns Details	Filters columns based on attribute importance.
Filter Rows	Filters rows from a data source based on some conditions. This is like using a WHERE clause.
Join	Allows you to join data sources together to create a new integrated data source.
Sample	Specifies what sampling criteria you want to apply to a data source.
Transform	Allows you to specify how you want to handle data based on statistical analysis. For example, you can specify which binning method to use and how to handle missing data, as well as configure data normalization, outline treatment, and custom data processing.

TABLE 4-1. *Components Workflow Editor Nodes* (continued)

Sections and Nodes	Description
Text	
Apply Text	Applies an existing text transformation from a previous node to new data.
Build Text	Prepares a data source that has one or more text columns so that the data can be used in the model build node.
Text Reference	Allows the referencing of text transformations that were defined in the current workflow or in a different workflow.
Models	
Anomaly Detection	Builds an anomaly detection model to identify rare occurrences using a One-Class Support Vector Machine.
Association	Builds an association rules model using the Apriori algorithm.
Classification	Builds classification models using the Generalized Linear Model, Support Vector Machine, Decision Tree, and Naïve Bayes algorithms.
Clustering	Builds clustering models using K-Means, O-Cluster, and Expectation Maximization algorithms.
Feature Extraction	Extracts features from a data source using Principal Component Analysis and Singular Value Decomposition algorithms.
Model	Allows you to add models to a workflow that were not built in the workflow. These models may have been created in the database using the PL/SQL CREATE_MODEL procedure.
Model Details	This node allows you to extract model details from a model build node or a model node. The details extracted give details about model attributes and their treatment by the algorithm.
Regression	Allows you to build regression models using the Generalized Linear Model and Support Vector Machine algorithms.

TABLE 4-1. *Components Workflow Editor Nodes* (continued)

Sections and Nodes	Description
Predictive Queries	
Anomaly Detection Query	Builds a predictive query for anomaly detection.
Clustering Query	Builds a predictive query for clustering.
Feature Extraction Query	Builds a predictive query for feature extraction.
Prediction Query	Builds a predictive query for classification.
Evaluate and Apply	
Apply	Applies a model from a model build node to new data.
Test	Allows for the testing of the classification and regression node, where separate data sources are used for model build and model testing.

TABLE 4-1. *Components Workflow Editor Nodes*

Summary

In this chapter, we looked at the different menus that are available when using the Oracle Data Miner tool in SQL Developer. We also looked at some of the initial steps you need to perform before you can actually start using the tool. These included creating a project and workflow. A useful feature for backing up your workflows and sharing them with other database users is the ability to export and import your workflows. Finally, you looked at the different nodes that are available in the Components Workflow Editor.

In the next chapter, you will look at how you can use Oracle Data Miner to perform some statistical analysis of the data and how you can use this important information to start creating a story about your data.

CHAPTER
5

Exploring Your Data

A s you embark on a data science project, one of the first tasks you will complete is to gather some statistical information about your data. You can combine this statistical information with other types of information on your data to begin the process of building a story about what is happening. You can use a variety of techniques to gather all of this information. With Oracle Data Miner, you can gather statistics about the attributes, produce graphs on each attribute, produce graphs comparing different attributes, and use advanced analytics features to gain a deeper insight into your data. This chapter explores each of these areas in Oracle Data Miner.

Gathering Statistics and Exploring Your Data

Before beginning any data science or data mining task, you need to perform some data investigations. These investigations enable you to explore the data and to gain a better understanding of the data values. You can discover a lot by doing this and it can help you to identify areas for improvement in the source applications, as well as identify data that does not contribute to solving your business problem (this is called *feature reduction*). Such investigations can allow you to identify data that needs reformatting into a number of additional features (*feature creation*). A simple example of this is a Date of Birth field; such a field may provide no real value, but by creating a number of additional attributes (features), you can use the field to determine the age group of various people.

The examples in the following sections illustrate how to define a data source, create and run the Explore Data node, use the statistics to build up a story about the data, and use some of the advanced analytics features to gain a deeper insight into the data. The data set used in these sections is from the Oracle Sample Schemas. When you followed the install instructions in Chapter 3, all the necessary permissions and views were set up for you.

Adding a Data Source

Before you can begin the data exploration, you need to identify the data you are going to use. To do this, you need to create a Data Source node on our Workflow Worksheet. Chapter 4 explained how to create a Workflow Worksheet called Explore Chapter. You can open this Workflow Worksheet or you can follow the same instructions to create a new workflow. When the Workflow Worksheet opens, so does the Components Workflow Editor. The Components Workflow Editor contains all the nodes that you can use to build up your Oracle Data Miner Workflow. The first category in the Components Workflow Editor is called Data. You can expand this category and display all the nodes that are available.

To create a Data Source node, you can click on the Data Source node in the Data category under the Components Workflow Editor, then move the mouse so that the onscreen point is located somewhere in the Workflow Worksheet. Then click your mouse again to create the Data Source node. Alternatively, you can click on the Data Source node and drag the icon onto the Workflow Worksheet. When the Data Source node is created, the Define Data Source window/wizard opens (see Figure 5-1). You can use this window/wizard to select the table or view that you want to use as your data source.

If the data source table or view is located in a different schema, you can click on the Add Schemas button (in the Step 1 of 2 window) and select the schema. The tables and views to which you have access are then displayed in the Available Tables/Views section of the Define Data Source Step 1 of 2 window.

When you have selected the table or view, you can then click on the Next button. In Figure 5-1, it shows the selection of the MINING_DATA_BUILD_V view. This view is used to illustrate the various data exploration features shown in this chapter.

After you have selected the table or view for your data source, click on the Next button to move on to the Step 2 of 2 window, where you can select what subset of attributes you would like to include for Oracle Data Miner. When this window opens, all the attributes are selected for inclusion. If you need to exclude any attributes, you can select these and move them to the Available Attributes list on the left-hand side. With the sample data, you will want to include all the attributes.

When you have finished selecting the attributes to include, you can click on the Finish button. The Data Source node is then renamed to have the same name as the table or view you have selected as the data source.

If you need to change the list of attributes, you can double-click on the Data Source node or you can right-click the node and select the option from the menu.

Data Source Properties

The Properties tab for the Data Source node allows you to edit the attribute list, specify whether you would like to use all the data or a sample of the data, and change the node details to include the node name and any comments you may have about the data source, as shown in Figure 5-2.

The Cache section of the Properties tab allows you to define how much of the underlying records should be used in Oracle Data Miner. If your table contains a very large number of records, you might want to use a subset of these for your initial work. By doing this, you can ensure that each of the nodes in your workflow runs quickly and allows you to get results promptly. As you progress through your data science project, you may want to increase the number of records. You can do this by changing the values in the Cache section and rerunning the workflow.

By default, the Cache section check box is unselected. This means that all the data will be used. To enable the Sampling of the records, you should select this check box.

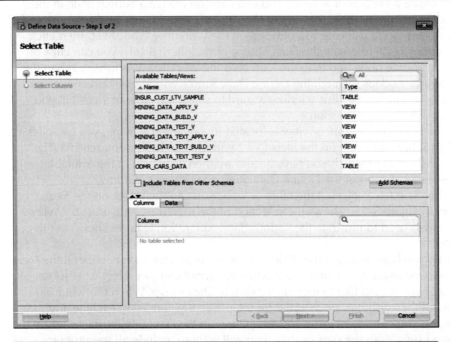

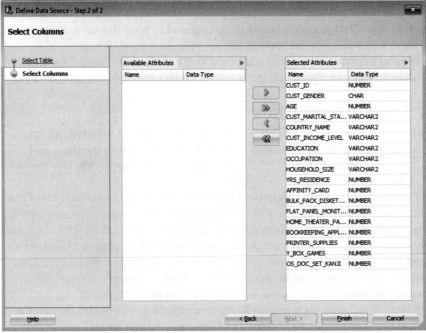

FIGURE 5-1. *Define Data Source window*

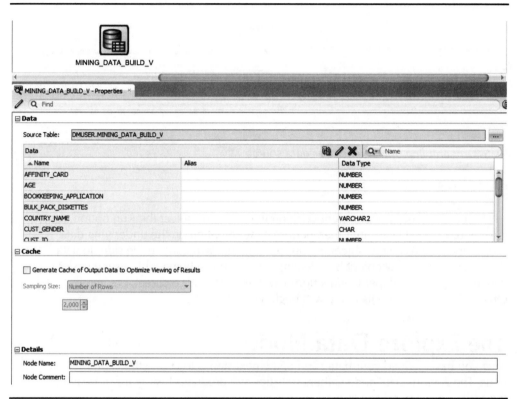

FIGURE 5-2. *Data Source node properties*

Two sampling methods are available. The first of these is to sample based on selecting a specified number of records, as shown in Figure 5-3. Alternatively, you can sample based on a percentage of the records. To select this option, change the Sampling Size drop-down list from Number of Rows to Percent. When you do this, a scroll bar appears below the drop-down list. You can adjust the sample size to the percentage you require. After adjusting the sample size, you need to run the node.

NOTE
There are options available to sample the data. The Explore Data node can generate statistics based on a sample of the data source records. There is a Sample node in the Transforms category of the Components Workflow Editor. It is recommended that, unless you are working with a very large data set, you should bring in all the data at the Data Source node and use the sample options available in the other nodes.

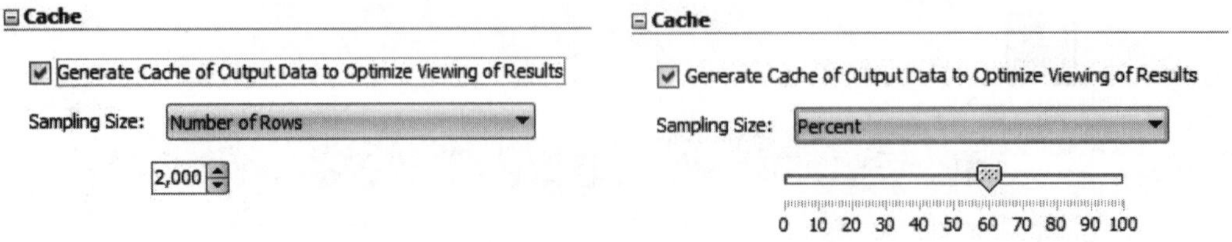

FIGURE 5-3. *Sampling options for your data source*

To run the node, you can right-click on the node and select the Run option from the menu. Oracle Data Miner then performs the sampling on the underlying data source and creates a new object in your schema that will contain the sample data. You can view this new object by selecting it from your schema table listing under your main SQL Developer Connections tab. It will be a table object, created by Oracle Data Miner, and its name will begin with "ODMRS."

The Explore Data Node

After you have defined your data source, the next step is to create the Explore Data node. The Explore Data node gathers statistics and produces histograms for each of the attributes in your data source.

The Explore Data node is located in the Data category of the Components Workflow Editor. To create the node on your Workflow Worksheet, click on the Explore Data node and then move your mouse to the Workflow Worksheet. Click again to create the node. The next step you need to perform is to connect the Data Source node to the Explore Data node. To do this, right-click on the Data Source node and select Connect from the menu. Then move the mouse to the Explore Data node and click again. A gray arrow line will be created between the two nodes. In the Properties tab for the Explore Data node, you can see the various properties relating to the data and the node (see Figure 5-4).

In the Properties tab, the main sections that you may be interested in are the Histogram and the Sample sections. As illustrated in the previous section, you can tell the Explore Data node to use all the data available in the data source or to sample the data. If you select to use sampling, the statistics and histograms calculated by the Explore Data node will be based on the sample. If you select to use all the data, then the statistics and histograms will be based on all the records. By default, a sample of 2,000 will be performed. You can change the number of records for the sample size or you can change the sample size to be based on a percentage of the number of records in the source table.

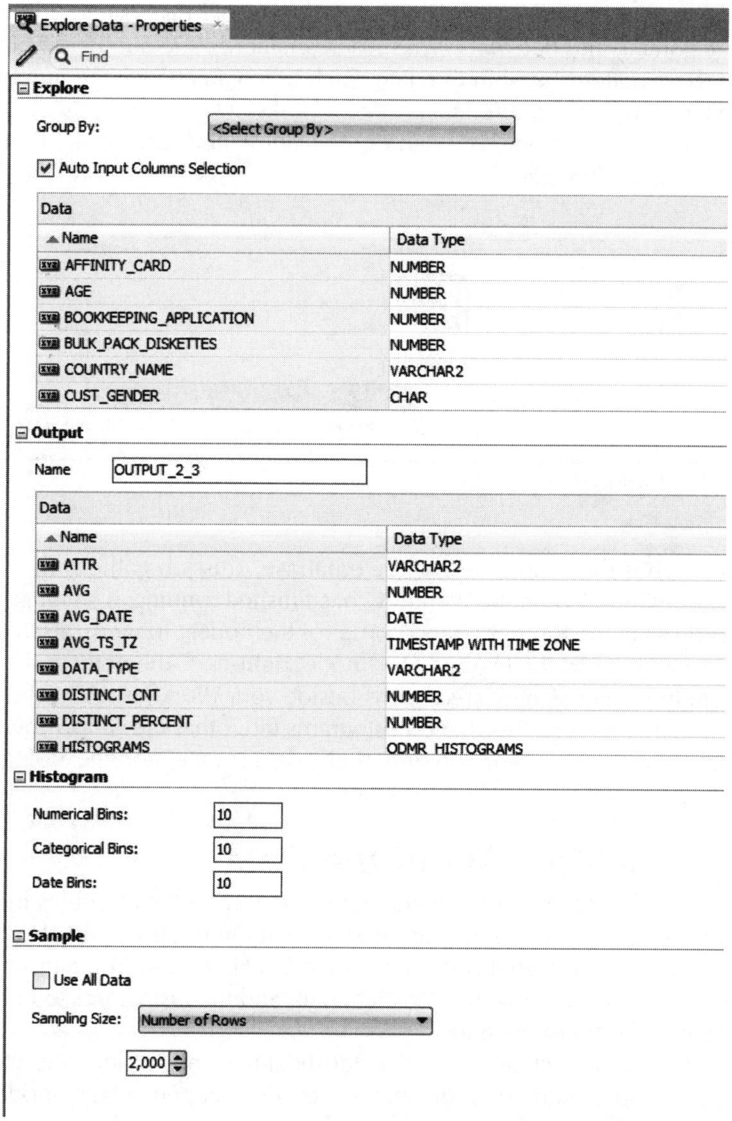

FIGURE 5-4. *Explore Data node Properties*

When the Explore Data node produces the histograms for each attribute, it bins the data into a specified number. By default, the number of bins is set to 10 for numerical, categorical, and date data types. You can change the number of bins to see whether certain patterns exist in the data. Each time you change the number of bins, you need to rerun the Explore Data node.

To run the Explore Data node, you can right-click the node and select Run from the menu, as illustrated in Figure 5-5.

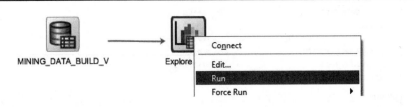

FIGURE 5-5. *Run the Explore Data node*

A workflow job is then submitted to the database. This job gathers all the statistics and histograms. When the workflow has finished running, a small green check mark appears at the top right-hand corner of the nodes. To view the statistics and histograms gathered by the Explore Data node, right-click the node and select View Data from the menu. A new area opens beside your Workflow Worksheet.

In addition to the main Statistics and Histograms tab, other tabs allow the user to view the data, the columns from the underlying data source, and the SQL query used to display information in the Statistics tab.

Building Up a Story About the Data

A lot of statistical information has been generated for each of the attributes in your Explore Data node. In addition to getting the statistical information, you also get a histogram of the attribute distributions, as illustrated in Figure 5-6. You can scroll through each attribute examining the statistical data and the histograms to build up a picture or an initial story of the data.

As you scroll through each attribute, the statistical information includes the data type, percentage of nulls, number of distinct values, distinct percentage, mode, average, median, minimum value, maximum value, standard deviation, variance, skewness, and kurtosis. The histogram presents, in a graphical form, the counts of the data values, based on the number of bins that was specified in the Properties section of the Explore Data node.

You can use this information to start to build up a story about your data. Using your knowledge of the domain where the data comes from, you can start to gain some insights into the data. For example, the sample data set MINING_DATA_BUILD_V contains data for an electronics goods store.

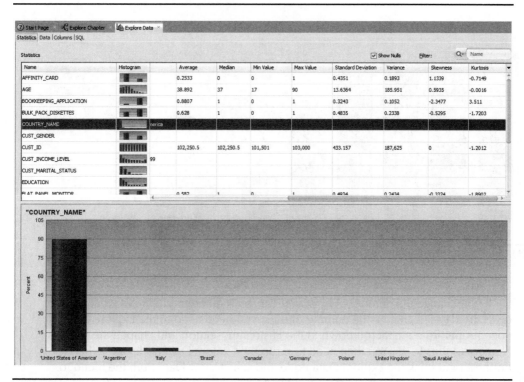

FIGURE 5-6. *Exploring the statistical information and histograms*

A few interesting things in the data are:

■ 90 percent of the data comes from the United States of America. Perhaps for your data mining models, you could just concentrate on these customers.

■ The PRINTER_SUPPLIES attribute only has one value. You can eliminate this from your data set as it does not contribute to the data mining algorithms.

■ The same applies to OS_DOC_SET_KENJI, which also has one value.

The histograms are based on a predetermined number of bins. This is initially set to 10, but you may need to increase or decrease this value to see whether a pattern exists in the data.

An example of this is if you select AGE and set the number of bins to 10, as shown in Figure 5-7. You get a nice histogram showing that most of your customers are in the 31 to 46 age ranges. So maybe you should be concentrating on these.

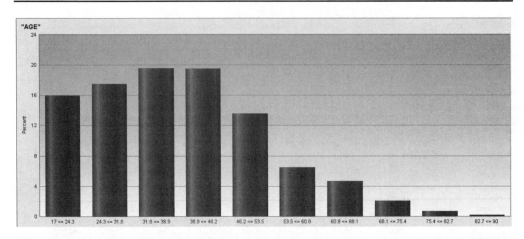

FIGURE 5-7. *Customer Age histogram*

If you change the number of bins, you can get a different picture of what is going on in the data. To change the number of bins, you need to go to the Explore Data node Properties pane. Scroll down to the Histogram section and change the Numerical Bins to 25. You then need to rerun the Explore Data node, and when it finishes, right-click the Explore Data node and select View Data from the menu to see the updated histogram, as shown in Figure 5-8.

Figure 5-8 shows that several important age groups stand out more than others. If you look at the 31 to 46 age range in Figure 5-7, you can see that there is not much change between each of the age bins. But when you look at Figure 5-8, for

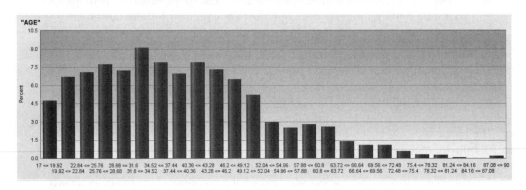

FIGURE 5-8. *Age histogram using 25 bins*

the same 31 to 46 age range, you get a very different view of the data. In Figure 5-8, you see that that the ages of the customers vary a lot. What does that mean? Well, it can mean lots of different things, and it all depends on the business scenario. In this example, you are looking at an electronic goods store. Figure 5-8 shows that there are a small number of customers up to about age 23. Then there is an increase. Is this due to people having obtained their main job after school and having some disposable income? This peak is followed by a drop-off in customers followed by another peak, drop-off, peak, drop-off, and so on. Maybe you can build a profile of your customers based on their age just like financial organizations do to determine what products to sell based on their customers' age and life stage.

In the current scenario of an electronics goods store, along with the statistical information and histograms, you could categorize the customers into the following:

- **Early 20s**   Finished with school, first job, disposable income.

- **Late 20s to early 30s**   Settling down, own home.

- **Late 30s**   Maybe kids, so less disposable income.

- **40s**   Maybe people are trading up and need new equipment. Or maybe the kids have now turned into teenagers and are encouraging their parents to buy up-to-date equipment.

- **Late 50s**   These could be empty nesters whose children have left home, maybe setting up home by themselves, and their parents are buying items for their children's home. Or maybe the parents are treating themselves to new equipment as they have more disposable income.

- **60s +**   Parents and grandparents buying equipment for their children and grandchildren. Or maybe these are very tech-oriented people who have just retired.

- **70+**   We have a drop-off here.

A lot can be discovered by changing the number of bins and examining the data. The important part of this examination is trying to relate what you are seeing from the graphical representation of the data on the screen back to the type of business you are examining. A lot can be discovered, but you will have to spend some time looking for it.

Exploring the Data Based on Attribute Grouping

The previous sections gave examples of how to use the Explore Data node to produce statistical information and histograms of the attribute values. They also showed that by changing the number of histograms in the Explore Data node Properties, you can gain a deeper insight into your data.

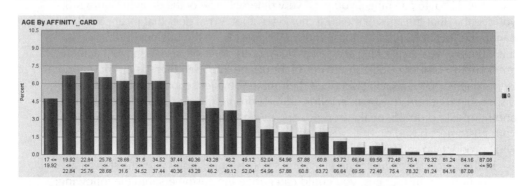

FIGURE 5-9.   *Histogram using a Group By attribute*

The Explore Data node also allows you to produce histograms that are based on an attribute, that is, Group By. For example, if you Group By the target attribute, you will get histograms that show the frequencies of the target attribute values for each of the attributes.

To change the Group By, you can double-click on the Explore Data node or go to the Explore Data node Properties. You can select one of the attributes from the Group By drop-down list, run the node again, and right-click on the node and select View Data from the menu. Figure 5-9 shows the histogram produced when the AFFINITY_CARD attribute was selected for the Group By. Figure 5-9 also shows for each Age bin how many customers have an affinity card and how many do not.

Graphs

Oracle Data Miner has a Graph node that allows you to create two-dimensional graphs of your data. The histogram produced in the Explore Data node has limited functionality. The Graph node allows you to create Line Plots, Scatter Plots, Bar Plots, Histograms, and Box Plots. The Graph node supports attributes with Number, Float, Date, and Timestamp data types.

The Graph node can be used at any point in your workflow to create graphs on data produced at any point of the workflow.

To create a Graph node in your workflow, you must first select the Graph node from the Data category of the Components Workflow Editor. You can select the node by clicking on it. Then move your mouse to your Workflow Worksheet and click again. The Graph node appears on the Workflow Worksheet. Next you need to connect the Graph node to the data source. The data source can be a Data Source node or another node that produces some data. To connect the nodes, right-click on the data source, select Connect from the menu, and then move the mouse to the

Graph node and click again. A gray arrow line is created between the data source and the Graph node.

The default setting is to create a sample of 2,000 records. If you want to use all the data for the graphs, you need to go to the Graph node Properties tab. In the section labeled Cache, you can change the drop-down list to Percent and move the slide to the 100 percent position. You are now ready to start creating your graphs, by double-clicking on the Graph node. A New Graph node window opens where you can select the type of graph you want to create; write a label for the graph; insert a comment; and specify the x-axis attribute and the y-axis attribute, the Group By column (if required), and any statistics that need to be used.

Creating a Graph

When the New Graph window opens, you are presented with a short list of required inputs. The first option you have to select is what type of graph you want to create. You can click on one of the buttons across the top of the Edit Graph window to select the type of graph you want to create. To create a graph, you need to select the attributes you want to use for your x-axis from the drop-down list, then the attribute you want for the y-axis from the scroll-down list. Be careful that you are selecting the correct attribute for each x-axis. You can choose a suitable name for the graph so that when you are looking at it later you will understand what the graph is showing. When finished, click the OK button to create the graph. Figure 5-10 shows the creation of a line graph.

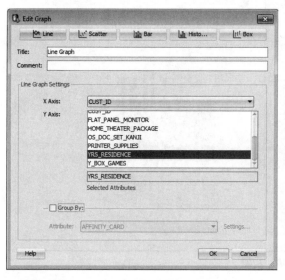
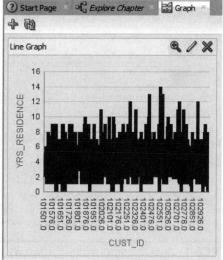

FIGURE 5-10. *Creating a line graph*

You can create a stacked line graph where you can use a number of attributes for your y-axis. To do this, you can hold down CTRL and select the attributes you want for the y-axis.

When the graph is drawn on the screen, you can zoom in on the graph by clicking the magnifying glass on the top right-hand corner of the graph. When the magnifying glass is clicked, the graph zooms out to occupy the full worksheet area. You can return the graph to the normal size by clicking on the magnifying glass again. If you need to change any of the graph settings, you can click on the yellow pencil on the top right-hand corner of the graph. This opens the Edit Graph window, where you can change the attributes and name, add a comment, and adjust Group By.

You can enhance your graph so that it contains more than one line or colored area. These lines and areas can be used to show the values from a particular attribute. To change a line graph so that it can represent the different values of an attribute, you can select the Group By check box. You then need to select an attribute from the drop-down list and then click the OK button to redraw the graph. In the example in Figure 5-11, the target attribute, AFFINITY_CARD, is selected from the drop-down list.

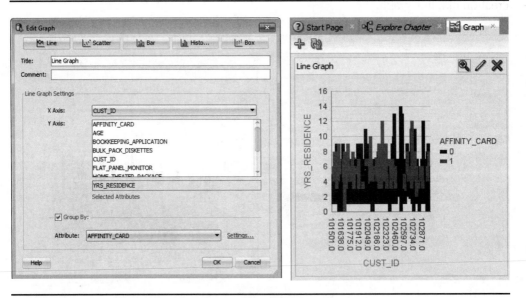

FIGURE 5-11. *Line graph with a Group By attribute*

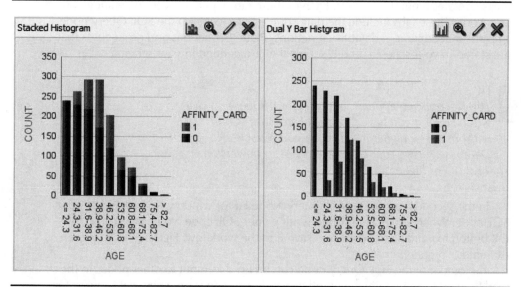

FIGURE 5-12. *Histogram graphs showing the different display options*

The redrawn graph has two lines, with one of these representing the zero value in the `AFFINITY_CARD` attribute and the other line representing the one value.

There is an additional display feature when you have specified a Group By attribute for the graph. When the graph is displayed, you will notice an additional icon (a small graph image) displayed along the top of the graph beside the magnifying glass. When you click on this graph icon, you can change the layout of the graph from being stacked to being side by side. Figure 5-12 shows an example of the same graph using the two display options.

SQL Query Node

The SQL Query node allows you to write your own SQL statements that you want executed on the data in your schema. When creating the SQL Query node, you have two options. The first option is to create the SQL Query node with no inputs. With this option, you can write a query (using SQL, PL/SQL, and an embedded R script) against any data that exists in your schema or to which you have access. The second option is when you attach a SQL Query node to a data source or model build nodes. With this second option, the code you specify in the SQL Query node will be only for the data source(s) to which the node is attached.

To create a SQL Query node, you can select it from the Data category in the Components Workflow Editor and then click your mouse again when it is over the Workflow Worksheet. Next you need to double-click on the node to open the SQL Query Node Editor window. This window has two main areas. The first of these areas contains a number of tabs. Each of these tabs can assist you in creating your SQL code. These tabs include the data sources connected to the SQL Query node, snippets that contain in-database functions, PL/SQL functions and procedures that are stored in your schema, and R scripts that are defined in your schema.

TIP
The R scripts tab appear only in the SQL Query Node Editor if you have Oracle R Enterprise (ORE) versions 1.3 or higher installed on your Oracle Database Server. Your Database needs to be version 11.2.0.3 or higher for ORE.

In the second area of the SQL Query Node Editor window, you can write your SQL code. When you have finished writing your SQL code, you can click on the OK button to validate the code and save it to the workflow. Figure 5-13 shows an example of a query.

The output of the SQL Query node can be used as input to other nodes in the workflow and can be joined with other data sources to form a new data source for your workflow.

If you have Oracle R Enterprise installed on your database server, you can embed your R scripts in the database. This will allow you to call these R scripts with SQL, using one of the following interfaces:

- `rqEval`

- `rqTableEval`

- `rqRowEval`

- `rqGroupEval`

Figure 5-14 shows the inclusion of R code in the SQL node.

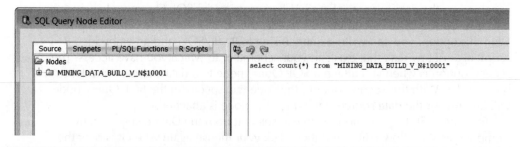

FIGURE 5-13. *SQL Query Node Editor window*

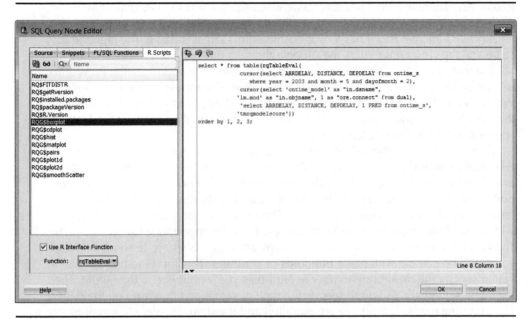

FIGURE 5-14. *SQL Query Node Editor using an embedded R script*

Feature Selection

After you have explored the data, you can identity some attributes and features that have just one value or mainly one value. In most of these cases, you know that these attributes will not contribute to the model build process, and you can remove these attributes as inputs to the data mining algorithms. The example data set includes a small number of attributes, so it is easy to work through the data and get a good understanding of some of the underlying information that exists in the data. Some of the aforementioned attributes were pointed out in the previous sections on exploring the data.

The reality is that your data sets can have a large number of attributes and features, so it will be very difficult or very time consuming to work through all of these to get a good understanding of what is a good attribute to use and to keep in your data set, and what attribute does not contribute and should be removed from the data set.

As your data evolves over time, the importance of the attributes will also evolve, with some becoming less important and some becoming more important. The Filter Columns node in Oracle Data Miner allows you to automate this work and can save you many hours, or even days, of your work on this task. The Filter Columns node uses the Minimum Description Length algorithm to determine the degree of importance for each attribute (Attribute Importance). The Attribute Importance is on a scale of zero to one. Any attribute with a negative value is reassigned to zero to indicate that the attribute does not have any relationship with the target variable. A positive ranking for an attribute indicates that it has a relationship with a target variable. The higher the value and the closer it is to one, the stronger the relationship.

To create the Filter Columns node, you need to select the node from the Transforms section of the Components Workflow Editor. Move the mouse to the Workflow Worksheet and click to create the node on the worksheet. Next you need to connect the Data Source node to the Filter Columns node. You can then connect the Data Source node to the Filter Columns node.

Figure 5-15 shows the default settings that are listed in the Properties tab for the Filter Columns node. You can modify these to match your requirements. The settings available include the Target; this is the target attribute that you will be using in your build node for classification. The Importance Cutoff indicates what should be the lowest value for the Attribute Importance. The node will not return any attributes with an Attribute Importance value that is less than the Importance Cutoff value. The Top N setting allows you to specify how many attributes to return. In some data sets, you could be dealing with many hundreds of attributes. This Top N setting allows you to specify the maximum number of attributes you would like in the output. The Sampling setting allows you to specify the type of sampling to perform on the data. The sampling methods available are Stratified and Random. The default sampling size is 2,000 records. You can adjust the sampling size to match your requirements.

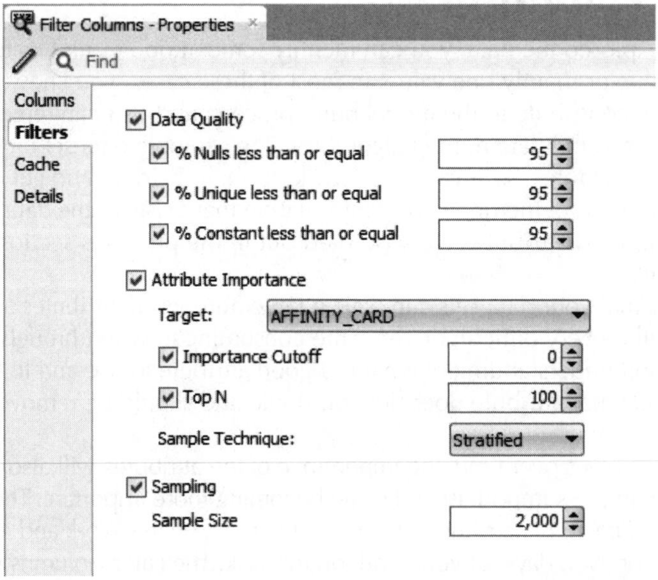

FIGURE 5-15. *Attribute Importance/Filter Columns node Properties*

TIP
You could create a number of Filter Columns nodes, each having a different sample size. This will allow you to see whether the attribute importance value increases or decreases as the sample size increases. Some attributes that may have an initial zero value may end up with a positive value as the number of records increases.

To run the Attribute Importance/Filter Columns node, you right-click on the node and select Run from the menu. When the node has completed, you see the small green check mark on the top right-hand corner of the node. To view the results, right-click on the node and select View Data from the pop-up menu. You then see the attributes listed in order of importance and their Importance measure as shown in Figure 5-16.

Target: AFFINITY_CARD

Attribute Ranking

Name	Type	▲ Rank	Importance
HOUSEHOLD_SIZE	VARCHAR2	1	0.159
CUST_MARITAL_STATUS	VARCHAR2	2	0.158
YRS_RESIDENCE	NUMBER	3	0.094
EDUCATION	VARCHAR2	4	0.086
AGE	NUMBER	5	0.085
OCCUPATION	VARCHAR2	6	0.075
Y_BOX_GAMES	NUMBER	7	0.063
HOME_THEATER_PACK...	NUMBER	8	0.056
CUST_GENDER	CHAR	9	0.035
BOOKKEEPING_APPLIC...	NUMBER	10	0.019
BULK_PACK_DISKETTES	NUMBER	11	0
COUNTRY_NAME	VARCHAR2	11	0
CUST_ID	NUMBER	11	0
CUST_INCOME_LEVEL	VARCHAR2	11	0
FLAT_PANEL_MONITOR	NUMBER	11	0
OS_DOC_SET_KANJI	NUMBER	11	0
PRINTER_SUPPLIES	NUMBER	11	0

FIGURE 5-16. *Attribute Importance results*

The Filter Columns node can be used as a data source for the various Data Mining model build nodes.

Summary

When starting out on your data science projects, it is important to explore your data in order to gain a good understanding of it. During the data exploration, you will discover what attributes are important, what the various data ranges are, what some of the correlations between attributes are, and more. You will use a variety of techniques to gain these insights and to help you to build up a picture of what is happening in your data. These are the first steps in creating the data story for your data science project. Oracle Data Miner has a number of features that facilitate the exploration of your data. These include enabling you to produce various statistics of the data, generate various graphs, write your own SQL code to extract the information you need, and use code written in R that is embedded in the database as part of Oracle R Enterprise. In addition, you can use advanced machine learning methods to extract what attributes are important for your data. By using all of these techniques and your domain knowledge, you can start your journey with your Oracle Data Science project.

CHAPTER
6

Data Preparation

Whan you start with any data science or data mining project, one of the stages that can take up a significant amount of time involves the preparation of the data. Data preparation can include many steps that involve merging and transforming the data in the formats that are required by the data mining algorithms. In addition to performing these data preparation steps you may want to work with a portion of the data, use data that is summarized to a certain level, use various filters, sample the data based on certain criteria, or transform attribute values into other values that are a bit more meaningful.

This chapter gives examples of the various data preparation nodes that are available in the Oracle Data Miner tool. You can find these data preparation nodes in the Transforms section of the Components Workflow Editor, as shown in Figure 6-1.

Aggregate

The Aggregate node allows you to create new attributes that are based on the data source. These new attributes contain values based on one or more of the defined aggregate functions or based on a user-defined function. For example, you can aggregate transaction data into monthly values. In addition to the typical type of aggregation, you can also create aggregate attributes that are aggregated at an additional level. This additional level of aggregation is stored in a nested column in the database. The following sections illustrate how you can use the Aggregate node to create aggregate attributes.

The Aggregate node requires a Data Source node or another node that already exists in your workflow and that contains the data that you want to aggregate. To create the Aggregate node, select the node from the Transforms section of the Components Workflow Editor, then create the node on the workflow. Then join

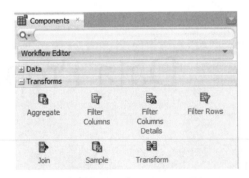

FIGURE 6-1. *Transforms section of the Components Workflow Editor*

the Data Source node (or another node that contains the data) to the Aggregate node by right-clicking on the Data Source node and selecting Connect from the menu; then move the mouse to the Aggregate node and click again. This creates the connection between the two nodes.

Using the Aggregation Wizard

To define the Aggregate node properties, you can double-click on the Aggregate node. This opens the Edit Aggregate Node window. The first step is to define the level at which you want the aggregation to occur. In the following example, MINING_DATA_BUILD_V is used to illustrate the creation of additional aggregate attributes. The example illustrated in Figure 6-2 shows the calculation of the average, minimum, and maximum age of the customers in the data set, aggregated based on the COUNTRY_NAME. To define the level of aggregation (COUNTRY_NAME in this example), select the Edit button beside the Group By field on the Edit Aggregate Node window illustrated in Figure 6-2a. This opens the Edit Group By window (Figure 6-2b). Select the attributes that define the level of aggregation. In this example, this is the COUNTRY_NAME attribute. Select this attribute and then move it to the panel on the right-hand side of the window. If you have more than one attribute that defines the level of aggregation, then select all necessary attributes and move them to the panel on the right.

When you have defined the level of aggregation, the next step is to define the attribute that you want to aggregate. To define this, you need to select the Aggregation Wizard icon or the Add Attribute icon, both of which are located under the Group By edit button in the Edit Aggregate Node window. The following example illustrates how to define the aggregation functions for the Age attributes as shown in Figure 6-3. To define the aggregate attributes using the Aggregation Wizard, click on the icon. The Aggregation Wizard window opens. In the first window, you can select the aggregation function you want to use. Depending on the data type of the attribute you want to aggregate, the aggregation functions for number data types and character data types are listed separately. Select all the aggregate functions you want to use. In the example shown in Figure 6-3a, you can select the MAX, AVG, and MIN functions from the list of numerical functions. Click the Next button to move to the next window, where you can select the attribute or attributes to which you want to apply the aggregation functions selected in the previous window. In the example shown in Figure 6-3b, the AGE attribute is selected and moved to the right-hand panel.

At this stage, you have defined what aggregation should be performed on the AGE attribute. You can ignore the remaining steps at this stage. Those steps of the Aggregate node are discussed in the next section, "Adding a New Aggregation-level Attribute." Click on the Finish button to close the Aggregation Wizard, then click on the OK button to close the Aggregate node.

To run the node and to produce the aggregate attributes, you need to run the Aggregate node by right-clicking it and selecting Run from the menu. When the

(a)

(b)

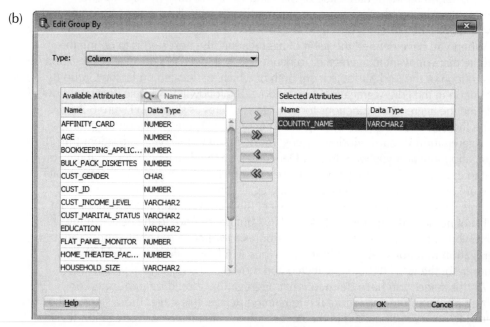

FIGURE 6-2. *Defining the level of aggregation of the Aggregate node*

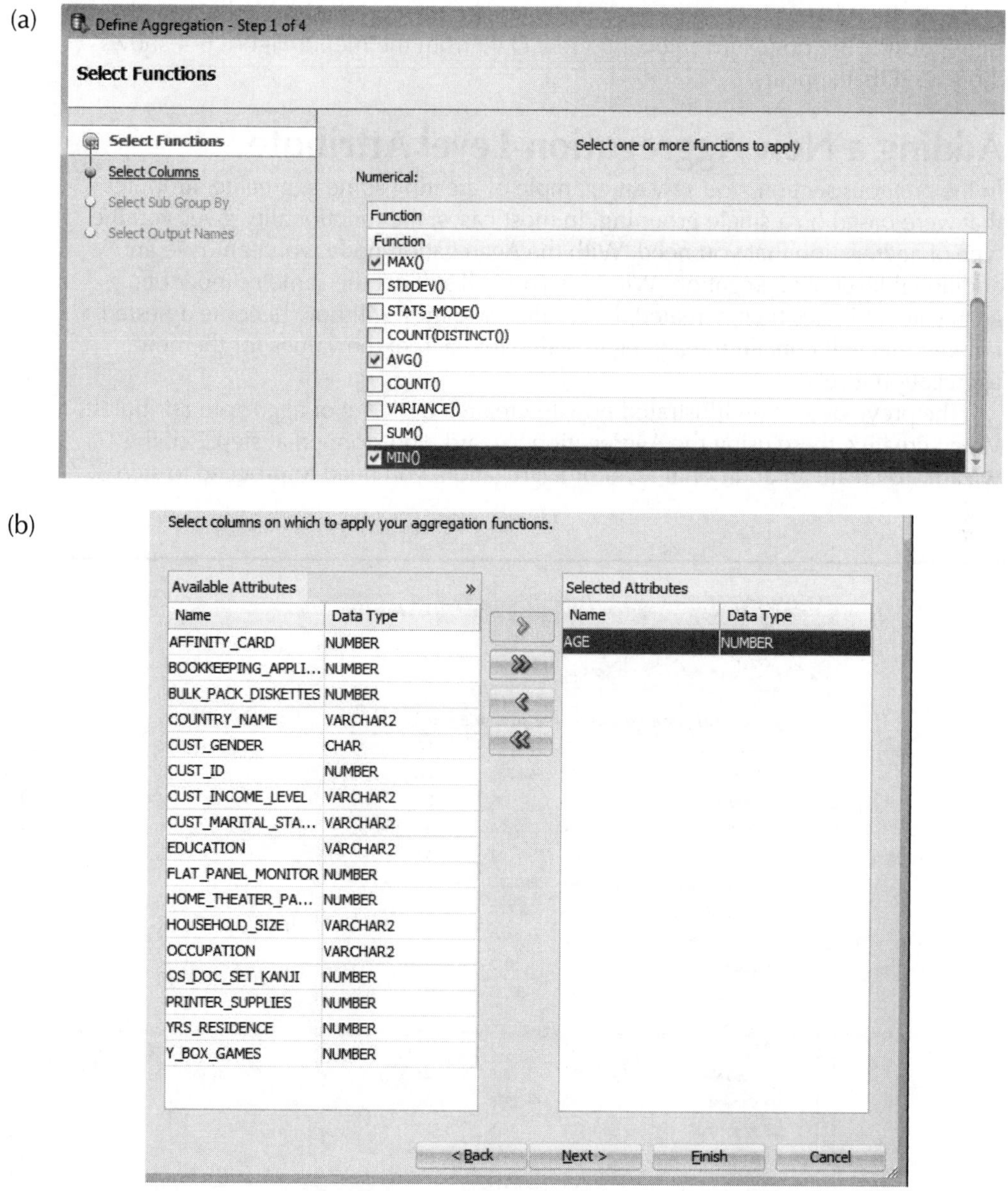

(a)

(b)

FIGURE 6-3. *Defining the aggregation attributes using the Aggregation Wizard; (a) select the aggregate functions; (b) select the attribute*

complete, a small green check mark appears on the top right-hand corner
.. node. When this appears, you can view the data produced by the node by
right-clicking the node and selecting View Data from the menu. Figure 6-4 shows
the screen that appears.

Adding a New Aggregation-Level Attribute

In the previous section, you saw an example of creating some aggregate attributes
that were based on a single grouping. In most cases, the functionality gives you the
type of aggregation that you need. With the Aggregation node, you can have an
additional level of aggregation. With this you will still get the same number of
aggregate attributes being created, but in this case they will now become a nested
column that will contain the aggregate value for each of the values for the new
aggregation levels.

The previous section illustrated how to create a basic set of aggregate attributes.
When creating these using the Aggregation Wizard, you stopped at step 2 of the
wizard. To create an additional level of aggregation, you need to proceed to step 3.

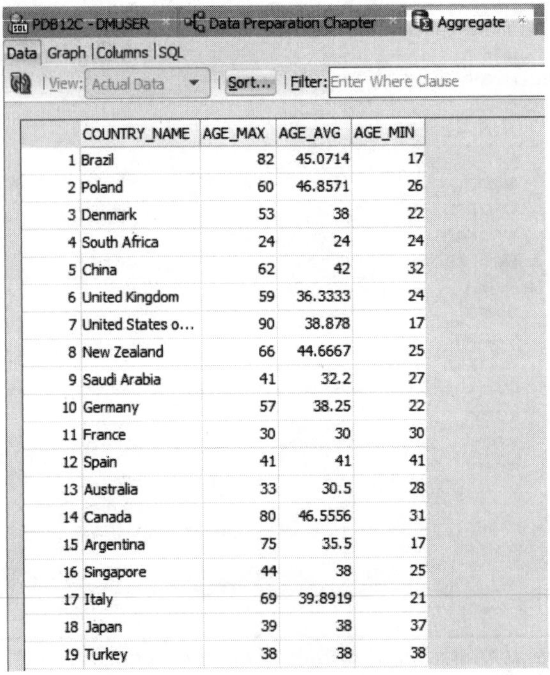

	COUNTRY_NAME	AGE_MAX	AGE_AVG	AGE_MIN
1	Brazil	82	45.0714	17
2	Poland	60	46.8571	26
3	Denmark	53	38	22
4	South Africa	24	24	24
5	China	62	42	32
6	United Kingdom	59	36.3333	24
7	United States o...	90	38.878	17
8	New Zealand	66	44.6667	25
9	Saudi Arabia	41	32.2	27
10	Germany	57	38.25	22
11	France	30	30	30
12	Spain	41	41	41
13	Australia	33	30.5	28
14	Canada	80	46.5556	31
15	Argentina	75	35.5	17
16	Singapore	44	38	25
17	Italy	69	39.8919	21
18	Japan	39	38	37
19	Turkey	38	38	38

FIGURE 6-4. *Results from Aggregation node*

Figure 6-5 shows step 3 of the Aggregation Wizard, where the CUST_GENDER is selected for the additional level of aggregation.

The last step of the Aggregation Wizard allows you to rename the names of the attributes that the node generates. To change the name, click on the cell that corresponds to the attribute name under the Output column. To finish with the Aggregation Wizard and complete the node setup, click the Finish button and then the OK button to close the Aggregate Node window. To run the node and to see the new aggregation attributes and values, right-click the Aggregation node, then select Run from the menu. After the node runs, you see a green check mark on the top right-hand corner of the node. To view the results, right-click the node, then select View Data from the menu. Figure 6-6 shows an example of the screen that View Data generates.

It can be seen in Figure 6-6 that the aggregated attributes contain nested data. To get a better view of the data that is contained in these attributes, you can use a query like the following to extract the aggregated data. But before you can run this query, you need to persist the data produced by the Aggregate node to the database

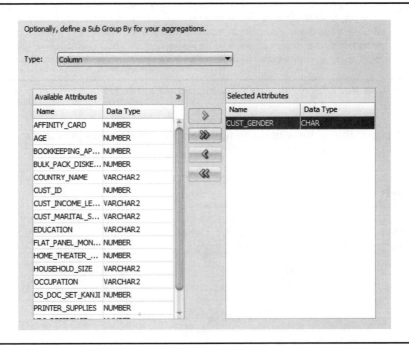

FIGURE 6-5. *Creating an additional aggregation level using the Aggregation Wizard*

	COUNTRY_NAME	AGE_MAX	AGE_AVG	AGE_MIN
1	Argentina	SYS.DM_NESTED_NUMERICALS(SYS.D...	SYS.DM_NESTED_NUMERICALS(SYS.D...	SYS.DM_NESTED_NUMERICALS(SYS.D...
2	Australia	SYS.DM_NESTED_NUMERICALS(SYS.D...	SYS.DM_NESTED_NUMERICALS(SYS.D...	SYS.DM_NESTED_NUMERICALS(SYS.D...
3	Brazil	SYS.DM_NESTED_NUMERICALS(SYS.D...	SYS.DM_NESTED_NUMERICALS(SYS.D...	SYS.DM_NESTED_NUMERICALS(SYS.D...
4	Canada	SYS.DM_NESTED_NUMERICALS(SYS.D...	SYS.DM_NESTED_NUMERICALS(SYS.D...	SYS.DM_NESTED_NUMERICALS(SYS.D...
5	China	SYS.DM_NESTED_NUMERICALS(SYS.D...	SYS.DM_NESTED_NUMERICALS(SYS.D...	SYS.DM_NESTED_NUMERICALS(SYS.D...
6	Denmark	SYS.DM_NESTED_NUMERICALS(SYS.D...	SYS.DM_NESTED_NUMERICALS(SYS.D...	SYS.DM_NESTED_NUMERICALS(SYS.D...
7	France	SYS.DM_NESTED_NUMERICALS(SYS.D...	SYS.DM_NESTED_NUMERICALS(SYS.D...	SYS.DM_NESTED_NUMERICALS(SYS.D...
8	Germany	SYS.DM_NESTED_NUMERICALS(SYS.D...	SYS.DM_NESTED_NUMERICALS(SYS.D...	SYS.DM_NESTED_NUMERICALS(SYS.D...
9	Italy	SYS.DM_NESTED_NUMERICALS(SYS.D...	SYS.DM_NESTED_NUMERICALS(SYS.D...	SYS.DM_NESTED_NUMERICALS(SYS.D...
10	Japan	SYS.DM_NESTED_NUMERICALS(SYS.D...	SYS.DM_NESTED_NUMERICALS(SYS.D...	SYS.DM_NESTED_NUMERICALS(SYS.D...
11	New Zealand	SYS.DM_NESTED_NUMERICALS(SYS.D...	SYS.DM_NESTED_NUMERICALS(SYS.D...	SYS.DM_NESTED_NUMERICALS(SYS.D...
12	Poland	SYS.DM_NESTED_NUMERICALS(SYS.D...	SYS.DM_NESTED_NUMERICALS(SYS.D...	SYS.DM_NESTED_NUMERICALS(SYS.D...
13	Saudi Arabia	SYS.DM_NESTED_NUMERICALS(SYS.D...	SYS.DM_NESTED_NUMERICALS(SYS.D...	SYS.DM_NESTED_NUMERICALS(SYS.D...
14	Singapore	SYS.DM_NESTED_NUMERICALS(SYS.D...	SYS.DM_NESTED_NUMERICALS(SYS.D...	SYS.DM_NESTED_NUMERICALS(SYS.D...
15	South Africa	SYS.DM_NESTED_NUMERICALS(SYS.D...	SYS.DM_NESTED_NUMERICALS(SYS.D...	SYS.DM_NESTED_NUMERICALS(SYS.D...
16	Spain	SYS.DM_NESTED_NUMERICALS(SYS.D...	SYS.DM_NESTED_NUMERICALS(SYS.D...	SYS.DM_NESTED_NUMERICALS(SYS.D...
17	Turkey	SYS.DM_NESTED_NUMERICALS(SYS.D...	SYS.DM_NESTED_NUMERICALS(SYS.D...	SYS.DM_NESTED_NUMERICALS(SYS.D...
18	United Kingdom	SYS.DM_NESTED_NUMERICALS(SYS.D...	SYS.DM_NESTED_NUMERICALS(SYS.D...	SYS.DM_NESTED_NUMERICALS(SYS.D...
19	United States o...	SYS.DM_NESTED_NUMERICALS(SYS.D...	SYS.DM_NESTED_NUMERICALS(SYS.D...	SYS.DM_NESTED_NUMERICALS(SYS.D...

FIGURE 6-6. *Results from Aggregation node using nested attributes*

using the Create Table or View node. In this example, the data was persisted to a table called `AGGREGATED_DATA`.

```
SELECT country_name, b.attribute_name CUST_GENDER, b.value MAX_CUST_AGE
FROM   aggregated_data,
       table(age_max)   b;


COUNTRY_NAME               CUST_GENDER     MAX_CUST_AGE
------------------------   -------------   ------------
Argentina                  F                         75
Argentina                  M                         65
Australia                  F                         28
Australia                  M                         33
Brazil                     F                         47
Brazil                     M                         82
Canada                     F                         72
Canada                     M                         80
China                      F                         33
China                      M                         62
Denmark                    F                         53
Denmark                    M                         49
...
```

An alternative to using the Aggregation Wizard is to select the Add Attribute icon (the green plus sign) in the Edit Aggregate Node window. This opens the Add Aggregate Element window and allows you to define and create a single aggregate attribute. The example shown in Figure 6-7 illustrates defining an aggregate attribute that calculates the average of the YRS_RESIDENCE attribute.

By default, the Aggregate Element window automatically generates the attribute name based on the function you select and the attribute to which it is to be applied. If you would like to use a different name, you can deselect the Auto Name check box. This makes the Output field editable and you can change the output attribute name. Additionally, you can also define the Sub Group for the additional levels of aggregation.

Adding an Aggregation Expression

Most of the types of aggregations you will want to define can be done using the Aggregation Wizard or by defining a new Aggregate Element. Both allow you to define an aggregation based on the standard list of numeric and character functions. But there can be occasions when you need to define a more complex aggregation that involves using a number of attributes or a number of functions and calculations. To do this, you can define an aggregate attribute using the Add Expression icon in the Edit Aggregate Node window.

When you click on this icon, the Add Aggregate Element window opens, as shown in Figure 6-8a. Here you can define the Output attribute name and then click on the pencil icon to open the Expression Builder window. The Expression Builder window, which is used in a number of other nodes, allows you to build up a SQL expression using the available attributes for the node and a range of functions and operations. Figure 6-8b illustrates an example of an expression using the

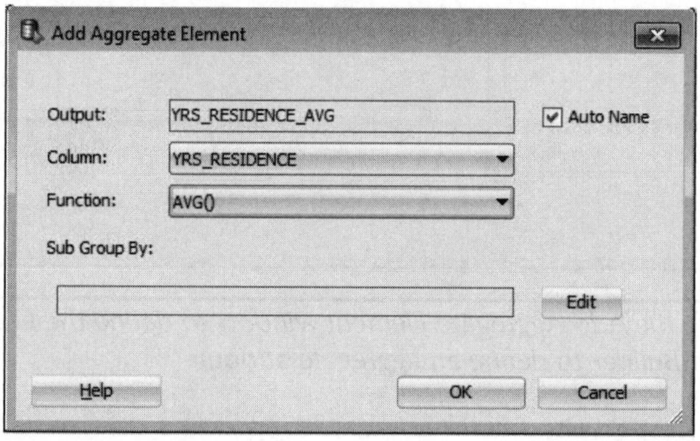

FIGURE 6-7. *Add Aggregate Element window*

(a)

(b)

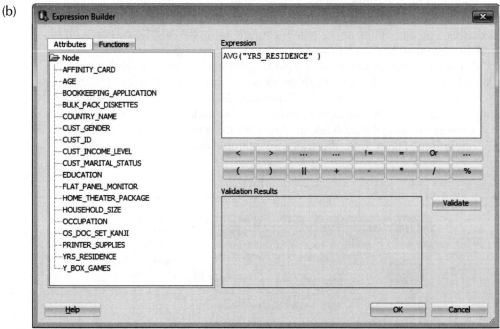

FIGURE 6-8. *(a) Using the Add Aggregate Element window to define the Output name; (b) using the Expression Builder to define an aggregate attribute*

Expression Builder window. It uses the AVG function that is listed under the analytical functions on the left-hand side of the window. You can validate the correctness of the expression by clicking on the Validate button after you have completed the expression. If the expression has any errors, these are reported in the Validation Results section of the window. An additional level of validation can be performed when you return to the Add Aggregate Element window.

CAUTION
The expression that you create using the Expression Builder should be a Group By expression and contain Group By functions.

Filter Columns

In Chapter 5, the section "Feature Selection" discussed the Filter Columns node. In that section, you learned how you can use the Filter Columns node to find out what attributes may contribute toward a particular attribute. This feature is called Attribute Importance and is based on the Minimum Description Length algorithm.

In addition to using this feature of the Filter Columns node, you can perform a number of additional filterings based on the columns and the values in them. The first of these Filter Columns settings can be found when you double-click on the Filter Columns node. The Edit Filter Columns Node window lists the attributes that are pipelined into the node from the previous node. If you decide not to include some of the attributes, you can click under the Output column for the attribute to exclude it from the output of the Filter Columns node. When you click under the Output column for an attribute, it changes from having an arrow to having an arrow with a red *X*.

The other types of filtering are available when you click on the Settings button in the Filter Columns Node window. The Define Filter Column Settings window, shown in Figure 6-9, then appears. Three types of filtering are available. One of these is the Attribute Importance. Chapter 5 details how to use this type of filtering. The Data Quality section allows you to specify certain criteria relating the percentage of null values in an attribute, the percentage of unique values, and the percentage of constant values value. You can specify an appropriate percentage level for each of these. Any attribute that does not match these percentages is outputted from the node.

You can also specify whether sampling should take place on the data so that a certain number of records will be outputted from the node. By default, the Filter Columns node has filtering turned on with a sample size of 2,000 records. This number of records can be altered to a number of your choice.

FIGURE 6-9. *Define Filter Column Settings window*

TIP
Disable the sampling in the Filter Columns node and use the Sample node to specify what sampling you want to perform on the data. The Sampling node gives you more options for sampling the data.

Filter Columns Details

The Filter Columns Details node allows you to filter the Attribute Importance information from the Filter Columns node. You should use the Filter Columns Details node only when you have enabled Attribute Importance and set the target attribute in the Filter Columns node. Figure 6-10 illustrates the output generated by the Filter Columns node that contains only the Attribute Importance information.

	ATTRIBUTE_NAME	RANK	IMPORTANCE_VALUE
1	HOUSEHOLD_SIZE	1	0.1589
2	CUST_MARITAL_...	2	0.1582
3	YRS_RESIDENCE	3	0.0941
4	EDUCATION	4	0.0863
5	AGE	5	0.0849
6	OCCUPATION	6	0.0752
7	Y_BOX_GAMES	7	0.063
8	HOME_THEATER...	8	0.0565
9	CUST_GENDER	9	0.0353
10	BOOKKEEPING_A...	10	0.0192
11	BULK_PACK_DIS...	11	0
12	CUST_INCOME_L...	11	0
13	OS_DOC_SET_K...	11	0
14	COUNTRY_NAME	11	0
15	PRINTER_SUPPLIES	11	0
16	CUST_ID	11	0
17	FLAT_PANEL_MO...	11	0

FIGURE 6-10. *Filter Columns Details node results showing the Attribute Importance results*

CAUTION
If you connect the Filter Columns Details node to the Filter Columns node but you have not turned on Attribute Importance, then you will not get any output for the Filter Columns Details node. But if you have previously enabled Attribute Importance and generated results and then disabled Attribute Importance. the Filter Columns Details node will show the previously generated Attribute Importance results.

The Filter Columns Details node can be connected only to the Filter Columns node. If you try to connect the Filter Columns Details node to another type of node, you will find that the connect arrow does not form.

To create the Filter Columns Details node, select it from the Transforms section of the Components Workflow Editor and click on your Workflow Worksheet to create the node. Then right-click on the Filter Columns node and select Connect from the menu. Move the mouse to the Filter Columns Details node and click again to form the connection. When you have enabled Attribute Importance in the Filter Columns node, you can right-click on the Filter Columns Details node to produce the node outputs. When the node has been run, a small green check mark appears on the top right-hand side of the Filter Columns Details node.

To view the Attribute Importance output, right-click on the Filter Columns Details node, then select View Data from menu. The results are displayed as illustrated in Figure 6-10.

Filter Rows

The Filter Rows node allows you to specify a restriction that you want to apply to the rows of the data from a previous node. This is like specifying a WHERE clause in the SELECT statement, but in this case you can specify it using the Expression Builder feature that is built into the Filter Rows node.

To create the Filter Rows node, you select it from the Transforms section of the Components Workflow Editor and click on your Workflow Worksheet. You then need to connect the Filter Rows node to the data source or other node that contains the data that you want to filter. To create this connection, select the node that contains the data to be filtered, right-click on this node, and select Connect from the menu. Then move the mouse to the Filter Rows node and click again to create the connection.

Double-click on the Filter Rows node to open it. When the Edit Filter Rows Node window opens, you can click on the pencil icon to create the filter condition. When you click the pencil icon, the Expression Builder window opens. Here you can write your filter condition or use the attributes, functions, and operators listed to build the filter condition. When you have created the filter condition, you can click on the Validate button to check the code you have written. When the filter condition is finished and validated, you can click on the OK button to return to the Edit Filter Rows Node window. Figure 6-11 shows the Edit Filter Rows Node and the Expression Builder window. The example illustrated in Figure 6-11 shows a filter that returned rows only where the country name (COUNTRY_NAME) is the "United States of America."

You can view the output of the Filter Rows node by running the node, right-clicking on the completed Filter Rows node, then selecting the View Data from the menu.

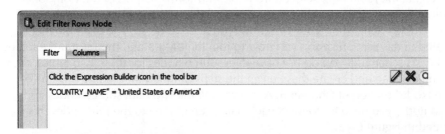

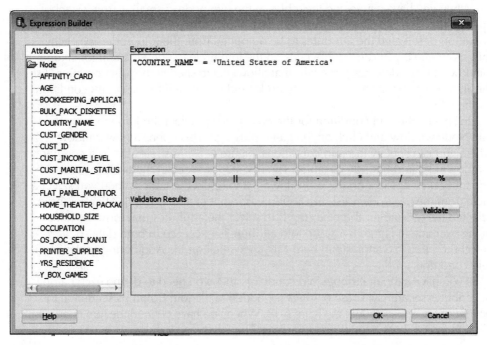

FIGURE 6-11. *Setting up a filter using the Filter Rows node*

Join

The Join node allows you to join two or more data sources together to form a new data set. When you use the Join node, you can specify the join conditions, identify the subset of the attributes you want to output, and apply a filter (i.e., a WHERE clause) to return records that match certain criteria.

To create the Join node, select it from the Transforms section of the Components Workflow Editor and then create it on your worksheet. If you do not have the data sources already defined on your workflow, you need to do so. The example that is illustrated in this section shows you how to join the SALES and the PRODUCTS tables from the SH schema. If you do not have data source nodes for these two tables, then you can go ahead and create these using the steps outlined in "Adding a Data Source Node" section of Chapter 5. After creating the two data source nodes and the Join node, you need to connect each data source node to the Join node. This is illustrated in Figure 6-12.

When you have connected the tables to the Join node, a small warning symbol appears on the node. This warning tells you that you have not specified the join condition or selected the attributes to be outputted from the Join node. To specify this information, you can double-click on the Join node to open the Edit Join Node window. This window has three tabs that allow you to specify the Join condition, list the attributes to be outputted from the node, and specify a filter or WHERE conditions for the join.

To specify the join condition for the data sources, select the Join tab in the Edit Join Node window and click on the green plus sign. This opens a new window where you can specify the join conditions. Figure 6-13 illustrates the join condition for the SALES and PRODUCTS tables. The first step is to select the table for Source 1 and for Source 2. Click on the drop-down list to select the table. When you select a table from the drop-down list, the attributes for that table are listed. After you have selected the two tables, the next step is to select the attributes that form the join. In the example in Figure 6-13, the join attribute is PROD_ID in both data sources. Select the PROD_ID attribute in both lists, then click on the Add button to define the join condition.

If you have a multi-attribute join condition, then you need to define each pairing of attributes separately. These pairings are added to the Join Columns section at the bottom of the screen shown in Figure 6-13. When you have defined the join condition, click on the OK button to return to the main Edit Join Node window.

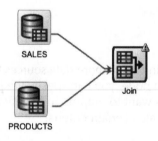

FIGURE 6-12. *Connecting the data sources to the Join node*

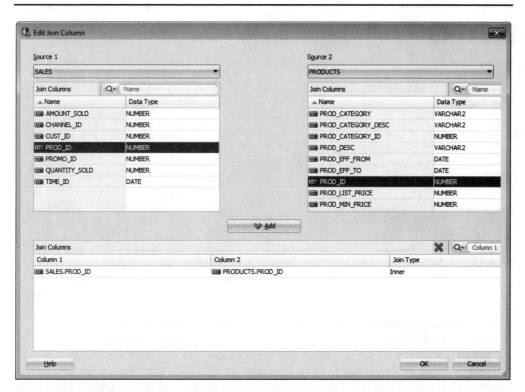

FIGURE 6-13. *Defining the join condition*

Click on the Columns tab in the Edit Join Node window to select the attributes you want outputted from the Join node. By default, all the attributes from your data sources are selected to be outputted from the Join node. In most cases, you will only want a subset of these attributes. To remove attributes from the list, you need to uncheck the Automatic Settings check box. Then select the attributes that you want to remove from the output and then click on the red *X* to remove these attributes from the list. In this sample scenario, you want the output to include all the attributes from the SALES table and the product name from the PRODUCTS table, as illustrated in Figure 6-14.

TIP
If you delete an attribute in error, you can list it again by clicking on the green X icon. A window opens that lists all the available attributes. Select the attribute you want, then move it to the Selected Attributes list.

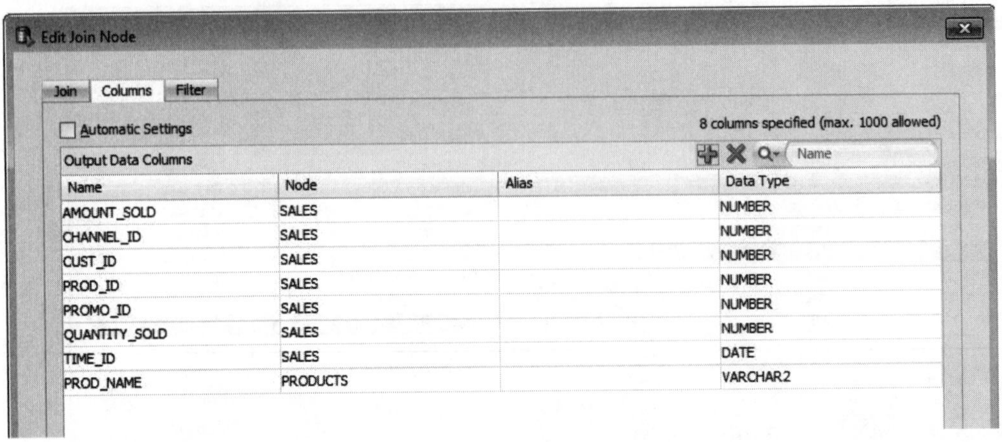

FIGURE 6-14. *Select the attributes to be outputted from the Join node*

If you need to apply a filter or WHERE clause to the join, you can define this by clicking on the Filter tab in the Edit Join Node window. To define the filter, click on the pencil icon to open the Expression Builder window. You can use the attribute list, functions list, and operator buttons to create the filter. The example shown in Figure 6-15 shows a filter that return records only where the PROMO_ID equals 33.

When you have defined the filter, you can validate the code by clicking on the Validate button. If the expression is valid, you get a "Validation successful" message in the Validation Results section. If there are any errors, these are also reported in this section. When you are finished, you can click on the OK button to return to the Edit Join node, then click on the OK button again to close the Edit Join node window.

To run the Join node, right-click on the node and select Run from the menu. When all the nodes have completed, a green check mark will appear on the top right-hand corner of the Join node. There is no option to view the results when the node has been run. If you want to see the results generated by the node, you need to create a new Create Table or View node, connect it to the Join node, and run it. When the node finishes running, you can view the output from the Join node.

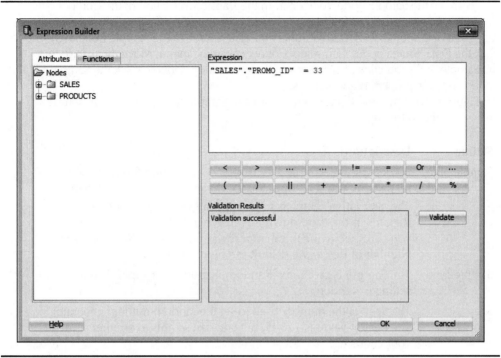

FIGURE 6-15. *Defining a filter for the Join node*

Sample

The Sample node allows you to extract a subset of the data from a data source, or some other input node, using one of three sampling techniques. The sampling techniques available include the following:

- **Random Sample** This is where every record in the data source has an equal chance of being selected.

- **Stratified Sample** This is where the data set is divided into subsets based on a particular attribute, and then random samples are taken from each of these subsets.

- **Top N Sample** This is where the first *N* values are selected from the data source.

To create the Sample node, select it from the Transforms section of the Components Workflow Editor and click on the worksheet to create the node. The Sample node requires a data source as input. To connect the data source to the Sample node, right-click the Data Source node, then select Connect from the menu. Move the mouse to the Sample node and click again to create the connection. Double-click the Sample node to edit the properties and settings.

Figure 6-16 shows the default settings for the Sample node. The default setting consists of the following:

Setting	Description
Sample Size	By default, the sample size is set to Percent and the size set to 60 percent. You can adjust this to whatever percentage you require. The alternative setting is to change Sample Size to Number of Records in the drop-down menu. When this setting is selected, you can specify the number of rows you want in the sample. For Number of Rows, the default setting is 2,000 rows.
Sample Type	The Sample Type can be Random, Stratified, or TopN. The default setting is Random.
Seed	The Seed is the number used to set the random number generator. The default value is 12345, but you can set this to another value of your choosing.
Case ID	The Case ID is an optional setting. You can set this to one of the attributes in your data source. The combination of the Seed value and the Case ID ensures that the data set produced is reproducible.

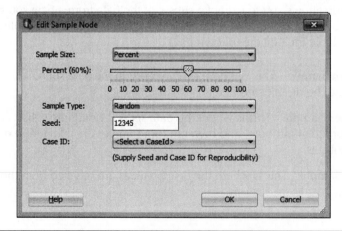

FIGURE 6-16. *Random sample setting in the Sample node*

If you want to perform stratified sampling and select this technique from the Sample Type drop-down list in Figure 6-16, you get the following additional node settings:

Stratified Sampling Settings	Description
Column	This is the column in your data set that will be used for the stratified sampling.
Distribution	This determines how the stratified sampling will be created. The following are possible values for this setting:

- **Original**   This is the default setting. It keeps the same distribution of values in the sample as what was in the data source based on the column. For example, if 30 percent of your customers come from the United States, then the sample data set will contain 30 percent of the records for the USA.

- **Balanced**   The distribution of the values of the column is equal in the sample, regardless of the distribution of the data. For example, if the column has two values, then the sample data set will have 50 percent of the records for each of these values regardless of the actual distribution in the data source.

- **Custom**   You can specify that the values of the column are distributed in the sample.

NOTE
You need to run the Sample node before you can edit the Custom Setting.

Figure 6-17 shows the settings used to generate a stratified sampling data set using the CUST_GENDER column and with the Case ID set to AFFINITY_CARD. After you run the node, you can view the statistics by double-clicking on the Sample node again.

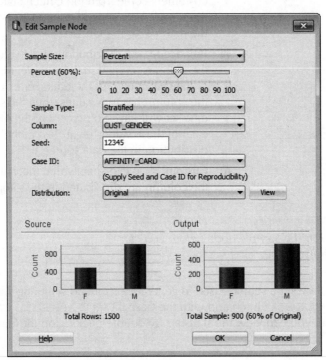

FIGURE 6-17. *Setting for stratified sampling*

Transform

The Transform node allows you to create new attributes that are based on some functions. Before you can define a new attribute, you need to run the Transform node. This gathers statistics about each of the attributes in your data source/input for the Transform node. You can use this statistical information to decide which transformations you want to implement. The typical type of transformations that you can implement include binning, missing value treatments, normalization, outlier treatment, and any other custom transformations.

You create the Transform node from the Transforms section of the Components Workflow Editor. Move the mouse to your worksheet and click to create the node. Next you connect your input data source node to the Transform node. In the example illustrated in Figure 6-18, the input data source is the MINING_DATA_BUILD_V view that comes as part of the sample data for ODM.

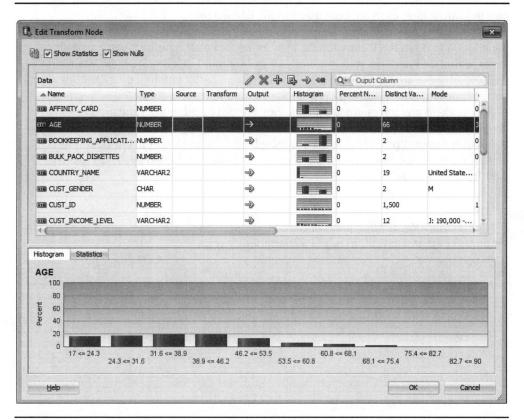

FIGURE 6-18. *Statistical information generated by the Transform node*

When you have connected your data input node to the Transform node, you need to run the node to generate the statistical information. This step is required before you can define any transformation nodes. Double-click on the Transform node to open the statistical information. Figure 6-18 shows the statistical information that was generated for the MINING_DATA_BUILD_V data source.

ODM will determine what type or types of data transformations it thinks would be useful for the data. To see the suggested transformation, double-click on an attribute. The Add Transform node opens displaying the statistical information and the binning it would create. The default setting is to accept this or you can create your own custom transformation. To create a custom transformation, click the Add Custom Transformation icon located on the Edit Transform Node window. Then when you create a new custom transformation, ODM creates a new attribute for it. The first step when adding a new custom transformation is to choose a meaningful attribute name. You do so in the Edit Transform window after you have clicked on the Add Custom Transformation icon. In the example in Figure 6-19, a new attribute and custom transformation is created for the AGE attribute. This custom transformation bins the values in the AGE attribute into specific labeled bins.

After adding the new attribute name in the Add Transform window, click on the pencil icon to open the Expression Builder. In the Expression Builder, you can define the SQL that will perform your required transformation. In Figure 6-19, the values in the AGE attribute are binned into new labeled groups. After entering the SQL code for the transformation, you can click on the Validate button to check the correctness of your code. If any errors are identified, they are displayed in the Validation Results box. If your code is valid, then you get a "Validation successful" message in the Validation Results box. When you are finished, you can click on the OK button to close the Expression Builder window, then click on the OK button again to close the Add Transform node.

TIP
Output only the attributes and custom transformation attributes that you want to use in a later node of your workflow.

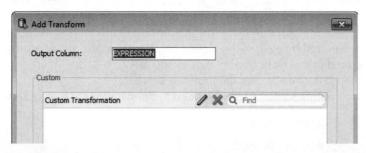

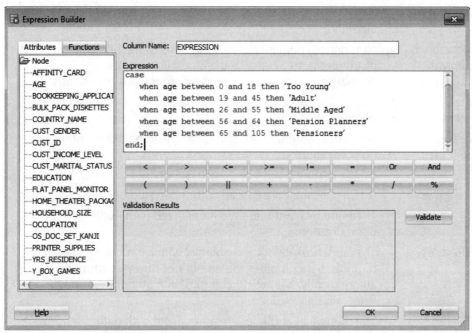

FIGURE 6-19. *Adding a custom transformation*

Automatic Data Preparation (ADP)

Most of the Oracle Data Mining algorithms require data to be transformed in some way. When a model is being built, Oracle Data Mining will automatically work out what transformations are required and apply these to the input data. The typical types of ADP transformations include binning, normalization, and outlier treatment.

Preparing data for input to the Data Mining algorithms can consume a lot of time and effort. Oracle has an in-database feature called Automatic Data Preparation (ADP). By default, ADP is enabled when you are using the Oracle Data Miner tool.

But when you are using the DBMS_DATA_MINING procedures, you need to enable ADP as part of the settings for each algorithm.

When ADP is active, Oracle Data Mining automatically performs the data transformations required by each of the algorithms. These transformation instructions become embedded in the Data Mining model and are automatically used and applied to the input data each time the model is used.

The following outlines what ADP is applied to the data for each algorithm.

Algorithm	ADP Applied
Apriori	ADP is not used.
Decision Tree	ADP is not used. All data preparation is performed by the algorithm.
Expectation Maximization	Non-nested, numerical single columns using the Gaussian distributions are normalized with outlier-sensitive normalization. ADP is not used for other types of columns.
GLM	Numerical attributes are normalized with outlier-sensitive normalization.
K-Means	Numerical attributes are normalized with outlier-sensitive normalization.
MDL	All the attributes are binned with supervised binning.
Naïve Bayes	All the attributes are binned with supervised binning.
NMF	The numerical attributes are normalized with outlier-sensitive normalization.
O-Cluster	The numerical attributes are binned with a form of equi-width binning that computes the number of bins per attribute automatically. Numerical columns with all nulls or a single value are removed.
SVD	The numerical attributes are normalized with outlier-sensitive normalization.
SVM	The numerical attributes are normalized with outlier-sensitive normalization.

Summary

Preparing your data for any data science or data mining project can consume a significant amount of time. Oracle Data Miner provides a range of data preparation and transformation nodes that allows you to easily prepare your data in the way that you and the data mining algorithms require, while at the same time keeping the amount of code you have to write to a minimum. In this chapter, you have seen how you can use these features. Some of these will be used in the following chapters when the different data mining algorithms are explained in detail.

CHAPTER
7

Association Rule Analysis

Association Rule Analysis is an unsupervised data mining technique that allows you to look for associations between items that are part of an event. This analysis is most typically applied in Market Basket Analysis, where an event would be a transaction. Although this is the most common application area of association rules, other application areas include financial product cross-selling, insurance claims analysis, packaging of products for mobile phone users, and more. Association Rule Analysis is implemented in Oracle Data Miner using the in-database Apriori algorithm. This chapter walks you through the steps required to set up and run an Association Rule Analysis, to analyze the results and to store these association rules for use by other applications.

What Is Association Rule Analysis?

Association Rule Analysis is an unsupervised data mining technique that looks for frequent itemsets in your data. This data mining technique is frequently used in the retail sector to discover what products are frequently purchased together. A common example used to illustrate Association Rule Analysis is that bread and milk are two products that are commonly purchased together in a grocery store. This type of data mining is very common in the retail sector and is sometimes referred to as Market Basket Analysis. By analyzing what products previous customers have bought, you can then prompt a new customer with products they might be interested in buying. Every time you look at a product—for example, a data mining book—on Amazon .com, the site also presents you with a list of other products that previous customers bought in addition to the product you are looking at. By using Association Rule Analysis, you can start to answer questions about your data and the patterns that may exist in the data. Some of these questions are illustrated in Figure 7-1 for a Market Basket Analysis scenario.

Other application areas include the following:

■ Telecommunication product analysis examines what products a customer typically has. This analysis can be used to identify new packages of products to sell to a customer or to identify products that can be removed from a package.

■ Insurance claims can be analyzed to see whether there are associations between products and claims.

■ Medical analysis determines whether there are interactions between existing and new treatments and medicines.

■ Banking and financial services can see what products customers typically have, then suggest these products to new or existing customers.

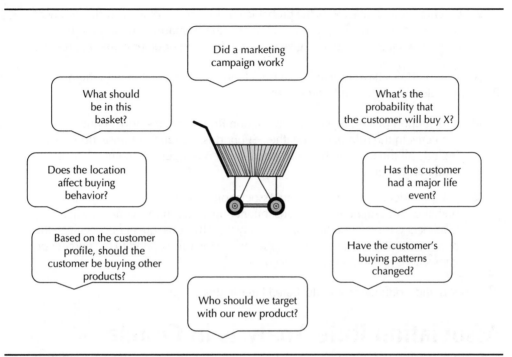

FIGURE 7-1. *Market Basket Analysis*

The Apriori algorithm is the main algorithm that most data mining software uses to produce the association rules in your data. The Apriori algorithm calculates rules that express probabilistic relationships between items in frequent itemsets. For example, a rule derived from frequent itemsets containing A, B, and C might state that if A and B are included in a transaction, then C is likely to also be included.

An Association Rule is of the form *IF antecedent, THEN consequent*. An Association Rule states that an item or group of items, the antecedent, implies the presence of another item, the consequent, with some probability. Unlike decision tree rules, which predict a target, Association Rules simply express correlation.

The Apriori algorithm has a two-step process, as follows:

1. Find all combinations of items in a set of transactions that occur with a specified minimum frequency. These combinations are called *frequent itemsets*.

2. Calculate rules that express the probable co-occurrence of items within frequent itemsets. The Apriori algorithm calculates the probability of an item being present in a frequent itemset, given that another item or other items are present.

Association Rules have two main statistical measures associated with them. These are called *Support* and *Confidence*:

■   The Support percentage of an Association Rule indicates how frequently the items in the rule occur together. Support is the ratio of transactions that include all the items in the antecedent and consequent to the number of total transactions.

■   The Confidence percentage of an Association Rule indicates the probability of both the antecedent and the consequent appearing in the same transaction. Confidence is the conditional probability that the consequent occurs given the occurrence of the antecedent. It is the ratio of the rule support to the number of transactions that include the antecedent.

Support and Confidence are illustrated later in this chapter.

Association Rule Analysis in Oracle

The current version of Oracle has the Apriori algorithm for generating association rules. The most commonly used algorithm for generating association rules, the Apriori algorithm, is implemented in most data mining applications. It is used for frequent itemset mining and association rule learning over transactional databases. The algorithm works in a bottom-up approach, where frequent subsets are extended one item at a time and groups of candidates are tested against the data. The algorithm terminates when no further successful extensions to the frequent subsets are found. It is available in the Oracle 11.2*g* and 12.1*c* Database Enterprise Edition.

To learn more details of how this algorithm is implemented, see the *Oracle Data Mining Concepts* book that is part of the Oracle documentation.

Building Association Rules Using ODM

When you build an Association Rules model in ODM, you use the Association node that is found under the Models menu of the Components Workflow Editor. The Association node offers only one algorithm, the Apriori algorithm.

In this section, we will walk through the steps to set up, run, and generate an Association Rules model in ODM. The data set that is used to illustrate the association rules is based on the sample Sales History (SH) schema.

The primary table of interest when you are building an Association Rules model is the table that contains the transactions for what you want to model. Typically, for a market basket type of scenario you want to use the table that contains all the items that were purchased. With most data mining produced, you would need to create

a single customer record that shows all the items purchased in a
attribute would exist for every product or product grouping in you
lead to a very large set of customer records, with many attributes
not having an applicable value. This is not the case in Oracle D
following sections show you how to create an Association Rules m
the minimum of data preparation.

As with all data mining projects, you need a worksheet that will contain your
workflows. You can either reuse an existing workflow that you have already used
for one of the other ODM exercises or you can create a new workflow called
Association Rules.

TIP
*Create separate ODM workflows for each of your
algorithms or problems that you are working on.
This allows you to organize your work into separate
worksheets and avoids the cluttering up of your
worksheets with too many workflows.*

Defining the Data Source

You start off by creating a Data Source node that points to a table or view that
contains your transaction records. To create the Data Source node, go to the
Components Workflow Editor and select the Data Source node from the Data
section. Then move your mouse to your worksheet area and click again. A Data
Source node is created and the Define Data Source window opens. The data source
that you will use in this chapter is located in the SH schema, so it is not listed in the
Available Tables/View list. The table you want to use is located in another schema. To
get access to this table, you need to click on the Add Schema button. The Edit Schema
List window opens. This window lists other schemas in your database from which
you can select data. Scroll down the list of available schemas until you find the SH
schema. Then click on the top arrow button to move the SH schema to the Selected
Schemas section on the right-hand side of the window, as shown in Figure 7-2.

When you click on the OK button, shown in Figure 7-2, you are brought back to
the Define Data Source window. The SH schema tables are not displayed. To get the
SH schema tables to display in the list, you need to select the Includes Tables from
Other Schemas check box. When this check box is selected, all tables and views
are relabeled to have their schema name at the start of the table or view name, as
shown in Figure 7-3. To locate the SH schema tables, you need to scroll down the
list of tables.

The table that contains the transaction records is the SH.SALES table. Select this
table from the list and click on the Next button. The next screen displays the list of
available columns in the table. You can exclude any columns you do not want to

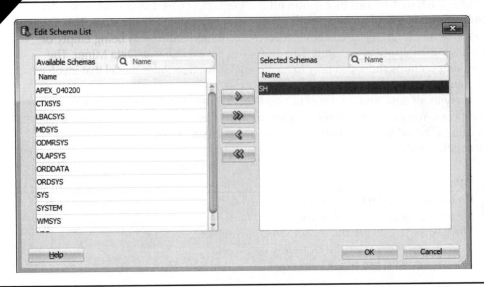

FIGURE 7-2. *Selecting a schema to make its data available for use in your workflows*

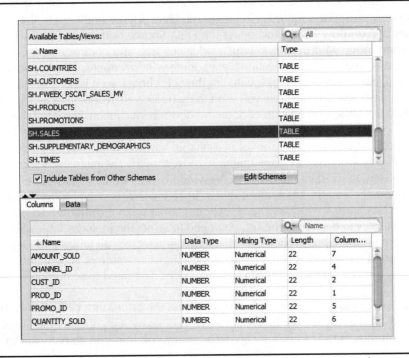

FIGURE 7-3. *Available tables and views, including tables from the SH schema*

use in your data mining node at this point. In the example SH.SALES table, you can keep all the attributes and click on the Finish button to create the node. The node is now created on the Workflow Worksheet and has been renamed to reflect the name of the schema.

TIP
If you need to give the Data Source node an alternative name, you can do this in the Details section of the Properties tab.

Creating the Association Node

After you have defined the data source that contains your transaction records, the next step is to create and set up the Association node in your workflow. The Association node is located in the Models section of the Components Workflow Editor. To add the Association node to the workflow, click on the node in the Components Workflow Editor, then move your mouse to your Workflow Worksheet. In keeping with the typical layout of workflows, which work in a left to right manner, position the mouse to the right of your data source and click again. The Association node is then created on your workflow.

The next step is to attach the data source to the Association node. This tells the workflow what data to pass to the algorithm in the Association node. To connect the Data Source node to the Association node, right-click on the Data Source node and select Connect from the menu. Then move the mouse to the Association node and click again to form the connection. When the connection is made, a window opens where you can specify attributes that are required as inputs to the algorithm. Table 7-1 details these parameters.

TIP
For the Value setting, if you select an attribute from the list, the attribute must have fewer than ten distinct values. Ten is the default for maximum distinct count. To change this value, you need to access the SQL Developer Preferences window by choosing Tools | Preferences. In the Preferences window, go to Oracle Data Miner | Node Settings | Models | Model Build | Association. You can then change the value.

Setting Name	Description
Transaction ID	This is the attribute or attributes that define a transaction. Oracle Data Miner allows you to have multiple input record transaction records in your data source. You can group the related transaction record based on the defining attribute(s). In your sample data set, the attributes identify a transaction at the Customer Identifier and the Time of the Transactions. All the items bought by the customer (in the customer's basket) are assigned the same customer number and time of purchase.
	To edit the Transaction ID attributes, you can click on the pencil icon to the right of the field.
Item ID	The Item ID identifies the attribute that contains the values that you want to link or associate using the Association Rules data mining algorithm. The sample data includes the different products that the customer bought at the same time. It is these products that you want the algorithm to analyze.
	To select the attribute, click on the drop-down list and select the appropriate attribute.
Value	This is the test that you want to perform on the related items. The default value is <Existence>. This tests whether the value of the attribute exists, such as whether Bread and Milk were bought together. For the majority of your analyses, this is the setting you will choose.
	In other scenarios, you may want to evaluate the number of items bought of each product, or conduct some other test. In this case, you can select one of your other attributes from the drop-down list.

TABLE 7-1. *Association Rules Node Settings*

Using the sample data that was set up in the previous section, you should adjust the Association node settings to the following values, as shown in Figure 7-4:

■ Transaction ID = CUST_ID and TIME_ID

■ Item ID = PROD_ID

■ Value = <Existence>

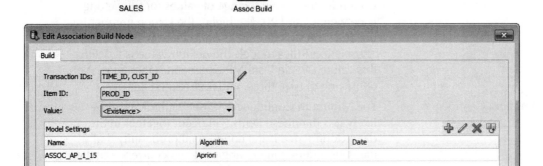

FIGURE 7-4. *Edit the Association node properties*

A feature of all the data mining model nodes is that you can create additional models based on the algorithm(s) for that type of data mining. In Oracle Data Miner, you can create an additional Apriori algorithm model. This new, additional model can be created using the green plus sign, located on the right-hand side of the Edit Association Build Node Properties window (see Figure 7-4). You can use this to create additional models of the Apriori algorithm by changing the internal algorithm settings. Before you run the Association node, you may want to inspect the Model Settings and the settings that are listed under the Properties tab. These are explained in the following sections. When you are ready to run your Association node, you should right-click on the node and select Run from the menu. Oracle Data Miner creates a job containing what is necessary to run each node of the workflow and submits this to the database. As each node is completed, a green check mark appears on the top right-hand corner of the node. When all nodes have been completed, you can then examine the data and results that were produced.

Model Settings

To access the Model Settings, you need to double-click on the model when you have the Edit Association Build Node window open, as shown in Figure 7-4. If you closed this window, then you can open the settings window by right-clicking the Association node and selecting Advanced Settings from the menu.

The Advanced Model Setting window for the Association node contains three settings and their default values. Table 7-2 describes each of these settings.

Setting Name	Description
Maximum Rule Length	This setting is the maximum number of attributes in each rule; the allowed range of values for this setting is between 2 and 20. The higher the setting number for this rule, the slower Oracle Data Miner will build the Association Rules model. The default value is 4. With this value, Oracle Data Miner generates the associations consisting of two, three, and four related items.
Minimum Confidence (%)	The Minimum Confidence (%) setting indicates how likely it is that these items will occur together in the data. Confidence is the conditional probability that the consequent will occur given the occurrence of the antecedent. The default value is 10%.
Minimum Support (%)	The Minimum Support (%) indicates how often these items occur together in the data set defined in your Data Source node.

TABLE 7-2. *Association Node Advanced Settings*

CAUTION
If a model has no rules, the following message is displayed in the rules tab of the mode viewer: "Model contains no rules." Consider rebuilding the model with lower Confidence and Support settings. Also, you may need to lower the percentage settings for the Minimum Confidence (%) and Minimum Support (%).

TIP
Start with the default setting and then adjust the Minimum Confidence (%) and the Minimum Support (%) based on the number of association rules that are produced by the Association node.

Association Node Properties Tab

The Association node Properties tab allows you to inspect what values were set up for the Association node when it was being created. You can use the Properties tab to edit this information. The Properties tab is node-sensitive and displays the properties

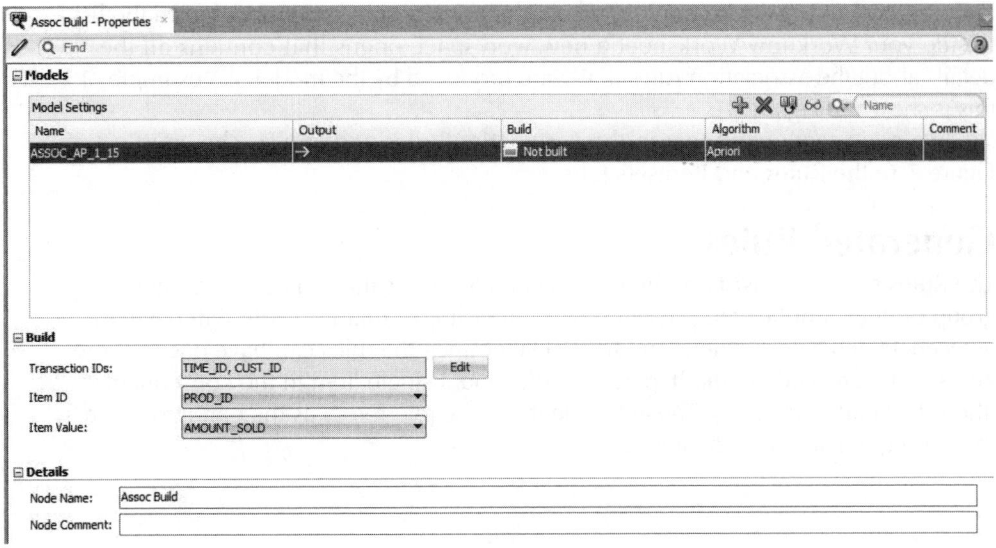

FIGURE 7-5. *Association node Properties tab*

for the current active node. You can make the Association node current by clicking on it in the Workflow Worksheet. The Properties tab then changes to contain the properties for the node.

If the Properties tab is not active and visible in your SQL Developer window, you can make it visible by choosing View | Properties. Figure 7-5 shows the Association node Properties tab. These are grouped into three sections: Models, Build, and Details.

The Models section contains the Apriori algorithms that have been set up for the Association node. You can edit these models, add new models, or remove a model (if you have created more than one). The Build section shows the attributes that were set up for each of the parameters. These include the Transaction IDs, the Item ID, and the Item Value. You can edit the listed attributes by clicking on the Edit button or the drop-down lists. The last section is the Details section, which allows you to change the label for the node and add a meaningful description.

Viewing the Association Rules

When the workflows consisting of the Data Source node and the Association node have been run and you see the green check marks on the top right-hand corner of the nodes, you are now ready to explore the association rules that were generated.

To view the generated association rules, you need to right-click on the Association node, select View Models from the menu, then finally select the model from the list. Beside your Workflow Worksheet a new workspace opens that contains all the details about the association rules that were produced by the model. An example of this is shown in Figure 7-6.

Two main sections appear in the Association Rules window, as shown in Figure 7-6: the Rules and Itemsets tabs.

Generated Rules

The Rules section consists of the set of generated rules that states that an item or group of items implies the presence of another item—that is, a rule will have an antecedent and a consequent. In Oracle Data Miner, the rules can have one or more items in the antecedent (the IF part of a rule) and a single item in the consequent (the THEN part of the rule). The antecedent may be referred to as the condition, and the consequent as the association.

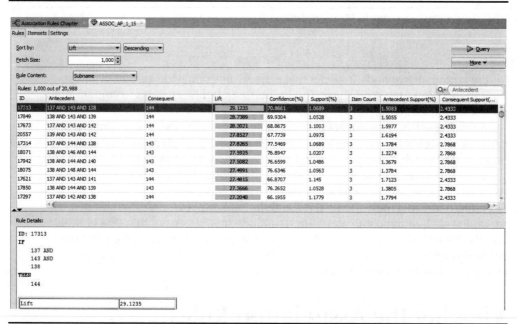

FIGURE 7-6. *Association Rules window*

Three main concepts are important in relation to association rules:

- **Support**   This is the proportion of transactions in the data set that contain the itemset, that is, the number of times the rule occurs.

- **Confidence**   This is the proportion of the occurrences of the antecedent that result in the consequent. For example, how many times do we get C when we have A and B? That is, {A, B} => C.

- **Lift**   This indicates the strength of a rule over the random co-occurrence of the antecedent and the consequent.

Support and Confidence are the primary measures that are used to access the usefulness of an association rule.

Figure 7-6 shows the rules that were generated for the sample data. When you look at the first rule displayed in Figure 7-6, you see the antecedent and the consequent has the form of an equation like the following:

```
IF
    137 AND
    143 AND
    138
THEN
    144
```

What this rule is saying is that if Product 137, Product 143, and Product 138 exist in the transaction—that is, the customer purchases these items together—then he or she will also purchase Product 144. The Confidence for this rule is 70.88 percent, which indicates that this happens in 70.88 percent of the cases when those three products are purchased. The Support value of 1 percent says that that rule occurs in just 1 percent of the rules.

The rules presented in Figure 7-7 show only the Product IDs. It can be difficult to fully understand what these mean when analyzing the rules. See the section "Adding a Data Source Node for Transaction Descriptions" to learn how you can improve the readability of the association rules.

Generated Itemsets

The association rules generated and shown in the previous section are calculated from the frequent itemsets that occur in the data. The Itemsets tab of the Association Rules window shows the values that occur most frequently together. The tab displays all the itemsets generated. These consist of the Product IDs that occur frequently together. Additional information for each itemset is the Support (%) and the number of items in the itemset.

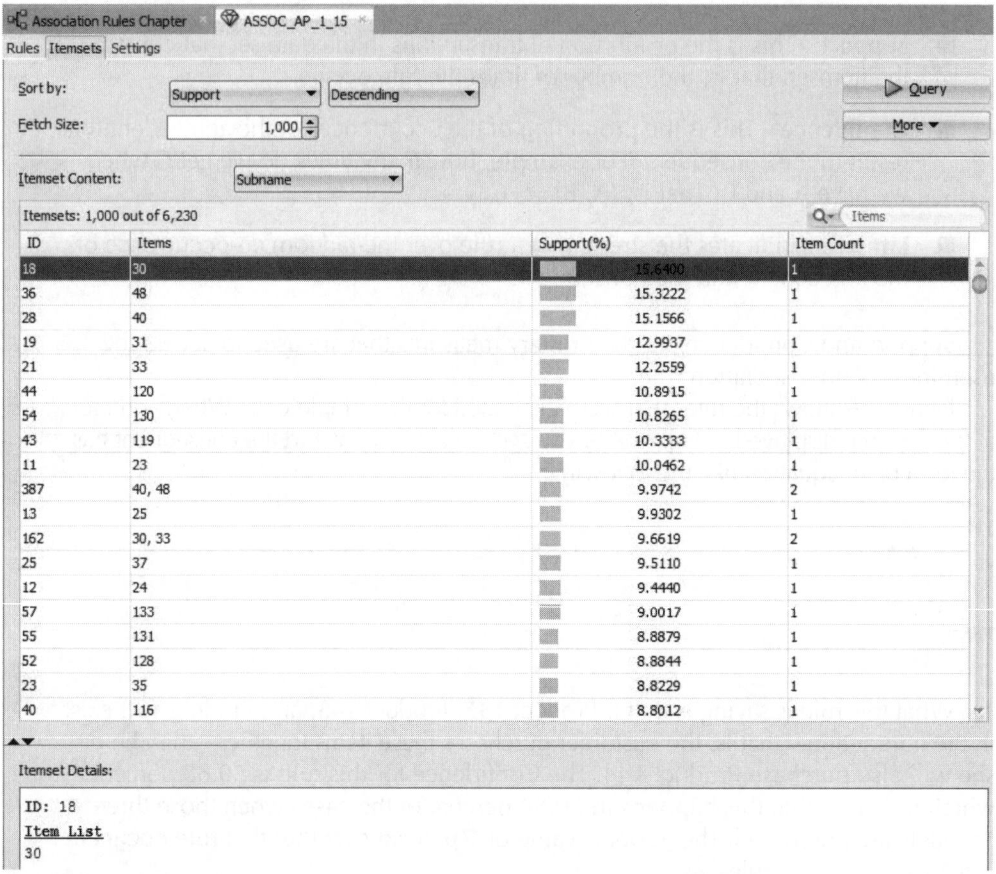

FIGURE 7-7. *Generated itemsets*

Adding a Data Source Node for Transaction Descriptions

In the previous section, you have seen how to build association rules (Market Basket Analysis) of transaction records that are in your sample data set. The association rules produced contain the product IDs, which consist of numbers. The association rules generated with product IDs can be difficult to understand without having to look up a description for each product ID.

To add the product names to the output, you need to add a new data source and rerun the Association node. Using the sample data set, you will need to add the new

Data Source node for the PRODUCTS table that is located in the SH schema. See the section "Defining the Data Source" earlier in this chapter to learn how to add a data source.

To add the product name as part of the input to the Association node, you need to create a Join node that joins the SALES and PRODUCTS tables. Before creating the Join node, you need to have the Data Source nodes created for the SALES and PRODUCTS tables. To create the Join node, select the Join node from the Transforms section of the Components Workflow Editor. Move your mouse to your workflow and click again to create the Join node on your workflow. Next you need to connect the SALES and PRODUCTS nodes to the Join node. For each Data Source node, you need to right-click on the node, select Connect from the menu, move the mouse to the Join node, and click again to form the connection.

After you have created the connections from the Data Source node, you now need to define the Join details. To do this, double-click on the Join node. The Edit Join node window opens. This consists of three tabs: Join, Columns, and Filter. To create the join condition between the two tables, click on the green plus sign that is located on the Join tab screen. This opens the Edit Join Column window as shown in Figure 7-8.

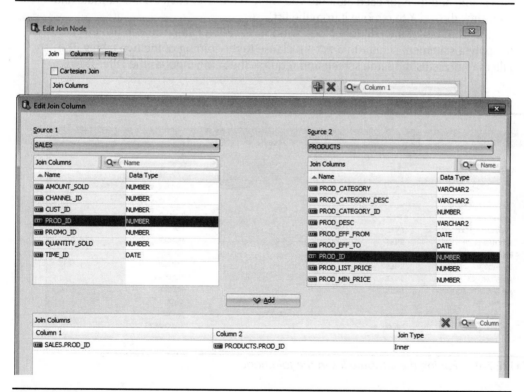

FIGURE 7-8. *Setting up the join condition for two data sources*

To create the join condition, you need to select one of the tables in the drop-down list for Source 1 (SALES) and the other table in the drop-down list for Source 2 (PRODUCTS). When the tables are selected, the Join Columns section displays their attributes. In each of the Join Columns sections, set the attributes that are needed to form the join. In the current example, you need to select the PROD_ID attribute in both column lists. Then to create the join, click the Add button. If you have more than one attribute involved in a join, you can create the additional entry for each pairing of attributes. When you have created the join, you can click the OK button to return to the Edit Join Node window.

When you click on the Columns tab, you get a list of all the attributes that the Join node will output. By default, all the attributes from the two tables being joined are listed. For the table that was listed as Source 2 (PRODUCTS in this example), the attribute used in the join condition will be relabeled with an alias. In this example, the new alias name is called PROD_ID1. You can accept this list of attributes to use an input to the next node of your workflow or you can edit the list, removing attributes that are not necessary for the next node. Figure 7-9 shows a reduced attribute listing that includes the attributes from the SALES table and just the PROD_NAME from the PRODUCTS table. To remove the attribute, you need to deselect the Automatic Settings check box, and then for each attribute you want to remove, click on the attribute and then click the red *X* to remove it from the list.

The third tab of the Edit Join Node window is called Filter. You can use this tab to apply a statement similar to a WHERE clause to the joining of the two tables. The Filter tab presents the same screen and requires the same input as the Filter Rows

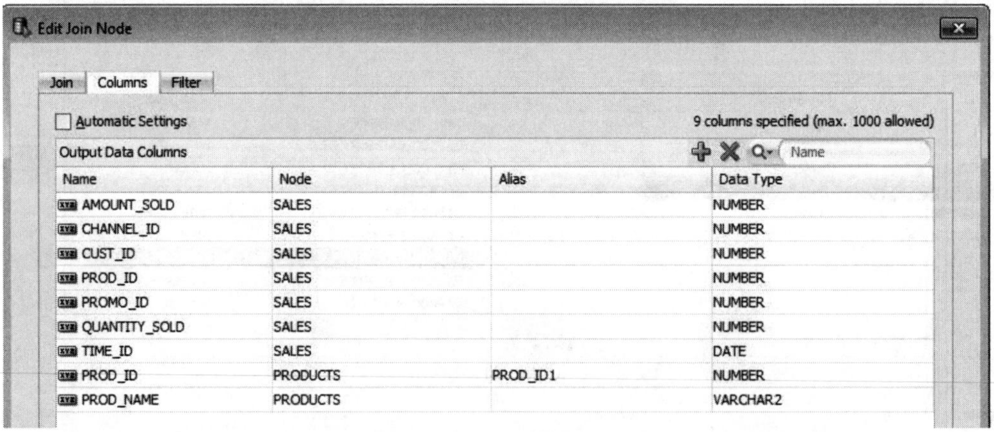

FIGURE 7-9. *Editing the attribute list in the Join node*

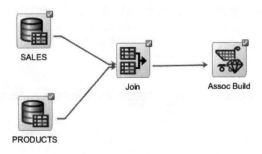

FIGURE 7-10.   *Association rule workflow with a Join node*

node. The details of how to create a filter are described in the Filter Rows node section in Chapter 6. For this example scenario, you do not need to apply a filter.

After the Join node is created, you need to create an Association node. See the section "Creating the Association Node" earlier in this chapter on how to create the Association node. This time, though, when setting up the parameter in the Edit Association Node window, set the Item ID to be PROD_NAME (which comes from the PRODUCT table). The following is a complete list of the settings for the Association node:

- `Transaction ID = CUST_ID` and `TIME_ID`

- `Item ID = PROD_NAME`

- `Value = <Existence>`

When all these nodes (two Data Source nodes, a Join node, and an Association node) have been created, you can run the workflow to generate the association rules for the data. Figure 7-10 shows the completed workflow, which consists of two Data Source nodes, a Join node, and the Association node. The next section, "Applying Filters to the Association Rules," describes the generated association rules with the product names instead of the product IDs.

Applying Filters to the Association Rules

Association Rule Analysis can generate many thousands of possible association rules and related information for a small data set, as shown in Figure 7-11.

In some cases, similar rules can appear, and lots of rules occur so infrequently that they are perhaps meaningless. Oracle Data Miner provides a number of filters that you can apply to look for the association rules that are of most interest to you.

ID	Antecedent	Consequent	Lift	Confidence(%)	Support(%)	Item Count	Antecedent Support(%)	Consequent Support(...
9136	128MB Memory Card AND Comic Book Heroes AND 2...	Fly Fishing	29.1235	70.8661	1.0689	3	1.5083	2.4333
10453	Bounce AND Comic Book Heroes AND 256MB Memory...	Fly Fishing	28.7389	69.9304	1.0528	3	1.5055	2.4333
9148	128MB Memory Card AND Martial Arts Champions AN...	Fly Fishing	28.3021	68.8675	1.1003	3	1.5977	2.4333
10465	Bounce AND Martial Arts Champions AND Comic Book...	Fly Fishing	27.8527	67.7739	1.0975	3	1.6194	2.4333
9133	Bounce AND 256MB Memory Card AND 128MB Me...	Comic Book Heroes	27.8265	77.5469	1.0689	3	1.3784	2.7868
9158	Fly Fishing AND Adventures with Numbers AND 256M...	Comic Book Heroes	27.5925	76.8947	1.0207	3	1.3274	2.7868
9109	Fly Fishing AND 256MB Memory Card AND Endurance...	Comic Book Heroes	27.5082	76.6599	1.0486	3	1.3679	2.7868
9013	Fly Fishing AND 256MB Memory Card AND Xtend Me...	Comic Book Heroes	27.4991	76.6346	1.0563	3	1.3784	2.7868
9064	Smash up Boxing AND Comic Book Heroes AND 128M...	Fly Fishing	27.4815	66.8707	1.145	3	1.7123	2.4333
10451	Bounce AND 256MB Memory Card AND Fly Fishing	Comic Book Heroes	27.3666	76.2652	1.0528	3	1.3805	2.7868
9140	128MB Memory Card AND Martial Arts Champions AN...	Fly Fishing	27.2040	66.1955	1.1779	3	1.7794	2.4333
9146	Fly Fishing AND Martial Arts Champions AND 128MB ...	Comic Book Heroes	27.0413	75.3589	1.1003	3	1.4601	2.7868
10405	Bounce AND Comic Book Heroes AND Smash up Boxing	Fly Fishing	27.0148	65.7351	1.1339	3	1.7249	2.4333
9100	Endurance Racing AND Comic Book Heroes AND 128...	Fly Fishing	27.0145	65.7343	1.2477	3	1.8982	2.4333
10441	Bounce AND Comic Book Heroes AND 128MB Memory...	Fly Fishing	26.9169	65.4969	1.2387	3	1.8912	2.4333
9060	Smash up Boxing AND 256MB Memory Card AND 128...	Fly Fishing	26.8379	65.3046	1.2058	3	1.8465	2.4333
9152	128MB Memory Card AND Adventures with Numbers ...	Fly Fishing	26.8197	65.2604	1.1995	3	1.8381	2.4333
9061	Fly Fishing AND 128MB Memory Card AND Smash up ...	Comic Book Heroes	26.8063	74.7037	1.145	3	1.5328	2.7868

FIGURE 7-11. *Association rules with the product descriptions*

To view the association rules, you need to right-click the Association node, select View Models, and then select the model name from the menu. A new tab area opens in Oracle Data Miner that displays the rules, as shown in Figure 7-11. You can apply filters to the rules by clicking on the More button, which is located just under the Query button.

You can refine your query of the association rules based on the various measures and the number of items in the association rule, as shown in Figure 7-12. In addition to this, you can also filter based on the values of the items. This is particularly useful if you want to concentrate on specific items (in this example, products). To illustrate this use, focus on the rules that involve the product "CD-RW, High Speed, Pack of 10." Click on the green plus sign on the right-hand side of the window to define a filter. Select "CD-RW, High Speed, Pack of 10" from the list provided, or you can search for it by clicking on the More button and entering the product name in the Name Filter field, and clicking the Query button. Next you need to decide whether you want this product involved in the antecedent or the consequent. For this example, select the consequent. This is located to the bottom-right of the window. Then click the OK button to return to the Association Rules Filter screen (see Figure 7-12). By clicking on the Query button on the Association Rules Filter screen, you enable Oracle Data Miner to update the list of association rules to list the rules that correspond with the new filter. These rules will have "CD-RW, High Speed, Pack of 10" as part of the consequent.

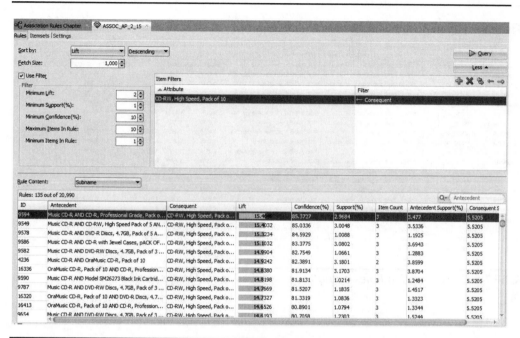

FIGURE 7-12. *Filtered association rules based on product name*

Outputting and Persisting the Association Rules

Association Rules are an unsupervised method of data mining. In Oracle Data Miner, you cannot use the Apply node to score new data. No representation of the association Rules exists in the database that can be applied to new data. What you have to do is to generate the rules, output them, and use these outputted rules in your applications.

The Model Details node is used when you want to extract the rules that are generated from the Association node. To create the Model Details node on your workflow, you need to click on the Model Details node in the Models section of the Components Workflow Editor, then click on your Workflow Worksheet to create the node. Next you need to connect the Association node with the Model Details node. To create the connection, you right-click the Association node, select Connect from the menu, then click on the Model Details node. When you run the Model Details node, it generates the Association Rules in a format that you can reuse. When the Model Details node has been run and you see the green check mark on the top right-hand corner of the node, you can view the outputs (shown in Figure 7-13)

	MODEL_SCHEMA	MODEL_NAME	ID	ANTECEDENT_ITEMS	CONSEQUENT_ITEMS	SUPPORT	CONFIDENCE	LIFT	ANTECEDENT_SUPPORT	CONSEQUENT_
1	DMUSER	ASSOC_AP_...	1	PROD_NAME.Music CD-R =	PROD_NAME.DVD-R Discs, 4.7GB, Pac...	0.0247	0.3266	4.252	0.0755	
2	DMUSER	ASSOC_AP_...	2	PROD_NAME.DVD-R Discs, 4.7GB, Pac...	PROD_NAME.Music CD-R =	0.0247	0.3211	4.252	0.0768	
3	DMUSER	ASSOC_AP_...	3	PROD_NAME.Music CD-R =	PROD_NAME.DVD-RW Discs, 4.7GB, P...	0.0181	0.2393	3.5326	0.0755	
4	DMUSER	ASSOC_AP_...	4	PROD_NAME.DVD-RW Discs, 4.7GB, P...	PROD_NAME.Music CD-R =	0.0181	0.2668	3.5326	0.0677	
5	DMUSER	ASSOC_AP_...	5	PROD_NAME.Music CD-R =	PROD_NAME.3 1/2" Bulk diskettes, Bo...	0.0176	0.233	3.0839	0.0755	
6	DMUSER	ASSOC_AP_...	6	PROD_NAME.3 1/2" Bulk diskett...	PROD_NAME.Music CD-R =	0.0176	0.2329	3.0839	0.0756	
7	DMUSER	ASSOC_AP_...	7	PROD_NAME.Music CD-R =	PROD_NAME.3 1/2" Bulk diskettes, Bo...	0.0155	0.2056	3.2156	0.0755	
8	DMUSER	ASSOC_AP_...	8	PROD_NAME.3 1/2" Bulk diskett...	PROD_NAME.Music CD-R =	0.0155	0.2428	3.2156	0.064	
9	DMUSER	ASSOC_AP_...	9	PROD_NAME.Music CD-R =	PROD_NAME.CD-R with Jewel Cases, ...	0.0635	0.8407	8.1359	0.0755	
10	DMUSER	ASSOC_AP_...	10	PROD_NAME.CD-R with Jewel Cases, ...	PROD_NAME.Music CD-R =	0.0635	0.6144	8.1359	0.1033	
11	DMUSER	ASSOC_AP_...	11	PROD_NAME.Music CD-R =	PROD_NAME.Model SM26273 Black In...	0.0212	0.2807	3.1591	0.0755	
12	DMUSER	ASSOC_AP_...	12	PROD_NAME.Model SM26273 Black In...	PROD_NAME.Music CD-R =	0.0212	0.2386	3.1591	0.0888	
13	DMUSER	ASSOC_AP_...	13	PROD_NAME.Music CD-R =	PROD_NAME.DVD-R Disc with Jewel C...	0.0182	0.2416	2.2185	0.0755	
14	DMUSER	ASSOC_AP_...	14	PROD_NAME.DVD-R Disc with Jewel C...	PROD_NAME.Music CD-R =	0.0182	0.1675	2.2185	0.1089	
15	DMUSER	ASSOC_AP_...	15	PROD_NAME.Music CD-R =	PROD_NAME.CD-R, Professional Grad...	0.0579	0.766	8.8758	0.0755	
16	DMUSER	ASSOC_AP_...	16	PROD_NAME.CD-R, Professional Grad...	PROD_NAME.Music CD-R =	0.0579	0.6703	8.8758	0.0863	
17	DMUSER	ASSOC_AP_...	17	PROD_NAME.Music CD-R =	PROD_NAME.Model CD13272 Tricolor ...	0.0183	0.2424	3.1456	0.0755	
18	DMUSER	ASSOC_AP_...	18	PROD_NAME.Model CD13272 Tricolor ...	PROD_NAME.Music CD-R =	0.0183	0.2376	3.1456	0.0771	
19	DMUSER	ASSOC_AP_...	19	PROD_NAME.Music CD-R =	PROD_NAME.DVD-RAM Jewel Case, D...	0.0118	0.1565	2.751	0.0755	

FIGURE 7-13. *Association Rules outputted using the Model Details node*

by right-clicking the Model Details node and selecting View Data. The output is displayed in columnar format.

To make the data in the Model Details node available, you can create a table in your schema to store the Association Rules. To do this, you create a Create Table or View node. This node is located in the Data section of the Components Workflow Editor. Create this node on your workflow and connect it to the Model Details node. You can specify which attributes you want in your output table. If you want to remove some attributes from the output table, you need to deselect the Auto Input Columns Selection check box, select the attributes you want to remove from the output table, then click the red *X* to remove them from the list. You can also give a meaningful name for the output table. In Figure 7-14, the output table is called AR_OUTPUT_RULES, and the output attributes include ANTECENDENT_ITEMS, CONSEQUENT_ITEMS, ID, LENGTH, CONFIDENCE, and SUPPORT.

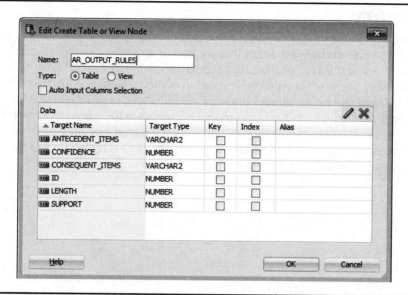

FIGURE 7-14. *Select the Model Details attributes to include in the output table*

To create the table and the records from the Model Details node, you need to run the Create Table node, called AR_OUTPUT_RULES. When this node completes, the table exists in your schema, and all the Association Rules exist as records in the table. Figure 7-15 shows the complete Association Rules workflow for this chapter.

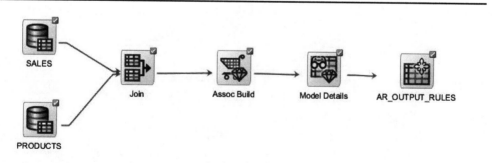

FIGURE 7-15. *Association Rules workflow*

Summary

Association Rule Analysis is an unsupervised data mining technique that allows you to look for associations between items that are part of an event. The most typical application area of this is in Market Basket Analysis. You see examples of its application every day when you purchase goods in our local grocery store or look at items on Amazon and in marketing from retail and financial organizations. With Association Rule Analysis in Oracle, no model is created in the database for you to use later. Instead, the data mining models tell you what patterns or associations exist in your data. What you do with these and how you use them is up to you, but they can be easily integrated into your applications.

CHAPTER

8

Classification

C lassification is one of the most common data mining techniques to use. It is widely implemented in problems where previous data is labeled to indicate a particular event has happened or not—for example, whether a customer has churned or not churned. Classification is an example of a supervised data mining exercise. This chapter will show how you can build classification models, how to evaluate them, and finally how to apply one of these models to new data.

What Is Classification?

Classification is a supervised data mining method that takes a data set of prelabeled data and builds a classification model, using one or more algorithms. The prelabeled data set is called the Training data set. The Training data set consists of the data for which you already know the outcome. For example, if you want to run a customer churn analysis, you would take all your customers who registered up to a certain date. You can write some code that can easily determine which of these customers have remained a customer—that is, who is still active—and those customers who are no longer active customers—that is, who has left. You create a new attribute for each customer. This attribute is typically called the *target variable*. It is this target variable that contains the label (0 or 1) that is used by the classification algorithms to build the models. You can then use one of these models to score a new group of customers and determine which customers are likely to stay and which will leave (churn).

We learn from the past to predict the future.

Classification typically involves three stages as described in Table 8-1.

The simplest type of classification problem is binary classification. In binary classification, the target attribute has only two possible values—for example, a credit rating that is considered either high or low. Multiclass targets have more than two values—for example, a credit rating that may be considered low, medium, high, or unknown.

Typical classification problems that you will encounter include marketing campaigns, loyalty cards, insurance, banking, retail stores, medical diagnostic, retention, churn, and more.

Stage	Definition
Stage One: Model Build	During the model build step, you will use a data set that contains your labeled data and input this to the data mining algorithms. Each algorithm will build a model based on this data and the algorithm parameter settings.
Stage Two: Testing	When the models have been built, the next step is to test how efficient the models are. To do this, you need a separate subset of your prelabeled data. Typically this data has not been used in the model build step. The default approach is to divide the labeled data set into two parts. The first part is used to build the model, and the second part is used to test the model. An alternative approach is for Build and Test data sets to be created separately.
	During the testing stage, the model is used to score the Test data set. It will be determined, using the model, what the target variable value should be for each record. The actual target variable is available for each of these records. The actual target value and the predicted target variable value are compared. A number of statistical tests will be carried out comparing the actual value to the predicted value. The results from these statistical tests are used to determine the efficiency of each model.
	Oracle Data Miner uses a 60:40 split. It will take 60 percent of the records in the Build data set as input for the model build and keep 40 percent of the records for the testing stage. These percentages can be adjusted and different selection methods can be used.
	You can also use separate data sets for building the models and for testing them.
Stage Three: Apply	In the apply stage, the model that was chosen as the most efficient is applied to our new unlabeled data. The Apply data set does not contain the target variable, as you do not know its value. The chosen data mining model is used to calculate or predict what this target value could be. In addition to predicting the target value, the model also calculates a probability percentage. This percentage tells you how strong the model thinks a prediction is, with 1 indicating that the model thinks it is 100 percent certain of its prediction.

TABLE 8-1. *Stages of Building a Classification Model*

Classification Methods Available in Oracle

Oracle has a number of classification algorithms available in the database. Table 8-2 lists the classification algorithms and provides a short description of each algorithm.

Building Classification Models

When building classification models in ODM, you use the Classification node that is found under the Models section of the Components Workflow Editor. By default, the Classification node lists all the classification algorithms that are available. You can select all or some of these and/or create additional versions of a model with different model settings.

In this section, you walk through the steps to set up, run, and generate classification models in ODM. The data set that is used to illustrate classification is based on the sample schemas in Oracle. When you were setting up your ODM schema (back in

Algorithm	Description
Decision Trees	A Decision Tree is a tree structure flow chart where each node represents a data rule and each branch represents an outcome of the rule. The rules produced are if-then-else expressions and explain the decisions that lead to the prediction.
Generalized Linear Model (GLM)	Generalized Linear Models implement logistic regression for classification of binary targets and linear regression for continuous targets, and are generalized versions of linear regression. GLM allows a categorical variable to be related to a set of predictor attributes in a manner similar to that of a modeling numeric target attribute using linear regression.
Naïve Bayes	Naive Bayes makes predictions using Bayes' Theorem, which derives the probability of a prediction from the underlying evidence, as observed in the data. It assumes that the effect of an attribute value on a given class of the target attribute is independent of the other attributes.
Support Vector Machine (SVM)	SVM transforms the training data set into separate groups based on the target attribute, where the hyperplane that separates the two groups is maximized. In Oracle, linear and Gaussian (nonlinear) kernels are supported.

TABLE 8-2. *Classification Algorithms Available in the Oracle Database*

Chapter 3), you created a number of views. These views look at different subsets of the SH (Sales History) schema. The data set that is used as input to the classification node is called DATA_MINING_BUILD_V. This view looks at a subset of the data in the Customer, Countries, and Supplementary Demographics tables in the SH schema. The scenario for this data is an electronic goods store. The data in the view contains details of customers who have taken up a loyalty card and those who did not take up a loyalty card following a marketing campaign. This is identified in the AFFINITY_CARD attribute. You want to use classification to build a model that represents and can identify each of these groups of people: the people who had taken up the offer of a loyalty card (represented by a 1) and those who did not take up the loyalty card (represented by a 0).

If you have completed Chapter 5, "Exploring Your Data," you already have the Data Source node set up and have attached DATA_MINING_BUILD_V to it. If you do not have this node set up yet, check Chapter 5 for the instructions on how to do so. Alternatively, you can create a new workflow that you can use to follow the examples in this chapter. You can call this new workflow "Classification Chapter."

After defining your data source, the next step is to create the Classification node. This node can be found under the Models section of the Components Workflow Editor. Click on the Classification node and move your mouse onto the worksheet. When you have the mouse located just to the right of the Data Source node, click again. The Classification node appears on your worksheet. The next step is to join the Data Source node to the Classification node. This tells ODM what data to use as input to each of the classification algorithms, as shown in Figure 8-1.

When you create the connect to the Classification node, the Edit Classification Build Node window opens, as shown in Figure 8-2. In this window, you can define the Case ID (primary key) of the input data, specify the target attribute, select what algorithms to use, and edit the algorithm settings. In this example scenario, the Target attribute is AFFINITY_CARD and the Case ID is CUST_ID. Select these attributes from the drop-down lists.

TIP
The Case ID/primary key needs to consist of one attribute from the table. If you have a multi-attribute primary key, then you need to generate an alternate key and use it as the Case ID.

MINING_DATA_BUILD_V   Class Build

FIGURE 8-1. *Classification node with a connected data source*

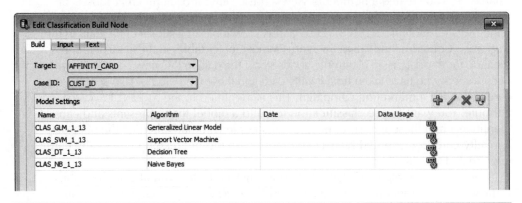

FIGURE 8-2. *Edit Classification Build Node*

When starting out with your data mining projects, you need to generate a model using each of the data mining algorithms. This allows you to see which algorithm performs best for your particular set of data.

If you are happy to use the Oracle defaults for each of the classification algorithms, then you are ready to run the Classification node and generate the models. But before you do this, you should review the settings for the Classification node in the Properties tab (see the section "Property Inspector" later in this chapter for details).

Model Settings

The Advanced Model Settings allow you to inspect and change the data usage, algorithm settings, and performance settings for each classification algorithm. Oracle has selected what it regards as the optimal settings that are suitable for most problems. Each algorithm comes with its own specific settings.

TIP
Change the algorithm settings only after you understand what the change means and why you are doing it. In most cases, you do not have to change these internal settings.

To change or view advanced settings, you can double-click on a model listed in the Edit Classification Build Node window. If you have closed this window, you can right-click the Classification node and select Advanced Settings from the context menu.

The Advanced Model Settings window lists all of the models in the node in the upper pane. To see and change the settings of these algorithms, click on each of the algorithms in turn. As you do this, you can select the Algorithm Settings and Performance Settings tabs.

GLM Algorithm Settings

The Generalized Linear Model algorithm has the following settings (see Figure 8-3):

- **Generate Row Diagnostics** By default, this is set off. You can view row diagnostics on the Diagnostics tab when you view the model. To further analyze row diagnostics, use the Model Details node to extract the row diagnostics table.

- **Confidence Level** This is a positive number that is less than 1. The setting indicates the degree of certainty that the true probability lies within the confidence bounds computed by the model. The default confidence is 0.95.

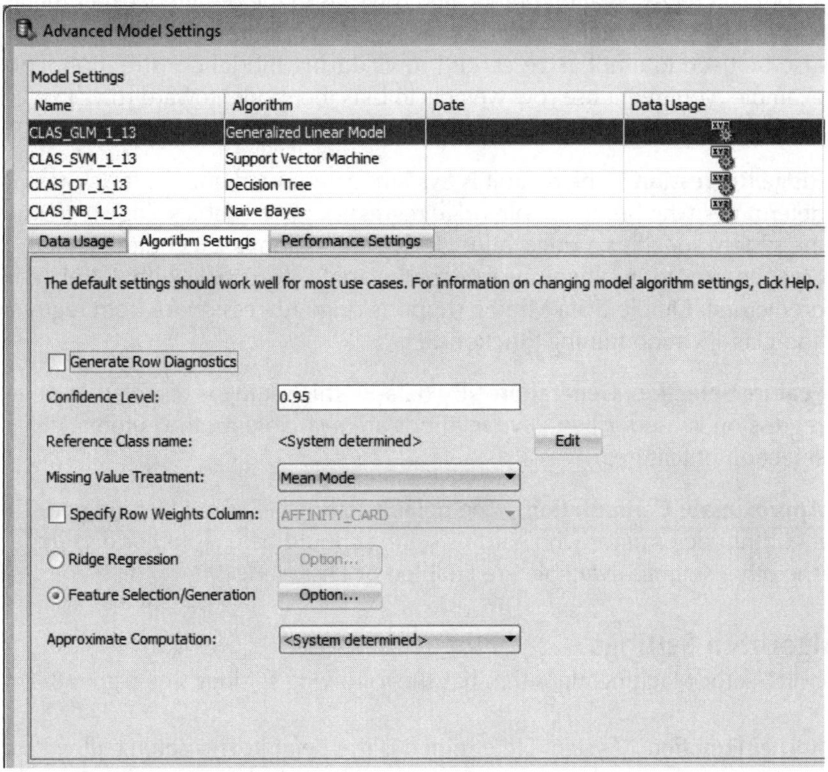

FIGURE 8-3. *GLM algorithm settings*

■ **Reference Class Name**   The Reference Target Class is the target value used as a reference in a binary logistic regression model. Probabilities are produced for the other (nonreference) class. By default, the algorithm chooses the value with the highest prevalence (the most cases). If there are ties, the attributes are sorted alphanumerically in ascending order. The default for Reference Class name is System Determined, that is, the algorithm determines the value.

■ **Missing Value Treatment**   The default setting is Mean Mode. It uses mean for numeric values and mode for categorical values. You can also select Delete Row to delete any row that contains missing values. If you delete rows with missing values, the same missing values treatment (Delete Rows) must be applied to any data to which you apply the model.

■ **Specify Row Weights Column**   The default is not to specify a Row Weights column. The Row Weights column is a column in the training data that contains a weighting factor for the rows. Row weights can be used as a compact representation of repeated rows, as in the design of experiments where a specific configuration is repeated several times. Row weights can also be used to emphasize certain rows during model construction. For example, you might use row weights to bias the model toward rows that are more recent and away from potentially obsolete data.

■ **Ridge Regression**   The default is System Determined, that is, the system determines whether to enable ridge regression; if it enables ridge regression, the system specifies a ridge value. Ridge regression is a technique that compensates for multicollinearity (multivariate regression with correlated predictors). Oracle Data Mining supports ridge regression for both regression and classification mining functions.

■ **Feature Selection/Generation**   By default, this setting is disabled as ridge regression is used. Alternative methods are available for the automatic selection of features.

■ **Approximate Computation**   The default setting is System Determined. The algorithm determines whether this setting should be enabled or disabled. The other settings available are Enabled or Disabled.

SVM Algorithm Settings

The Support Vector Machine algorithm has the following settings (see Figure 8-4):

■ **Kernel Function**   System Determined is the default. This setting allows ODM to work out which of the kernel functions it should use. The kernel functions available include Linear and Gaussian. When the model is built, the kernel used is displayed in the settings in the model viewer.

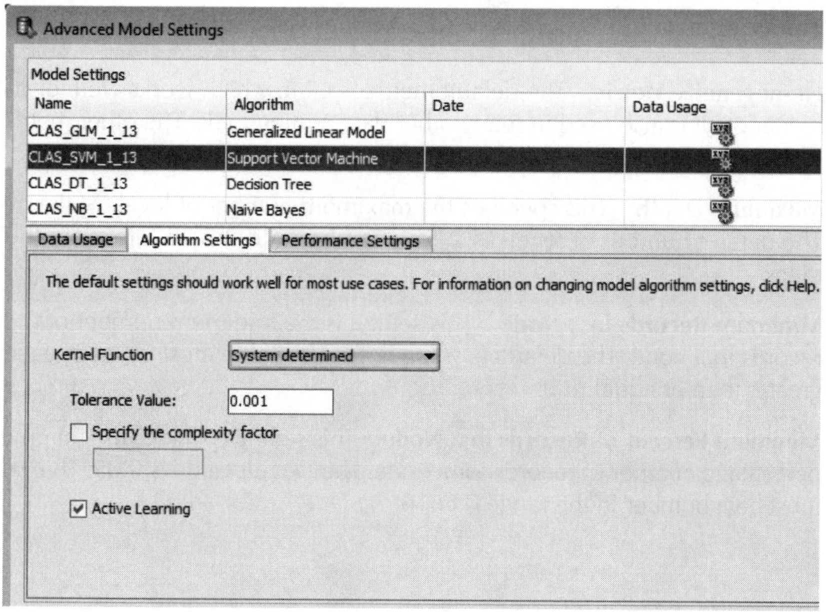

FIGURE 8-4.   *SVM algorithm settings*

For System Determined and Linear, you can modify the Tolerance Value, specify the complexity factor, and set active learning. If you change the Kernel Function setting to Gaussian, you get the following additional parameters: the standard deviation for the Gaussian kernel and cache size.

- **Tolerance Value**   This is the maximum size of a violation of convergence criteria such that the model is considered to have converged. The default value is 0.001. Larger values imply faster building but less accurate models.

- **Specify the Complexity Factor**   This determines the trade-off between minimizing model error on the training data and minimizing model complexity. The setting is responsible for avoiding over-fit (an over-complex model fitting noise in the training data) and under-fit (a model that is too simple). The default is to specify no complexity factor, in which case the system calculates a complexity factor. If you do specify a complexity factor, specify a positive number.

- **Active Learning**   This forces the SVM algorithm to restrict learning to the most informative examples and not to attempt to use the entire body of data. In most cases, the resulting models have predictive accuracy comparable to that of the standard (exact) SVM model.

Decision Tree Algorithm Settings

The Decision Tree algorithm has the following settings (see Figure 8-5):

■ **Homogeneity Metric** The default metric is Gini, which works well for most scenarios. It is also used in many other data mining tools. The other metric is Entropy.

■ **Maximum Depth** This specifies the maximum number of levels of the tree. The default number of levels is 7. The number must be an integer in the range 2 to 20.

■ **Minimum Records in a Node** This setting is the minimum number of records in a node. The default is value is 10. The value must be an integer greater than or equal to 0.

■ **Minimum Percent of Records in a Node** This setting specifies the minimum percentage number of records for a node. The default value is 0.05. The value must be a number in the range 0 to 10.

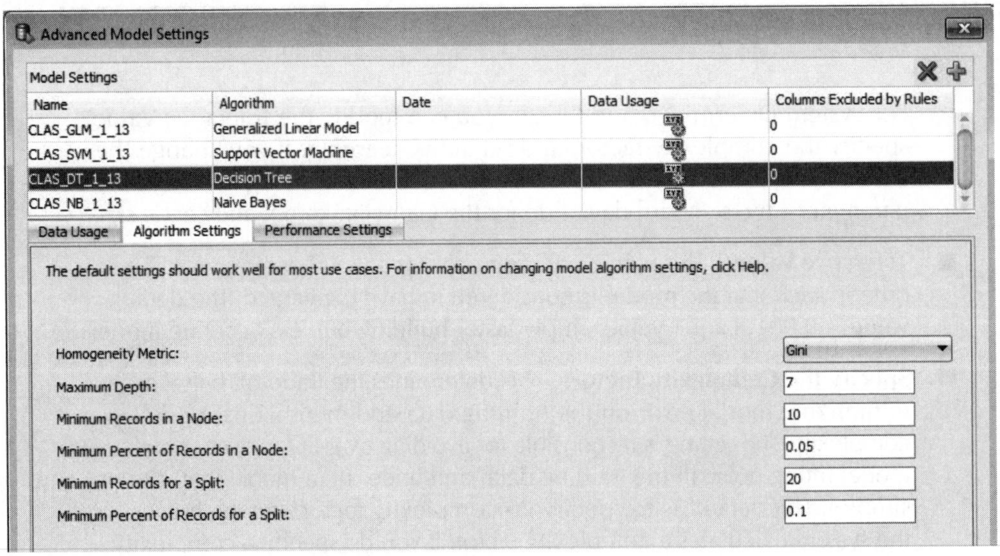

FIGURE 8-5. *Decision Tree algorithm settings*

- **Minimum Records for a Split**   This is the minimum number of records for a node to split. The default value is 20. The value must be an integer greater than or equal to 0.

- **Minimum Percent of Records for a Split**   This setting specifies the minimum percentage of records for a node to split. The default value is 0.1. The value must be a number in the range 0 to 20.

Naïve Bayes Algorithm Settings

The Naïve Bayes algorithm has the following settings (see Figure 8-6):

- **Singleton Threshold**   This is the minimum percentage of singleton occurrences required for including a predictor in the model.

- **Pairwise Threshold**   This setting specifies the minimum percentage of pairwise occurrences required for including a predictor in the model.

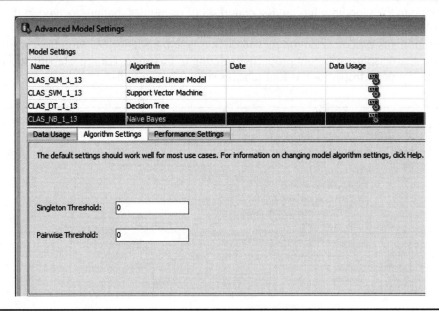

FIGURE 8-6.   *Naïve Bayes algorithm settings*

Performance Settings

The Performance Settings tab defines the performance objective for the Classification model build. The default setting is Balanced and allows ODM to determine the best approach to take. Select one of these settings:

- **Balanced**   This is the default setting. ODM attempts to find the best overall accuracy across all the target class values. This is done in different ways depending on the algorithm being used.

- **Natural**   This setting allows the model to be built without any biasing, so that the model uses its natural view of the data to build an accurate model.

- **Custom**   This allows you enter a set of weights for each target value. One way to get started defining custom weights is to click Balanced or Natural, just above the Weights grid. Either of these buttons generates weights similar to those that would result in either Balanced or Natural performance. You can then change these weights to different values.

Property Inspector

Each node in the workflow has an associated set of properties that are located in the Properties tab. This is a dockable area and typically appears below or to the side of the Components Workflow Editor. As you click on each node in your workflow, the Properties tab displays different properties relating to the node. For the Classification node, the Property Inspector has four tabs, as shown in Figure 8-7.

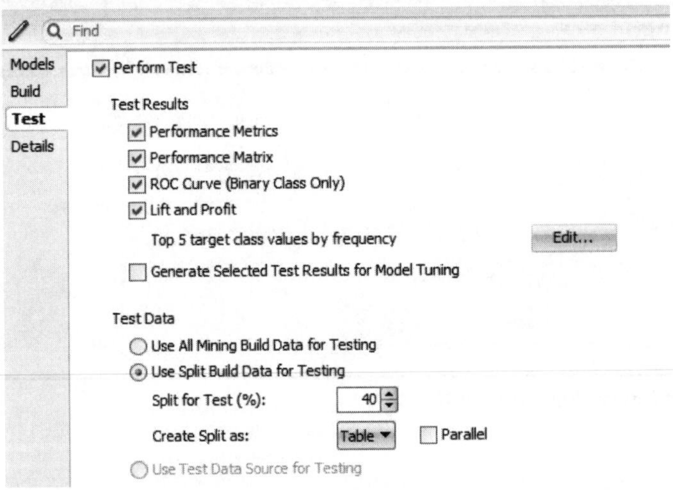

FIGURE 8-7.   *Classification node Property Inspector, showing the Test tab*

The Classification node Property Inspector has the following tabs:

- **Models**   This lists the models that are part of the Classification node. Models can be removed from the list, and new models can be added. Details of the current status of each model are included.

- **Build**   The build information includes the Target variable and the Case ID. These are common for all the Classification models listed in the Models tab.

- **Test**   This tab contains the details of what data will be used for testing the models. The default option is to split the data supplied in the Data Source node into model build data and model test data. The default setting for this is to keep 40 percent of the data for testing. You can change this percentage; for example, if you want to use 70 percent of the data for building the models and 30 percent for testing the models, you would change this Test value to 30. Other options include using all the data for building the models.

- **Details**   The Details tab allows you to change the default name to a name that is more meaningful for your scenario. You can also add a description for the node to include all relevant details and design decisions.

Using Different Build and Test Data Sets

There are two approaches you can take to define the data you want to use for your classification work. The typical method is to use a single data source that contains the data for the build and testing stages of the Model Build node. Using this method, you can specify what percentage of the data in the data source to use for the build step, and the remaining records will be used for testing the model. The default is a 60:40 split, as shown in Figure 8-7, but you can change this to whatever percentage you think is appropriate (such as 70:30). The records are split randomly into the Build and Test data sets.

The second way to specify the data sources is to use a separate data source for the build and a separate data source for the testing of the model. To do this, you need to add a new additional data source (containing the Test data set) and connect it to the Model Build node, as shown in Figure 8-8. ODM assigns a label (Test) to the connector for the second data source.

If the label is assigned incorrectly, you can swap the data sources. To do this, right-click on the Model Build node, then select Swap Data Sources from the menu.

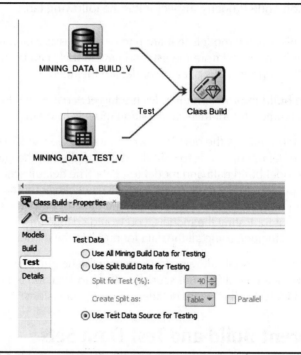

FIGURE 8-8. *Classification Build node with separate Build and Test data sets*

CAUTION
The label on the connection between the Data Source node that contains the Test data set and the Classification node might disappear after you close and reopen the workflow. You need to keep a note of which data source is being used for building the model and which data source is being used for the testing of the model. You can enter this information in the Details tab of the Property Inspector for the Classification node.

This label might also disappear after you have run your workflow.

Creating Additional Models and Removing Unwanted Models

When creating a Classification Model node, Oracle Data Miner defaults to creating a model for each of the classification algorithms. Depending on your project, you might want to create only one model—for example, just a Decision Tree. To remove the other models from the Classification Build node, you need to have the Build section in the Properties tab of the Classification node active.

The Models section of the Properties tab lists the models that will be built (see Figure 8-9). To remove a model, click on the model name, then click on the red X that is just above the model listing. This removes the model from the list in the Models tab. You can repeat this for each of the models you want to remove from the Classification Build node.

If you want to add extra models to the Classification Build node, you can use the green plus sign. Click on the icon to open the Add Model window. In this window, you can select the algorithm you want to use, specify the name for the new model, and enter a comment. A default name is generated and entered in the Name field. You can overwrite this with something that is meaningful to you. An example of an instance where you might want to add another model is when you want to create an additional Decision Tree with different properties, such as being shallower or deeper than the other Decision Tree. When you have the new model listed in the Models tab, you then need to change the settings of the newly created Decision Tree. In the example in Figure 8-10, a new decision tree called DECISION_TREE_2 is created.

To change the settings, you need to right-click on the Classification Build node (on the workflow) and select Advanced Settings from the menu. The Advanced Model Settings window opens. Scroll down to the new model (DECISION_TREE_2) and click on the Algorithm Settings tab to make the necessary changes to the algorithm, such as to change the Maximum Depth of the Decision Tree.

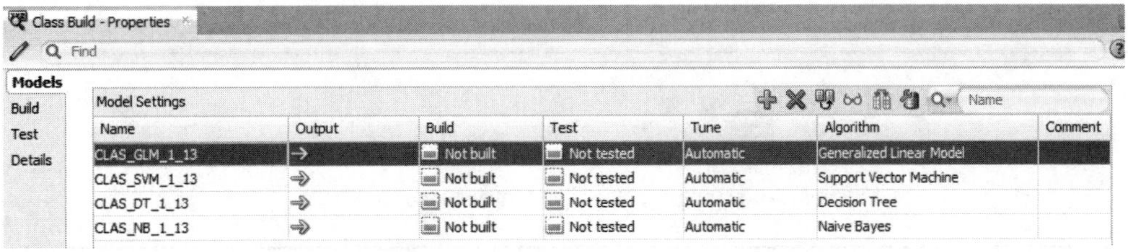

Name	Output	Build	Test	Tune	Algorithm	Comment
CLAS_GLM_1_13	→	Not built	Not tested	Automatic	Generalized Linear Model	
CLAS_SVM_1_13	→	Not built	Not tested	Automatic	Support Vector Machine	
CLAS_DT_1_13	→	Not built	Not tested	Automatic	Decision Tree	
CLAS_NB_1_13	→	Not built	Not tested	Automatic	Naive Bayes	

FIGURE 8-9. *Adding and removing models from the Classification Build node*

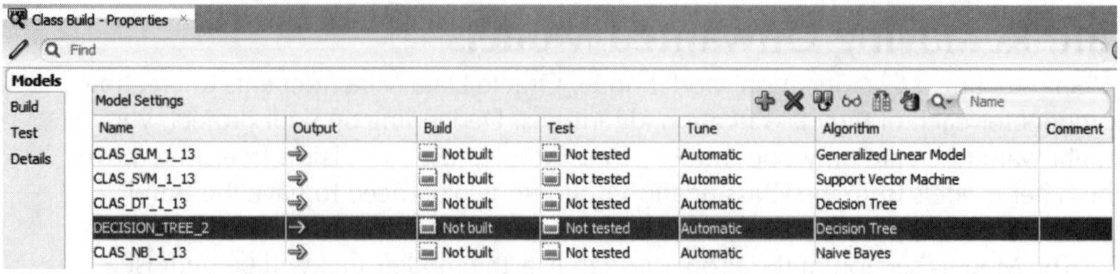

Class Build - Properties ×							
🖉 Q Find							

Models	Model Settings					✚ ✖ 🗑 ∞ 🗎 🔧 Q▾	Name

Models								
Build	Name	Output	Build	Test	Tune	Algorithm	Comment
Test	CLAS_GLM_1_13	⇒	🖾 Not built	🖾 Not tested	Automatic	Generalized Linear Model	
Details	CLAS_SVM_1_13	⇒	🖾 Not built	🖾 Not tested	Automatic	Support Vector Machine	
	CLAS_DT_1_13	⇒	🖾 Not built	🖾 Not tested	Automatic	Decision Tree	
	DECISION_TREE_2	→	🖾 Not built	🖾 Not tested	Automatic	Decision Tree	
	CLAS_NB_1_13	⇒	🖾 Not built	🖾 Not tested	Automatic	Naive Bayes	

FIGURE 8-10. *Adding a new Decision Tree to the Classification Build node*

Generating the Models

When you have set up your training and test data, identified the algorithms you want to use to generate your models, and configured the algorithm settings, you are now ready to run the Classification Build node. To run the node, right-click on the Classification Build node, then select Run from the menu. Alternatively, you can click on the green arrow on the Workflow Worksheet menu.

After you have clicked Run, Oracle Data Miner looks back along the workflow, packages up all the steps, and then submits these to the database as a process using DBMS_JOBS.

As each step of the workflow is processed, you see a green wheel on the top right-hand corner of the node. When a node has been completed, the green wheel appears on the next node in the workflow. After all the nodes have been completed, you see a green check mark in the top right-hand corner of the node, as shown in Figure 8-11.

If an error occurs when processing a node, a red *X* appears on the top right-hand corner of the node. To see the error messages for this node, right-click on the node, then select Show Errors from the menu.

MINING_DATA_BUILD_V   Class Build

FIGURE 8-11. *Completed workflow with generated models*

Evaluating the Classification Models

Evaluating the models produced by the Classification Build node is an important step. It enables you to identify the most efficient model. An efficient model is one that gives the best accuracy for your scenario and the data used to generate the model. As you gather more data, with the target variable defined, you can regenerate your models. When you do this, you may find that the same algorithm still produces the best model, or perhaps that one of the other algorithms gives a better result.

The following sections describe the different evaluation methods available in Oracle Data Miner. Using a combination of these evaluation methods allows you to select the best or most efficient model for your scenario.

The results displayed in each of the model evaluation screens are based on the data that was defined for testing in the Classification Build node. If you chose the default settings, Oracle Data Miner kept a random sample of 40 percent of the data that is a stratified sample across the target values.

To view the model evaluation results, right-click on the Classification Build node. This should have the green check mark on the top right-hand corner of the node. From the menu, select Compare Test Results. The following sections explain what is displayed for each of the model evaluation screens.

Performance

The Performance screen (see Figure 8-12) gives an overall summary of the performance of each model generated. A number of graphs and some statistics are given for each model. You can use this information to get an initial impression of how well each model performed using the Test data set. The graphs give a visualization of the summary results, and you can easily see the differences between each model.

The visualizations and statistics include the following for each model:

- **Predictive Confidence (%)**   This gives an estimate of the overall quality of the model. It indicates how much better the predictions are than the predictions made by a naïve model.

$$\text{Predictive Confidence} = \text{MAX}\left[\left(1 - \frac{\text{error of model}}{\text{error of naïve model}}\right), 0\right] \times 100$$

- **Overall Accuracy (%)**   This is the average per-class accuracy percentage of correct predictions made by the model when compared to the actual classifications in the testing data set.

- **Average Accuracy (%)**   This gives the percentage of correct predictions made by the model when compared with the actual classifications in the testing data set.

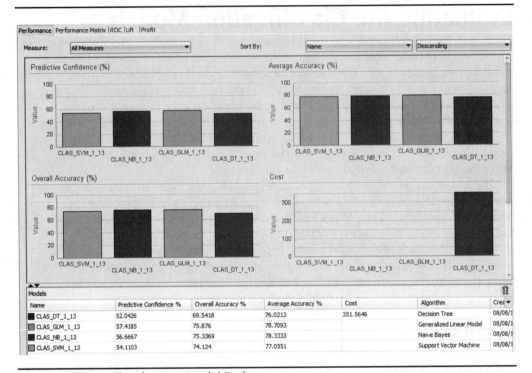

FIGURE 8-12. *Classification Model Performance screen*

NOTE
You may get slightly different results from the models. The results vary slightly due to the version of the database, the data set being used, the parameter settings, and so on.

Performance Matrix

The Performance Matrix tab on the Compare Test Results screen shows the details of the likelihood for each model of predicting the correct or incorrect target variable. The Performance Matrix is commonly referred to as the Confusion Matrix.

In the Display drop-down list in this screen, the default setting is Compare Models (see Figure 8-13). This gives, for each model, the number of records used for testing each model. This result is the same for each model. The Compare Models setting also gives the number of correct predictions. This number is the overall total for each target value. The setting also gives the percentage of correct predictions.

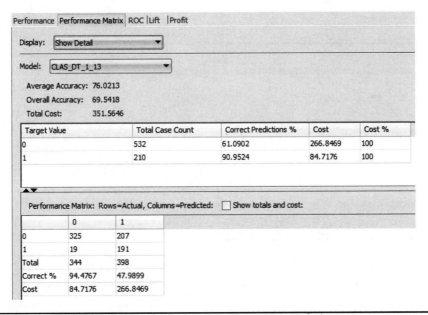

FIGURE 8-13. *Performance Matrix*

The Performance Matrix is calculated by applying the model to the testing data set. The values of the target attribute are already known. These known values are compared with the values predicted by the model.

A detailed Performance Matrix can be displayed by changing the Display drop-down list to Show Detail (as shown in Figure 8-13). This gives for each model a breakdown of the number of records it correctly predicted and incorrectly predicted for each of the target attribute values. You can view the Performance Matrix for each model by changing the model in the Model drop-down list.

In the example shown in Figure 8-13, you can see that the Decision Tree model achieves a high accuracy percentage for predicting the target value of 1.

ROC

The Receiver Operating Characteristic (ROC) curve provides a way to compare individual models based on predicted and actual target values in a model. The ROC curve is a statistical method dating back to World War II, where it was developed to access the ability of radar operators to identify indicators correctly on a radar screen. The ROC curve is used to represent the relationship between the false positive rate and the false negative rate for each model.

The horizontal axis of an ROC graph measures the false positive rate as a percentage. The vertical axis shows the true positive rate. The top left-hand corner

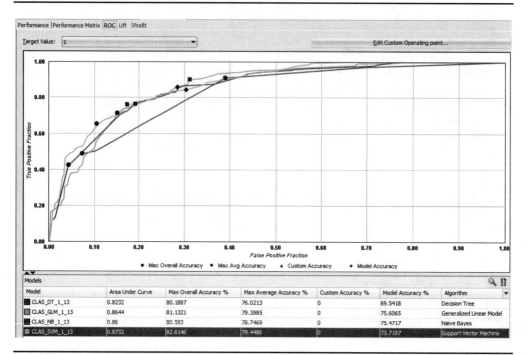

FIGURE 8-14. *ROC curve*

is the optimal location in an ROC curve, indicating a high true positive rate versus a low false positive rate.

The maximum overall accuracy, maximum average accuracy, custom accuracy, and model accuracy are indicated the ROC curves.

You can change the custom operating point by clicking on the Edit Custom Operating Point button on the top right-hand corner of the screen (see Figure 8-14).

The Edit Custom Operating Point dialog box allows you to edit the custom operating point for all models in the node. To change Hit Rate or False Alarm, click the appropriate radio button and adjust the slider to the value that you want to use. It is best to change this setting in small increments. The ROC curve is updated to show the custom accuracy points. Alternatively, you can specify the false positive/false negative ratio.

Lift

Lift measures the degree to which the predictions of a classification model are better than randomly generated predictions, as indicated by the diagonal line in Figure 8-15. The Lift chart is similar to the ROC curve, as it is a means of comparing individual models.

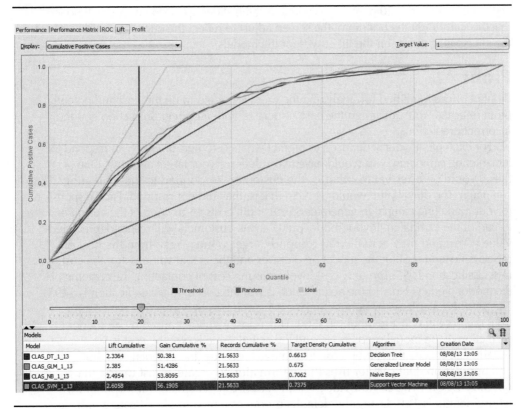

FIGURE 8-15. *Lift chart*

To calculate the lift and to draw the Lift chart, Oracle Data Miner takes the predicted and actual target values from the Testing data set, sorts the predicted results by the probability of making a positive prediction, divides the ranked list into ten quantiles, and then counts the actual positive values in each quantile.

The diagonal line in the chart indicates a random approach. For example, if you are running a marketing campaign and targeted 10 percent of the population, you would get 10 percent of our target customers. Similarly, if you targeted 50 percent of the population, you would get 50 percent of your target customers. You can use the Lift chart to see which of the models gives you the best lift in comparison to the random approach. The greater the lift, the greater the number of customers you could be targeting.

In this example, you can adjust the slider that is located under the graph. The slider represents the percentage of your target audience. The vertical line shows you where it intersects with the lift curve for each model. The initial position of the vertical blue line is at 20 percent. As you adjust the slider up or down, you will notice that the statistics at the bottom of the screen adjust to reflect the current position and the intersecting points on the lift curves for the models.

Profit

Profit provides a method for analyzing the models to determine the cost and potential profit returned. You can assign the cost associated with a correct prediction and the incorrect predictions.

For example, if your scenario is to predict what customers are likely to respond to a marketing campaign, you would have two values for your target attribute. One of these would be a Yes value—that is, the customers responded to the marketing campaign. The other value would be No—that is, they did not respond. Each response to your marketing campaign generates $500, and it costs $5 to contact the customer as part of the campaign. If your model predicts that customers will respond (predicted value = Yes) and they actually did respond (target value = Yes), then the cost of misclassification is $0. If the model predicts Yes and the actual value is No, the cost of misclassification is $5. The only cost involved is the cost of contacting the customer. If the model predicts No and the actual value is Yes, the cost of misclassification is $495. The $495 is calculated by subtracting the $5 saved by not contacting the customer from the potential lost revenue of $500. This is lost revenue caused by an incorrect prediction. If the model predicts No and the actual value is No, the cost is $0.

You can specify the startup cost, incremental revenue, incremental cost, budget, and population. Data Miner uses this information to create a cost matrix that optimizes profit. The default value for all variables is 1, except for population, whose default is 100. Using the defaults produces a meaningless Profit graph, so unless you have actual values to use here, this screen will not contribute to your analysis of the model.

To set up the costs for your model, you need to click on the Profit Settings button on the Profit screen. This opens the Profit Setting Dialog, where you can enter the appropriate costs. Using the marketing campaign example, you could enter the following, as shown in Figure 8-16:

- **Startup Cost** This is the fixed cost of setting up the project. For example, it could cost $10,000 to get the project to the point of starting the marketing campaign.

- **Incremental Revenue** This is the estimated revenue that results from a sale or new customer. In this example, this amount is $495.

- **Incremental Cost** This is the estimated cost that is associated with promoting a sale or contacting the customer. In this example, this cost is $5.

- **Budget** This is the amount of money you have for the project. It is used to calculate how much of the customer population can be covered based on the other variables. In this example, you can set this amount to $12,000.

- **Population** This is the number of cases or customers you want to consider. In this example, you will consider 1,000 customers.

The Profit chart is redrawn based on these values, as shown in Figure 8-16. You will see that the Profit chart flattens out at approximately the 60 percent of the population mark. A vertical line is drawn on the graph to indicate the point at which you have reached or used up the budget. This is shown as the vertical line on the right of the chart in Figure 8-16. From the Profit Matrix below the graph, you can see how much total profit each model will potentially give you. At the point where you have used up the budget, you will have reached approximately 40 percent of your population, and the best models will produce approximately $95,410 in profit. This is given by the Naïve Bayes and the Support Vector Machine models.

TIP
The values you enter into the Profit Setting Dialog are not saved in Oracle. If you restart SQL Developer, you have to enter the values again.

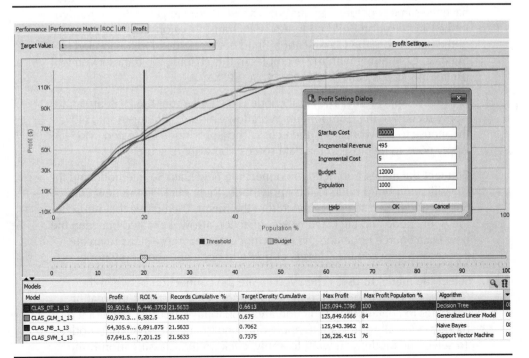

FIGURE 8-16. *Profit chart with Profit Setting Dialog*

Applying a Classification Model to New Data

After you have analyzed the different models that were produced by the Classification Build node, you should be able to identify which of the models best suits your scenario. The chosen model has modeled the past behavior of your data based on a target variable. You can now use this model or models on new data. Using the Oracle Data Miner tool, you can take new data that exists in a table and score/label it with a predicted value. In addition to yielding the predicted value, Oracle Data Miner also gives the predictive probability for this score. The predictive probability is a measure of how sure Oracle is of its prediction. A predictive probability value of one (1) indicates that Oracle thinks that this prediction is 100 percent correct. The range of values of the predictive probability ranges from zero to one.

The following outlines the steps you need to perform to score a new data set:

1. **Define the data source.** You need to create a new Data Source node that contains the new data that you want to score. Select the Data Source node from the Data section of the Components Workflow Editor. Move your mouse to the worksheet and click. The Data Source node opens and the Define Data Source wizard opens. Select the table or view that contains the data and the attributes that you want to use. This new table or view should have the same structure and attributes as were used to generate the models in the Classification Build node. Any data transformations that were applied to the data before the Classification Build node also need to be applied to the data. Continuing with the examples in this chapter, the data set you will use for this step is called `MINING_DATA_APPLY_V`.

2. **Create the Apply node.** The Apply node is located under the Evaluate and Apply section of the Components Workflow Editor. Select this node, move the mouse to the worksheet, then click. The Apply node is created. Move the Apply node to be close to the data source you want to score.

3. **Connect the nodes.** You need to connect the new Data Source node and the Classification Build node to the Apply node. Right-click on the new Data Source node, then select Connect from the menu. Then move the mouse to the Apply node and click again. A connection arrow is created between the new Data Source node and the Apply node. Repeat these steps to create a connection between the Classification Build node and the Apply node.

4. **Select the model to use.** When you create the connection between the Classification Build node and the Apply node, ODM defaults to creating attributes to contain the prediction and probability values for each of the models. Typically you want to apply only one (or a couple) of your models. To select the model you want to apply, click on the Classification Build

node. In the Models section of the Properties tab is a column called Output. For each model you will see a green arrow. This arrow indicates that the model will be used in the Apply node and will create the associated output columns for each model. To remove the necessary models from the output, click on each green arrow. For example, in the current scenario, you want to use the Support Vector Machine model. As you click on the other models, the green arrow changes to a red *X*, leaving the Support Vector Machine model with the full green arrow.

5. **Select the attributes for output.** After selecting the model, click on the Apply node. The Properties tab for the Apply node now displays the output columns for the Support Vector Machine. These are the Prediction and the Prediction Probability columns. In addition to choosing these attributes, you can select what attributes from the Apply Data node to include in the output. For example, you need the Primary Key attribute from the Apply data set. This attribute allows you to link the prediction back to the record for which it was made. To select the Apply data set attributes to include in the Apply output, go to the Additional Output section of the Properties tab. Alternatively, double-click on the Apply node and go to the Additional Output tab. To add the columns, click on the green plus sign. A window opens listing all the attributes in the Apply data set. Select the columns you want to include in the output—for example, CUST_ID—and move them to the right-hand side of this window. When you are finished selecting the attributes, click on the OK button(s). The attributes selected now appear in the Data tab of the Property Inspector.

6. **Run the Apply node.** When you have selected the model(s) you want to apply to your new data and the attributes you want as part of the output, the next step is to run the Apply node. To do so, right-click on the Apply node, then select Run from the menu. ODM creates a workflow job that constitutes the different elements that need to be run. These are packaged up and submitted to the database to be run. While the workflow is running, a rotating wheel appears on the top right-hand corner of each node as it is being processed. When the workflow is finished, a green tick mark appears on the top right-hand corner of the nodes and in particular the Apply node.

7. **View the results.** To view the results from the Apply node, applying the data mining model to your new data, right-click on the Apply node and select View Data from the menu. In the current example, three columns are displayed: CUST_ID, the Predicted value by the SVM, and the Prediction Probability. CUST_ID allows you to link the prediction information back to the original data and records. The Predicted value is the class value that the classification model has predicted. The Prediction Probability is the percentage probability that Oracle thinks that its Predicted value is correct. You can order the data grid showing the results by double-clicking on a column heading or by using the Sort filter.

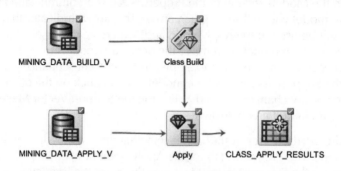

MINING_DATA_BUILD_V   Class Build

MINING_DATA_APPLY_V   Apply   CLASS_APPLY_RESULTS

FIGURE 8-17. *The complete classification workflow*

8. **Persist the results.** The results are not persisted in the database. If you would like to use these results at a later time or to use the results in another schema or database, you need to persist the results in a table. To persist the data, you need to create a new table and store the results in it. From the Data menu on the Components Workflow Editor, select Create Table or View, move your mouse to be beside the Apply node, then click again. A new node is created with a name beginning with OUTPUT_ and followed by some numbers. Click on this node, then in the Table section of the Properties tab change the name of the table to something meaningful, such as CLASS_APPLY_RESULTS. Next you need to connect the Apply node to the CLASS_APPLY_RESULTS node. Right-click on the Apply node, select Connect from the menu, then click on the CLASS_APPLY_RESULTS node. A connection arrow is created. To persist the results, right-click on the CLASS_APPLY_RESULTS node, then select Run from the menu. When the workflow is finished, a green tick mark appears at the top right-hand corner of the node. The CLASS_APPLY_ RESULTS table now exists in your schema. Figure 8-17 shows the complete classification workflow.

Summary

Classification is a very powerful technique that you can use in your data science projects. It allows you to find patterns that exist in your current data. You can then use these patterns to label new data to see how it fits into your existing groups. Typical application areas for classification include marketing campaigns, loyalty cards, insurance, banking, retail stores, medical diagnostic, retention, churn, and more. This chapter showed you how to use the Oracle Data Miner tool, which is part of SQL Developer, to build up a classification workflow. In Chapter 15 you will see how to use the in-database SQL functions and procedures to create and use classification models.

CHAPTER

9

Clustering

C lustering is an unsupervised data mining technique. You can use the clustering algorithms to find groupings of data that are more related to each other (a cluster) and less related to other groupings (other clusters). Examples of when the clustering data mining technique is used include customer segmentation, marketing, insurance claims analysis, outlier detection, image pattern recognition, biology, security, and more.

What Is Clustering?

Clustering is a process of dividing the data into smaller related subsets. Each of these subsets is called a *cluster*. For each cluster, the data in the cluster are very similar to each other, but also dissimilar to the data in the other clusters. The clustering algorithms in Oracle form a hierarchical structure similar to what is illustrated in Figure 9-1.

Different clustering algorithms may generate different clusters on the same data. Clustering is an unsupervised data mining method that aims to find data that is closely related to each other. The clusters produced by the algorithms are the groupings that exist in the data. No explanation is given as to why these clusters exist. The algorithms give a set of rules that explain each cluster. These rules consist of the attributes and the values of those attributes that determine whether a record belongs to a particular cluster. What a cluster means or represents in a business context is left to the data scientist to explore and discover. From this process, the data scientist can add a label to each cluster to represent what it means and he or she can combine clusters that have a very similar meaning.

Clustering is a very useful method for exploring your data to find whether there are any clusters in the data. Typically, you will use clustering with other data mining algorithms as part of your data science projects.

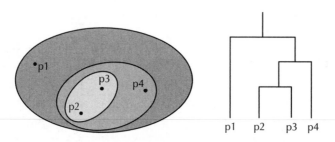

FIGURE 9-1.   *Hierarchical clustering and dendrogram*

There are a number of clustering algorithms available in Oracle Data Mining, and these use different approaches to calculating the clusters. Oracle Data Mining supports three approaches to clustering:

- **Distance Based**   This approach uses a distance measure to calculate the similarity or dissimilarity between data items. The distance measure is a measurement of the distance from the centroid of the cluster to the data item. This measurement can be used to determine the cluster to which the data item belongs. This approach is used in the enhanced *K*-Means algorithm.

- **Grid Based**   This approach involves dividing the data set into hyper-rectangular cells, discarding cells where there is a low density and combining adjacent high-density cells to form clusters. This approach is used in the O-Cluster algorithm.

- **Density Based**   This approach finds the distribution of the data and estimates the areas of high density in the data. High-density areas are interpreted as clusters.

Clustering Methods Available in Oracle

Oracle has a number of clustering algorithms available. Table 9-1 lists the Clustering algorithms available in Oracle and briefly describes each.

Algorithm	Description
K-Means	Oracle Data Miner runs an enhanced version of the typical *K*-means algorithm. ODM builds models in a hierarchical manner, using a top-down approach with binary splits and refinements of all nodes at the end. The centroid of the inner nodes in the hierarchy is updated to reflect changes as the tree grows. The tree grows one node at a time. The node with the largest variance is split to increase the size of the tree until the desired number of clusters is reached. The algorithm evolves producing the number of clusters specified by the data scientist. The number of clusters to be produced is set as part of the algorithm parameters.
	The enhanced *K*-Means algorithm uses a density-based distance measure, can handle data sets of any size but with a low number of attributes, and produces a user-defined number of clusters.

TABLE 9-1.   *Clustering Algorithms Available in the Oracle Database* (continued)

Algorithm	Description
O-Cluster	O-Cluster is an Orthogonal Partitioning Clustering method that creates a hierarchical grid-based clustering model. The algorithm uses axis-parallel unidimensional data projections to identify the areas of density. The algorithm looks to find cluster splitting points that result in distinct clusters that do not overlap and are balanced in size. The O-Cluster algorithm operates recursively, generating a hierarchical structure. The resulting clusters define dense areas. The algorithm automatically determines the number of clusters to produce.
	The O-Cluster works with a fixed-sized buffer. The data is loaded into this buffer for processing. If the data set is too large to fit into this buffer, active sampling is performed to set the data for clustering. After the initial data set is processed, the algorithm continues to sample the data set to obtain new cases that will contribute to the cluster generation and splitting.
	The O-Cluster algorithm uses a grid-based approach, is suitable for data sets with more than 500 cases and have a high number of attributes, and automatically determines the number of clusters in the data set.
Expectation Maximization	The Expectation Maximization algorithm is available in Oracle version 12c. This is based on a probabilistic, density estimation clustering algorithm. The Expectation Maximization algorithm starts with an initial set of parameters and iterates until the clustering cannot be improved or until the clustering converges. This is an iterative approach that involves two steps for each iteration:
	1. The expectation step places data in clusters according to the parameters of probabilistic clustering.
	2. The maximization step finds new clusters or parameters that maximize the clusters.
	Oracle Data Miner has implemented an enhanced version of the Expectation Maximization algorithm to allow it to be scalable using the database parallel processing. It can handle high-dimensional data for single-attribute and nested data, and the number of components is automatically calculated by the algorithm.

TABLE 9-1. *Clustering Algorithms Available in the Oracle Database* (continued)

To read more details of these algorithms, see the *Oracle Data Mining Concepts* book that is part of the Oracle documentation.

When preparing your data for input to the Oracle Data Mining clustering algorithms, you need to prepare one record for each case. Each case requires a single attribute that is unique. This attribute is called the Case ID. If you have a record where the primary key is a multi-attribute primary key, you need to generate a new attribute that is unique, and that attribute is the Case ID.

Building Clustering Models

When you build clustering models in ODM, you use the Clustering node. The Clustering node is located under the Models section of the Components Workflow Editor. By default, the Clustering node lists the clustering algorithms that are available. You can select all of these, remove them, or create additional versions of a model with different model settings. For example, you can create a clustering model with a different number of clusters using the K-Means algorithm.

In this section, you walk through the steps to set up, run, and generate clustering models in Oracle Data Miner. The data set that is used to illustrate clustering is the INSUR_CUST_LTV_SAMPLE table. You created this table back in Chapter 3 when you created your DMUSER schema to access the ODM Repository and sample schemas.

The INSUR_CUST_LTV_SAMPLE table contains records for an example financial company. Each customer has one record, which contains some personal, demographic, account, customer interactions, life time value (LTV) information, as well as whether the customer bought insurance in the past. You will use the clustering features in Oracle to see whether there are natural groups (clusters) in the data. The INSUR_CUST_LTV_SAMPLE table was created when you first set up your schema to use Oracle Data Miner.

When using Oracle Data Miner, it can be useful to separate your work into separate workflows. Before you create your clustering models, it is recommended that you create a separate workflow that will contain all your clustering work. In the following sections, you perform all your work in a new workflow called "Clustering Chapter," which is created under the "ODM Book" project. To get more detail on how to create a workflow, see Chapter 4.

As with all data mining work using Oracle Data Miner, you need to define a new data source. To create the data source for the INSUR_CUST_LTV_SAMPLE table, you need to select the Data Source node from the Data section of the Components Workflow Editor. Click on the Data Source node, then move the mouse to the worksheet and click again. The Data Source node is created and the Define Data Source window opens. In the Define Data Source window, select INSUR_CUST_LTV_SAMPLE from the list of tables. Click on the Next button to move to the attribute selection window. You want to include all the attributes and then click the Finish button. The Data Source node is renamed INSUR_CUST_LTV_SAMPLE.

FIGURE 9-2. *Data Source and Clustering nodes*

The next step is to create the Clustering node. The Clustering node is located under the Models section of the Components Workflow Editor. To create this node in your worksheet, click on the Clustering node, move your mouse to the worksheet (ideally just to the right of the data node), then click on the worksheet. The Clustering node appears on your worksheet. The next step is to join the Data Source node to the Clustering node. Right-click on the Data Source node, then select Connect from the menu. Then move your mouse to the Clustering node and click again. A connection line is drawn between the two nodes on the worksheet, as illustrated in Figure 9-2.

To edit the properties and the algorithm settings for the Clustering node, you must double-click the Clustering node. The Edit Clustering Build Node window opens (see Figure 9-3). In the Edit Clustering Build Node window, you can define the Case ID of the input data, change the settings for each of the Clustering algorithms, and add or remove models from the list.

TIP
The Case ID/primary key needs to consist of one attribute from the table. If you have a multi-attribute primary key, then you need to generate an alternate key and use this as the Case ID.

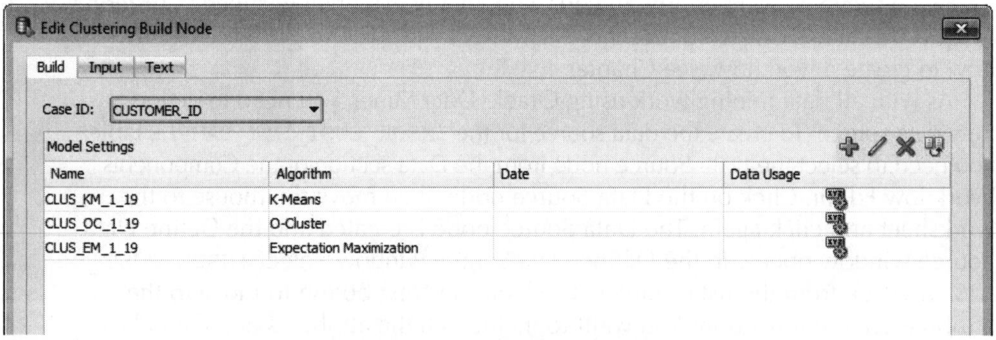

FIGURE 9-3. *Edit Clustering Build Node*

For the INSUR_CUST_LTV_SAMPLE table, the Case ID is the CUSTOMER_ID attribute. This is shown in Figure 9-3.

When starting out with your data mining projects, you want to generate a model using each of the data mining algorithms. This allows you to see which algorithm performs best for your particular set of data.

If you are happy to use the Oracle default setting for each of the clustering algorithms, then you are ready to run the Clustering node and generate the models.

Model Settings

The Advanced Model Settings allow you to inspect and change the data usage and algorithm settings for each clustering algorithm. Oracle has selected what it regards as the optimal settings suitable for most problems. Each algorithm comes with its own specific settings. You can modify the defaults to alter the internal processing of the clustering algorithms.

TIP
Change the algorithm settings only when you understand what the change means and why you are doing it. In most cases, you do not need to change these internal settings.

To change or view Advanced Model Settings, open the Edit Clustering Build Node window and double click on one of the listed algorithms (see Figure 9-3). If you have closed this window, you can right-click the Classification node, then select Advanced Settings from the context menu.

The Advanced Model Settings window lists all of the models in the node in the upper pane. To view and change the settings of these algorithms, click on each of the algorithms in turn. As you do this, you can select the Algorithm Settings tab to see the settings for each algorithm.

K-Means Algorithm Settings

The K-Means algorithm has the following settings (see Figure 9-4):

- **Number of Clusters**   This is the number of hierarchical leaf clusters to generate. The default number is 10.

- **Growth Factor**   This is the growth factor for allocating memory to hold the cluster data. The default value is 2. The setting can have a value in the range 1 to 5.

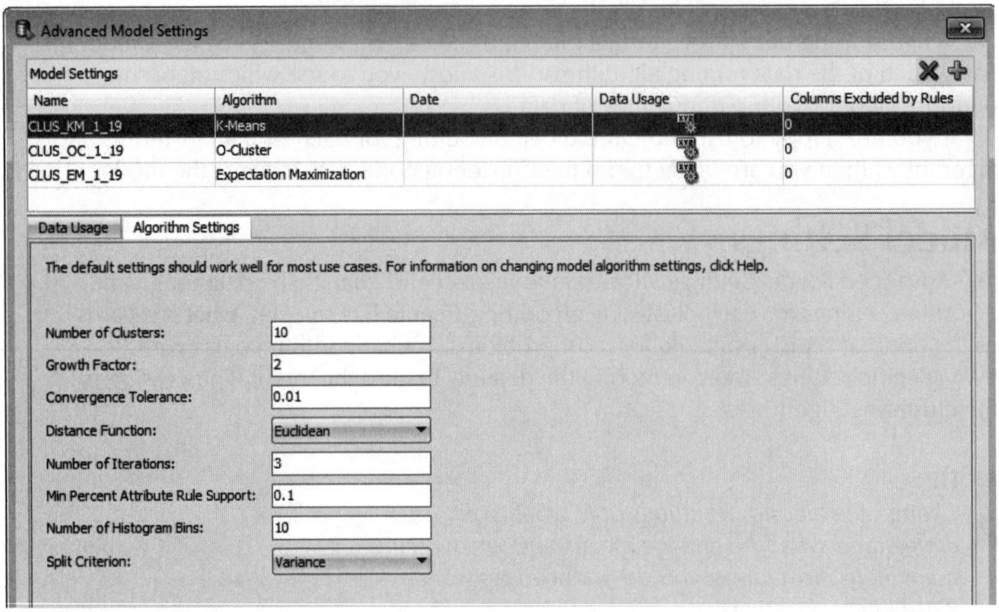

FIGURE 9-4. *K-Means algorithm settings*

■ **Convergence Tolerance**   This value determines how fast a build will be.
There is a balance between build speed and accuracy. The slower the build,
the higher the accuracy, and vice versa. The default value is 0.01. The setting
can have a value in the range 0.001 (slow build) and 0.1 (fast build).

■ **Distance Function**   This is the distance measure to use when assessing the
clusters. The default value is Euclidean. Other distance measures include
Cosine and Fast Cosine.

■ **Number of Iterations**   This is the number of iterations the K-Means
algorithm will perform. The default value is 3. The setting can have a value
in the range 2 (slow build) and 30 (fast build).

■ **Min Percent Attribute Rule Support**   This percentage is used to filter rules
that do not meet the support threshold. If the value is set too high, you get a
small set of rules. The default value is 0.1. The setting can have values in the
range 0.0 to 1.0.

- **Number of Histogram Bins**   This is the number of bins in the attribute histogram produced by the K-Means algorithm. Binning is performed automatically, with a binning method of equi-width. The default value is 10. The setting must be a positive value.

- **Split Criterion**   The default value is Variance. The alternative value is Size.

O-Cluster Algorithm Settings
The O-Cluster algorithm has the following settings (see Figure 9-5):

- **Number of Clusters**   This is the maximum number of leaf clusters that the O-Cluster algorithm will generate. The default value is 10.

- **Buffer Size**   This is the maximum size of the memory buffer that the O-Cluster algorithm will use. The bigger the buffer, the larger the number of records that it can use before active sampling is activated. The default is 10,000 records.

- **Sensitivity**   This value specifies the peak density required for separating a cluster. The default value is 0.5. The setting can have a value in the range 0 (fewer clusters) and 1 (more clusters).

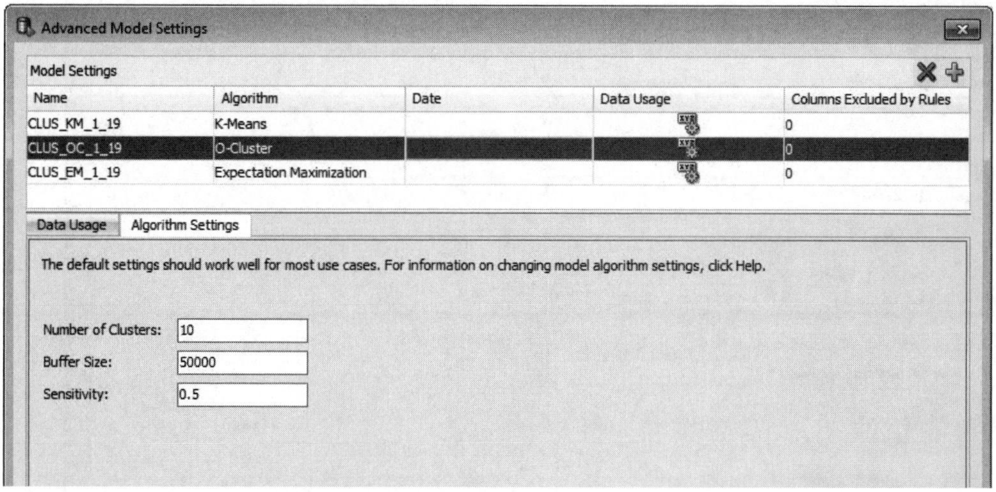

FIGURE 9-5.   *O-Cluster algorithm settings*

Expectation Maximization Algorithm Settings

The Expectation Maximization algorithm is available only in version 12c and has the following settings (see Figure 9-6):

■ **Number of Clusters** This is the maximum number of leaf clusters that the Expectation Maximization algorithm will generate. The algorithm may return fewer clusters than the setting specified. The default value setting is System Determined. Alternatively, you can specify a maximum number, and this value should be greater than zero.

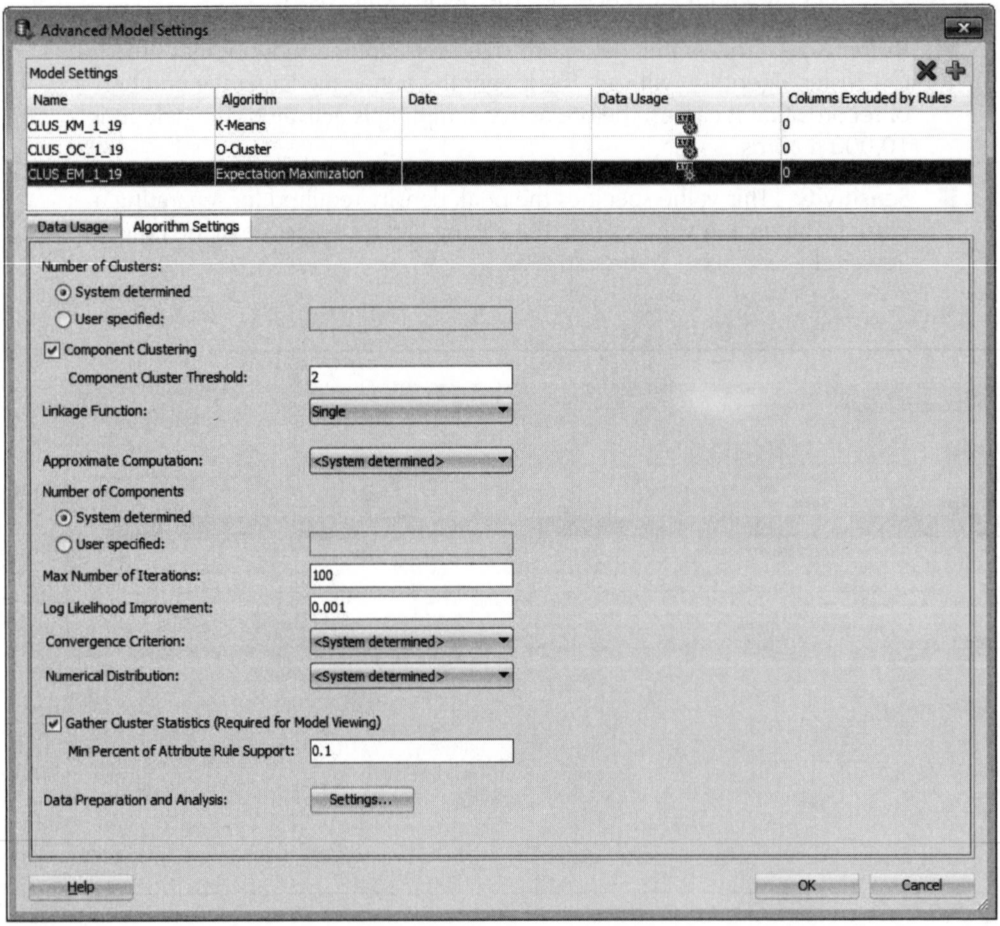

FIGURE 9-6. *Expectation Maximization algorithm settings*

■ **Component Clustering**   If component clustering is to be used, you can specify the Component Cluster Threshold. The default value is 2.

■ **Linkage Function**   This setting enables you to specify the linkage function for the agglomerative clustering step. There are three functions available:

  ■ **Single**   This function uses the nearest distance with the branch. With this function, the clusters are generally larger and have arbitrary shapes.

  ■ **Average**   This function uses the average distance with the branch. With this function, there are fewer chaining effects and the clusters are more compact.

  ■ **Complete**   This function uses the maximum distance with the branch. With this function, the clusters are smaller and require strong component overlap.

  The default value is Single.

■ **Approximate Computation**   This allows you to specify whether the algorithm should use approximate computations to improve performance. The default value is System Determined, with other values being Enabled and Disabled.

■ **Number of Components**   This setting allows you to specify the number of components in the model. The default setting is System Determined.

■ **Max Number of Iterations**   This setting specifies the maximum number of iterations in the Expectation Maximization algorithm. The default value is 100.

■ **Log Likelihood Improvement**   This is the percentage improvement in the value of the log likelihood function required to add a new component to the model. The default value is 0.001.

■ **Convergence Criterion**   The default value for the convergence criterion is System Determined. The other values are Bayesian Information Criterion and Held-Aside Dataset.

■ **Numerical Distribution**   This setting specifies the distribution method for modeling numeric attributes. The default value is System Determined. The other values are Bernoulli and Gaussian.

■ **Gather Cluster Statistics**   The default setting is enabled, which tells ODM to gather descriptive statistics for the clusters produced by the algorithm. When this setting is enabled, you can specify a value for Min Percent of Attribute Rule Support. The default value for this setting is 0.1. If the Gather

Cluster Statistics check box is disabled, the algorithm produces smaller models that contain minimal information. In this case, you will not be able to view the model.

■ **Data Preparation and Analysis** This allows you to specify the setting for data preparation and analysis. The settings include how to handle equi-width bins, top-N bins, quantile bins, nested data, and two-dimensional (2D) attributes.

TIP
You need to scroll down the settings window to see all the algorithm settings. Alternatively, you can use your mouse to increase the size of the window. Figure 9-6 shows all the algorithm settings when the window size has been increased.

Property Inspector

Each node in the workflow has an associated Property Inspector. This is a dockable area and typically appears below the Components Workflow Editor. As you click on each node in your workflow, different properties relating to the node are displayed in the Property Inspector. For the Clustering node, the Property Inspector has three tabs, as shown in Figure 9-7.

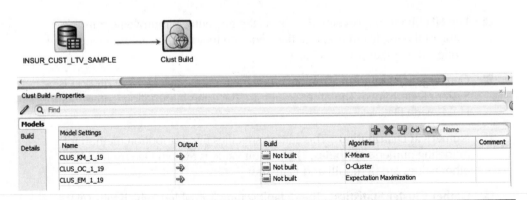

FIGURE 9-7. *Clustering node Property Inspector showing the Test tab*

The Clustering node Property Inspector has the following tabs:

■ **Models** This lists the models and algorithms that are part of the Clustering node. You can remove models from the list or add new ones. Details of the current status of each model are included.

■ **Build** The Build information includes Case ID. This is common for all the Clustering models listed in the Models tab. You can change the Case ID, and this change is then applied to all the models the next time the node is run.

■ **Details** The Details tab allows you to change the default name to a name that is more meaningful for your scenario. You can also add a description for the node to include all relevant details and design decisions.

Creating Additional Models and Removing Unwanted Models

When creating the Clustering node, Oracle Data Miner defaults to creating a model for each of the clustering algorithms. Depending on your project, you many want to create only one clustering model, for example, just a K-Means with ten clusters. Or your project might require a number of clustering models with different numbers of clusters. To add or remove models for the Clustering Build node, you can use the Models tab of the Property Inspector. The Models tab lists the current models that will be built when the Clustering node is run. Alternatively, you can double-click on the Clustering node to open the Edit Clustering Build Node window.

To remove a model, click on the model name, then click on the red *X* that is just above the model listing. This removes the model from the list in the Models tab. You can repeat this for each of the models you want to remove from the Classification Build node.

If you want to add extra models to the Clustering node, you can use the green plus sign. Click on the green plus sign to open the Add Model window. In this window, you can select from the drop-down list the algorithm you want to use, specify the name for the new model, and add some comments in the comment area. A default name is generated and entered in the Name field. You can rename the model something that is meaningful to you. An example of when you might want to add an additional model is when you want to create a number of different cluster models, each having a different number of clusters. When you have the new model listed in the Models tab, you then need to change the settings of the newly created cluster models. The example in Figure 9-8 shows a new K-Means called CLUS_KMEANS_5_CLUSTERS.

When a new model is created, the default settings for the algorithm are assigned. While still in the Advanced Model Settings window, you need to double-click on the newly created clustering model to edit the default settings. For example, you can change the number of clusters setting to 5.

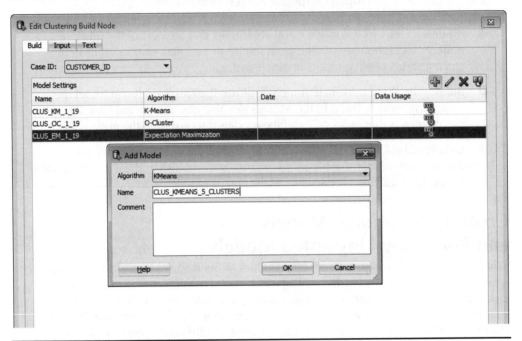

FIGURE 9-8.   *Adding a new cluster model*

Generating the Models

After you have set up your data, specified the Case ID, identified the algorithms you
want to use to generate your models, and configured the algorithm settings, you are
now ready to run the Cluster Build node. To run the node, right-click on the Cluster
Build node, then select Run from the menu. Alternatively, you can click on the green
arrow on the Workflow Worksheet menu.

After you click Run, Oracle Data Miner looks back along the workflow, packages
up all the steps, and then submits these to the database as a process using DBMS_JOBS
and DBMS_SCHEDULER.

As each step of the workflow is processed, you see a green wheel on the top
right-hand corner of the node that is being processed. When a node has been
completed, a green check mark appears at the top right-hand corner of the node, as
shown in Figure 9-9.

If an error occurs while ODM is processing a node, a red *X* appears on the top
right-hand corner of the node. To see the error messages for the node, right-click on
the node, then select Show Errors from the menu.

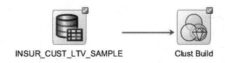

INSUR_CUST_LTV_SAMPLE   Clust Build

FIGURE 9-9. *Completed workflow with generated models*

Evaluating the Classification Models

Evaluating the models produced by the Cluster Build node is an important step. It allows you to identify the cluster model that gives the most information about your data.

The following sections show you how to examine the cluster models that were produced by Oracle Data Miner. Using a combination of approaches, you can select the cluster model that best fits your data.

View Your Cluster Models

To view the cluster models, you need to right-click the Cluster Build node, then select View Models from the drop-down list. An additional drop-down menu opens to display the names of the cluster models that were produced by Oracle. If you performed the steps outlined in the previous section, three cluster models should appear. One of these will be a K-Means model, another for the O-Cluster model, and the third one being the additional K-Means model with five clusters.

If you did not give specific names to your cluster models, then you see models with names consisting of the cluster algorithm name (CLUST_KM, CLUS_OC, or CLUS_EM) followed by some sequence numbers. Oracle Data Miner generates these sequence numbers internally to uniquely identify each cluster model. You may get cluster model names different than those shown in Figure 9-10.

To view the details of a model, you can select it from the menu list. In the following examples, the K-Means model is used (CLUS_KM_1_19 in Figure 9-10).

CAUTION
If you have followed the previous steps to create your clustering models, you may have the same cluster model but with a different sequence number as part of the name.

When the CLUS_KM_1_19 model is selected from the menu, the workflow area is replaced with a graphical representation of the hierarchical K-Means model, as

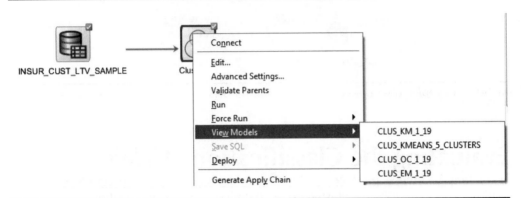

FIGURE 9-10. *Viewing the cluster models*

shown in Figure 9-11. You might need to resize the display and decrease the size of some of the other panes to get a good view of the model.

You will see that ten terminating nodes (nodes with no branches) are created. One of the algorithm settings was for the number of clusters to produce. The default setting for this was 10. By exploring the nodes in the hierarchy, you can see what the split decisions were and what rules were used to determine whether a record or case belongs to a particular cluster.

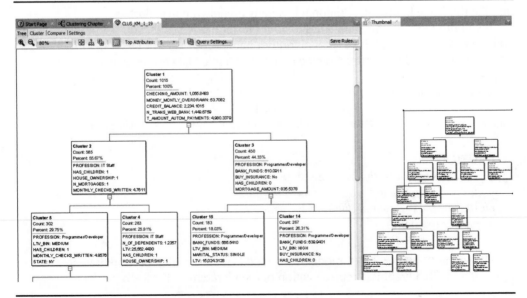

FIGURE 9-11. *Hierarchical view of K-Means model*

With Oracle Data Miner, you cannot modify the cluster hierarchy by splitting nodes, merging nodes, altering the split values, or taking similar actions. Oracle simply shows you what it found; it is now up to you to decide how you are going to use the information.

To see the cluster rules that were produced by Oracle, you can click on a Clustering node. When you do so, you should see the contents of the pane (under the cluster diagram) change to reflect the rules for the cluster. This pane contains two tabs, Centroid and Rule. The Centroid tab, shown in Figure 9-12, provides a list of the attributes that best define the selected cluster, along with a measure of the attribute importance, along with the mode, mean, and variance values for each of the attributes.

The Rule tab, shown in Figure 9-13, contains the rule for the Clustering node. It is in the form of an IF/THEN statement consisting of the attributes defined in the Centroid tab. Not all the attributes listed in the Centroid tab are used in the cluster rule. By default, only the top five most important attributes are included in the rule. You can change this using the Top Attributes drop-down to select the number of attributes you want to include in the cluster rule. Figure 9-13 shows all the attributes used for the cluster and the Wrap check box is selected to make the rule appear in the display area.

As you work your way down the tree exploring each of the clusters produced, you can see the number of records that correspond to each node and the percentage of the overall number of records. You also can see that the number of cases and the percentage decrease.

Cluster Details

When you have the Cluster model open displaying the hierarchical structure of the model, a number of additional options are available to you to examine the clusters in more detail. You can access these by using the tabs that appear across the top of

Centroid	Rule			
Name	▼ Importance	Mode	Mean	Variance
PROFESSION	0.7500	Nurse		
TIME_AS_CUSTOMER	0.7500	2		
MARITAL_STATUS	0.6667	SINGLE		
LTV	0.6000		16,467.2406	4,922,582.3196
BUY_INSURANCE	0.5000	No		
CHECKING_AMOUNT	0.5000		2,730.5849	29,658,270.3628
HAS_CHILDREN	0.5000	1		
HOUSE_OWNERSHIP	0.5000	0		
LTV_BIN	0.5000	MEDIUM		
MORTGAGE_AMOUNT	0.5000		0	0

FIGURE 9-12. *Centroid details for a Clustering node*

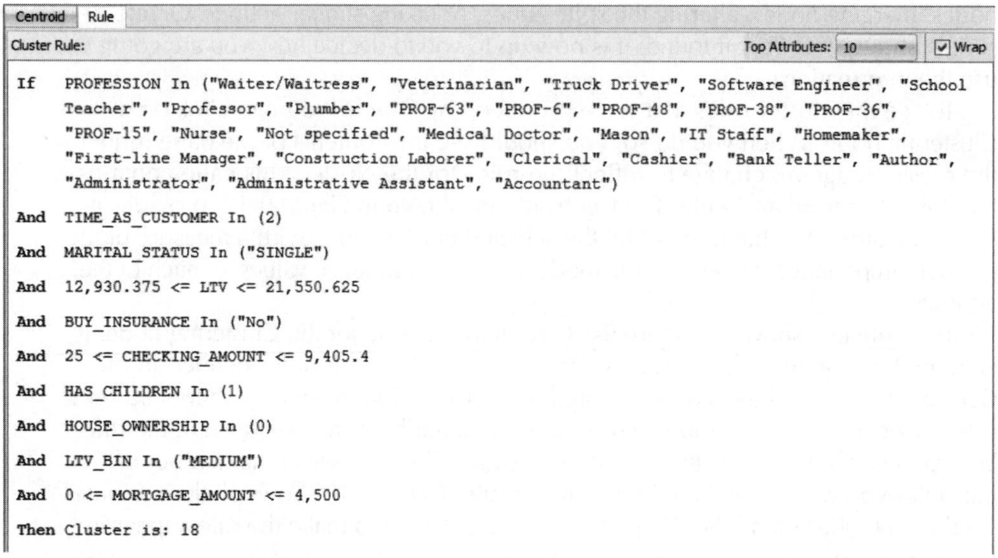

Centroid	Rule			
Cluster Rule:		Top Attributes:	10 ▼	☑ Wrap

```
If    PROFESSION In ("Waiter/Waitress", "Veterinarian", "Truck Driver", "Software Engineer", "School
      Teacher", "Professor", "Plumber", "PROF-63", "PROF-6", "PROF-48", "PROF-38", "PROF-36",
      "PROF-15", "Nurse", "Not specified", "Medical Doctor", "Mason", "IT Staff", "Homemaker",
      "First-line Manager", "Construction Laborer", "Clerical", "Cashier", "Bank Teller", "Author",
      "Administrator", "Administrative Assistant", "Accountant")
And   TIME_AS_CUSTOMER In (2)
And   MARITAL_STATUS In ("SINGLE")
And   12,930.375 <= LTV <= 21,550.625
And   BUY_INSURANCE In ("No")
And   25 <= CHECKING_AMOUNT <= 9,405.4
And   HAS_CHILDREN In (1)
And   HOUSE_OWNERSHIP In (0)
And   LTV_BIN In ("MEDIUM")
And   0 <= MORTGAGE_AMOUNT <= 4,500
Then  Cluster is: 18
```

FIGURE 9-13. *Rule information tab*

the worksheet. The first tab is called Tree, which displays the hierarchical cluster tree as shown in Figure 9-11. The next tab is called Cluster. This section looks at the cluster evaluation features available in this Cluster tab. The next tab is called Compare; this Compare tab is discussed in the next section, "Comparing Clusters: Multicluster-Multivariable Comparison."

The Cluster tab allows you to examine the attributes and the values for the attributes for each of the clusters produced by the algorithm. The screen is divided into two parts. The top part contains the Cluster check box, the Fetch Size setting, and the Query button. When you select the Cluster check box, ODM lists all the cluster leaf nodes. You can use the Fetch Size setting to specify the maximum number of attributes to include in the display. After you have specified the cluster leaf node and the number of attributes to include, you need to click the Query button to update the display in the bottom part of the screen. You need to do this every time you change the cluster leaf node you want to look at or if you use the Fetch Size setting to change the number of attributes to display. Figure 9-14 shows the details of Clustering Node 4.

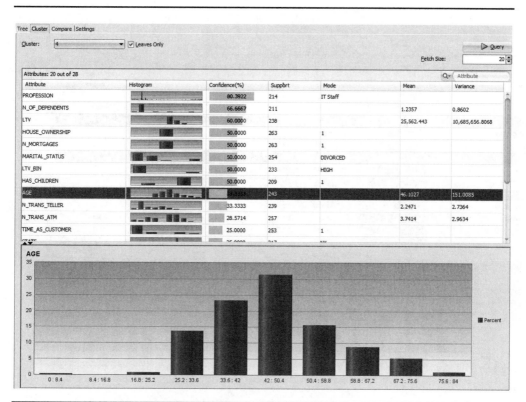

FIGURE 9-14. *Examining the Clustering node details*

You can examine the attributes and the values for these attributes that apply to the node. When you click on each attribute, you see that the histogram will be updated to represent the data for the attribute. You can increase the size of the histogram area to get the details of each bar area by holding the mouse over each bar.

An additional level of analysis that you can perform here is to compare several attributes at the same time. To do so, select the attributes you want to compare by holding down CTRL while clicking the attributes with the mouse. As you do this, the histogram area will will be updated to display the histograms for each of the selected attributes. Figure 9-15 shows how this looks when the Age, Marital Status, and LTV attributes have been selected.

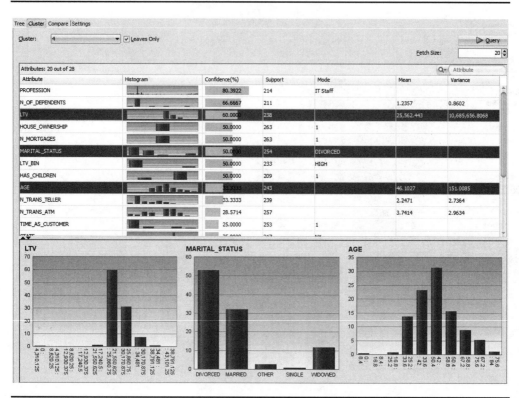

FIGURE 9-15. *Displaying multiple-attribute histograms for a cluster*

Comparing Clusters: Multicluster-Multivariable Comparison

The Compare tab allows you to compare two clusters of the same model and to identify similarities or differences. Similar to the Cluster tab, the Compare tab is available only when you have opened a cluster, as illustrated in the previous sections. The Compare screen is laid out in three sections. The first section provides the Cluster 1 and Cluster 2 controls to enable you to select the clusters you want to compare, the Fetch Size setting so you can specify the number of attributes you want to display for the clusters, and the Query button. Whenever you change the clusters to be compared or the Fetch Size, you need to click on the Query button to refresh the display in the other sections of the screen. The second section of the screen displays the attributes and centroid details for each attribute of the cluster. The third part of the screen displays the histogram for each attribute. The histogram has the distribution of

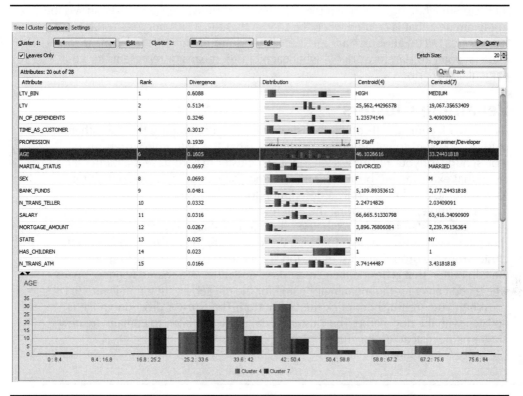

FIGURE 9-16. *Comparing two clusters in a model*

values for each cluster colored red or blue. Figure 9-16 gives an example of comparing two clusters that are in the cluster model illustrated in this chapter.

CAUTION
If you have been following the steps outlined in this chapter, you might get slightly different values for your cluster models, including clusters, attributes, and other values. This might be due to different versions of the database, sample data, and parameter settings.

An additional level of comparison you can perform across the two clusters is to compare several attributes at the same time. For example, if you want to compare the several attributes and their histograms, you can select the attributes you are interested in while holding down CTRL. The example shown in Figure 9-17 shows the histogram area that is created when the LTV_BIN, AGE, TIME_AS_CUSTOMER, and MARITAL_STATUS attributes are selected. By performing this level of comparison of clusters, you can start to work out what each cluster means or represents for your particular scenario.

Renaming Clusters

As you work your way through the list of clusters and compare them to other clusters, you start to get an understanding of what the different clusters are representing for your business scenario. Each cluster may represent a particular group that exists in your business scenario, and you can apply a description for each scenario and hence apply a description for each cluster.

For example, after exploring the different clusters in your model, you might decide that Cluster 4 can be relabeled "Short Term Value Customers" and Cluster 7 "Long Term Value Customers." To assign these labels to the clusters, you select the cluster from the drop-down list in the top section of the Compare screen, then click the Edit button that is beside the Cluster drop-down list. A Rename window opens where you can enter the meaningful name for the cluster, as shown in Figure 9-18.

When you are finished, click the OK button. The Cluster drop-down list is updated with the new name. The cluster model is also updated to contain the new cluster name instead of the cluster number.

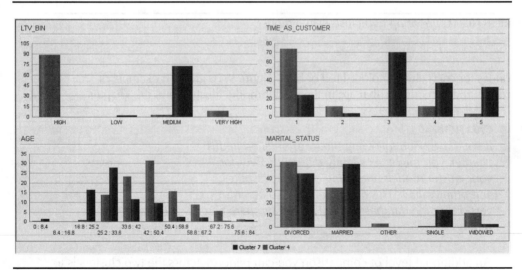

FIGURE 9-17. *Comparing multiple attributes for two clusters in a model*

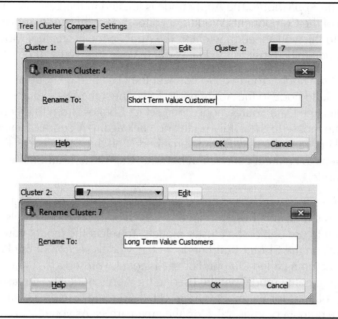

FIGURE 9-18.   *Renaming a cluster with a meaningful name*

Applying a Clustering Model to New Data

After you have analyzed the various cluster models you have produced, you decide which one best fits your scenario. You can use this cluster model to segment and label the data based on the model. You can use Oracle Data Miner to apply your model to new data that already exists in a table in your database.

The following steps outline what you need to perform to apply a cluster model to new data:

1. *Define the data source.* When using Oracle Data Miner to label new data using a cluster model, you need to define a Data Source node for the table that contains the data. Any data transformations that were applied to data before you created the Cluster Build node also need to be applied to the new Data Source node. The new Data Source node should contain only the data to which you want to apply the cluster model.

2. *Create the Apply node.* The Apply node is located in the Evaluate and Apply section of the Components Workflow Editor. Select this node, move the mouse to the worksheet, then click. The Apply node is created. Move the Apply node to be close to the Data Source node that you will be using.

3. *Connect the nodes.* You need to connect the Data Source node and the Cluster Build node to the Apply node. To connect the Data Source node, you right-click the Data Source node, then select Connect from the menu. Then move the mouse to the Apply node and click again. A connection arrow is created between the new Data Source node and the Apply node. Repeat these steps to create a connection between the Cluster Build node and the Apply node.

4. *Select the cluster model to use.* By default, the Apply node contains attributes that match those produced by each of the cluster models. Typically you want to use one of the cluster models. To select the model you want to use, click on the Cluster Build node. In the Models section of the Properties tab is a column called Output. For each model, you see a green arrow. This indicates that the model will be used in the Apply node and the associated output columns for the models are created. To remove the necessary models from the output columns, click on the green arrow. As you click on the models that you want to exclude from the Apply node, the green arrow changes to a red *X*.

5. *Select the attribute for output.* After selecting the cluster model you want to use in the Apply node, you can now specify what attributes should be included in the output of the Apply node. When you click on the Apply node, the Properties tab is updated to list only the model output columns for the model you selected in the previous step. The attributes created by each cluster model include the Cluster ID and the Cluster Probability. Alternatively, you can double-click on the Apply node. The Predictions tab lists the output columns that the cluster model will produce. To add other attributes from the data source, you need to click on the Additional Output tab. Then click on the green plus sign to list the attributes you want to include in the output. These attributes will typically include the primary key attribute(s) and other identifying attributes.

6. *Run the Apply node.* After completing the preceding steps, you are now ready to run the Apply node. To run the Apply node, you can right-click on it, then select Run from the menu. Oracle Data Miner packages up all the necessary steps, which it submits as a job to the database. When all the steps are completed, you will see a green check mark on the top right-hand corner of the Apply node.

7. *View the results.* To view the data produced by the Apply node, you can right-click the Apply node, then select View Data from the menu. A new work area opens that displays the data for each record. This data includes the identifying attributes selected in previous steps as well as the cluster model–specific attributes.

8. *Persist the results.* You can persist the results to a table in your schema by creating a Create Table or View node from the Data section of the Components Workflow Editor. You need to connect the Apply node to the Create Table or View node, and you should give the output table a meaningful name. You can then run the node to create the new table and save the records to the new table.

 NOTE
The output columns, when viewed from the Apply node, might be in a different order from the order of the columns when the data is persisted to the database using the Create Table or View node.

Summary

Clustering is an unsupervised data mining technique where the clustering algorithms find groupings of data that are more related to each other (a cluster) and less related to other groupings (other clusters). The typical application areas for clustering are customer segmentation, marketing, insurance claims analysis, outliner detection, image pattern recognition, biology, security, and so on. This chapter showed you how to use Oracle Data Miner to build a number of clustering models, how to evaluate the individual clusters, how to compare clusters, and finally how to apply a cluster model to new data. In Chapter 16, you learn how to use the in-database SQL and PL/SQL functions and procedures to create and apply cluster models.

CHAPTER
10

Regression

Regression is a data mining technique that is very similar to classification. With regression, you use the regression algorithms to predict a value of an attribute based on the other attributes in your data set. The predicted attribute is a continuous value attribute, which is unlike the target attribute used in classification. Typical examples of where regression can be used is in data preparation to determine missing data, calculation of dosages for prescriptions, financial predictions based on previous history, credit limits, life time values, and more.

What Is Regression?

Regression in data mining is a data mining technique that is used to predict a continuous value. Traditionally, regression is used to form a relationship between a predictor attribute and a target attribute. The two main types of regression are linear regression and nonlinear regression. An example of a linear regression problem is the prediction of the tilt of the Leaning Tower of Pisa. You could take the tilt of the tower from previous years (the previously recorded data) and use regression to predict the tilt at different future dates (see Figure 10-1).

For typical data mining problems, you can use a number of possible attributes as input to the regression algorithm. In these kinds of scenarios, the type of regression is called *multivariate linear regression*.

Not all problems follow a linear pattern, as shown in Figure 10-2. These kinds of problems are called nonlinear regression, and as with the multivariate linear

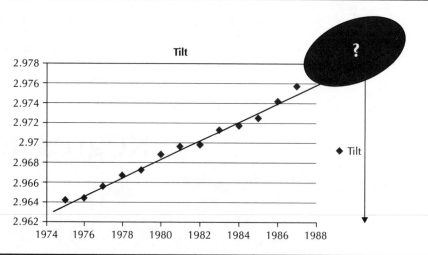

FIGURE 10-1. *Predicting the tilt of the Leaning Tower of Pisa*

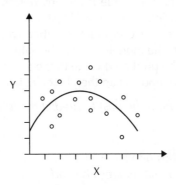

FIGURE 10-2. *Example of nonlinear regression using a single predictor*

regression problems, you can use many attributes as input. When multiple input attributes are used, it is called *multivariate nonlinear regression*.

NOTE
Multiple regression is another name that is commonly used for multivariate linear and multivariate nonlinear regression.

Regression prediction is similar in approach to the classification problems you have looked at in previous chapters. Typically with classification, multiple input attributes are used to determine the value of a target attribute. With regression prediction, you are looking to predict a value of some continuous value attribute. An example of this is to calculate the life time value (LTV) of a customer. As with typical classification problems, with regression prediction, you have a set of data with the LTV value already determined. You input into the regression algorithm this data set, which contains many attributes about each customer (also called a *case record*). The regression algorithm then works out how each of these attributes and the values that they contain contribute toward the value in the LTV attribute.

Regression prediction can be used in a wide variety of problems and can also be used as part of your data preparation before being used as input into other data mining algorithms. Typical regression prediction problems include calculating profit, sales, values, sizes, distances, volumes, and such. Regression can be used in a variety of applications, including trend analysis, business planning, marketing, financial forecasting, time series prediction, and more.

The process of building, testing, and applying a regression model follows the same process that is used for classification. You use a data set that contains the continuous value attribute, and this value is already determined. The regression algorithms divide this data set into training and test data sets. The training data set is used to train and build the regression model. You then apply the new regression model against the test data set. The model predicts the value of the continuous value attribute and then compares the predicted value to the actual value in the data set. The accuracy of the regression models can then be calculated.

We learn from the past to predict the future.

NOTE
Like the other chapters in this book, this chapter does not cover the detailed mathematics behind each of the algorithms. There are plenty of books that cover the mathematics in lots of detail. The aim of this book is to help you understand how you can apply these techniques using the in-database implementations of these mathematical functions.

Regression Methods Available in Oracle

Oracle has a number of regression data mining algorithms available in the database. Table 10-1 lists the regression algorithms and briefly describes each.

Algorithm	Description
Generalized Linear Model (GLM)	A Generalized Linear Model implements logistic regression for classification of binary targets and linear regression for continuous targets, and is a generalized version of linear regression. GLM allows a categorical variable to be related to a set of predictor attributes in a manner similar to modeling a numeric target attribute using linear regression.
Support Vector Machine (SVM)	SVM regression supports two kernels: the Gaussian kernel for nonlinear regression, and the linear kernel for linear regression. SVM also supports active learning. SVM regression tries to find a continuous function such that the maximum number of data points lie within the epsilon-wide insensitivity tube. Predictions falling within epsilon distance of the true target value are not interpreted as errors.

TABLE 10-1. *Regression Algorithms Available in the Oracle Database*

Preparing Your Data for Regression

Preparing your data for regression is very similar to the preparation involved for all the other data mining algorithms and techniques. You extract the data from your data sources and integrate them to form your analytical record. Regression is very similar to classification (see Chapter 8), except for the target variable. In classification, your target variable typically is a binary value. With regression, it is a continuous value variable, in that it will have some number value. For example, the target variable for regression might be an amount that is calculated to represent the LTV of a customer over a defined period of time.

The sample data set used in this chapter to illustrate regression is the INSUR_ CUST_LTV_SAMPLE table. You created this table in the DMUSER schema when you granted the DMUSER access to the Oracle Data Miner Repository, during the creation of the schemas in Chapter 3. The INSUR_CUST_LTV_SAMPLE table contains historical information for each customer of an insurance company, and each customer is represented by one record. The table contains an attribute called LTV. This is the historically calculated value for each customer. For regression, this is your target variable. This is the attribute that you want the regression data mining algorithms to determine what attributes and the values of these attributes contribute toward the value in the target variable.

When you explore INSUR_CUST_LTV_SAMPLE using the Explore Data node and the Graph node, you can start to build up a picture of what data you have. This can be used to supplement your existing domain knowledge. From your exploration of the data, you might discover some attributes that can be excluded from the data set. In your sample data set, there is an attribute called LTV_BIN, shown in Figure 10-3.

The LTV_BIN attribute is very closely correlated to the LTV attribute. When you have attributes like LTV_BIN that are closely correlated to the target variable/attribute, these attributes should be removed from the data before the data is inputted to the data mining algorithms. If these closely correlated attributes are left in the data set, then the data mining algorithm will produce a model that contains only these attributes. This is not what you want to achieve.

To remove this attribute as an input to the data mining algorithms, you can either go back to the Data Source node and exclude the LTV_BIN attribute from the list of attributes from the table, or you can use the Filter Columns node to exclude the attribute. To create the Filter Columns node, go to the Transforms section of the Components Workflow Editor, click on the Filter Columns node, then move your mouse to your workflow and click again. Next you need to join the Data Source node to the Filter Columns node by right-clicking the Data Source node, then select Connect from the menu. Then move the mouse to the Filter Columns node and click again. A connection line is created joining the two nodes. To edit the list of input

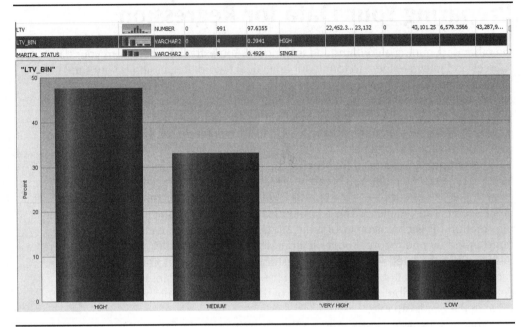

LTV		NUMBER	0	991	97.6355		22,452.3...	23,132	0	43,101.25	6,579.3566	43,287,9...
LTV_BIN		VARCHAR2	0	4	0.3941	HIGH						
MARITAL_STATUS		VARCHAR2	0	5	0.4926	SINGLE						

FIGURE 10-3. *LTV_BIN attribute is closely correlated to the LTV attribute*

attributes, you need to double-click on the Filter Columns node to open the Edit Filter Columns Node window. Scroll down the Columns list until you find the LTV_ BIN attribute. To deselect this attribute so that it is not used in later nodes, you need to click on the green arrow under the Output column. This changes the green arrow to a red *X*, as shown in Figure 10-4. The LTV_BIN attribute will not be outputted from the Filter Columns node, while all the other attributes will be outputted from the node and used as input to another node.

The final step in preparing the data for input to the regression data mining algorithms is to run the Filter Columns node. When complete, the Filter Columns node will have a green tick mark on the top right-hand corner of the node.

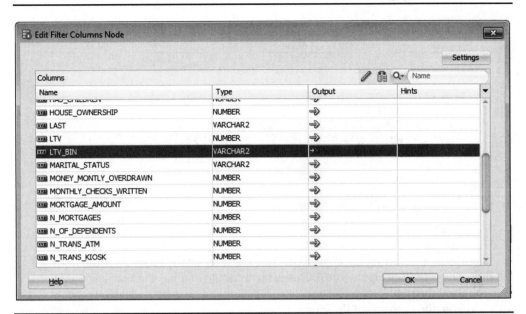

FIGURE 10-4. *Excluding the* LTV_BIN *attribute using the Filter Columns node*

Building Regression Models

To add the regression node to your workflow, you need to select the Regression node from the Models section of the Components Workflow Editor. You can then add it to the workflow by moving the mouse to the workflow and clicking again. The Regression node will be created. The next step is to connect your data set to the Regression node. If you have completed the steps outlined in the section on "Preparing Your Data for Regression," you can connect the Filter Columns node to the Regression node as illustrated in Figure 10-5.

When you connect the data source to the Regression node, the Edit Regression Node window opens automatically. If this does not happen, then you can double-click on the Regression node to open the window. By default, the Regression node creates two regression models. One of these is built using the Generalized Linear Model algorithm, and the second model is built using the Support Vector Machine algorithm. You can add additional regression models using these algorithms with different settings by clicking on the green plus sign. Alternatively, if you want to build only one regression model, then you can select the model you want to remove and click on the red *X*.

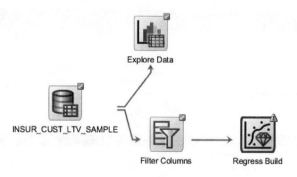

FIGURE 10-5. *Regression node added to the workflow*

In addition to selecting the algorithms, you can also set the target attribute from the drop-down list (see Figure 10-6). This is the attribute that has the numeric value that you want the model to determine. In this example, you want to select the LTV attribute from the drop-down list for the target.

The Case ID can be set to the primary key or identifying attribute for the data set. Only one attribute can be selected for the Case ID. If one unique attribute does not exist in your data set, you might need to create one when you are preparing the data for your data mining task. The Case ID can be left null with a setting of <none>. It is advisable to always have a Case ID for your data sets.

CAUTION
If a Case ID is not supplied, Oracle Data Miner creates a new table for all the input data that contains a generated Case ID using a row number. This table is used as the source to create the build and test random sample views. The generated Case ID is constant for all queries. This ensures that consistent test results are generated.

Using the sample data set, you can set the Case ID to CUSTOMER_ID, as shown in Figure 10-6.

Regression Model Settings

To view the settings for each of the regression models, you can double-click on a model while you have the Edit Regression Build Node window open. The Advanced Model Settings window then opens. This window enables you to inspect and change

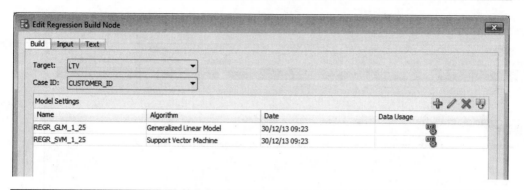

FIGURE 10-6.   *Edit Regression Build Node window*

the data usage and algorithm settings for each regression algorithm. Oracle has selected what it regards as the optimal settings suitable for most problems. Each algorithm comes with its own specific settings.

If you have closed the Edit Regression Build Node window, you can right-click on the Regression node, then select Advanced Model Settings from the context menu.

The Advanced Model Settings window lists all of the models in the node in the upper pane. To see and change the settings of these algorithms, click on each of the algorithms in turn. As you do this, you can select the Algorithm Settings tabs.

GLM Algorithm Settings
The Generalized Linear Model algorithm has the following settings (see Figure 10-7):

- **Generate Row Diagnostics**   By default, this setting is disabled. If you enable it, you can view Row Diagnostics on the Diagnostics tab when you view the model. To further analyze row diagnostics, use the Model Details node to extract the Row Diagnostics table.

- **Confidence Level**   The value of this setting is a positive number that is less than 1. This value indicates the degree of certainty that the true probability lies within the confidence bounds computed by the model. The default confidence is 0.95.

- **Missing Value Treatment**   The default is Mean Mode. This setting uses mean for numeric values and mode for categorical values. You can also select Delete Row to delete any row that contains missing values. If you delete rows with missing values, the same missing values treatment (Delete Row) must be applied to any data to which the model is applied.

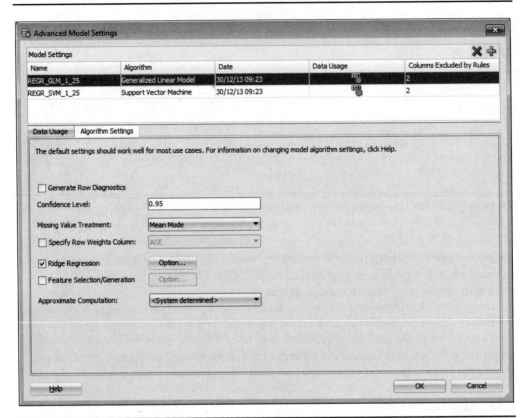

FIGURE 10-7. *GLM Algorithm Settings for regression*

- **Specify Row Weights Column**   The default is to not specify a Row Weights column. The Row Weights column is a column in the training data that contains a weighting factor for the rows. Row weights can be used as a compact representation of repeated rows, as in the design of experiments where a specific configuration is repeated several times. Row weights can also be used to emphasize certain rows during model construction. For example, you might bias the model toward rows that are more recent and away from potentially obsolete data.

- **Ridge Regression**   The default is System Determined, that is, the system determines whether to enable ridge regression; if the system enables ridge regression, the system specifies a ridge value. Ridge regression is a technique that compensates for multicollinearity (multivariate regression with correlated predictors). Oracle Data Mining supports ridge regression for both regression and classification mining functions.

- **Feature Selection/Generation** By default, this is disabled as ridge regression is used. Alternative methods are available for the automatic selection of features.

- **Approximate Computation** The default setting is System Determined. The algorithm determines whether this setting should be enabled or disabled. The other settings available are Enabled or Disabled.

SVM Algorithm Settings

The Support Vector Machine algorithm has the following settings (see Figure 10-8):

- **Kernel Function** System Determined is the default. This setting allows ODM to work out which of the kernel functions it should use. The functions available include Linear and Gaussian. When the model is built, the kernel used is displayed in the settings in the model viewer.

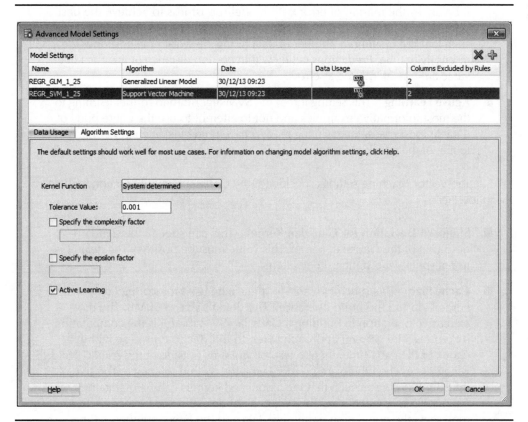

FIGURE 10-8. *SVM Algorithm Settings for regression*

For System Determined and Linear, you can modify the Tolerance Value, specify the complexity factor, and set active learning. If you change the Kernel Function setting to Gaussian, you get the following additional parameters: the standard deviation for the Gaussian kernel and cache size.

- **Tolerance Value**   This is the maximum size of a violation of convergence criteria such that the model is considered to have converged. The default value is 0.001. Larger values imply faster-building but less accurate models.

- **Specify the Complexity Factor**   This setting determines the trade-off between minimizing model error on the training data and minimizing model complexity. Its responsibility is to avoid overfit (an overcomplex model fitting noise in the training data) and underfit (a model that is too simple). The default is to specify no complexity factor, in which case the system calculates a complexity factor. If you do specify a complexity factor, specify a positive number.

- **Specify the Epsilon Factor**   This is a regularization setting for SVM regression. It balances the margin of error with model robustness to achieve the best generalization to new data. SVM regression tries to find a continuous function such that the maximum number of data points lie within the epsilon-wide insensitivity tube. Predictions falling within epsilon distance of the true target value are not interpreted as errors.

- **Active Learning**   This setting forces the SVM algorithm to restrict learning to the most informative examples and not to attempt to use the entire body of data. In most cases, the resulting models have predictive accuracy comparable to that of the standard (exact) SVM model.

Support Vector Machine settings specific for the Gaussian kernel function include the following:

- **Standard Deviation for Gaussian Kernel**   This can specify the standard deviation of the Gaussian kernel. This value must be positive. The default is to not specify the standard deviation.

- **Cache Size**   This specifies a size for the cache used for storing computed kernels during the build operation. The default size is 50MB. The most expensive operation in building a Gaussian SVM model is the computation of kernels. The general approach taken to build is to converge within a chunk of data at a time, then to test for violators outside of the chunk. Build is complete when there are no more violators within tolerance. The size of the chunk is chosen such that the associated kernels can be maintained in memory in a kernel cache. The larger the chunk size, the better the chunk represents the population of training data and the fewer number of times new chunks must be created. Generally, larger caches imply faster builds.

Property Inspector

Each node in the workflow has an associated set of properties that are located in the Properties tab. This is a dockable area that typically appears below or to the side of the Components Workflow Editor. As you click on each node in your workflow, the Properties tab displays different properties relating to the node. For the Regression node, the Property Inspector has four sections, as shown in Figure 10-9.

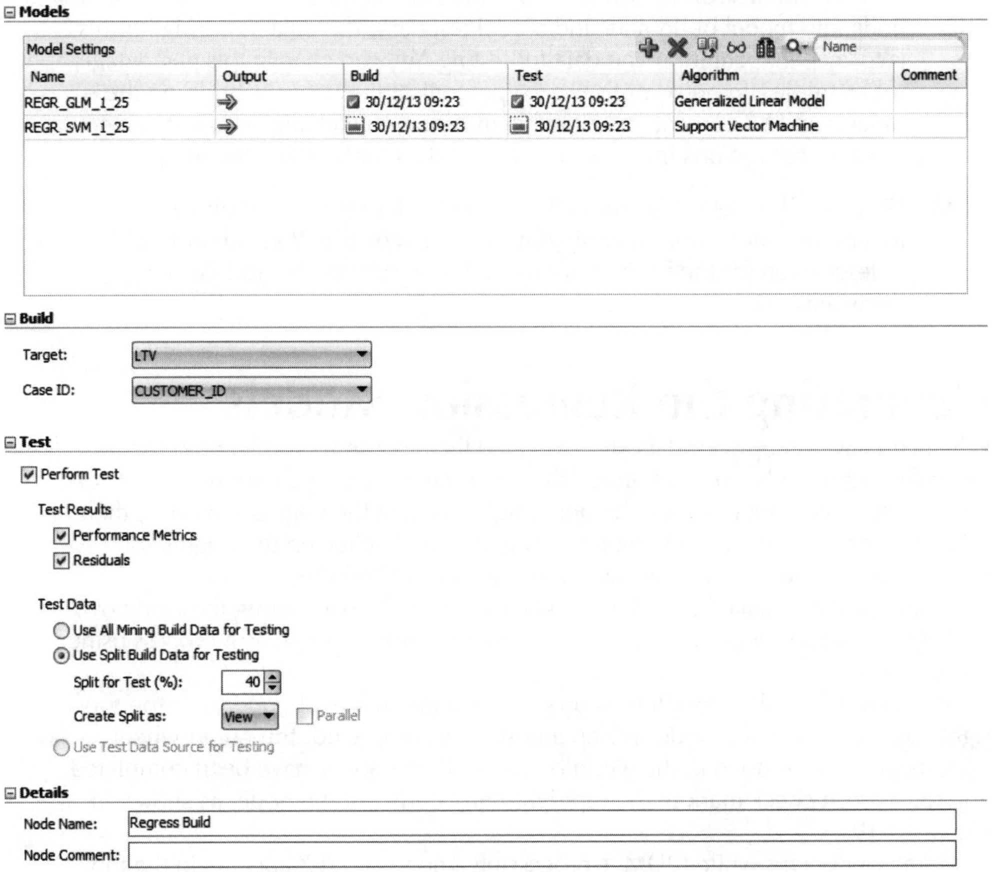

Models

Name	Output	Build	Test	Algorithm	Comment
REGR_GLM_1_25	→	☑ 30/12/13 09:23	☑ 30/12/13 09:23	Generalized Linear Model	
REGR_SVM_1_25	→	30/12/13 09:23	30/12/13 09:23	Support Vector Machine	

Model Settings

Build

Target: LTV

Case ID: CUSTOMER_ID

Test

☑ Perform Test

Test Results
    ☑ Performance Metrics
    ☑ Residuals

Test Data
    ○ Use All Mining Build Data for Testing
    ◉ Use Split Build Data for Testing
        Split for Test (%):   40
        Create Split as: View   ☐ Parallel
    ○ Use Test Data Source for Testing

Details

Node Name: Regress Build

Node Comment:

FIGURE 10-9. *Regression node Property Inspector*

The Regression node Property Inspector has the following sections:

- **Models**   This lists the models that are part of the Regression node. Models can be removed from the list or new models can be added. Details of the current status of each model are included.

- **Build**   The build information includes the target variable and the Case ID. These are common for all the regression models listed in the Models section.

- **Test**   This contains the details of what data will be used for testing the models. The default option is to split the data supplied in the Data Source node into model build data and model test data. The default setting for this is to keep 40 percent of the data for testing. You can change this percentage; for example, if you want to use 70 percent of the data for building the models and 30 percent for testing them, you would change this Test value to 30. Other options include using all the data for building the models.

- **Details**   The Details section allows you to change the default name to a name that is more meaningful for your scenario. You can also add a description for the node to include all relevant details and design decisions.

Generating the Regression Models

When you have set up your data set, identified the algorithms you want to use to generate your models, and configured the algorithm settings, you are now ready to run the Regression node. To run the node, right-click on the Regression node, then select Run from the menu. Alternatively, you can single-click on the Regression node, then click on the green arrow on the Workflow Worksheet menu.

After you have clicked Run, Oracle Data Miner looks back along the workflow, packages up all the steps, and then submits these to the database as a process using DBMS_JOBS.

As each step of the workflow is processed, a green wheel appears at the top right-hand corner of the node. When a node has completed, the green wheel appears on the next node in the workflow. After all the nodes have been completed, you see a green check mark in the top right-hand corner of the node, as shown in Figure 10-10.

If an error occurs while ODM is processing a node, a red *X* appears in the top right-hand corner of the node. To see the error messages for this node, right-click on the node, then select Show Errors from the menu.

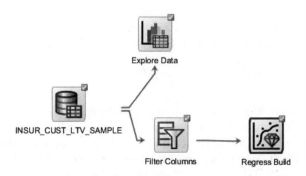

FIGURE 10-10. *Completed regression workflow with generated models*

Viewing the Regression Models

When the Regression node has finished and the green check mark appears in the top right-hand corner of the node, you can view the details of the regression models that were produced. The Regression node had listed for models to be created using the Generalized Linear Model and Support Vector Machine algorithms.

This section looks at the model details of each regression model produced. To access the models produced by the Regression node, you can right-click on the Regression node, then select View Models from the menu, as shown in Figure 10-11.

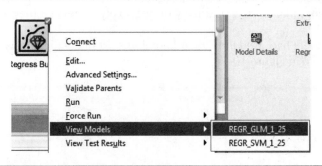

FIGURE 10-11. *Selecting the regression models*

NOTE
The model names shown in Figure 10-11 may be slightly different from the names of your regression models. The numbers that are part of the model name are system-generated, and new numbers are generated for each new data mining model.

The first regression model that you will look at is the model produced using the GLM. Select this model from the list of models as shown in Figure 10-11. After you select this model. the Oracle Data Miner tool opens a new window that contains all the details about the GLM model. The GLM window includes three tabs for Details, Coefficients, and Settings. When the window opens, it defaults to the Coefficients tab.

The Details tab contains a listing of various statistics that are generated to describe the GLM model, as shown in Figure 10-12a.

The Coefficients tab (shown in Figure 10-12b) lists the attributes, the values of the attributes, and the coefficient values that have been generated by the model. You can sort the data by absolute value by clicking the Sort by Absolute Value setting or in ascending or descending order by double-clicking on the column headings.

The Settings tab (shown in Figure 10-12c) shows what settings were actually used to generate the model. For example, if you select a setting to be System Determined, then you will see the actual value that the system used to produce the model. The settings are divided into General and Algorithm.

When you view the details of the SVM regression model, you see only two tabs, as shown in Figure 10-13. If the SVM regression algorithm chooses to build the model using the Gaussian kernel, your output will look similar to what is shown in Figure 10-13. When the Gaussian kernel is used, no coefficients are produced, nor does the algorithm indicate how positively or negatively correlated they are to the target attribute.

If the SVM model had used the Linear kernel, the set of coefficients would be produced as shown in Figure 10-14.

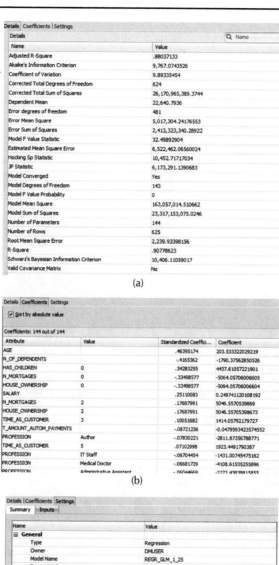

FIGURE 10-12. *GLM model information: (a) Details, (b) Coefficients, and (c) Settings*

Name	Value
General	
Type	Regression
Owner	DMUSER
Model Name	REGR_SVM_1_25
Target Attribute	LTV
Creation Date	30/12/13
Duration(Minutes)	0.1167
Size(MB)	0.2524
Comment	
Algorithm	
Active Learning	Enable
Algorithm Name	Support Vector Machine
Automatic Preparation	On
Complexity Factor	0.450764
Kernel Cache Size	50000000
Kernel Function	Gaussian
SVMS_EPSILON	0.006248
Standard Deviation	2.971519
Tolerance	0.001

(a)

Name	Data Type	Mining Type	Target	Data Preparation
AGE	NUMBER	Numerical		Yes
BANK_FUNDS	NUMBER	Numerical		Yes
BUY_INSURANCE	VARCHAR2	Categorical		Yes
CAR_OWNERSHIP	NUMBER	Categorical		Yes
CHECKING_AMOUNT	NUMBER	Numerical		Yes
CREDIT_BALANCE	NUMBER	Numerical		Yes
CREDIT_CARD_LIMITS	NUMBER	Numerical		Yes
HAS_CHILDREN	NUMBER	Categorical		Yes
HOUSE_OWNERSHIP	NUMBER	Categorical		Yes
LTV	NUMBER	Numerical	✔	Yes
MARITAL_STATUS	VARCHAR2	Categorical		Yes
MONEY_MONTLY_OVE...	NUMBER	Numerical		Yes
MONTHLY_CHECKS_W...	NUMBER	Numerical		Yes
MORTGAGE_AMOUNT	NUMBER	Numerical		Yes
N_MORTGAGES	NUMBER	Categorical		Yes
N_OF_DEPENDENTS	NUMBER	Numerical		Yes
N_TRANS_ATM	NUMBER	Numerical		Yes
N_TRANS_KIOSK	NUMBER	Numerical		Yes
N_TRANS_TELLER	NUMBER	Numerical		Yes
N_TRANS_WEB_BANK	NUMBER	Numerical		Yes
PROFESSION	VARCHAR2	Categorical		Yes
REGION	VARCHAR2	Categorical		Yes
SALARY	NUMBER	Numerical		Yes
SEX	VARCHAR2	Categorical		Yes

(b)

FIGURE 10-13. *SVM model (Gaussian kernel) information: (a) Summary, (b) Inputs*

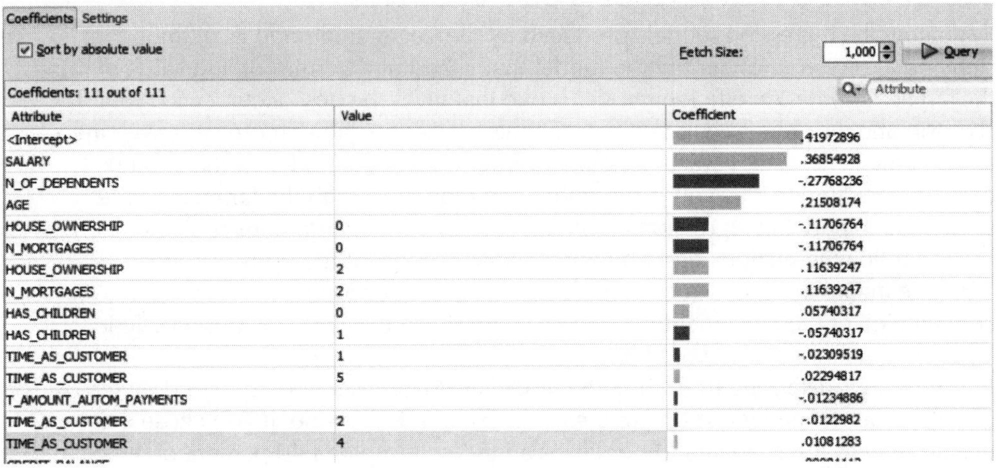

(a)

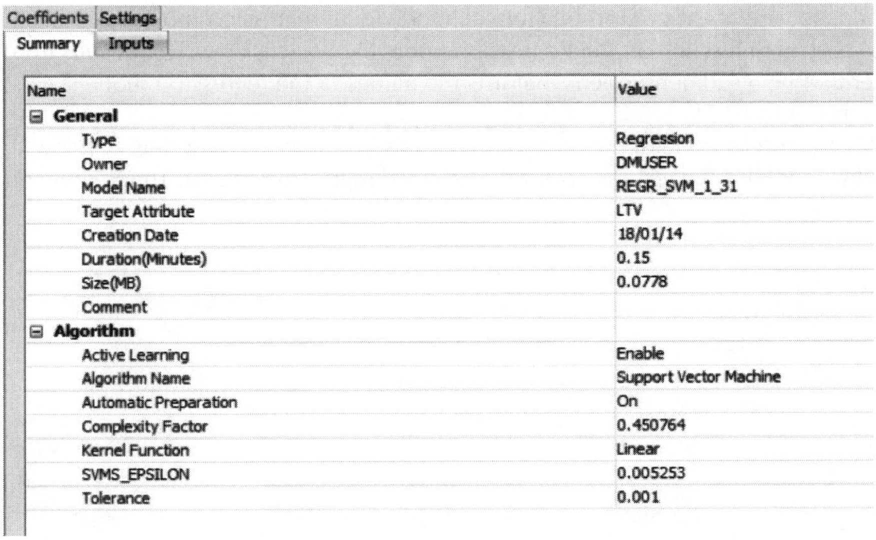

(b)

FIGURE 10-14.   *SVM model (Linear kernel) information: (a) Coefficients, (b) Settings*

Regression Model Test Results

Evaluating the regression models produced by the Regression node is an important step and allows you to identify the model that is best at determining the value of the target attribute. An efficient model is one that gives the best accuracy for your scenario and the data used to generate the model. As you gather more data, with the target variable defined, you can regenerate your regression models. When you do this, you may find that as you gather more and more data with the target attribute value determined, the regression algorithms become more and more accurate.

The following sections describe the different evaluation methods that are available in Oracle Data Miner for evaluating your regression models. Using a combination of these evaluation methods enables you to select the most efficient regression model for your scenario.

The results displayed in each of the model evaluation screens are based on the data that was defined for testing in the Classification Build node. If you chose the default settings, Oracle Data Miner keeps a random sample of 40 percent of the data that is a stratified sample across the target values.

There are two ways to view the regression model evaluation results. The first method is to view the model results for each individual regression model. To view these, you can right-click on the Regression node, then select View Test Results from the menu. A new submenu opens that lists the names of the regression models, as shown in Figure 10-15.

When you select one of the regression models from the menu, a new window opens that contains the test results for the selected regression model. The Regression

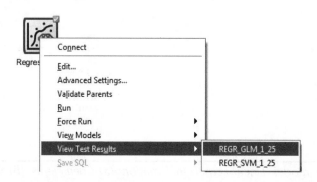

FIGURE 10-15. *Selecting to view an individual regression model's results*

Results window presents two tabs, Performance and Residual. The Performance tab contains some statistical information about the regression model and on the accuracies of the predictions of the target attributes values. Table 10-2 lists the statistical information produced for each regression model.

The Residual tab gives a graphical representation of the results from using the testing data set. The default plot shown when the tab is activated is called the *residual plot*. The residual plot is a scatter plot of the residuals. Each residual is the difference between the actual value and the value predicted by the model. Residuals can be positive or negative. If residuals are small (close to 0), the predictions are accurate. A residual plot may indicate that predictions are better for some classes of values than for others.

You can alter the residual plot to have different values represented for the x-axis and the y-axis. An example of a very useful graph is one that plots the actual values on the y-axis versus the predicted values on the x-axis, as shown in Figure 10-16.

After you have evaluated each of the regression models to assess their performance at predicting the target attribute values, you want to compare how the regression models performed compared to each other. To open the Compare Test Results window,

Regression Model Statistics	Description
Predictive Confidence	This measures how much better the predictions of the model are than those of the naive model. Predictive Confidence for regression is the same measure as Predictive Confidence for classification.
Mean Absolute Error	This is the average of the absolute value of the residuals (error). The Mean Absolute Error is very similar to the Root Mean Square Error but is less sensitive to large errors.
Root Mean Square Error	This is the square root of the average squared distance of a data point from the fitted line.
Mean Predicted Value	Mean Predicted Value is the average of the predicted values.
Mean Actual Value	This is the average of the actual values from the testing data set.

TABLE 10-2. *Statistical Information Produced for Each Regression Model*

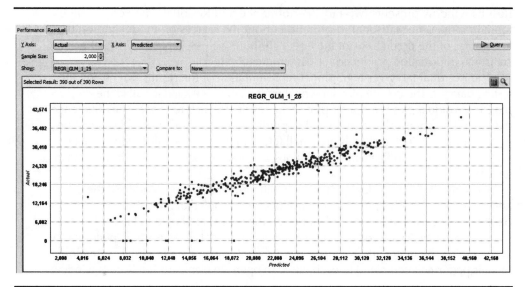

FIGURE 10-16. *Actual versus predicted regression model scatter plot*

right-click on the Regression node on your workflow, then select Compare Test Results from the menu. A window opens that shows the performance results and graph comparisons for the regression models that were produced. The Compare Test Results window has two tabs, Performance and Residual. The Performance tab displays the statistical information of your regression models in both graphical and tabular form. This Performance tab is very similar to the one that is displayed for a single regression model and presents the same statistical information.

The Residual tab for the Compare Test Results window displays the scatter plots for your regression models. By default, the scatter plots are based on the residual values. You can alter the x-axis and y-axis using the drop-down lists and then clicking the Query button to update the scatter plots. To compare the scatter plots of two regression models, you can select the relevant regression model names in the Show and Compare To drop-down lists, as shown in Figure 10-17.

Using the statistical information and the scatter plots in Figure 10-16, you might determine that the SVM regression model gives the best results, as the error rates are smaller and the scatter plot shows a smaller scatter range compared to the GLM regression model. The SVM regression model is used in the next section to illustrate how you can apply it to new data to score the new data with an LTV value.

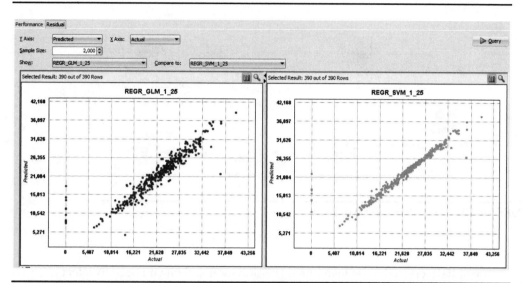

FIGURE 10-17. *Compare test results for your regression models.*

Applying a Regression Model to New Data

After you have generated your regression model, you are ready to apply it to new data and to score the new data with the predicted value. This section describes the steps required to apply a regression model to new data. For simplicity, the same data set is used for the apply process as what was used to build the regression model. In your real-world scenario, you will collect new data on a daily basis.

The first step is to create a Data Source node for your data set. The Data Source node can be found in the Data section of the Components Workflow Editor. Click on this node, then move the mouse to the workflow and click again. When the Data Source node is created, you can define the table to be used. In this example, the table is INSUR_CUST_LTV_SAMPLE. Select all the attributes to be included in the node.

The second step is to create an Apply node on your workflow. The Apply node can be found in the Evaluate and Apply section of the Components Workflow Editor. Click on this node, then move the mouse to the Workflow Worksheet and click again. This creates the Apply node on your workflow. Next you need to connect the new Data Source node and the Regression node to the Apply node. This tells the Apply node what regression model should be applied to what data set. Figure 10-18 shows the completed workflows before the node has been run.

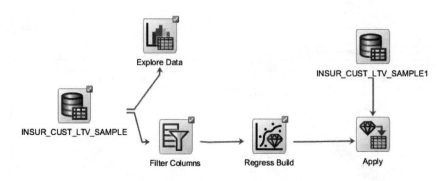

FIGURE 10-18. *The regression workflow*

If you have created more than one regression model, then you need to select the one you want to apply to the data. You can do this by clicking (a single click) on the Regression node and then in the Output column of the Property Inspector deselecting the model you do not want to use. In the previous section, the SVM regression model was identified as the preferred regression model. Figure 10-19 shows the selection of the SVM regression model to be used in the Apply node.

When the new Data Source node and the Regression node have been connected to the Apply node, you can double-click on the Apply node to edit and define what attributes you want the Apply node to produce. You can open the Edit Apply Node window by double-clicking on the Apply node. By default, the Apply node produces a prediction attribute for the GLM and SVM models. For the GLM model, two additional attributes are created. These attributes contain the Lower and Upper Bounds prediction confidence percentages. In addition to needing the prediction attribute(s), you also need to define which attributes from your data set you want to

Models

Model Settings					✛ ✗ ⬚ ∞ ⬚ ⬚ Name	
Name	Output	Build	Test	Algorithm	Comment
REGR_GLM_1_25	→·	☑ 30/12/13 09:23	☑ 30/12/13 09:23	Generalized Linear Model	
REGR_SVM_1_25	⇒	☑ 30/12/13 10:29	☑ 30/12/13 10:29	Support Vector Machine	

FIGURE 10-19. *Selecting the regression model to use in the Apply node*

include in the output of the Apply node. Typical attributes include the primary key, other identifying attributes, and other attributes that you require. You can add these attributes by clicking on the Additional Output tab of the Edit Apply Node window, as shown in Figure 10-20.

You are now ready to run the Apply node. To do so, right-click on the node, then select Run from menu or select the Run icon at the top of the window. Oracle Data Miner now packages all the required steps into a job that it schedules to run in the database. When everything is complete, a green check mark appears on the top right-hand corner of the Apply node, as shown in Figure 10-21.

NOTE
When the regression model is applied to new data, it looks only at the attributes that are defined in the model. Your new data source will have more attributes than what was used to create the regression model. When the model is applied, it will ignore these attributes.

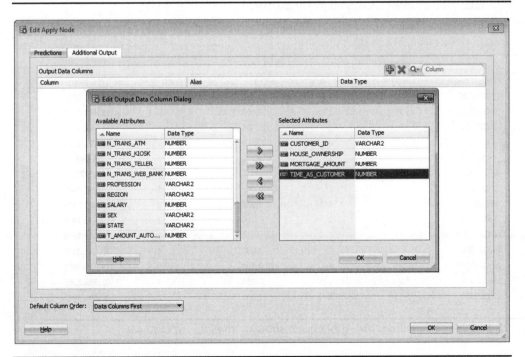

FIGURE 10-20. *Creating the additional output columns*

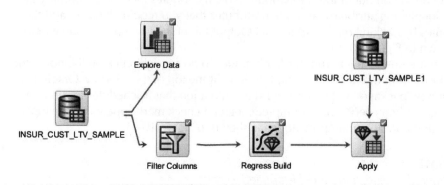

FIGURE 10-21. *The completed regression workflow*

To view the results from the completed Apply node, right-click the Apply node, then select View Data from the menu. The results of the Apply node then appear in a new data grid window, as shown in Figure 10-22.

	CUSTOMER_ID	HOUSE_OWNERSHIP	MORTGAGE_AMOUNT	TIME_AS_CUSTOMER	REGR_SVM_1_25_PRED
1	CU13388	0	0	2	19,777.3212
2	CU13386	1	3,000	3	22,483.3498
3	CU6607	1	980	3	19,103.3054
4	CU7331	0	0	2	22,301.6513
5	CU2624	1	5,000	5	16,946.73
6	CU6389	0	0	2	16,392.596
7	CU100	1	2,000	2	24,968.0901
8	CU8653	1	1,000	3	19,465.6779
9	CU2639	0	0	2	19,534.7426
10	CU1330	0	0	1	19,794.9929
11	CU6308	1	7,000	4	29,537.2545
12	CU15141	1	2,500	4	24,922.7009
13	CU15960	1	250	4	23,638.8567
14	CU2806	1	2,000	2	30,141.4692

FIGURE 10-22. *Results from the Apply node showing the labeled data set*

Summary

This chapter presented an example of how you can build a regression model to predict the life time value (LTV) of a customer. The regression model took into account the other attributes that were part of the data set and determined how they contribute toward predicting the required attribute. The process of creating and using a regression model is very similar to classification, where an existing data set with determined values for the target attribute is available. Chapter 17 also looks at regression, exploring how you can build, evaluate, and apply a regression model using the in-database SQL and PL/SQL procedures and functions.

Summary

CHAPTER
11

Anomaly Detection

A nomaly detection is a method that allows you to use Oracle Data Mining to identify records that are slightly different (anomalous) from the main set of records in your data set. Anomaly detection is commonly used in the financial industry to identify potentially fraudulent or money laundering transactions. Anomaly detection can also be used as part of your data exploration to identify data that can be used as input to other data mining techniques or to identify records that can be removed from the data set.

What Is Anomaly Detection?

When you are analyzing data, there are times when you want to identify what data items or records are different from the other data items or records. Anomaly detection is the searching for and identification of case records that do not conform to the typical pattern of case records. These nonconforming cases are often referred to as *anomalies* or *outliers*.

Anomaly detection can be applied to many problem domains, including the following:

- Financial transaction monitoring by clearinghouses to identify transactions that require further investigation for potentially fraudulent or money laundering transactions

- Detection of fraudulent credit card transactions

- Insurance claims analysis to identify possible claims that are not in keeping with their typical claims

- Network intrusion to detect possible hacking or untypical behavior by employees.

With the preceding examples, the types of transactions that you are interested in discovering are uncommon or rare. They occur only in a very small percentage of the cases, but they may have a high impact for the scenario. An alternative approach would be to use classification, but this approach can be used only if you have a sufficient number of case records for the rare or anomalous cases you are interested in.

If a sufficient number of case records do not exist, then the use of classification is of limited value. For example, if the types of cases you are interested in only occur in 1 or 2 percent of your data, then classification may not be able to produce a model to represent these. Also the number and types of different anomalous events may not be determinable, and you are left with an insufficient number of cases for the typical classification approach to work.

For anomaly detection, you need to use a different approach toward modeling your data. With this approach, the anomaly detection algorithm examines your data as one unit, that is, a single class. It then identifies the core characteristics and expected behavior of the cases. The algorithm then labels the data to indicate how similar or dissimilar each case record is from the core characteristics and expected behavior. You can then use this information to identify what case records—that is, anomalous records—warrant further investigation.

Anomaly Detection in Oracle

In Oracle Data Mining, anomaly detection is implemented using a *One-Class Support Vector Machine*. With this, the data set does not have a target attribute defined and it is assumed that all the case records in the data set belong to the same class. The algorithm allows you to set an Outlier percentage. The algorithm uses this percentage to identify an approximate number of cases in your data set that correspond with the percentage. The default value for the Outlier percentage is 10 percent. In most cases, this value is probably set too high and you will need to adjust it to a lower value that is in keeping with your domain knowledge of possible anomalous transactions.

The anomaly detection model, when it is applied to the data, labels the data with a prediction and a prediction probability score. If the prediction score is 1, the case record is considered to be typical. If the prediction score is 0, then the case record is considered anomalous.

Building an Anomaly Detection Model

To build an anomaly detection model in the Oracle Data Miner tool, you use the Anomaly Detection node that is located in the Models section of the Components Workflow Editor. In this section, instructions are given on how to set up an anomaly detection model, configure the settings, generate the model, and then apply the anomaly detection model to your data. Details of how to examine the output of the anomaly detection model are given in the next section, "Model Settings."

Before you can create your anomaly detection model, you need to set up the data that contains the case records that you want to analyze. The example data set used in this chapter to illustrate anomaly detection is the data contained in the CLAIMS data set. This data set is available on the Oracle Data Mining OTN web page and on the Oracle ODM Blog (https://blogs.oracle.com/datamining/entry/fraud_and_anomaly_detection_made_simple). The CLAIMS data set contains records of car insurance claims. You will use this car insurance claims data set to identify any anomalous claims that might exist in the data set. You can import this data set into your DMUSER schema, or you can use the data import feature in SQL Developer to create and load the table into your schema.

CAUTION
When importing the CLAIMS data using the SQL Developer Import wizard, four of the columns need to have their data sizes adjusted to change the default values, as follows:
POLICYNUMBER VARCHAR2(3) needs to be changed to VARCHAR2(4).
ADDRESSCHANGE_CLAIM VARCHAR2(12) needs to be changed to VARCHAR2(14).
NUMBEROFCARS VARCHAR2(10) needs to be changed to VARCHAR2(11).
MARITALSTATUS VARCHAR2(7) needs to be changed to VARCHAR2(8).

As with the previous ODM examples that have been shown in this book, you need to create a new workflow or use an existing Workflow Worksheet for your work. When you have created your workflow (I've called mine "Anomaly Detection Chapter"), the next step is to create a Data Source node for the CLAIMS table. To create this node, select the Data Source node from the Data section of the Components Workflow Editor, then create the node on your worksheet. Complete the Data Source node creation steps by selecting all the attributes and closing the Create Data Source window.

At this point, you are ready to create the anomaly detection model, but before you do this, you might want to explore the data to gain a better understanding. Use the Explore Data node and the Graph node to see what initial insights you might gather from the data.

To create the anomaly detection model, you need to create the Anomaly Detection node on your Workflow Worksheet. The Anomaly Detection node can be located in the Models section of the Components Workflow Editor. Select the Anomaly Detection node, then move your mouse to the worksheet and click again. The Anomaly Detection node is created. The next step is to connect the CLAIMS Data Source node to the Anomaly Detection node. This tells the anomaly detection algorithm what data to use to build the model. To create this connection, right-click on the CLAIMS node, then select Connect from the menu. Then move the mouse to the Anomaly Detection node and click again. A connection arrow is created, as shown in Figure 11-1. You are now ready to set up and configure the Anomaly Detection node. Double-click on the Anomaly Detection node to edit its settings.

The following sections take you through the steps required to set up, generate, and apply the anomaly detection model.

CLAIMS   Anomaly Build

FIGURE 11-1.   *Initial setup of the anomaly detection workflow*

Model Settings

When the Edit Anomaly Detection Build Node window opens, you can edit the options available. The first option that you can edit is the Case ID. This is the identifying attribute from your data set that is unique for each case or record. In some data sets, you may not have an attribute for this, and in these situations you can leave the Case ID with the default value of <None>; otherwise, select the Case ID attribute from the drop-down list. In the sample data set being used in this chapter, the CLAIMS table has a POLICYNUMBER attribute that can be used for the Case ID.

By default, only one anomaly detection model is created. If you want to create a number of models with each having slightly different settings, you can create these in the Edit Anomaly Detection Build Node window (see Figure 11-2).

To edit the model settings, you can double-click on the anomaly detection model name under the Model Settings section in Figure 11-2. This opens the Advanced Settings window for the algorithm. When you click on the Algorithm Settings tab, you see the available settings that you can modify for the algorithm.

FIGURE 11-2.   *Edit Anomaly Detection Build Node window*

Figure 11-3 shows the algorithm settings for the single-class Support Vector Machine used by ODM for anomaly detection, which are as follows:

- **Kernel Function** System Determined is the default. This setting enables ODM to work out which of the kernel functions it should use. The kernel functions available include Linear and Gaussian. When the model is built, the kernel used is displayed in the settings in the model viewer. You should change the Kernel Function setting to Linear for anomaly detection.

  For Rate of Outliers, System Determined, and Linear, you can modify the Tolerance Value, specify the complexity factor, and set Active Learning. If you change the Kernel Function setting to Gaussian, you get two additional parameters: the standard deviation for the Gaussian kernel and cache size.

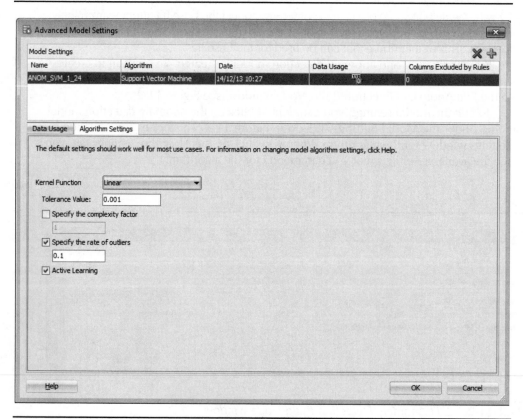

FIGURE 11-3. *Anomaly detection Algorithm Settings*

- **Tolerance Value** This is the maximum size of a violation of convergence criteria such that the model is considered to have converged. The default value is 0.001. Larger values imply faster-building but less accurate models.

- **Specify the Complexity Factor** This setting determines the trade-off between minimizing model error on the training data and minimizing model complexity. Its responsibility is to avoid overfit (an overcomplex model fitting noise in the training data) and underfit (a model that is too simple). The default is to specify no complexity factor, in which case the system calculates a complexity factor. If you do specify a complexity factor, specify a positive number.

- **Specify the Rate of Outliers** This setting enables you to set the approximate rate of outliers (negative predictions) produced by a one-class SVM model on the training data. The rate is a number greater than 0 and less than or equal to 1; the default value is 0.1. This rate indicates the percent of suspicious records. If you do not want to specify the rate of outliers, deselect Specify the Rate of Outliers.

- **Active Learning** This forces the SVM algorithm to restrict learning to the most informative examples and not to attempt to use the entire body of data. In most cases, the resulting models have predictive accuracy comparable to that of the standard (exact) SVM model.

For anomaly detection, you should change the Kernel Function setting to Linear for an anomaly detection model, as shown in Figure 11-3. If you do not make this change and leave the Kernel Function setting to the default value of System Determined, when you run the Anomaly Detection node Oracle Data Miner will probably choose Linear for the Kernel Function setting. If you did not set the Kernel Function setting to Linear, you should select the setting after the Anomaly Detection node has been run, to ensure that ODM chooses the correct function. If it didn't, you should change the parameter setting and rerun the node.

Setting the Kernel Function setting to Linear generates the coefficients for each anomalous and nonanomalous case record.

CAUTION
The default value for the Specify the Rate of Outliers is 0.1 or 10 percent. This value in most cases is too high and should be adjusted to an appropriate value that best fits with your particular scenario.

When you have selected and specified the algorithm setting you want to use, you can then close the Advanced Model Settings window and the Edit Anomaly Detection Build Node window.

Property Inspector

Each node in the workflow has an associated set of properties that is located in the Properties tab. This is a dockable area and typically appears below or to the side of the Components Workflow Editor. As you click on each node in your workflow, different properties relating to the node are displayed in the Properties tab.

For the Anomaly Detection node, the Property Inspector has the following three sections, as shown in Figure 11-4:

- **Models** This lists the models that are part of the Classification node. You can remove models from the list or add new ones. Details of the current status of each model are included.

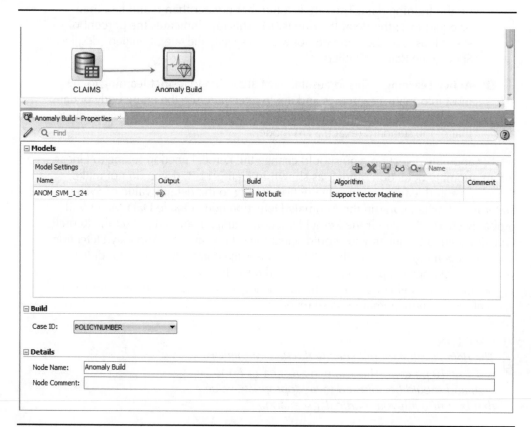

FIGURE 11-4. *Anomaly Detection node Property Inspector*

■ **Build** The build information includes the Case ID. This will be common for all the models you have defined in the Models tab.

■ **Details** The Details tab allows you to change the default name to a name that is more meaningful for your scenario. You can also add a description for the node to include all relevant details and design decisions.

Generating the Models

After you have set up your data and specified the settings for the algorithm, you are now ready to run the Anomaly Detection node to build the model. The results that are shown in the following sections are based on using the default settings, which include the Specify the Rate of Outliers setting of 10 percent. As mentioned previously, this value is probably too high and should be set to a lower percentage.

To run the Anomaly Detection node, right-click on the node, then select Run from the menu. Alternatively, you can click on the green arrow on the Workflow Worksheet menu.

After you click Run, Oracle Data Miner looks back along the workflow, packages up all the steps, submits these to the database as a process using DBMS_JOBS, and schedules these jobs to run in the database.

As each step of the workflow is processed, you see a green wheel on the top right-hand corner of the node. When a node is completed, the green wheel appears on the next node in the workflow. After all the nodes have been completed, you see a green check mark in the top right-hand corner of the node, as shown in Figure 11-5.

At this stage, you have completed the first part of the anomaly detection model process. This step builds the model based on the data set. The second step is to apply the model to the same data set to identify the anomalous cases.

CLAIMS   Anomaly Build

FIGURE 11-5. *Completed anomaly detection workflow with generated models*

Evaluating the Anomaly Detection Model

After the anomaly detection model has been generated, you can view the coefficients for the anomalous cases and for the nonanomalous cases. To view the model details, right-click on the completed Anomaly Detection node, then select View Models from the pop-up menu. Then select the model from the list. There will be only one model listed unless you created a number of different anomaly detection models.

When you select the model name, a new tab area opens that contains all the coefficient details. The Anomaly Detection model tab area includes three sections. The first section is the Coefficients tab, the second tab section is Compare, and the third tab section is called Settings.

The first tab, Coefficients, allows you to see the attributes, their values, and the coefficient values that determine whether a case record is part of the predicted class. In anomaly detection, the predicted class is either a nonanomalous or homological record that has a value of Normal or 1, or an anomalous record that has a value of 0. Figure 11-6 shows the attributes, the attribute value, and the coefficient values for the Normal (1) records.

To switch between the attributes and coefficients for the Normal records to the nonanomalous records, you can change the value of the Predictive Class drop-down list to Anomalous (0). The coefficient grid is then updated with the attributes, the attribute values, and the coefficient values for the anomalous records.

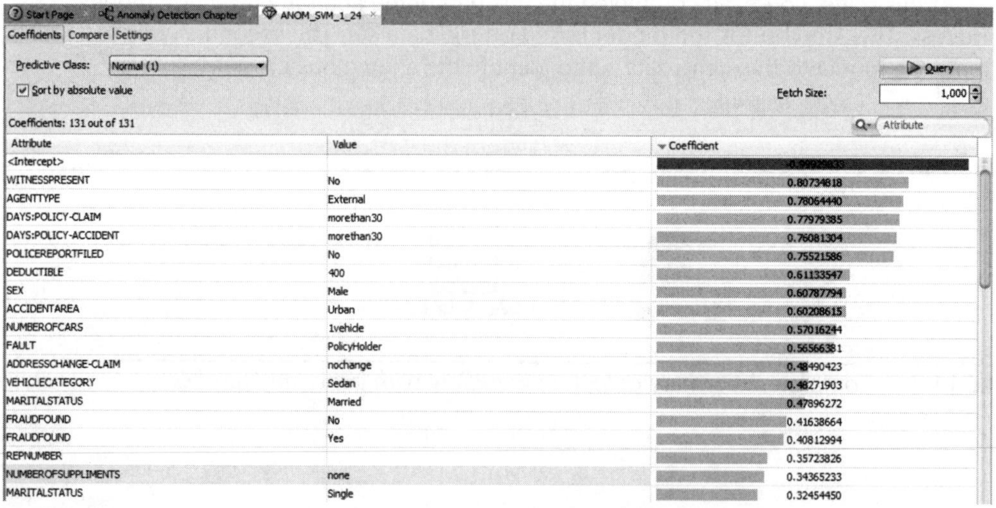

FIGURE 11-6. *Anomaly detection model attributes, values, and coefficients for Normal cases*

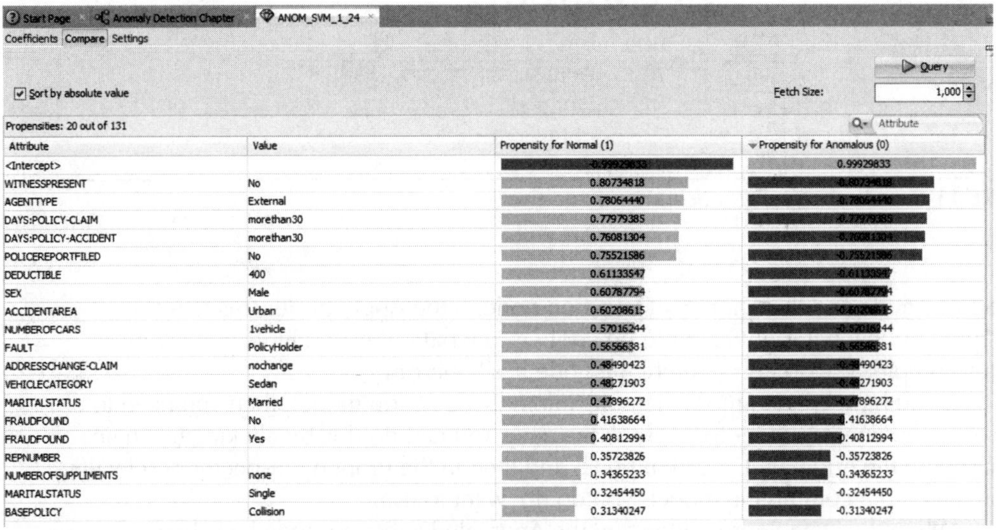

FIGURE 11-7. *Comparing the coefficients of an anomaly detection model*

You can compare the anomalous and normal attributes, values, and coefficients by selecting the Compare tab at the top of the window. This opens the Compare window, which displays the anomalous and normal case coefficient values side-by-side, as shown in Figure 11-7.

The Compare window shows the attribute, the attribute value, and the propensity value for each of the predictive classes (Normal or Anomalous). Propensity is intended to show for a given attribute/value pair which of the two target values has a more predictive relationship. Propensity can be measured in terms of being predicted for or against a target value. If propensity is against a value, the number is negative.

Applying the Model to Your Data

After generating your anomaly detection model, you are ready to complete the second part of the anomaly detection process. This is the applying of the Anomaly Detection model to your original data set to identify possible anomalous records.

To identify these anomalous records, you need to perform a number of steps. The first step is to create an Apply node on your workflow. The Apply node can be found in the Evaluate and Apply section of the Components Workflow Editor. Click on this node, then move the mouse to the Workflow Worksheet and click again. This creates the Apply node on your workflow. Next you need to connect the Data

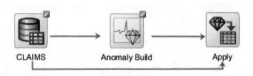

FIGURE 11-8. *Anomaly detection workflow*

Source node and the Anomaly Detection node to the Apply node. This tells the Apply node what model should be applied to what data set. Figure 11-8 shows the completed workflows before the node has been run

If you have created more than one anomaly detection model, then you need to select the one you want to apply to the data. You can do this by clicking (a single click) on the Anomaly Detection node, and then in the Property Inspector deselecting in the output column the models you do not want to use.

When the Data Source node and the Anomaly Detection node have been connected to the Apply node, you can double-click on the Apply node to edit and define the attributes you want the Apply node to produce. You can open the Edit Apply Node window by double-clicking on the Apply node. By default, the Apply node produces attributes for Prediction and Prediction Probability for the selected model(s). But by default, the node does not produce any additional attributes. So you have to do this manually by clicking on the Additional Output tab of the Edit Apply Node window, as shown in Figure 11-9.

TIP
In the Edit Apply Node window, set the Default Column Order setting, on the Predictions tab, to Apply Columns First. This places the Prediction and Prediction Probability attributes to the first attributes outputted. This saves some time with scrolling over and back as you examine the outputs of the Apply node.

To add the extra attributes, click on the green plus sign in the Additional Output tab screen. This opens the Edit Output Data Column Dialog window. Move all the attributes to the right-hand column by clicking on the double arrow pointing to the right, as shown in Figure 11-9. When you have selected all the attributes you want included in the output, click on the OK buttons to close the windows and return to the Workflow Worksheet.

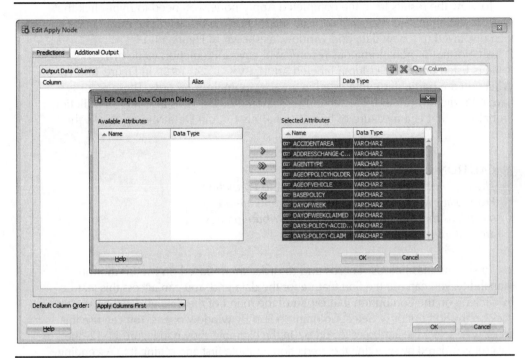

FIGURE 11-9. *Creating the additional output columns for the Anomaly Detection nodes*

You are now ready to run the Apply node. To do so, right-click on the node, then select Run from the menu or select the Run icon at the top of the window. Oracle Data Miner now packages all the required steps into a job and schedules this job to run in the database. When everything is complete, a green check mark appears at the top right-hand corner of the Apply node, as shown in Figure 11-10.

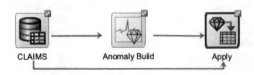

FIGURE 11-10. *Completed anomaly detection workflow*

To view the results from the completed Apply node, you need to right-click the Apply node, then select View Data from the menu. The results of the Apply node are then displayed in a new data grid window, as shown in Figure 11-11.

All Normal or nonanomalous records will have a Prediction value of 1. This value is listed under the column labeled `ANOM_SVM_1_24_PRED` in Figure 11-11. What you are particularly interested in are the anomalous records. These records have a Prediction value of 0. Each of these anomalous records also has a Prediction Probability that is a measure of how anomalous Oracle Data Mining thinks the record is.

CAUTION
The attribute names for the Prediction and Prediction Probability will be different when you generate a model, as the numbers shown in the attribute names are system-generated.

To see the anomalous records and to order them based on the Prediction Probability, you can use the Sort feature for the data grid. You can access this feature by clicking on the Sort button that is part of the menu of the data grid. When you click on the Sort button, a Select Columns to Sort By window opens. You can use this window to select the attributes to sort by. In the example shown in Figure 11-12, the data set is ordered by selecting the Prediction attribute first and setting it to Ascending order. This setting lists the anomalous records first. Then select the Prediction Probability attribute and set it to Descending order. This setting orders the anomalous records with the most anomalous records being displayed first and in descending order of the possibility of their being anomalous.

	ANOM_SVM_1_24_PRED	ANOM_SVM_1_24_PROB	NUMBEROFSUPPLIMENTS	REPNUMBER	FAULT	FRAUDFOUND
1	0	0.6251831232030544	none	12	PolicyHolder	No
2	1	0.5311321724735222	none	9	PolicyHolder	Yes
3	0	0.5146837014795069	3to5	4	PolicyHolder	Yes
4	1	0.5560990178594477	3to5	13	PolicyHolder	Yes
5	1	0.5278905141908866	morethan5	10	ThirdParty	No
6	1	0.5415945140138595	3to5	7	PolicyHolder	Yes
7	1	0.5868448494004973	none	7	PolicyHolder	Yes
8	1	0.5179025661999153	morethan5	2	PolicyHolder	Yes
9	0	0.5069826679447413	none	10	PolicyHolder	Yes
10	1	0.532226911248571	3to5	4	PolicyHolder	No

FIGURE 11-11. *Results from the Apply node showing the labeled data set*

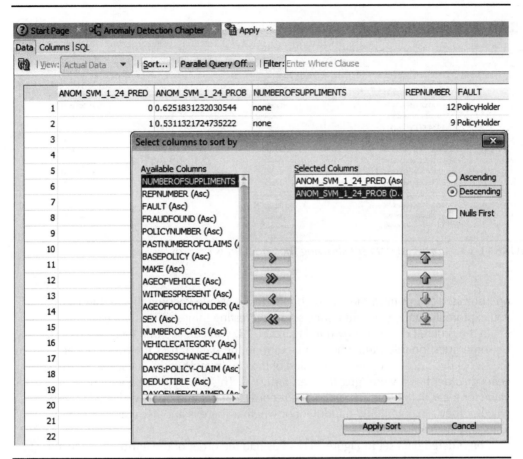

FIGURE 11-12. *Selecting the attribute sort by order for the anomalous records*

With most data mining approaches, the models are used to identify records that are of interest. The models do not tell you why those particular records are of interest or any other reason. This is the same with anomaly detection. The model produced identifies records that seem to be different or even slightly different to the core pattern of the data set. It is your job as a data scientist to explore the records that have been identified to see what the distinguishing characteristics are that makes these anomalous records interesting.

When you examine the ordered anomalous data set, you start to look at the attributes and their values for clues as to why these records were identified as anomalous. An import aspect of this process is that you will bring in some of your domain knowledge to use during this investigation. This example's data set is based

	ANOM_SVM_1_24_PRED	ANOM_SVM_1_24_PROB	MAKE	AGEOFVEHICLE	VEHICLEPRICE	
1	0	0.6374311401940357	Honda	5years	more than 69_000	
2	0	0.6251831232030544	Honda	3years	more than 69_000	
3	0	0.6115639569173855	Toyota	5years	20_000 to 29_000	
4	0	0.609465919432898	Saturn	7years	40_000 to 59_000	
5	0	0.6090623853501513	Pontiac	7years	20_000 to 29_000	
6	0	0.596938102299814	Chevrolet	7years	more than 69_000	
7	0	0.5791871168934224	Chevrolet	morethan7	40_000 to 59_000	
8	0	0.5791263931306097	Pontiac	5years	30_000 to 39_000	
9	0	0.5772515970910052	Honda	5years	more than 69_000	
10	0	0.5757654791195084	Mazda	5years	20_000 to 29_000	
11	0	0.5744811917244084	Accura	5years	more than 69_000	
12	0	0.5738300699103734	Dodge	7years	30_000 to 39_000	
13	0	0.5694824951719468	Toyota	morethan7	30_000 to 39_000	

FIGURE 11-13. *Ordered data set showing the anomalous records*

on insurance claims from the automobile industry. While keeping this in mind as you explore the data, you will notice some interesting things start to appear.

In the ordered data set shown in Figure 11-13, you can see that there seems to be some questionable data when you examine the data across the make of car, the age of the car, and the reported value of the car. In most cases, a car that is five years or older has a value greater than $40,000. This seems to be a very high value for a car of that age. These are the records that need to be investigated to see whether they are potentially fraudulent or whether there is another reason for these unusually high valuations.

The ordered data set in Figure 11-13 has had the order of the attributes changed to show the car make, car age, and car value side-by-side. This makes it a bit easier to see potential issues.

Summary

Anomaly detection is a very useful data mining technique that can be used to explore your data to gain a deeper insight into what is going on in your data. You can use anomaly detection to identify records that can be used as input to other data mining techniques, or you can use it by itself to identify potentially fraudulent cases in your data. In this chapter, a data set that contained case records from an insurance company was explored. Oracle Data Miner was used to build an anomaly detection model, which applied to the data set to identify potentially fraudulent records that require further investigation. In Chapter 18, examples show how you can build and apply an anomaly detection model using the SQL and PL/SQL Oracle Data Mining functions that are in the database.

PART
III

Data Mining Using SQL and PL/SQL

CHAPTER
12

The ODM Data
Dictionary, SQL,
and PL/SQL Packages

Oracle Data Miner comes with a number of Data Dictionary views, SQL functions, and PL/SQL packages to help you prepare data for data mining, build a data mining model, modify and tune the settings of a data mining algorithm, analyze and evaluate the models, and then apply these models to your new data. As Oracle Data Miner is an in-database data mining tool, all objects and models created with it are stored in the database. This allows you to use SQL as the main interface for performing your data mining tasks. This chapter provides an overview of the ODM Data Dictionary views, the various SQL scoring functions, and the main PL/SQL packages. Many examples are given in the various chapters of this section of the book on how to use these Data Dictionary views and PL/SQL packages.

ODM Data Dictionary Views

The Oracle Data Mining models and other objects reside in the schema in which they were created. They can be shared, queried, and used by any schema in the database that has been given access to them. A number of Oracle Data Dictionary views exist that allow you to query the Oracle Data Mining models and their various properties. Table 12-1 lists the Data Dictionary views that are specific to Oracle Data Miner. There are three versions of these views (except for the DBA_MINING_MODEL_SETTINGS). They enable you to see what ODM objects you have access to

Dictionary View Name	Description
*_MINING_MODELS	This view contains the details of each of the Oracle Data Mining models that have been created. This information includes the model name, the data mining type (or function), the algorithm used, and some other high-level information about the models. This view has the following attributes: OWNER *(for DBA_ and ALL_)* MODEL_NAME MINING_FUNCTION ALGORITHM CREATION_DATE BUILD_DURATION MODEL_SIZE COMMENTS

TABLE 12-1.   *Data Dictionary Views*

Dictionary View Name	Description
*_MINING_MODEL_ATTRIBUTES	This view contains the details of the attributes that have been used to create the Oracle Data Mining model. If an attribute is used as a target, the Target column indicates this. This view has the following attributes: OWNER *(for DBA_ and ALL_)* MODEL_NAME ATTRIBUTE_NAME ATTRIBUTE_TYPE DATA_TYPE DATA_LENGTH DATA_PRECISION DATA_SCALE USAGE_TYPE TARGET ATTRIBUTE_SPEC
*_MINING_MODEL_SETTINGS	This view contains the algorithm settings that were used to generate the Oracle Data Mining model for a specific algorithm. This view has the following attributes: OWNER *(for DBA_ and ALL_)* MODEL_NAME SETTING_NAME SETTING_VALUE SETTING_TYPE
DBA_MINING_MODEL_TABLES	This view, which is accessible only by users with DBA privileges, lists all the tables that contain the metadata that is related to the data mining models that exist in the database. This view has the following attributes: OWNER MODEL_NAME TABLE_NAME TABLE_TYPE

Where * can be replaced by

- ALL_ contains the Oracle Data Mining information that is accessible to the user.
- DBA_ contains the Oracle Data Mining information that is accessible to DBA users.
- USER_ contains the Oracle Data Mining information that is accessible to the current user.

TABLE 12-1.   *Data Dictionary Views*

in your local schema (using USER_), what ODM objects you have access to within the database (using ALL_), and what ODM objects are available to database administrators (DBAs) (using DBA_).

Examples of how to use the ODM-related Data Dictionary views are given throughout the chapters in Part III. These example will demonstrate how to find what data mining models you have, what are the properties of the algorithms used, what attributes are used, and more.

The following example shows a query that can be used to retrieve all the classification data mining models in your schema as well as the data mining models for which you have been granted privileges:

```
column model_name format a25
SELECT model_name,
       algorithm,
       build_duration,
       model_size
FROM ALL_MINING_MODELS
WHERE mining_function = 'CLASSIFICATION';
```

MODEL_NAME	ALGORITHM	BUILD_DURATION	MODEL_SIZE
CLAS_GLM_1_13	GENERALIZED_LINEAR_MODEL	13	.1611
CLAS_NB_1_13	NAIVE_BAYES	13	.061
CLAS_DT_1_13	DECISION_TREE	13	.0886
CLAS_SVM_1_13	SUPPORT_VECTOR_MACHINES	13	.0946

ODM SQL Functions

One of the most powerful features of Oracle Data Miner is the ability to use SQL to run and score your data using the data mining models with SQL functions. The functions, listed in Table 12-2, can apply a mining model schema object to the data, or they can dynamically mine the data by executing an analytic clause. SQL functions are available for all the data mining algorithms that support the scoring operation. By using these SQL functions, you can easily embed data mining functionality into all parts of your Oracle environment, be that your batch processing tasks, your reporting tools, your analytical dashboards, or your front-end applications.

The main functions that you will use are PREDICTION and PREDICTION_ PROBABILITY. The PREDICTION function is used to determine the predicted value that the Oracle Data Mining model has calculated for your input data. The PREDICTION_PROBABILITY function tells you how strong of a prediction this value is. The following example shows you how you can use these two functions when using a classification model on your data (a subset of the results are shown). This

Function Name	Description
PREDICTION	Returns the best prediction for the target.
PREDICTION_PROBABILITY	Returns the probability of the prediction.
PREDICTION_BOUNDS	Returns the upper and lower bounds of the interval wherein the predicted values (linear regression) or probabilities (logistic regression) lie. This function applies only to Generalized Linear Model (GLM) models.
PREDICTION_COST	Returns a measure of the cost of incorrect predictions.
PREDICTION_DETAILS	Returns detailed information about the prediction.
PREDICTION_SET	Returns the results of a classification model, including the predictions and associated probabilities for each case.
CLUSTER_ID	Returns the ID of the predicted cluster.
CLUSTER_DETAILS	Returns detailed information about the predicted cluster.
CLUSTER_DISTANCE	Returns the distance from the centroid of the predicted cluster.
CLUSTER_PROBABILITY	Returns the probability of a case belonging to a given cluster.
CLUSTER_SET	Returns a list of all possible clusters to which a given case belongs along with the associated probability of inclusion.
FEATURE_ID	Returns the ID of the feature with the highest coefficient value.
FEATURE_DETAILS	Returns detailed information about the predicted feature.
FEATURE_SET	Returns a list of objects containing all possible features along with the associated coefficients.
FEATURE_VALUE	Returns the value of the predicted feature.

TABLE 12-2. *ODM SQL Functions*

example shows how the GLM classification model that was produced in Chapter 8 can be used.

```
column probability format 9.9999
SELECT cust_id,
       prediction(CLAS_GLM_1_13 USING *)  predicted_value,
       prediction_probability(CLAS_GLM_1_13 USING *) probability
FROM   mining_data_apply_v;

    CUST_ID PREDICTED_VALUE PROBABILITY
---------- --------------- -----------
    100617               0       .9266
    100618               0       .6956
    100619               0       .5733
    100620               1       .6570
    100621               1       .7245
    100622               0       .7692
    100623               0       .9272
    100624               0       .8181
    100625               0       .6648
    100626               1       .7719
    100627               0       .6963
    100628               0       .6783
    ...
```

The other SQL functions allow you to gain additional information about the predicted value that the Oracle Data Mining model has come up with. You can use this additional information to process your data or customer ID in a specific way.

Examples of how to use most of these functions are given through the various chapters in Part III of this book.

ODM PL/SQL Packages

Oracle Data Miner comes with some in-database PL/SQL packages. These packages allow you to perform all of your data mining tasks. There are three PL/SQL packages associated with Oracle Data Miner:

- DBMS_DATA_MINING

- DBMS_DATA_MINING_TRANSFORM

- DBMS_PREDICTIVE_ANALYTICS

The DBMS_DATA_MINING PL/SQL package is the main package that you will use to perform your data mining tasks. These tasks include creating new models, evaluating and testing the models, and applying the models to new data. An overview of this package is given in the following section, "DBMS_DATA_MINING PL/SQL Package," and examples of how to use the various procedures in this package are given in the various chapters in Part III.

The DBMS_DATA_MINING_TRANSFORM PL/SQL package allows you to define various data transformations that can be applied to your data sets to prepare them for input to the data mining algorithms. Examples of how to use this PL/SQL package are given in Chapter 13.

The DBMS_PREDICTIVE_ANALYTICS PL/SQL package contains a number of procedures that allow you to perform an automated form of data mining. When you use this PL/SQL package, you enable the Oracle Data Miner engine to determine what algorithm and settings to use. The output from the procedures consists of the results, and any model produced will not exist after the procedure has completed. This PL/SQL package differs significantly from the DBMS_DATA_MINING package, as that package allows you to determine the algorithm, define the setting, investigate the model performance results, and so on. Examples of how to use the DBMS_PREDICTIVE_ANALYTICS PL/SQL package are given in the section "DBMS_PREDICTIVE_ANALYTICS PL/SQL Package" later in this chapter.

DBMS_DATA_MINING PL/SQL Package

The DBMS_DATA_MINING PL/SQL package contains the main procedures that allow you to create your data mining models, define all the necessary algorithm settings, investigate the results to determine the efficiency of the models, and apply the data mining models to your data. The Oracle Data Miner graphical user interface (GUI) tool that is part of SQL Developer is built upon this package and the procedures that it contains.

Table 12-3 lists all the procedures in the DBMS_DATA_MINING PL/SQL package.

The following chapters in Part III provide a number of examples of how you can use most of the procedures in the DBMS_DATA_MINING package that involve various data mining algorithms and data sets.

Two of the most commonly used procedures in the DBMS_DATA_MINING PL/SQL package are the CREATE_MODEL and APPLY procedures. The CREATE_MODEL procedure allows you to create a data mining model. A prerequisite to using this procedure is that you need to have some of the algorithm settings defined in a table. The following chapters in Part III show you how you can set up this table of settings for the algorithms for each type of data mining you want to perform. Then examples will show how you can define the model build using the CREATE_MODEL

Function/Procedure	Description
ADD_COST_MATRIX	Adds a cost matrix to a classification model
ALTER_REVERSE_EXPRESSION	Changes the reverse transformation expression to an expression that you specify
APPLY	Applies a model to a data set (scores the data)
COMPUTE_CONFUSION_MATRIX	Computes the confusion matrix for a classification model
COMPUTE_LIFT	Computes lift for a classification model
COMPUTE_ROC	Computes Receiver Operating Characteristic (ROC) for a classification model
CREATE_MODEL	Creates a model
DROP_MODEL	Drops a model
EXPORT_MODEL	Exports a model to a dump file
GET_ASSOCIATION_RULES	Returns the rules from an association model
GET_FREQUENT_ITEMSETS	Returns the frequent itemsets for an association model
GET_MODEL_COST_MATRIX	Returns the cost matrix for a model
GET_MODEL_DETAILS_AI	Returns details about an attribute importance model
GET_MODEL_DETAILS_EM	Returns details about an Expectation Maximization model
GET_MODEL_DETAILS_EM_COMP	Returns details about the parameters of an Expectation Maximization model
GET_MODEL_DETAILS_EM_PROJ	Returns details about the projects of an Expectation Maximization model
GET_MODEL_DETAILS_GLM	Returns details about a GLM
GET_MODEL_DETAILS_GLOBAL	Returns high-level statistics about a model
GET_MODEL_DETAILS_KM	Returns details about a K-Means model
GET_MODEL_DETAILS_NB	Returns details about a Naive Bayes model
GET_MODEL_DETAILS_NMF	Returns details about a Non-Negative Matrix Factorization model
GET_MODEL_DETAILS_OC	Returns details about an O-Cluster model

TABLE 12-3. *DBMS_DATA_MINING PL/SQL Package Procedures and Functions* (continued)

Function/Procedure	Description
GET_MODEL_DETAILS_SVD	Returns details about a Singular Value Decomposition (SVD) model
GET_MODEL_DETAILS_SVM	Returns details about a Support Vector Machine (SVM) model with a linear kernel
GET_MODEL_DETAILS_XML	Returns details about a Decision Tree model
GET_MODEL_TRANSFORMATIONS	Returns the transformations embedded in a model
GET_TRANSFORM_LIST	Converts between two different transformation specification formats
IMPORT_MODEL	Imports a model into a user schema
RANK_APPLY	Ranks the predictions from the Apply results for a classification model
REMOVE_COST_MATRIX	Removes a cost matrix from a model
RENAME_MODEL	Renames a model

TABLE 12-3.   *DBMS_DATA_MINING PL/SQL Package Procedures and Functions*

procedure. The following code segment illustrates the CREATE_MODEL procedure. This code example is taken from Chapter 15.

```
BEGIN
    DBMS_DATA_MINING.CREATE_MODEL(
        model_name              => 'DEMO_CLASS_DT_MODEL',
        mining_function         => dbms_data_mining.classification,
        data_table_name         => 'mining_data_build_v',
        case_id_column_name     => 'cust_id',
        target_column_name      => 'affinity_card',
        settings_table_name     => 'demo_class_dt_settings');
END;
```

This example illustrates the creation of a classification model using a Decision Tree algorithm. The details of the Decision Tree algorithm and its settings are contained in a table called 'demo_class_dt_settings'. Check out Chapter 15 for the full details of building a classification model and how to use the APPLY procedure to apply the model and score new data with the model.

DBMS_PREDICTIVE_ANALYTICS PL/SQL Package

The DBMS_PREDICTIVE_ANALYTICS PL/SQL package is very different from the DBMS_DATA_MINING PL/SQL package. The DBMS_PREDICTIVE_ANALYTICS PL/SQL package includes routines for predictive analytics, an automated form of data mining. With predictive analytics, you do not need to be aware of what algorithm or settings are needed for the model build and scoring of data. All mining activities are handled internally and automatically by the predictive analytics procedures.

Predictive analytics routines prepare the data, determine what algorithm to use, determine what algorithm settings are necessary, build a model, score the model, and return the results of model scoring. When the procedure completes, all details of the algorithm, the settings, and the model are deleted along with any supporting objects in the database.

The DBMS_PREDICTIVE_ANALYTICS PL/SQL package comes with the functions EXPLAIN, PREDICT, and PROFILE. Details of how to use each of these procedures are given in the following sections.

You can query the database to get some of the details of each of the procedures in the package. These details include the parameter names, the data type, and the direction of the parameter. The following example illustrates how you can obtain this information:

```
SQL> desc dbms_predictive_analytics
PROCEDURE EXPLAIN
 Argument Name                   Type                     In/Out Default?
 ------------------------------  -----------------------  ------ --------
 DATA_TABLE_NAME                 VARCHAR2                 IN
 EXPLAIN_COLUMN_NAME             VARCHAR2                 IN
 RESULT_TABLE_NAME               VARCHAR2                 IN
 DATA_SCHEMA_NAME                VARCHAR2                 IN     DEFAULT

PROCEDURE PREDICT
 Argument Name                   Type                     In/Out Default?
 ------------------------------  -----------------------  ------ --------
 ACCURACY                        NUMBER                   OUT
 DATA_TABLE_NAME                 VARCHAR2                 IN
 CASE_ID_COLUMN_NAME             VARCHAR2                 IN
 TARGET_COLUMN_NAME              VARCHAR2                 IN
 RESULT_TABLE_NAME               VARCHAR2                 IN
 DATA_SCHEMA_NAME                VARCHAR2                 IN     DEFAULT

PROCEDURE PROFILE
 Argument Name                   Type                     In/Out Default?
 ------------------------------  -----------------------  ------ --------
 DATA_TABLE_NAME                 VARCHAR2                 IN
 TARGET_COLUMN_NAME              VARCHAR2                 IN
 RESULT_TABLE_NAME               VARCHAR2                 IN
 DATA_SCHEMA_NAME                VARCHAR2                 IN     DEFAULT
```

EXPLAIN Procedure

The EXPLAIN procedure creates an attribute importance model. Attribute importance uses the Minimum Description Length algorithm to determine the relative importance of attributes in predicting a target value. The EXPLAIN procedure returns a list of the attributes ranked in relative order of their impact on the prediction. This information is derived from the model details for the attribute importance model.

Attribute importance models are not scored against new data. They simply return the model details about the data you provided. The EXPLAIN procedure ranks attributes in order of influence in explaining a target column.

The syntax of the function is

```
DBMS_PREDICTIVE_ANALYTICS.EXPLAIN (
        data_table_name       IN VARCHAR2,
        explain_column_name   IN VARCHAR2,
        result_table_name     IN VARCHAR2,
        data_schema_name      IN VARCHAR2 DEFAULT NULL);
```

The parameters for the EXPLAIN procedure are detailed in Table 12-4.

The following code example illustrates how you use the EXPLAIN procedure to run against the data defined by the MINING_DATA_BUILD_V view. In addition to defining the input data, you also need to specify the target attribute. In this example, the target attribute is AFFINITY_CARD. Finally, you also need to specify the name of the table to create that will store the results from the EXPLAIN procedure. In this example, the table is PA_EXPLAIN.

```
BEGIN
    DBMS_PREDICTIVE_ANALYTICS.EXPLAIN(
        data_table_name       => 'mining_data_build_v',
        explain_column_name   => 'affinity_card',
        result_table_name     => 'PA_EXPLAIN');
END;
/
```

Parameter	Description
data_table_name	The name of input table or view.
explain_column_name	The name of column to be explained.
result_table_name	The name of table where the results are saved. It creates a new table in your schema.

TABLE 12-4. *EXPLAIN Procedure Parameters*

When the procedure has completed, you can then select from the results table (PA_EXPLAIN in the preceding example) to see the results:

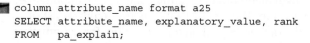

```
column attribute_name format a25
SELECT attribute_name, explanatory_value, rank
FROM   pa_explain;

ATTRIBUTE_NAME              EXPLANATORY_VALUE        RANK
--------------------------  -----------------   ----------
HOUSEHOLD_SIZE                    .194540348           1
CUST_MARITAL_STATUS              .193586215           2
YRS_RESIDENCE                    .115114555           3
EDUCATION                       .105578426           4
AGE                             .103917188           5
OCCUPATION                      .092052058           6
Y_BOX_GAMES                     .077157404           7
HOME_THEATER_PACKAGE            .069102344           8
CUST_GENDER                     .043162087           9
BOOKKEEPING_APPLICATION          .02350555          10
FLAT_PANEL_MONITOR                        0          11
OS_DOC_SET_KANJI                          0          11
COUNTRY_NAME                              0          11
CUST_INCOME_LEVEL                         0          11
BULK_PACK_DISKETTES                       0          11
PRINTER_SUPPLIES                          0          11
CUST_ID                                   0          11
```

As the results are ranked, the lower the rank number, the more important that particular attribute is. In addition to the RANK attribute, the EXPLANATORY_VALUE gives a measure of importance of the attribute. EXPLANATORY_VALUE ranges from 1 to 0, and the higher the value, the more important the attribute is. In some data mining applications, you will find a similar feature and in some cases that feature lists attributes with a negative value. In Oracle, all the negative values are discarded as they are not considered important.

PREDICT Procedure

The PREDICT procedure can be used only for a classification problem and an appropriate data set. The procedure creates a classification model based on the supplied data (your input data set or table) that contains a target value. PREDICT works out which of the in-database classification algorithms to use and what parameter settings are necessary. The procedure then returns a scored data set in a new table. When using PREDICT, you do not get to select an algorithm like you can when using the DBMS_DATA_MINING package. When the results are generated, the model and its associated objects no longer exist in the database.

The input data source should contain records that already have the target value populated. It can also contain records that do not have a target variable. In this case, the PREDICT function uses the records that have a target value to generate the model. The generated model then is used to score or label all the records with the predicted target value.

CAUTION
The input data set should have a reasonable percentage of records that already have the target variable defined. In most cases, more than 50 percent of the records have the target variable defined. Anything less than this will lower the accuracy of the generated model.

The syntax of the PREDICT procedure is as follows:

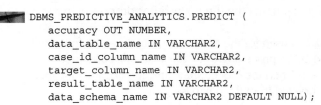

```
DBMS_PREDICTIVE_ANALYTICS.PREDICT (
    accuracy OUT NUMBER,
    data_table_name IN VARCHAR2,
    case_id_column_name IN VARCHAR2,
    target_column_name IN VARCHAR2,
    result_table_name IN VARCHAR2,
    data_schema_name IN VARCHAR2 DEFAULT NULL);
```

Table 12-5 explains the parameters for the PREDICT procedure.

Parameter	Description
accuracy	This is an output parameter from the procedure. You do not pass anything into this parameter. The accuracy value returned is the predictive confidence of the model generated/used by the PREDICT procedure.
data_table_name	This is the name of the table that contains the data you want to use.
case_id_column_name	This is the Case ID for each record. This parameter is unique for each record/case.
target_column_name	This is the name of the column that contains the target column to be predicted.
result_table_name	This is the name of the table that will contain the results. This table should not exist in your schema, otherwise an error will occur.
data_schema_name	This is the name of the schema where the table containing the input data is located. This parameter is probably in your current schema, so you can leave this parameter NULL.

TABLE 12-5. *PREDICT Procedure Parameters*

Attribute Name	Description
CASE_ID	This is the Case ID of the record from the original `data_table_name`. This attribute allows you to link up the data in the source table to the prediction in the `result_table_name`.
PREDICTION	This attribute is the predicted value of the target attribute.
PROBABILITY	This is the probability of the prediction being correct.

TABLE 12-6. *Attributes of the PREDICT Procedure's Output Table*

The PREDICT procedure produces an output table as defined by the `result_table_name` parameter. This table contains the three attributes described in Table 12-6.

Using the sample data set that was used for the EXPLAIN procedure, the following code illustrates how to use the PREDICT procedure to create a classification model and apply this model to the data set. When the procedure is finished, the classification model and associated objects are deleted from the database.

```
set serveroutput on
DECLARE
    v_accuracy NUMBER(10,9);
BEGIN
    DBMS_PREDICTIVE_ANALYTICS.PREDICT(
        accuracy => v_accuracy,
        data_table_name => 'mining_data_build_v',
        case_id_column_name => 'cust_id',
        target_column_name => 'affinity_card',
        result_table_name => 'PA_PREDICT');
    DBMS_OUTPUT.PUT_LINE('Accuracy of model = ' || v_accuracy);
END;
/
```

The procedure has one return parameter. This parameter returns a figure in the range of 0 to 1 that represents the overall accuracy of the model. The higher the accuracy value, the better the model is at making the predictions. When you run the preceding code on the sample data set, you get an accuracy value of 0.60766.

To view the predictions and the results from the PREDICT procedure, you need to query the PA_PREDICT table. This table contains one record for each case record in the original database, and for each of these records it has the predicted target value and the probability of that prediction being correct. A subset of the results is shown in the following output listing:

```
column probability format 9.9999
SELECT * FROM PA_PREDICT
WHERE rownum <= 12;
```

```
   CUST_ID PREDICTION PROBABILITY
---------- ---------- -----------
    102212          1       .5829
    102673          0       .8174
    102676          1       .4418
    102681          1       .8749
    102683          0       .9506
    102687          1       .8588
    102689          0       .9070
    102695          1       .7943
    102696          1       .7438
    102700          1       .9345
    102701          0       .9462
    102703          0       .9655
```

The final step that you might be interested in is to compare the original target value with the prediction value:

```
SELECT v.cust_id,
       v.affinity_card,
       p.prediction,
       p.probability
FROM   mining_data_build_v  v,
       pa_predict p
WHERE  v.cust_id = p.cust_id
AND    rownum <= 12;
```

```
   CUST_ID AFFINITY_CARD PREDICTION PROBABILITY
---------- ------------- ---------- -----------
    102262             0          0       .8647
    102272             0          0       .9816
    102273             0          0       .9187
    102277             1          1       .8175
    102280             1          0       .9138
    102285             0          0       .8174
    102286             0          0       .8952
    102293             0          0       .9904
    102294             0          0       .9213
    102296             0          0       .9840
    102297             0          0       .9760
    102299             0          0       .8224
```

So you have to be careful about when you use the PREDICT function and on what data. Would you use this function as a way to explore your data and to see whether predictive analytics/data mining might be useful for you? Yes, you would.

Would you use it in a production scenario? The answer is maybe, but it depends on the scenario. In reality, if you want to use this function in a production environment, you need to put some work into developing data mining models that best fit your data. To do this, you will need to move on to the ODM tool and the DBMS_DATA_ MINING package. But the PREDICT function is a quick way to get some small data scored (in some way) based on your existing data. It may not give you the most accurate of results, but it does give you results that you can start using quickly.

TIP
There is a new feature available in Oracle 12c called Predictive Queries. These perform similar functionality to what the PREDICT procedure does. But with Predictive Queries, you can build temporary models for anomaly detection, clustering, classification, and regression. See Chapter 20 for some examples of Predictive Queries.

PROFILE Procedure

Like the EXPLAIN procedure, the PROFILE procedure works only with classification type of problems. The PROFILE procedure works out some rules that determine a particular target value. For example, it might ascertain what rules determine whether a customer will or will not take up an affinity card. So, as happens when you use the EXPLAIN procedure, you will get a prelabeled data set with the value of the target attribute already determined. The PROFILE procedure examines the records for each target value and determines what rules best describe the combinations of attributes and the values in these attributes for each target value.

Oracle does not tell us what algorithm it uses to calculate these rules, but they are similar to the rules that are produced by some of the classification algorithms illustrated in other chapters.

The syntax of the PROFILE procedure is as follows:

```
DBMS_PREDICTIVE_ANALYTICS.PROFILE (
        data_table_name         IN VARCHAR2,
        target_column_name      IN VARCHAR2,
        result_table_name       IN VARCHAR2,
        data_schema_name        IN VARCHAR2 DEFAULT NULL);
```

Table 12-7 explains the parameters for the PREDICT procedure.

The PROFILE procedure produces an output table called result_table_name in your schema. The table contains three attributes, described in Table 12-8.

Parameter	Description
data_table_name	This is the name of the table that contains the data that you want to analyze.
target_column_name	This parameter sets the name of the target attribute.
result_table_name	This is the name of the table that will contain the results. This table should not exist in your schema; otherwise, an error will occur.
data_schema_name	This parameter sets the name of the schema where the table containing the input data is located. This is probably in your current schema, so you can leave this parameter NULL.

TABLE 12-7. *Parameters of the* PROFILE *Procedure*

Attribute	Description
PROFILE_ID	This is the PK/unique identifier for the profile/rule.
RECORD_COUNT	This is the number of records that are described by the profile/rule.
DESCRIPTION	This is the profile rule. It is in XML format and has the following XSD:

```
<xs:element name="SimpleRule">
    <xs:complexType>
        <xs:sequence>
            <xs:group ref="PREDICATE"/>
            <xs:element ref="ScoreDistribution"
                minOccurs="0" maxOccurs="unbounded"/>
        </xs:sequence>
        <xs:attribute name="id"
            type="xs:string" use="optional"/>
        <xs:attribute name="score"
            type="xs:string" use="required"/>
        <xs:attribute name="recordCount"
            type="NUMBER" use="optional"/>
    </xs:complexType>
</xs:element>
```

TABLE 12-8. *Attributes of* result_table_name

The following example code illustrates how to use the PROFILE procedure to examine the MINING_DATA_BUILD_V data set that has a target attribute of 'affinity_card'. The generated set of rules is stored in a table called 'PA_PROFILE'.

```
BEGIN
    DBMS_PREDICTIVE_ANALYTICS.PROFILE(
        DATA_TABLE_NAME     => 'mining_data_build_V',
        TARGET_COLUMN_NAME  => 'affinity_card',
        RESULT_TABLE_NAME   => 'PA_PROFILE');
END;
/
```

To see the results that the PROFILE procedure creates, you can query the results table, PA_PROFILE. The output for the DESCRIPTION attribute is in XML format using the XSD format given above. The following code example illustrates some of the rules that were generated by the PROFILE procedure:

```
SET trimspool ON
SET pages 10000
SET long 10000
SET pagesize 10000
SET linesize 90
SELECT *
FROM pa_profile
WHERE rownum <= 3;


PROFILE_ID RECORD_COUNT
---------- ------------
DESCRIPTION
----------------------------------------------------------------------------
         1          135
<SimpleRule id="1" score="0" recordCount="135">
  <CompoundPredicate booleanOperator="and">
    <SimpleSetPredicate field="HOUSEHOLD_SIZE" booleanOperator="isIn">
      <Array type="string">&quot;3&quot; &quot;4-5&quot; </Array>
    </SimpleSetPredicate>
    <SimpleSetPredicate field="EDUCATION" booleanOperator="isIn">
      <Array type="string">
        &quot;10th&quot; &quot;11th&quot; &quot;12th&quot;
        &quot;1st-4th&quot; &quot;5th-6th&quot;
        &quot;7th-8th&quot; &quot;9th&quot; &quot;&lt; Bach.&quot;
        &quot;Assoc-V&quot; &quot;HS-grad&quot; &quot;Presch.&quot;
      </Array>
    </SimpleSetPredicate>
    <SimplePredicate field="YRS_RESIDENCE" operator="lessOrEqual" value="3.5"/>
  </CompoundPredicate>
  <ScoreDistribution value="0" recordCount="116"/>
  <ScoreDistribution value="1" recordCount="19"/>
</SimpleRule>
```

```
        2           328
<SimpleRule id="2" score="0" recordCount="328">
  <CompoundPredicate booleanOperator="and">
    <SimpleSetPredicate field="HOUSEHOLD_SIZE" booleanOperator="isIn">
      <Array type="string">&quot;3&quot; &quot;4-5&quot; </Array>
    </SimpleSetPredicate>
    <SimpleSetPredicate field="EDUCATION" booleanOperator="isIn">
      <Array type="string">
          &quot;10th&quot; &quot;11th&quot; &quot;12th&quot;
          &quot;1st-4th&quot; &quot;5th-6th&quot;
          &quot;7th-8th&quot; &quot;9th&quot;
          &quot;&lt; Bach.&quot; &quot;Assoc-V&quot;
          &quot;HS-grad&quot; &quot;Presch.&quot;
      </Array>
    </SimpleSetPredicate>
    <SimplePredicate field="YRS_RESIDENCE" operator="greaterThan" value="3.5"/>
  </CompoundPredicate>
  <ScoreDistribution value="0" recordCount="197"/>
  <ScoreDistribution value="1" recordCount="131"/>
</SimpleRule>


        3           243
<SimpleRule id="3" score="1" recordCount="243">
  <CompoundPredicate booleanOperator="and">
    <SimpleSetPredicate field="HOUSEHOLD_SIZE" booleanOperator="isIn">
      <Array type="string">&quot;3&quot; &quot;4-5&quot; </Array>
    </SimpleSetPredicate>
    <SimpleSetPredicate field="EDUCATION" booleanOperator="isIn">
      <Array type="string">
          &quot;Assoc-A&quot; &quot;Bach.&quot;
          &quot;Masters&quot; &quot;PhD&quot; &quot;Profsc&quot;
      </Array>
    </SimpleSetPredicate>
  </CompoundPredicate>
  <ScoreDistribution value="1" recordCount="179"/>
  <ScoreDistribution value="0" recordCount="64"/>
</SimpleRule>
```

TIP
*Oracle has a significant number of statistical
functions built into all versions of the database.
These come as standard in the database and do not
involve any additional license fees.*

TIP
In addition to the PL/SQL packages listed in this chapter, there are a number of other PL/SQL packages that you might be interested in exploring. These packages are not part of Oracle Data Miner, but the functionality that they contain may be of some use to you as part of your data science projects. These packages are the following:

*CTX_* * (the Oracle Text Packages)*
DBMS_CUBE
DBMS_FREQUENT_ITEMSET
DBMS_RANDOM
DBMS_STATS_FUNCTIONS

Check out the Oracle Database PL/SQL Packages and Types Reference *book, which comes with the Oracle documentation, for more details on what these packages contain and how to use them.*

Summary

There are a number of Data Dictionary views available in the Oracle Database that enable you to see what data mining objects you have and what their various properties are. Additionally, a number of PL/SQL packages come with Oracle Data Miner. This chapter provided examples of how you can use the DBMS_PREDICTIVE_ANALYTICS package. An overview was given of the procedures in the DBMS_DATA_MINING packages. Examples will be given in each of the chapters in Part III demonstrating how you can use these procedures. In the next chapter, you can find details of how to use the DBMS_DATA_MINING_TRANSFORM package.

CHAPTER
13

Data Preparation

F or all data mining projects, the data preparation stage can take the most amount of time and can involve a number of people. Chapter 6 gave examples of how you can use some of the data preparation/transform nodes that are available in the Oracle Data Miner tool. In this chapter, examples are given on how to use some of the typical SQL functions. Not all of the functions will be demonstrated, but you will see how to use some of the main ones. Oracle Data Mining comes with a number of PL/SQL packages. For data preparation and transformation, there is DBMS_DATA_MINING_TRANSFORM. Examples are given on how you can use most of the procedures that come with this package and how you can use these transformations to prepare your data for data mining. Additionally, you can also embed transformations into your data mining model. Again, the chapter provides examples to illustrate this process.

Data Preparation for Data Mining

Data mining algorithms typically require your data to be prepared in a manner where there is one record for each case you want to feed as input to the data mining algorithms. Each of these case records typically has a unique identifier that is called the CASE_ID. This case identifier can be based on one of a number of attributes that form the case record, or it can be generated automatically in some way by yourself or by a developer.

Typically when you are constructing the case records that you are going to use as your input data set to the data mining algorithm, you may want to perform a number of data preparation steps to get the data into the format that you require. The Oracle Data Miner tool comes with a number of data preparation/transformation nodes. Chapter 6 looked at how you can use these nodes to create and modify a data set for data mining.

In this chapter, the following sections outline some of the typical tasks in data preparation and give some examples of how you can perform these tasks using the various functions that are available in SQL and PL/SQL. The data preparation steps or methods demonstrated in the following sections do not constitute a comprehensive list of data preparation tasks, but they do cover the main tasks that you will encounter.

Data Sampling

When your data sets are relatively small, consisting of a hundred thousand records or fewer, you can explore the data in a relatively short period of time and build your data mining models using the entire data set. But if your data sets become larger than that, particularly as the size of your company increases, and taking into account all the data that might be available when you include the various Big Data data sources, you encounter a new difficulty. This new difficulty is that it can now take a considerable amount of time to analyze the data and to build your data mining models. Sampling is a technique that you can use to work with a subset of the data while maintaining the same characteristics of the entire data set. This technique takes a "random" selection of records from your data set using a specified selection criteria. For some of the data mining techniques, sampling can be used to divide your data set into two separate data sets that can be used for building your models and then for testing the effectiveness of the models.

In Oracle, the SAMPLE function takes a percentage figure. This is the percentage of the entire data set you want to have in the sampled result.

```
SELECT count(*)
FROM   mining_data_build_v
SAMPLE (20);

  COUNT(*)
----------
       319
```

CAUTION

The SAMPLE function returns an estimate of the records for the sample size. Each time you run the preceding query, it returns a slightly different number of records, as Oracle completes an estimate that is based on the sample size as well as the default SEED value used for the function.

There is a variant of the SAMPLE function called SAMPLE BLOCK. In this case, you can still define a percentage value, but Oracle takes a random sample that closely relates to the percentage value from each block for the table.

```
SELECT count(*)
FROM   mining_data_build_v
SAMPLE BLOCK (20);

  COUNT(*)
----------
       150
```

CAUTION

Just like the SAMPLE function, the SAMPLE BLOCK command returns a different number of records each time you use it.

Each time you use the SAMPLE function, Oracle generates a random SEED number that it uses as a seed for the function. If you omit a SEED number (as in the preceding examples), you get a different result set in each case, and each result set will have a slightly different number of records. If you run the preceding sample code over and over again, you will see that the number of records returned varies by a small amount.

If you want the same SAMPLE data set returned each time, then you need to specify a SEED value. The SEED must be an integer between 0 and 4294967295.

```
SELECT count(*)
FROM   mining_data_build_v
SAMPLE (20) SEED (124);


  COUNT(*)
----------
       350
```

Again, if you run this query multiple times, it still returns a slightly different number each time, but the results are not as varied as they are when the SEED is not used.

An alternative to using the SAMPLE function is to use the ORA_HASH function. The ORA_HASH function generates a hash value for a given expression, and can be very useful when you want to generate a random sample based on a particular attribute. The following example illustrates how you can generate a subset of your data set consisting of 60 percent of the data that can be used for building your data mining model. The ORA_HASH value has three parameters. The first is the CASE_ID for the data set/table. The second is the number of hash buckets that can be created. The numbering for the buckets starts at zero, so having a value of 99 indicates to the ORA_HASH function to create 100 buckets. The third parameter is the SEED value. In the following example, this value is zero:

```
CREATE VIEW BUILD_DATA_SET_V
AS SELECT * FROM mining_data_build_v
WHERE ORA_HASH(CUST_ID, 99, 0) <= 60;
```

The rest of the original data set can then be used for your testing data set, as illustrated in the following example when a different range of the ORA_HASH values is used:

```
CREATE VIEW TEST_DATA_SET_V
AS SELECT * FROM mining_data_build_v
WHERE ORA_HASH(CUST_ID, 99, 0) > 60;
```

Data Aggregation and Pivoting the Data

A common task in preparing your data set is to create new attributes (or features) that contain values that have been calculated from a variety of data that is available within your organization. A method that is regularly used to populate these new fields is to aggregate the data and present it in a flattened format.

Oracle has a number of data aggregation functions, and the most commonly used ones are MIN, MAX, SUM, AVG, and COUNT. These are used in conjunction with the

HAVING and ORDER BY clauses in SELECT statements to return single-row results based on these functions, clauses, and the WHERE clause. The output of these aggregate functions can then be used to populate new attributes in your data set for data mining.

The PIVOT command can be very useful in preparing the data, as it allows you to aggregate the data and reformat the output. This reformatted output can be very easily used as input to the case record format. For example, you might want to aggregate the data for a customer based on his or her monthly spending over a 12-month period. By using the PIVOT command, you can display each of the values for each of the months as columns in the results rather than in rows. The following example illustrates how the PIVOT command can be used.

In this example, a view has been defined that already has sales data aggregated by customer, product, country, channel, and quarter. This example is based on the data that can be found in the SH schema sample data sets.

```
Name                                      Null?     Type
-------------------------------------     --------  ------------
CUSTOMER                                  NOT NULL  NUMBER
PRODUCT                                   NOT NULL  VARCHAR2(50)
COUNTRY                                   NOT NULL  VARCHAR2(40)
CHANNEL                                   NOT NULL  NUMBER
QUARTER                                             VARCHAR2(2)
AMOUNT_SOLD                                         NUMBER
QUANTITY_SOLD                                       NUMBER
```

Using the aggregate functions, you can get the total sales for each customer by quarter. The results are returned with one row per quarter per customer:

```
SELECT customer, quarter, sum(amount_sold)
FROM    sales_view
WHERE   customer in (942, 1255, 1267)
GROUP BY customer, quarter
ORDER BY customer, quarter;

CUSTOMER   QU  SUM(AMOUNT_SOLD)
---------  --  ----------------
     942   01           3003.29
     942   02           6179.69
     942   03           9967.38
     942   04           3521.05
    1255   01           9710.03
    1255   02           2951.51
    1255   03           3666.97
    1255   04            4294.9
    1267   01            4103.6
    1267   02           1308.21
    1267   03            532.69
    1267   04          21068.85
```

By using the `PIVOT` function, you can convert the data so that the quarters appear as columns in the result:

```
SELECT *
FROM
    (SELECT customer, quarter, quantity_sold
     FROM sales_view
     where  customer in (942, 1255, 1267))
     PIVOT (sum(quantity_sold)
       FOR quarter IN ('01', '02', '03', '04'))
ORDER BY customer;

  CUSTOMER         '01'         '02'         '03'         '04'
---------- ----------- ----------- ----------- -----------
       942          31           40           39           45
      1255          74           42           62           66
      1267          93           39           13           83
```

When you are writing your code to create each of the individual case records, you can see that by using the `PIVOT` function you can easily reduce the amount of code you need to write to retrieve the data, extract the necessary information, and reformat it so that it can be inserted into your case records attributes/features.

Handling Missing Data

Missing data occurs when you have no value recorded for a particular attribute or feature, that is, you have a null for the attribute. Traditionally, data mining applications do not like to have null as a data value as they can be unsure of how to handle them. Programmers then had to write some application code to work out what value should be inputted into the attribute.

The Oracle Data Miner tool includes as part of the Filter Columns node a feature that performs an assessment of the missing data for each attribute. If the attribute has certain missing values greater than the defined percentage, then the Filter Columns node excludes those attributes from the rest of the workflow.

In the cases where you have no values recorded for some of the attributes, you want to determine what would be a suitable default value for these attributes. One option is to enter a default value of `'UNKNOWN'` or zero for a numeric attribute, or some other similar value, using the `NVL` function that is available in Oracle. If there was a particular reason why no value was recorded, perhaps due to some business logic, then you can enter a suitable value to represent this scenario. In other situations, you might want to calculate a value based on the values used in the other case records of your data set.

For most numeric attributes, you can calculate the mean value and use this as a default value for the attribute that has a missing value. If you have a categorical attribute, then you can use the mode value.

If a case record has a high number of attributes that have null values, then you need to consider removing that record from the data set, as it is of very low quality.

Histograms and Binning

When exploring your data, it is useful to group values together into a number of buckets or to enter a generalized value based on specific ranges or business rules. One approach to this is to define the number of buckets or bins you want the data to be divided into. For example, suppose that you are building data mining models using customer data, and one of these attributes contains the customer's date of birth or age. Perhaps the use of the actual age is too specific of a value to use. If the customer is aged 24 today but in a week's time will be 25, does that change the behavior of the customer? What you might find more interesting is to allocate a customer to a particular age range that is defined by what is called a bucket or bin.

There is a SQL function called WIDTH_BUCKET that allows you to process an attribute and determine what bucket or bin it belongs to. The WIDTH_BUCKET function takes the following inputs:

- Expression   This is the expression or attribute on which the you want to build the histogram.

- Min Value   This is the lower or starting value of the first bucket.

- Max Value   This is the last or highest value for the last bucket.

- Num Buckets   This is the number of buckets you want created.

Typically the Min Value and the Max Value can be calculated using the MIN and MAX functions. As a starting point, you generally would select 10 for the number of buckets. This value can be changed to suit your particular business requirement.

The following example illustrates how you can take an age attribute and calculate what age bin the customer should be in. In this example, the number of buckets or bins is set to 10. When you use WIDTH_BUCKET, each bucket or bin is equally long.

```
SELECT cust_id,
       age,
       width_bucket(age,
                    (SELECT min(age) from mining_data_build_v),
                    (select max(age)+1 from mining_data_build_v),
                    10)  bucket
FROM mining_data_build_v
GROUP BY cust_id, age;
```

```
CUST_ID        AGE       BUCKET
----------  ----------  ----------
   102772        30           2
   102780        58           6
   102786        53           5
   102768        37           3
   102776        54           6
   102761        18           1
   102804        71           8
   102777        21           1
   102783        59           6
   102788        27           2
   102798        31           2
   102766        31           2
...
```

In the preceding example, all the buckets or bins are of equal width. In some scenarios, this is a suitable approach to use. In others, it may not be, as it does not fit in with the general groupings that are used within your company or by the wider business domain. In cases like this, you need to define explicitly what the lower and upper boundaries of each bin are. The following example illustrates how you can use the CASE statement to define what bucket or bin a customer should be placed in based on his or her age:

```
SELECT cust_id, age,
    CASE
        when age between 0 and 18 then 'Too Young'
        when age between 19 and 45 then 'Adult'
        when age between 26 and 55 then 'Middle Aged'
        when age between 56 and 64 then 'Pension Planners'
        when age between 65 and 105 then 'Pensioners'
    END AGE_BIN
FROM mining_data_build_v;

    CUST_ID      AGE AGE_BIN
 ---------  ---------- ----------------
    102767       51 Middle Aged
    102770       36 Adult
    102774       53 Middle Aged
    102775       25 Adult
    102779       54 Middle Aged
    102781       36 Adult
    102787       38 Adult
    102791       47 Middle Aged
    102792       33 Adult
    102797       62 Pension Planners
```

Creating a Target Variable/Attribute

A significant number of data mining projects are focused on using the data mining techniques of classification and regression. The aims of these techniques are to build a model and then to apply this model to new data so that a prediction can be made. With classification and regression, the data mining algorithms need to have one particular attribute in your data set that indicates whether a particular event has happened or not (this is for classification) or has a numeric measure that means something (this is for regression).

Every data mining project begins with defining what problem will be solved. This is what the first two stages of the CRISP-DM process are focused on. For classification and regression problems, you can spend a significant amount of time refining the problem definition so that you have a very clear view of what you want to focus on and what you want to achieve. For classification problems, you want to define a target variable (or attribute or feature) that indicates whether a particular event has occurred or not. For example, you might need to determine whether a customer insurance claim is fraudulent or not. For regression, this is a numeric measure, such as a customer's life time value (LTV).

After you define the target variable, you should have a clear set of instructions that define how the data in your databases can be used to indicate what the target variable value should be for a case record. This set of instructions can be given to your Oracle Database programmer or used by yourself to write the application code that populates the target variable for each case record. Typically you will be using PL/SQL to write this code to query your Oracle Database, examine the data, apply the set of rules to determine the target variable value, and then write the target variable value to the case record.

NOTE
All of the preceding sections have given you some examples of the type of data processing that you need to complete to create your data set of data mining. If you are working with data in Oracle Databases, the primary skill you use is PL/SQL programming. PL/SQL is a very powerful language that enables you to perform almost any task or data modification needed to create your case records.

NOTE
The data preparation techniques outlined in this chapter are examples of some of the techniques you may need to use. They do not by any means constitute an exhaustive list of techniques, and you will need to use a variety of techniques to get the data into the format that you want.

Automatic Data Preparation in ODM

In Oracle, most of the data mining algorithms require some form of data transformation to be performed before the model is built. Oracle has built a lot of the necessary processing into the database, and the required data transformations are automatically performed on the data. This reduces the amount of time you have to spend preparing the data for data mining and frees up this time for you to concentrate on your data mining project and its goals. Oracle Data Miner calls this Automatic Data Preparation (ADP).

During the building of a model, Oracle takes the specific data transformations that each algorithm requires and applies these to the input data. You can supplement these embedded data transformations with additional ones of your own, or you can choose to manage all the transformations yourself.

ADP looks at the requirements of each algorithm and the input data set and then applies the necessary data transformations, which may include binning, normalization, and outlier treatment.

Table 13-1 summarizes the ADP that is performed for each algorithm.

When you use the Oracle Data Miner tool, the Automatic Data Preparation feature is automatically turned on in each of the model build nodes. You can turn this off by double-clicking on the model build node and the Input tab.

When you are using the Oracle Data Miner PL/SQL package `DBMS_DATA_MINING` to create your model, the default setting for Automatic Data Preparation is off (`PREP_AUTO_OFF`). You need to turn ADP on (`PREP_AUTO_ON`) by including a record in a settings table. Various chapters in Part III of this book provide several examples of this. The following example is taken from Chapter 15:

```
-- create the settings table for a Decision Tree model
CREATE TABLE demo_class_dt_settings
( setting_name  VARCHAR2(30),
  setting_value VARCHAR2(4000));

-- insert the settings records for a Decision Tree.
-- Decision Tree algorithm. By default Naive Bayes is used for classification
-- ADP is turned on. By default ADP is turned off.
BEGIN
  INSERT INTO demo_class_dt_settings (setting_name, setting_value)
  VALUES (dbms_data_mining.algo_name, dbms_data_mining.algo_decision_tree);

  INSERT INTO demo_class_dt_settings (setting_name, setting_value)
  VALUES (dbms_data_mining.prep_auto, dbms_data_mining.prep_auto_on);
END;
/
```

ADP with Transformation Lists

If you choose to create your own set of transformations either to complement or replace ADP, you need to ensure that these same set of transformations are applied in the same manner as the data set used to build your data mining model, test the model, and apply it to new data.

Algorithm	What ADP Is Performed
Apriori	ADP has no effect on association rules.
Decision Tree	ADP has no effect on Decision Tree. Data preparation is handled by the algorithm.
Expectation Maximization	Single-column (not nested) numerical columns that are modeled with Gaussian distributions are normalized with outlier-sensitive normalization. ADP has no effect on the other types of columns.
GLM	Numerical attributes are normalized with outlier-sensitive normalization.
K-Means	Numerical attributes are normalized with outlier-sensitive normalization.
MDL	All attributes are binned with supervised binning.
Naïve Bayes	All attributes are binned with supervised binning.
NMF	Numerical attributes are normalized with outlier-sensitive normalization.
O-Cluster	Numerical attributes are binned with a specialized form of equi-width binning, which automatically computes the number of bins per attribute. Numerical columns with all nulls or a single value are removed.
SVD	Numerical attributes are normalized with outlier-sensitive normalization.
Support Vector Machines	Numerical attributes are normalized with outlier-sensitive normalization.

TABLE 13-1. *Effect of ADP on Various Algorithms*

One option that is available to you is to embed these transformations into your model when it is being created using the CREATE_MODEL procedure. This ensures that the transformations are applied in a consistent manner. The details of how to build these transformation lists are given later in this chapter. When these transformations are included in the model, they are applied before any of the ADP transformations. If ADP is disabled and a transformation list is embedded in the model, then only the transformation list is performed.

By default, if no transformation list is embedded in the model and ADP is turned on, then only the default transformations for the algorithm are performed.

Using DBMS_DATA_MINING_TRANSFORM PL/SQL Package

The DBMS_DATA_MINING_TRANSFORM PL/SQL package provides a number of procedures and functions that allow you to perform certain types of data transformations on your data set. This PL/SQL package can be used with the other types of transformations that you need to perform on your data.

There are two different ways of using the DBMS_DATA_MINING_TRANSFORM package. The first way is to use the package to define a list of transformations. These transformations form a list of what needs to be performed on the data. The output from this list of transformations is a database view. This database view can then be used as the data source for your data mining algorithm. Every time you want to use the data mining model to score new data, you need to apply the list of transformations to the data before applying the model to the transformed data.

The second way to use this package is to define the list of transformations and then pass this list of transformations as a parameter to the CREATE_MODEL procedure that is used to create the data mining model. When you use this approach, the list of transformations is embedded into the data mining model. So when you want to apply the model to new data, you do not have to run the list of transformations. Instead, the model applies the embedded transformations to the data before applying the model.

CAUTION
When you embed the transformations in the data mining model, you may still need to run some data transformations on the data set. This is because the DBMS_DATA_MINING_TRANSFORM PL/SQL package can handle only a certain set of transformations. Using this PL/SQL package can form one part of your data transformations.

TIP
When ADP is enabled, the embedded transformation list is executed before the ADP transformations.

The procedures and functions in the DBMS_DATA_MINING_TRANSFORM package can be grouped into the following types of transformations.

■ **Binning** A number of different binning techniques are supported that enable you to map the attribute values into a number of defined bins (or buckets). The binning techniques include the following:

■ **Supervised Binning** This is where the binning is based on the intrinsic relationships that exist in the data as determined by a Decision Tree model.

■ **Top-N Frequency for Categorical Binning**   This is based on the number of cases in each category. The procedure computes the bin boundaries based on the frequency counts.

■ **Equi-width for Numerical Binning**   This is where the bins are created using an equal range of values. The minimum and maximum values are determined and used to define the bin boundaries for the required number of bins.

■ **Quantile Numerical Binning**   The bins are created based on the quantities computed using the SQL NTILE function. This function orders the data and divides it equally into the specified number of bins—in this case, quantiles.

■ **Linear Normalization**   Normalization is the process of scaling continuous values down to a specific range, often between 0 and 1. Normalization transforms each numerical value by subtracting a number, called the *shift*, and dividing the result by another number called the *scale*. The normalization techniques include the following:

■ **Min-Max Normalization**   There is where the normalization is based on using the minimum value for the shift and the maximum-minimum for the scale.

■ **Scale Normalization**   This is where the normalization is based on 0 being used for the shift, and the value is calculated using max[abs(max), abs(min)] for the scale.

■ **Z-Score Normalization**   This is where the normalization is based on using the mean value for the shift and the standard deviation for the scale.

■ **Outliner Treatment**   The PL/SQL package supports the identification of outliers and their treatment using the following techniques:

■ **Winsorizing**   This is where the outliers (tail values) are replaced by the nearest value that is not an outlier.

■ **Trimming**   This is where the outliers (tail values) are set to null.

■ **Missing Value Treatment**   The PL/SQL package supports the missing value treatment by providing two procedures that can be used to calculate a replacement value. For numeric attributes, the mean value is calculated from the data set. This is used to replace the missing numeric value. For categorical attributes, the mode value is calculated and used to replace the missing categorical value.

List of Package Procedures and Functions

Table 13.2 describes the procedures and functions that are part of the DBMS_DATA_ MINING_TRANSFORM package.

Procedure Name	Description
CREATE_BIN_CAT	Creates a transformation definition table for categorical binning
CREATE_BIN_NUM	Creates a transformation definition table for numerical binning
CREATE_CLIP	Creates a transformation definition table for clipping
CREATE_COL_REM	Creates a transformation definition table for column removal
CREATE_MISS_CAT	Creates a transformation definition table for categorical missing value treatment
CREATE_MISS_NUM	Creates a transformation definition table for numerical missing value treatment
CREATE_NORM_LIN	Creates a transformation definition table for linear normalization
DESCRIBE_STACK	Describes the transformation list
GET_EXPRESSION	Returns a VARCHAR2 chunk from a transformation expression
INSERT_AUTOBIN_NUM_EQWIDTH	Inserts numeric automatic equi-width binning definitions in a transformation definition table
INSERT_BIN_CAT_FREQ	Inserts categorical frequency-based binning definitions in a transformation definition table
INSERT_BIN_NUM_EQWIDTH	Inserts numeric equi-width binning definitions in a transformation definition table
INSERT_BIN_NUM_QTILE	Inserts numeric quantile binning expressions in a transformation definition table
INSERT_BIN_SUPER	Inserts supervised binning definitions in numerical and categorical transformation definition tables

TABLE 13-2. *DBMS_DATA_MINING_TRANSFORM Package Functions and Procedures* (continued)

Procedure Name	Description
INSERT_CLIP_TRIM_TAIL	Inserts numerical trimming definitions in a transformation definition table
INSERT_CLIP_WINSOR_TAIL	Inserts numerical Winsorizing definitions in a transformation definition table
INSERT_MISS_CAT_MODE	Inserts categorical missing value treatment definitions in a transformation definition table
INSERT_MISS_NUM_MEAN	Inserts numerical missing value treatment definitions in a transformation definition table
INSERT_NORM_LIN_MINMAX	Inserts linear min-max normalization definitions in a transformation definition table
INSERT_NORM_LIN_SCALE	Inserts linear scale normalization definitions in a transformation definition table
INSERT_NORM_LIN_ZSCORE	Inserts linear z-score normalization definitions in a transformation definition table
SET_EXPRESSION	Adds a VARCHAR2 chunk to an expression
SET_TRANSFORM	Adds a transformation record to a transformation list
STACK_BIN_CAT	Adds a categorical binning expression to a transformation list
STACK_CLIP	Adds a clipping expression to a transformation list
STACK_COL_REM	Adds a column removal expression to a transformation list
STACK_MISS_CAT	Adds a categorical missing value treatment expression to a transformation list
STACK_MISS_NUM	Adds a numerical missing value treatment expression to a transformation list
STACK_NORM_LIN	Adds a linear normalization expression to a transformation list
XFORM_BIN_CAT	Creates a view of the data table with categorical binning transformations
XFORM_BIN_NUM	Creates a view of the data table with numerical binning transformations

TABLE 13-2. *DBMS_DATA_MINING_TRANSFORM Package Functions and Procedures* (continued)

Procedure Name	Description
XFORM_CLIP	Creates a view of the data table with clipping transformations
XFORM_COL_REM	Creates a view of the data table with column removal transformations
XFORM_EXPR_NUM	Creates a view of the data table with the specified numeric transformations
XFORM_EXPR_STR	Creates a view of the data table with the specified categorical transformations
XFORM_MISS_CAT	Creates a view of the data table with categorical missing value treatment
XFORM_MISS_NUM	Creates a view of the data table with numerical missing value treatment
XFORM_NORM_LIN	Creates a view of the data table with linear normalization transformations
XFORM_STACK	Creates a view of the transformation list

TABLE 13-2. *DBMS_DATA_MINING_TRANSFORM Package Functions and Procedures*

Example of Using the DBMS_DATA_MINING_TRANSFORM Package

The DBMS_DATA_MINING_TRANSFORM PL/SQL package comes with an extensive range of procedures and functions. The following example illustrates how you can use some of these procedures and functions to transform the data and prepare it for data mining. Not all of the procedures and functions are illustrated. The example shows how you can transform missing data, normalize data, and handle outliers. The results from these transformations can then be used as input to the CREATE_MODEL procedure that will be used to generate the data mining model.

TIP
Later chapters in Part III of this book will include examples of how to use the CREATE_MODEL procedure that is part of the DBMS_DATA_MINING PL/SQL package.

TIP
You might need to go through the other chapters in Part III first and then try out the examples that are illustrated in the following examples.

Transform Missing Data

When you want to transform the data to replace the missing data with a mean or mode value, you need to follow a three-stage process. The first stage is to create a table that contains the updated transformed data. The second stage is to run the procedure that calculates the replacement value and then to create the necessary records in the table created in the first stage. These two stages need to be followed for both numerical and categorical attributes. For stage three, you need to create a new view that contains the data from the original table and has the missing data rules generated in the second stage applied to it. The following example illustrates these two stages for numerical and categorical attributes in the MINING_DATA_BUILD_V data set.

```
-- Transform missing data for numeric attributes
-- Stage 1 : Create the tables that will store the
--    transformed missing data for numeric and categorical
--    attributes.
-- Stage 2 : Perform the transformations
--    Exclude any attributes you don't want transformed
--       e.g. the case id and the target attribute
BEGIN
   --
   -- Clean-up : Drop the previously created tables
   --
   BEGIN
      execute immediate 'drop table TRANSFORM_MISSING_NUMERIC';
   EXCEPTION
      WHEN others THEN
         null;
   END;
   BEGIN
      execute immediate 'drop table TRANSFORM_MISSING_CATEGORICAL';
   EXCEPTION
      WHEN others THEN
         null;
   END;
```

```
--
-- Transform the numeric attributes
--
dbms_data_mining_transform.CREATE_MISS_NUM (
   miss_table_name => 'TRANSFORM_MISSING_NUMERIC');

dbms_data_mining_transform.INSERT_MISS_NUM_MEAN (
 miss_table_name => 'TRANSFORM_MISSING_NUMERIC',
 data_table_name => 'MINING_DATA_BUILD_V',
 exclude_list    => DBMS_DATA_MINING_TRANSFORM.COLUMN_LIST (
                    'affinity_card',
                    'cust_id'));


--
-- Transform the categorical attributes
--
dbms_data_mining_transform.CREATE_MISS_CAT (
   miss_table_name => 'TRANSFORM_MISSING_CATEGORICAL');

dbms_data_mining_transform.INSERT_MISS_CAT_MODE (
   miss_table_name => 'TRANSFORM_MISSING_CATEGORICAL',
   data_table_name => 'MINING_DATA_BUILD_V',
   exclude_list    => DBMS_DATA_MINING_TRANSFORM.COLUMN_LIST (
                    'affinity_card',
                    'cust_id'));
END;
/
```

When the preceding code finishes running, the two transformation tables are in your schema. When you query these two tables, you find the attributes (numeric or categorical) listed along with the value to be used to relate the missing value. For example, the following illustrates the missing data transformations for the categorical data:

```
column col format a25
column val format a25
SELECT col, val FROM transform_missing_categorical;

COL                      VAL
------------------------ ------------------------
CUST_GENDER              M
CUST_MARITAL_STATUS      Married
COUNTRY_NAME             United States of America
CUST_INCOME_LEVEL        J: 190,000 - 249,999
EDUCATION                HS-grad
OCCUPATION               Exec.
HOUSEHOLD_SIZE           3
```

For stage three, you need to create a new view (MINING_DATA_V) that contains the data from the original table and has the missing data rules generated in the second stage applied to it. This is built in stages with an initial view (MINING_DATA_MISS_V) created that merges the data source and the transformations for the missing numeric attributes. MINING_DATA_MISS_V then has the transformations for the missing categorical attributes applied to create a new view called MINING_DATA_V that contains all the missing data transformations.

```
BEGIN
    -- xform input data to replace missing values
    -- The data source is MINING_DATA_BUILD_V
    -- The output is MINING_DATA_MISS_V
    DBMS_DATA_MINING_TRANSFORM.XFORM_MISS_NUM(
        miss_table_name => 'TRANSFORM_MISSING_NUMERIC',
        data_table_name => 'MINING_DATA_BUILD_V',
        xform_view_name => 'MINING_DATA_MISS_V');

    -- xform input data to replace missing values
    -- The data source is MINING_DATA_MISS_V
    -- The output is MINING_DATA_V
    DBMS_DATA_MINING_TRANSFORM.XFORM_MISS_CAT(
        miss_table_name => 'TRANSFORM_MISSING_CATEGORICAL',
        data_table_name => 'MINING_DATA_MISS_V',
        xform_view_name => 'MINING_DATA_V');
END;
/
```

You can now query the MINING_DATA_V view and see that the data displayed does not contain any null values for any of the attributes.

Transform Outliers

The following example shows you how you can transform the data to identify outliers and to transform them. In the example, the Winsorizing transformation is performed, in which the outlier values are replaced by the nearest value that is not an outlier. The transformation process takes place in three stages. For the first stage, a table is created that contains the outlier transformation data. The second stage calculates the outlier transformation data and stores these in the table created in stage one. One of the parameters to the outlier procedure requires you to list the attributes you do not want the transformation procedure applied to (this is instead of listing the attributes you do want it applied to). The third stage is to create a view (MINING_DATA_V_2) that contains the data set with the outlier transformation rules applied. The input data set to this stage can be the output from a previous transformation process (for example, DATA_MINING_V).

```
BEGIN
    -- Clean-up : Drop the previously created tables
    BEGIN
        execute immediate 'drop table TRANSFORM_OUTLIER';
    EXCEPTION
        WHEN others THEN
            null;
    END;

    -- Stage 1 : Create the table for the transformations
    -- Perform outlier treatment for: AGE and YRS_RESIDENCE
    --
    DBMS_DATA_MINING_TRANSFORM.CREATE_CLIP (
        clip_table_name => 'TRANSFORM_OUTLIER');

    -- Stage 2 : Transform the categorical attributes
    --    Exclude the number attributes you do not want transformed
    DBMS_DATA_MINING_TRANSFORM.INSERT_CLIP_WINSOR_TAIL (
        clip_table_name => 'TRANSFORM_OUTLIER',
        data_table_name => 'MINING_DATA_V',
        tail_frac       => 0.025,
        exclude_list    => DBMS_DATA_MINING_TRANSFORM.COLUMN_LIST (
                            'affinity_card',
                            'bookkeeping_application',
                            'bulk_pack_diskettes',
                            'cust_id',
                            'flat_panel_monitor',
                            'home_theater_package',
                            'os_doc_set_kanji',
                            'printer_supplies',
                            'y_box_games'));

    -- Stage 3 : Create the view with the transformed data
    DBMS_DATA_MINING_TRANSFORM.XFORM_CLIP(
        clip_table_name => 'TRANSFORM_OUTLIER',
        data_table_name => 'MINING_DATA_V',
        xform_view_name => 'MINING_DATA_V_2');
END;
/
```

The view MINING_DATA_V_2 now contains the data from MINING_DATA_
BUILD__V, which has been transformed to process missing data for numeric and
categorical data and also has an outlier treatment for the AGE attribute.

Normalize the Data

The normalize procedures and the process of performing this transformation on your
data follow a similar process to the other transformations previously described. There
is a three-stage process. The first stage involves the creation of a table that contains
the normalization transformation data. The second stage applies the normalization

procedures to your data source, defines the normalization required, and inserts the required transformation data into the table created during the first stage. The third stage involves the defining of a view that applies the normalization transformations to your data source and displays the output via a database view. The following example illustrates how you can normalize the AGE and YRS_RESIDENCE attributes. The input data source is the view that was created as the output of the previous transformation (MINING_DATA_V_2). The final output from this transformation step and all the other data transformation steps is MINING_DATA_READY_V.

```
BEGIN
    -- Clean-up : Drop the previously created tables
    BEGIN
        execute immediate 'drop table TRANSFORM_NORMALIZE';
    EXCEPTION
        WHEN others THEN
            null;
    END;

    -- Stage 1 : Create the table for the transformations
    -- Perform normalization for: AGE and YRS_RESIDENCE
    dbms_data_mining_transform.CREATE_NORM_LIN (
        norm_table_name => 'MINING_DATA_NORMALIZE');

    -- Step 2 : Insert the normalization data into the table
    dbms_data_mining_transform.INSERT_NORM_LIN_MINMAX (
        norm_table_name => 'MINING_DATA_NORMALIZE',
        data_table_name => 'MINING_DATA_V_2',
        exclude_list    => DBMS_DATA_MINING_TRANSFORM.COLUMN_LIST (
                            'affinity_card',
                            'bookkeeping_application',
                            'bulk_pack_diskettes',
                            'cust_id',
                            'flat_panel_monitor',
                            'home_theater_package',
                            'os_doc_set_kanji',
                            'printer_supplies',
                            'y_box_games'));

    -- Stage 3 : Create the view with the transformed data
    DBMS_DATA_MINING_TRANSFORM.XFORM_NORM_LIN (
        norm_table_name => 'MINING_DATA_NORMALIZE',
        data_table_name => 'MINING_DATA_V_2',
        xform_view_name => 'MINING_DATA_READY_V');

END;
/
```

You can now use the MINING_DATA_READY_V view as the data source to the Oracle Data Mining algorithms.

Using the Transformed Data as Input to `CREATE_MODEL`

When you have prepared your data, performing all the necessary transformations on it, you are now ready to use the data as an input to the data mining algorithms. The following chapters present examples of how to use the various algorithms. For more details on how to set up the algorithms, see Chapters 14 through 18 for each of the data mining techniques.

The following example illustrates how the transformed data that was created in the preceding sections can be added as a data source to the data mining algorithms. Before you can create a data mining model, you need to create a settings table that contains all the algorithm settings necessary to create the model. The following example illustrates the creation of a settings table for a Decision Tree classification model:

```
-- create the settings table for a Decision Tree model
CREATE TABLE demo_class_dt_settings
 (setting_name  VARCHAR2(30),
  setting_value VARCHAR2(4000));

-- insert the settings records for a Decision Tree.
-- Decision Tree algorithm. By default Naive Bayes is used for classification
-- ADP is turned on. By default ADP is turned off.
BEGIN
  INSERT INTO demo_class_dt_settings (setting_name, setting_value)
  values (dbms_data_mining.algo_name, dbms_data_mining.algo_decision_tree);

  INSERT INTO demo_class_dt_settings (setting_name, setting_value)
  VALUES (dbms_data_mining.prep_auto,dbms_data_mining.prep_auto_on);
END;
/
```

After you have defined the settings, you can use the `CREATE_MODEL` procedure that is part of the `DBMS_DATA_MINING` PL/SQL package to create your data mining model. The following example shows how the `CREATE_MODEL` procedure uses the preceding settings table and uses `MINING_DATA_READY_V` as the data source to build the model:

```
BEGIN
    DBMS_DATA_MINING.CREATE_MODEL(
        model_name        => 'DEMO_CLASS_DT_MODEL',
        mining_function   => dbms_data_mining.classification,
        data_table_name   => 'MINING_DATA_READY_V',
        case_id_column_name   => 'cust_id',
        target_column_name    => 'affinity_card',
        settings_table_name   => 'demo_class_dt_settings');
END;
/
```

TIP
It is important to keep track of the order in which you process the transformations you want to perform, as you will need to run them in the same order every time you want to generate a model or apply the model to your new data. This ensures that the new data is formatted correctly and in exactly the same way as when you built the data mining model.

Embedding Transformation List into the Model

The data transformations illustrated in the previous section showed how you can create the transformations, apply these to the data set, and then through a number of steps apply the transformations, ending up with a database view that can be used as the input data set to the CREATE_MODEL procedure. This transformed data set includes the various transformations. These are in addition to the more structural transformation you might need to write in PL/SQL (or in some other programming language) to create.

If you have a well-defined list of transformations, you might consider embedding them in your data mining model. To do this, you can pass a parameter that contains the list of transformations to the CREATE_MODEL procedure. The form of this parameter is as follows:

```
xform_list              IN TRANSFORM_LIST DEFAULT NULL
```

where TRANSFORM_LIST has the following structure:

```
TRANSFORM_REC      IS RECORD (
      attribute_name        VARCHAR2(4000),
      attribute_subname     VARCHAR2(4000),
      expression            EXPRESSION_REC,
      reverse_expression    EXPRESSION_REC,
      attribute_spec        VARCHAR2(4000));
```

You can use the SET_TRANSFORM procedure (in DBMS_DATA_MINING_TRANSFORM) to defined the transformations required. The following example illustrates the transformation of converting the BOOKKEEPING_APPLICATION attribute from a number data type to a character data type:

```
DECLARE
    transform_stack    dbms_data_mining_transform.TRANSFORM_LIST;
BEGIN
    dbms_data_mining_transform.SET_TRANSFORM(transform_stack,
                        'BOOKKEEPING_APPLICATION',
                        NULL,
                        'to_char(BOOKKEEPING_APPLICATION)',
                        'to_number(BOOKKEEPING_APPLICATION)',
                        NULL);
END;
/
```

Alternatively, you can use the SET_EXPRESSION procedure to create the transformation.

You can stack the transformations together. Using the preceding example, you could express a number of transformations and have these stored in the TRANSFORM_ STACK variable. You can then pass this variable to your CREATE_MODEL procedure and embed these transformations in your data mining model (DEMO_TRANSFORM_MODEL). This is illustrated in the following example:

```
DECLARE
    transform_stack    dbms_data_mining_transform.TRANSFORM_LIST;
BEGIN
    -- Define the transformation list
    dbms_data_mining_transform.SET_TRANSFORM(transform_stack,
                        'BOOKKEEPING_APPLICATION',
                        NULL,
                        'to_char(BOOKKEEPING_APPLICATION)',
                        'to_number(BOOKKEEPING_APPLICATION)',
                        NULL);
    -- Create the data mining model
    DBMS_DATA_MINING.CREATE_MODEL(
        model_name          => 'DEMO_TRANSFORM_MODEL',
        mining_function         => dbms_data_mining.classification,
        data_table_name         => 'MINING_DATA_BUILD_V',
        case_id_column_name     => 'cust_id',
        target_column_name      => 'affinity_card',
        settings_table_name     => 'demo_class_dt_settings',
        xform_list               => transform_stack);
END;
/
```

The previous section showed examples of how you can create various transformations on your data set. These transformations were then used to create a view of the data set that included these transformations. If you want to embed these transformations in your data mining model instead of having to create the various views, you can use the STACK procedures in the DBMS_DATA_MINING_TRANSFORM package. The following examples illustrate the stacking of the transformations created in the previous section. These transformations are added (or stacked) to a transformation list. Then the transformations listed are used in the CREATE_MODEL procedure call to embed these transformations in the model (MINING_STACKED_MODEL).

```
DECLARE
    transform_stack    dbms_data_mining_transform.TRANSFORM_LIST;
BEGIN
    -- Stack the missing numeric transformations
    dbms_data_mining_transform.STACK_MISS_NUM (
        miss_table_name    => 'TRANSFORM_MISSING_NUMERIC',
        xform_list         => transform_stack);

    -- Stack the missing categorical transformations
    dbms_data_mining_transform.STACK_MISS_CAT (
        miss_table_name    => 'TRANSFORM_MISSING_CATEGORICAL',
        xform_list         => transform_stack);

    -- Stack the outlier treatment for AGE
    dbms_data_mining_transform.STACK_CLIP (
        clip_table_name    => 'TRANSFORM_OUTLIER',
        xform_list         => transform_stack);

    -- Stack the normalization transformation
    dbms_data_mining_transform.STACK_NORM_LIN (
        norm_table_name    => 'MINING_DATA_NORMALIZE',
        xform_list         => transform_stack);

    -- Create the data mining model
    DBMS_DATA_MINING.CREATE_MODEL(
        model_name          => 'DEMO_STACKED_MODEL',
        mining_function     => dbms_data_mining.classification,
        data_table_name     => 'MINING_DATA_BUILD_V',
        case_id_column_name    => 'cust_id',
        target_column_name     => 'affinity_card',
        settings_table_name    => 'demo_class_dt_settings',
        xform_list          => transform_stack);
END;
/
```

To view the embedded transformations in your data mining model, you can use the GET_MODEL_TRANSFORMATIONS procedure that is part of the DBMS_DATA_MINING_TRANSFORM PL/SQL package. The following example illustrates the embedded transformations that were added to the data mining model DEMO_STACKED_MODEL:

```
SELECT TO_CHAR(expression)
FROM TABLE (dbms_data_mining.GET_MODEL_TRANSFORMATIONS('DEMO_STACKED_MODEL'));

TO_CHAR(EXPRESSION)
--------------------------------------------------------------------------------
(CASE  WHEN (NVL("AGE",38.892)<18) THEN 18 WHEN (NVL("AGE",38.892)>70) THEN 70 E
LSE NVL("AGE",38.892) END -18)/52

NVL("BOOKKEEPING_APPLICATION",.880667)
NVL("BULK_PACK_DISKETTES",.628)
NVL("FLAT_PANEL_MONITOR",.582)
NVL("HOME_THEATER_PACKAGE",.575333)
NVL("OS_DOC_SET_KANJI",.002)
NVL("PRINTER_SUPPLIES",1)
(CASE  WHEN (NVL("YRS_RESIDENCE",4.08867)<1) THEN 1 WHEN (NVL("YRS_RESIDENCE",4.
08867)>8) THEN 8 ELSE NVL("YRS_RESIDENCE",4.08867) END -1)/7

NVL("Y_BOX_GAMES",.286667)
NVL("COUNTRY_NAME",'United States of America')
NVL("CUST_GENDER",'M')
NVL("CUST_INCOME_LEVEL",'J: 190,000 - 249,999')
NVL("CUST_MARITAL_STATUS",'Married')
NVL("EDUCATION",'HS-grad')
NVL("HOUSEHOLD_SIZE",'3')
NVL("OCCUPATION",'Exec.')
```

Summary

There is no avoiding the need to have a good developer help you to prepare the data for data mining. Maybe you have the skills yourself. The examples given in this chapter illustrate how you can apply some of the SQL and PL/SQL functions and procedures that are available in the database to prepare your data. This chapter has not presented an exhaustive list of the available SQL functions and procedures, but has demonstrated how to use the main functions and procedures that are part of the DBMS_DATA_MINING_TRANSFORM PL/SQL package. You can use these transformations to create transformation lists and then embed these in your data mining models.

CHAPTER
14

Association Rule Analysis

Association rule analysis is a very popular data mining technique that is used to find associations of items that are grouped together. Typical scenarios include Market Basket Analysis, financial product analysis, telecommunications, and so on. Chapter 7 explored how you can build an association rules analysis model using the Oracle Data Miner tool and extract the rules for later use in your applications. In this chapter, you will learn how you can perform the same steps using the functions available in PL/SQL and SQL.

Setting Up Your Data

Typically, for most data mining algorithms, you need to set up one case record per customer for the scenario that you want to model. This case record is a flattened structure that merges all necessary records and attributes into a single record.

With association rule analysis in Oracle, you do not need to do this. Instead of having one record per customer or event—for example a shopping basket—in Oracle you can use a table that contains many records per customer or event. Using the shopping basket scenario, you may have many records that represent the items that the customer purchased. Each product in the shopping basket would be one record in the transaction table. Allowing this transaction table to be the input to the association rule algorithm removes the need to produce a single, sparsely populated record per transaction. This reduces considerably the amount of data processing that you would have to do compared to that required with other data mining applications.

When preparing your data, you need to ensure that you have the following:

- Attributes that can identify the transaction, such as Customer and the Date/Time of the transaction

- One record per product or whatever you are going to analyze

- The product or another attribute that you test for the association

Unlike other directed or supervised data mining techniques, association rule analysis with Oracle does not require a target attribute to indicate an event. The existence of a transaction record makes this possible.

The examples in this chapter use the SALES and PRODUCT tables from the SH (Sales History) schema. If you look at the data in the SALES table (shown in Figure 14-1), you can see the individual transaction records.

In Figure 14-1, you can see that you can have multiple records per event. These multiple records are from the transaction or shopping basket in this case. Oracle Data Miner can process these multiple transaction records as one unit.

PROD_ID	CUST_ID	TIME_ID	CHANNEL_ID	PROMO_ID	QUANTITY_SOLD	AMOUNT_SOLD
118	465	01-JAN-98	4	999	1	8.26
118	465	01-JAN-98	3	999	1	8.26
118	465	01-JAN-98	2	999	1	8.26
119	465	01-JAN-98	4	999	1	7.15
119	465	01-JAN-98	2	999	1	7.23
114	465	01-JAN-98	3	999	1	19.64
114	465	01-JAN-98	2	999	1	19.64
115	465	01-JAN-98	3	999	1	9.3
116	465	01-JAN-98	3	999	1	12.4
117	465	01-JAN-98	4	999	1	9.3
117	465	01-JAN-98	3	999	1	9.3

FIGURE 14-1.   *Transaction records from the SALES table in the SH schema*

The Apriori algorithm requires the input table or view to have a Case ID and the attribute that is to be evaluated. In the example data, the Case ID is formed by concatenating the CUST_ID and the TIME_ID attributes, and the Product ID is the item for which you want the Apriori algorithm to discover the association rules. You can create a view of the SH.SALES table to contain these attributes:

```
CREATE VIEW ASSOC_DATA_V AS (
    SELECT CUST_ID||TIME_ID CASE_ID,
           t.PROD_ID
    FROM SH.SALES t );
```

Oracle has a feature called Automatic Data Preparation (ADP). This has a number of built-in data processing functions that are dependent on the data mining algorithm being processed. The default setting for ADP is OFF. ADP is not required for association rule analysis. You do not need to create a record in your settings table for the algorithm.

Settings Table

Before you can create a data mining model in Oracle, you need to define the various parameter settings for the data mining algorithm. For each data mining model or data mining scenario, you need to create a settings table to store the specific algorithm settings for each model and scenario. To specify the settings, you will need to create a table that contains one record for each setting. The settings table will have two attributes:

- **`setting_name`**   This contains the name of the setting parameter.

- **`setting_value`**   This contains the value of the setting parameter.

TIP
Do not reuse a settings table from a previous model build. Create a new settings table, even if you have the same settings. As you develop and evolve your models, the settings will change. If you were to use the same settings table for an association rules scenario, then you might introduce conflicts with a model built for one scenario versus another.

You can define the name of the settings table. As you may have a number of these tables in your schema, you need to ensure that they have unique names and that the name is meaningful.

For an association rule analysis model, you need to create a record in the settings table for each of the following:

- Algorithm Name

- Set Automatic Data Preparation Off (this is optional as this is the default setting in the database)

- The attribute for which you want to discover the association rules

For association rule analysis, Oracle offers an Apriori algorithm, `ALGO_APRIORI_ASSOCIATION_RULES`. The Apriori algorithm has a number of settings, as described in Table 14-1. A record can be created in the settings table for each of these settings, if the value you want to use is different from the default setting.

Setting	Values and Default Value
ASSOC_MAX_RULE_LENGTH	This is the maximum rule length for the association rules. The value is the maximum number of items that will be included in the rules. The default value is 4.
ASSOC_MIN_CONFIDENCE	This setting establishes the minimum confidence for the association rules. The default value is 0.1.
ASSOC_MIN_SUPPORT	This is the minimum support for the association rules. The default value is 0.1.
ODMS_ITEM_ID_COLUMN_NAME	This value should contain the name of the attribute that contains the items in a transaction. This is equivalent to using the <Existence> setting when using the Association node in the ODM tool. When using this setting, the algorithm expects the data to be presented as two columns: Case ID or Transaction ID Item ID – the attribute specified by this setting
ODMS_ITEM_VALUE_COLUMN_NAME	This will contain the name of the attribute that contains the value associated with each item in a transaction. When using this setting the algorithm will expect the data to be presented as three columns: Case ID or Transaction ID Item ID – the attribute specified by ODMS_ITEM_ID_COLUMN_NAME Item Value – the attribute specified by this setting

TABLE 14-1. *Apriori Algorithm Settings*

The following code creates a settings table for this chapter's association rule analysis example. It inserts three settings records, and the other settings use the default values.

```
-- create the settings table for the Association Rules model
CREATE TABLE demo_ar_settings
 (setting_name  VARCHAR2(30),
  setting_value VARCHAR2(4000));

-- insert the settings records for the Apriori Algorithm
BEGIN
    INSERT INTO demo_ar_settings (setting_name, setting_value) VALUES
    (dbms_data_mining.algo_name, dbms_data_mining.ALGO_APRIORI_ASSOCIATION_RULES);

    INSERT INTO demo_ar_settings (setting_name, setting_value) VALUES
    (dbms_data_mining.prep_auto, dbms_data_mining.prep_auto_off);

    INSERT INTO demo_ar_settings (setting_name, setting_value) VALUES
    (dbms_data_mining.ODMS_ITEM_ID_COLUMN_NAME, 'PROD_ID');

    INSERT INTO demo_ar_settings (setting_name, setting_value) VALUES
    (dbms_data_mining.ASSO_MIN_SUPPORT, 0.01);
END;
/

-- Select from the settings table to see the records
SELECT *
FROM   demo_ar_settings;

SETTING_NAME                      SETTING_VALUE
--------------------------------  ---------------------------------------------
ALGO_NAME                         ALGO_APRIORI_ASSOCIATION_RULES
PREP_AUTO                         OFF
ODMS_ITEM_ID_COLUMN_NAME          PROD_ID
ASSO_MIN_SUPPORT                  .01
```

CAUTION
The default SUPPORT value is set at 0.1, or 10 percent. This is a very high percentage for this value and can result in a small set of outputs from the algorithm. It is advisable to set this to a lower value in your settings table, as shown in the preceding code.

Creating the Association Rule Analysis Model

To create the association rule analysis model in Oracle Data Mining, you use the CREATE_MODEL procedure that is part of the DBMS_DATA_MINING package. The CREATE_MODEL procedure accepts the parameters described in Table 14-2.

Parameter	Description
model_name	This parameter specifies the name of the model you are creating. This is a meaningful name you want to give to the model.
mining_function	This is the data mining function you want to use. The possible values are ASSOCIATION, ATTRIBUTE_ IMPORTANCE, CLASSIFICATION, CLUSTERING, FEATURE_EXTRACTION, and REGRESSION.
data_table_name	This parameter sets the name of the table or view that contains the build data set.
case_id_column_name	This is the Case ID (PK) for the build data set.
target_column_name	This parameter identifies the name of the target attribute in the build data set. This can be left NULL, as there is no target column for association rule analysis.
settings_table_name	This is the name of the settings table. In the current example, this table is called DEMO_AR_SETTINGS.
data_schema_name	This parameter specifies the schema where the build data set is located. This can be left NULL if the build data set is in the current schema.
settings_schema_name	This is the schema where the settings table is located. You can leave this value NULL if the settings table is in the current schema.
xform_list	If you have a set of transformations you want to embed into the model, then you can specify them here. These transformations can be used instead of or in conjunction with the transformations performed by the ADP.

TABLE 14-2.   *CREATE_MODEL Parameters*

The syntax of the CREATE_MODEL procedure is as follows:

```
DBMS_DATA_MINING.CREATE_MODEL (
    model_name              IN VARCHAR2,
    mining_function         IN VARCHAR2,
    data_table_name         IN VARCHAR2,
    case_id_column_name     IN VARCHAR2,
    target_column_name      IN VARCHAR2 DEFAULT NULL,
    settings_table_name     IN VARCHAR2 DEFAULT NULL,
    data_schema_name        IN VARCHAR2 DEFAULT NULL,
    settings_schema_name    IN VARCHAR2 DEFAULT NULL,
    xform_list              IN TRANSFORM_LIST DEFAULT NULL);
```

The following example shows you how to generate an association rules analysis model using the CREATE_MODEL procedure and the settings table DEMO_AR_SETTINGS:

```
BEGIN
  DBMS_DATA_MINING.CREATE_MODEL(
      model_name           => 'ASSOC_MODEL_2',
      mining_function      => DBMS_DATA_MINING.ASSOCIATION,
      data_table_name      => 'ASSOC_DATA_V',
      case_id_column_name  => 'CASE_ID',
      target_column_name   => null,
      settings_table_name  => 'demo_ar_settings');
END;
/
```

The association rules generated by the model are stored in the Oracle Data Miner Repository.

Viewing the Association Rule Model Item Sets and Rule

Two different sets of outputs are generated for the association rule model. The first of these is the Frequent Item Sets that are found in the data. You can use the GET_FREQUENT_ITEMSETS procedure to retrieve these outputs from the Oracle Data Miner Repository. The second output generated is the association rules. These are the rules that conform with the Support and Confidence values that are specified by the default values or are specified in the settings table. This section shows you how to extract and view the Frequent Item Sets and the association rules for your model.

Viewing the Frequent Item Sets

To return the Frequent Item Sets produced by the association rules model, you need to use the GET_FREQUENT_ITEMSETS function. The syntax of this function is as follows:

```
DBMS_DATA_MINING.GET_FREQUENT_ITEMSETS (
    model_name          IN VARCHAR2,
    topn                IN NUMBER DEFAULT NULL,
    max_itemset_length  IN NUMBER DEFAULT NULL)
RETURN DM_ITEMSETS PIPELINED;
```

Table 14-3 describes the parameters for the function.

Parameter	Description
model_name	This is the name of the association rule model that was created using the CREATE_MODEL procedure. If the model is located in a different schema than the one you were using for the GET_FREQUENT_ITEMSETS procedure, you can include the schema name as part of the model name, as in dmuser.assoc_model_2.
topn	If you only want a certain number of frequent itemsets returned, you can use this parameter to specify the number. It returns the top N frequent itemsets ordered by their support value and in descending order.
	If you do not enter a value for this parameter, the procedure returns all frequent itemsets.
max_itemset_length	You can specify the maximum number of items for the Frequent Item Sets using this parameter. If you do not enter a value for this parameter, all Frequent Item Sets are returned based on the previous parameters.

TABLE 14-3. *GET_FREQUENT_ITEMSETS Parameters*

The following examples show you the various ways of calling the GET_ FREQUENT_ITEMSETS procedure using the different parameter inputs:

```
--
-- Select all the Item Sets for the ASSOC_MODEL_2 model
--
SELECT itemset_id, items, support, number_of_items
FROM TABLE(DBMS_DATA_MINING.GET_FREQUENT_ITEMSETS('assoc_model_2'));


--
-- Select all the top 10% of Item Sets based on the Support value
--
SELECT itemset_id, items, support, number_of_items
FROM TABLE(DBMS_DATA_MINING.GET_FREQUENT_ITEMSETS('assoc_model_2', 10));


--
-- Select all the Item Sets that have up to a maximum of 3 items
--
SELECT itemset_id, items, support, number_of_items
FROM TABLE(DBMS_DATA_MINING.GET_FREQUENT_ITEMSETS('assoc_model_2',null, 3));
```

The following is an extract from the rows returned by the first query, to illustrate the format of the Frequent Item Sets:

```
ITEMSET_ID
----------
ITEMS(ATTRIBUTE_NAME, ATTRIBUTE_SUBNAME, ATTRIBUTE_NUM_VALUE, ATTRIBUTE_STR_VALU
-------------------------------------------------------------------------------
   SUPPORT NUMBER_OF_ITEMS
---------- ---------------
        72
DM_ITEMS(DM_ITEM('PROD_ID', '13', NULL, NULL), DM_ITEM('PROD_ID', '20', NULL, NULL))
.010681925               2

        73
DM_ITEMS(DM_ITEM('PROD_ID', '13', NULL, NULL), DM_ITEM('PROD_ID', '30', NULL, NULL))
.017675127               2

       786
DM_ITEMS(DM_ITEM('PROD_ID', '13', NULL, NULL), DM_ITEM('PROD_ID', '33', NULL, NULL),
DM_ITEM('PROD_ID', '30', NULL, NULL))
.013029293                  3

       787
DM_ITEMS(DM_ITEM('PROD_ID', '13', NULL, NULL), DM_ITEM('PROD_ID', '40', NULL, NULL),
DM_ITEM('PROD_ID', '30', NULL, NULL))
.011653009                  3

      2969
DM_ITEMS(DM_ITEM('PROD_ID', '13', NULL, NULL), DM_ITEM('PROD_ID', '48', NULL, NULL),
DM_ITEM('PROD_ID', '40', NULL, NULL), DM_ITEM('PROD_ID', '30', NULL, NULL))
.010528228                  4

      2970
DM_ITEMS(DM_ITEM('PROD_ID', '19', NULL, NULL), DM_ITEM('PROD_ID', '26', NULL, NULL),
DM_ITEM('PROD_ID', '25', NULL, NULL), DM_ITEM('PROD_ID', '23', NULL, NULL))
.010262752                  4
```

NOTE
The preceding results are what you will see in SQL*Plus. When you run the query in SQL Developer, you will not get the values for ITEM *displayed in the results. To see the individual results for this nested attribute, you need to click on each result cell in SQL Developer.*

The preceding output listing illustrates Frequent Item Sets with two, three, and four items. This listing illustrates the use of a nested column. In this case, the nested column is used to contain items that are associated together. The Nest column in this case has a data type of DM_ITEMS and has the following structure for occurrence in the nested column:

```
(attribute_name       VARCHAR2(4000),
 attribute_subname    VARCHAR2(4000),
 attribute_num_value  NUMBER,
 attribute_str_value  VARCHAR2(4000))
```

The use of the nested column is ideal for Frequent Item Sets and association rules as there is an unknown number of possible occurrences. The GET_FREQUENT_ITEMSETS procedure returned records with the structure of DM_ITEMSETS and consists of the following:

```
(itemsets_id       NUMBER,
 items             DM_ITEMS,
 support           NUMBER,
 number_of_items   NUMBER)
```

Viewing the Association Rules

To return the association rules produced by the association rules model that are based on the Support and Confidence settings, you need to use the GET_ASSOCIATION_RULES function. Rather than returning all the association rules, this procedure can be used to filter the required subset of the rules. The syntax of this function is as follows:

```
DBMS_DATA_MINING.GET_ASSOCIATION_RULES (
     model_name          IN VARCHAR2,
     topn                IN NUMBER              DEFAULT NULL,
     rule_id             IN NUMBER (38)         DEFAULT NULL,
     min_confidence      IN NUMBER              DEFAULT NULL,
     min_support         IN NUMBER              DEFAULT NULL,
     max_rule_length     IN NUMBER (38)         DEFAULT NULL,
     min_rule_length     IN NUMBER (38)         DEFAULT NULL,
     sort_order          IN ORA_MINING_VARCHAR2_NT DEFAULT NULL,
     antecedent_items    IN DM_ITEMS            DEFAULT NULL,
     consequent_items    IN DM_ITEMS            DEFAULT NULL,
     min_lift            IN NUMBER              DEFAULT NULL)
  RETURN DM_RULES PIPELINED;
```

The only mandatory parameter is the model name. All the other parameters are optional. Table 14-4 describes the parameters for the function.

Parameter	Description
model_name	This is the name of the association rule model for which you want to extract the association rules. If the model is located in a different schema than the one you were using for the GET_ASSOCIATION_RULES procedure, you can include the schema name as part of the model name, as in dmuser .assoc_model_2.
topn	This parameter is used to specify the top N association rules to return. The returned association rules are ordered by Confidence and then Support, in descending order.
rule_id	This is the identifier of the rule that you want to return. The parameter is used only if you want to see the details of a specific rule. You should not specify the other parameter settings when using this parameter.
min_confidence	This parameter returns the rules that have a Confidence value greater than or equal to this number.
min_support	This returns the rules that have a Support value greater than or equal to this number.
max_rule_length	This returns the rules that have up to this maximum number of items.
min_rule_length	This returns the rules that have this number of items or greater.
sort_order	You can sort the rules based on the values in one or more of the returned columns, in ascending or descending order.
antecedent_items	This parameter returns the rules with these items in the antecedent.
consequent_items	This returns the rules with this item in the consequent.
min_lift	This parameter returns the rules with a lift value greater than or equal to this number.

TABLE 14-4. *GET_ASSOCIATION_RULES Parameters*

The following examples show you the various ways of calling the GET_ ASSOCIATION_RULES procedure using the different parameter inputs:

```
--
-- Select all the Item Sets for the ASSOC_MODEL_2 model
--
SELECT rule_id, antecedent, consequent, rule_support, rule_confidence
FROM TABLE(DBMS_DATA_MINING.GET_ASSOCIATION_RULES('assoc_model_2'));


--
-- Select all the top 10% of Item Sets based on the Support value
--
SELECT rule_id, antecedent, consequent, rule_support, rule_confidence
FROM TABLE(DBMS_DATA_MINING.GET_ASSOCIATION_RULES('assoc_model_2', 10));


--
-- Select all the Item Sets that have 2 or 3 items
--
SELECT rule_id, antecedent, consequent, rule_support, rule_confidence
FROM TABLE(DBMS_DATA_MINING.GET_ASSOCIATION_RULES('assoc_model_2', null,
          null, null, null, 3, 2));
```

NOTE
When the preceding queries are run in SQL Developer, the values for the antecedent and consequent attributes are not displayed, as they are nested attributes. You need to click in each attribute cell to see the values. Alternatively, you can run the results in SQL*Plus to see the nested attribute values.

The GET_ASSOCIATION_RULES procedure returns records with the structure of DM_RULES, which consists of the following:

```
(rule_id              INTEGER,
 antecedent           DM_PREDICATES,
 consequent           DM_PREDICATES,
 rule_support         NUMBER,
 rule_confidence      NUMBER,
 rule_lift            NUMBER,
 antecedent_support   NUMBER,
 consequent_support   NUMBER,
 number_of_items      INTEGER )
```

The antecedent and the consequent columns are defined as the nested column called DM_PREDICATES, which has the following structure:

```
(attribute_name          VARCHAR2(4000),
 attribute_subname        VARCHAR2(4000),
 conditional_operator     CHAR(2)/*=,<>,<,>,<=,>=*/,
 attribute_num_value      NUMBER,
 attribute_str_value      VARCHAR2(4000),
 attribute_support        NUMBER,
 attribute_confidence     NUMBER)
```

The following example illustrates how you can format the outputs of the antecedent and the consequent to show each item separately for one particular association rule (rule id = 18273). This example also illustrates how you can use an attribute defined as a nested column data type as a table.

```
SELECT a.attribute_name, a.conditional_operator oper, a.attribute_subname,
       b.attribute_name, b.conditional_operator coper, b.attribute_subname
FROM TABLE(DBMS_DATA_MINING.GET_ASSOCIATION_RULES('assoc_model_2')) t,
          table(t.antecedent) a,
          table(t.consequent) b
WHERE t.rule_id = 18273;
```

ATTRIBUTE_NAME	OPER	ATTRIBUTE_SUBNAME	ATTRIBUTE_NAME	COPE	ATTRIBUTE_SUBNAME
PROD_ID	=	114	PROD_ID	=	119
PROD_ID	=	118	PROD_ID	=	119
PROD_ID	=	115	PROD_ID	=	119

Summary

Association rule analysis is a common data mining technique that is used to find associations with the occurrences of items that happen together. Typical scenarios include Market Basket Analysis, financial product analysis, telecommunications, and so on. This chapter presented examples of how you can build an association rules model using the functionality that is available in PL/SQL. Examples were also given of how you can extract and use these rules and the information that they contain.

CHAPTER
15

Classification

Classification is one of the most common data mining techniques to use. In Chapter 8, you learned how you can build classification models using the Oracle Data Miner tool and to apply one of these models to your new data. In this chapter, you learn how you can perform the same steps using the functions available in PL/SQL and SQL. The data sets used in this chapter are the same as were used in Chapter 8. Using the contents of this chapter, you should be able to easily understand what is happening under the hood of the Oracle Data Miner tool and be able to modify the ODM workflows to suit your data, your project, and your scenario.

Setting Up Your Data

For classification-type problems in Oracle, you need a case table or view. The case table or view contains the data set you want to use to build and test your classification data mining models. This case table should contain the following:

- One record per case

- One attribute as the primary key or the Case ID

- A target attribute

To prepare your case table or view, you need a very clear definition of the question that you are asking, as this determines what value should be in the target attribute. For example, you might be asking whether a customer will take up an affinity card or not. Having a clearly defined question also enables you to clearly define the steps required to produce the required target attribute value.

Most of the work in preparing the case table or view can be completed using SQL and PL/SQL programs. These take merged data from various sources together to form one record to represent a case. These programs then work out the value for the target variable.

In addition to writing the programs to do this processing, you may also want to reformat the data in a variety of ways. For example, you may not be interested in a person's age, but you might be more interested in what age band they might fit in; for example, the age bands could be <=18, >18 and <=26, >26 and <=34, >= 35 and <=52, and >52. This type of data processing is called *binning* the data.

Oracle has a feature called Automatic Data Preparation (ADP). This has a number of built-in data processing functions that are dependent on the data mining algorithm being processed. By default, ADP is turned on when you are using the

Algorithm	ADP Performed
Naïve Bayes	All attributes are binned with supervised binning.
Generalized Linear Model	Numerical attributes are normalized.
Support Vector Machine	Numerical attributes are normalized.
Decision Tree	The Decision Tree algorithm handles the data preparation.

TABLE 15-1. *ADP Processing for Classification Algorithms*

Oracle Data Mining tool, but when you are using the PL/SQL functions to create a model, you need to turn it on explicitly (see the next section, "Settings Table").

Table 15-1 shows the ADP processing performed for the classification algorithms.

Settings Table

To use a data mining algorithm to build a model, you need to list the settings you want to use for the algorithm. To specify the settings, you must create a table that contains one record for each setting. The settings table will have two attributes:

- `setting_name`   This contains the name of the setting parameter.

- `setting_value`   This contains the value of the setting parameter.

You can define the name of the settings table. As you may have a number of these tables in your schema, you need to ensure that they have unique names and that the names are meaningful.

Typically the settings table has two records in it. One of these records specifies the algorithm that you want to use when building the model, while the second record specifies whether you want to use the ADP feature. ADP is turned on automatically when you are using the Oracle Data Miner tool, but when using the CREATE_MODEL PL/SQL function, ADP is turned off by default.

The following example gives the code to create a settings table and inserts two settings records. These records specify the use of the Decision Tree algorithm and then turn on the ADP. This code can be run using a SQL worksheet in SQL Developer or using SQL*Plus. The schema that you use should be set up with the necessary

permissions to use Oracle Data Miner; for example, you could use the
DMUSER schema.

```
-- create the settings table for a Decision Tree model
CREATE TABLE demo_class_dt_settings
( setting_name  VARCHAR2(30),
  setting_value VARCHAR2(4000));

-- insert the settings records for a Decision Tree.
-- Decision Tree algorithm. By default Naive Bayes is used for classification
-- ADP is turned on. By default ADP is turned off.
BEGIN
  INSERT INTO demo_class_dt_settings (setting_name, setting_value)
  VALUES (dbms_data_mining.algo_name, dbms_data_mining.algo_decision_tree);

  INSERT INTO demo_class_dt_settings (setting_name, setting_value)
  VALUES (dbms_data_mining.prep_auto,dbms_data_mining.prep_auto_on);
END;
/
SELECT *
FROM   demo_class_dt_settings;

SETTING_NAME                    SETTING_VALUE
------------------------------- -------------------------------------------
ALGO_NAME                       ALGO_DECISION_TREE
PREP_AUTO                       ON
```

If you want to perform your own data preparation, then you don't need to
include the second INSERT statement or you can change the setting value to
PREP_AUTO_OFF.

You need to create a separate settings table for each algorithm you want to use.
In the current example, we are only specifying the settings for creating a Decision
Tree model. If you want to create additional classification models at the same time,
then you need to create a separate settings table for each of the other algorithms.

Table 15-2 lists the algorithms available in Oracle.

Algorithm Name	Description
ALGO_DECISION_TREE	Decision Tree
ALGO_GENERALIZED_LINEAR_MODEL	Generalized Linear Model
ALGO_NAIVE_BAYES	Naïve Bayes
ALGO_SUPPORT_VECTOR_MACHINES	Support Vector Machine

TABLE 15-2. *Oracle Algorithms*

Each algorithm has its own settings. Table 15-3 shows the settings for each classification algorithm and its default value.

Algorithm	Setting	Values and Default Value
Naïve Bayes	NABS_PAIRWISE_THRESHOLD	The value of the pairwise threshold for the algorithm. Values >= 0 and <= 1 0.001 (default)
	NABS_SINGLETON_THRESHOLD	The value of the singleton threshold for the algorithm. Values >= 0 and <= 1 0.001 (default)
Generalized Linear Model	GLMS_CONF_LEVEL	The confidence level for the intervals. Values > 0 and < 1 0.95 (default)
	GLMS_DIAGNOSTICS_TABLE_NAME	The name of the table that contains row-level diagnostic information, which is created during the model build. Default is determined by the algorithm.
	GLMS_REFERENCE_CLASS_NAME	The target value to be used as the reference value in a logistic regression model. Default is determined by the algorithm.
	GLMS_RIDGE_REGRESSION	The value determines whether ridge regression is enabled: GLMS_RIDGE_REG_ENABLE GLMS_RIDGE_REG_DISABLE Default is determined by the algorithm.

TABLE 15-3. *Oracle Algorithm Settings and Values* (continued)

Algorithm	Setting	Values and Default Value
	`GLMS_RIDGE_VALUE`	The value of the ridge parameter used by the algorithm; this should be set only when ridge regression is enabled.
		Values > 0
		Default is determined by the algorithm if set automatically; otherwise, a value must be provided.
	`GLMS_VIF_FOR_RIDGE`	The value specifies whether Variance Inflation Factor statistics are created when ridge is used:
		`GLMS_VIF_RIDGE_ENABLE` `GLMS_VIF_EIDGE_DISABLE` (default)
Support Vector Machine	`SVMS_ACTIVE_LEARNING`	This value determines whether active learning is enabled or disabled:
		`SVMS_AL_DISABLE` `SVMS_AL_ENABLE` (default)
	`SVMS_COMPLEXITY_FACTOR`	The value of the complexity factor.
		Values > 0
		Default value is estimated by the algorithm.
	`SVMS_CONV_TOLERANCE`	The convergence tolerance for the algorithm.
		Values > 0
		0.001 (default)
	`SVMS_EPSILON`	The value of the epsilon factor.
		Values > 0
		Default value is estimated by the algorithm.

TABLE 15-3. *Oracle Algorithm Settings and Values* (continued)

Algorithm	Setting	Values and Default Value
	`SVMS_KERNEL_CACHE_SIZE`	The value of the kernel cache size; for Gaussian kernels only. Values > 0 50MB (default)

	`SVMS_KERNEL_FUNCTION`	The kernel used by the algorithm.
		
		`svm_gaussian`
		`svm_linear`
		Default is determined by the algorithm.

	`SVMS_OUTLINER_RATE`	The rate of outlines in the training data for one-class models. Values > 0 and < 1 1 (default)
	`SVMS_STD_DEV`	The value of standard deviation for the algorithm using the Gaussian kernel. Values > 0 Default is estimated by the algorithm.
Decision Tree	`TREE_IMPURITY_METRIC`	The value specifies the algorithm used to determine the best way to split the data for each node: `TREE_IMPURITY_GINI` (default) `TREE_IMPURITY_ENTROPY`
	`TREE_TERM_MAX_DEPTH`	Maximum depth of the tree, that is, the number of nodes between root and the leaf nodes. Values >= 2 and <= 20 7 (default)

TABLE 15-3. *Oracle Algorithm Settings and Values* (continued)

Algorithm	Setting	Values and Default Value
	TREE_TERM_MINPCT_NODE	Child nodes will not have a percentage record count below this value. Values >= 0 and <= 10 0.5 (default)
	TREE_TERM_MINREC_SPLIT	Minimum number of records in a parent node before a split will be considered. Values >= 0 and <= 20 20 (default)
	TREE_TERM_MINREC_NODE	Child nodes will not be created where the record count is below this value. Values >= 0 10 (default)
	TREE_TERM_MINPCT_SPLIT	Minimum percentage of records needed to split a node. Values >= 0 .1 (default)

TABLE 15-3. *Oracle Algorithm Settings and Values*

Creating the Classification Models

To create a new Oracle Data Mining model, you will use the CREATE_MODEL procedure that is part of the DBMS_DATA_MINING package. Table 15-4 describes the parameters that the CREATE_MODEL procedure accepts.

The syntax of the CREATE_MODEL procedure is as follows:

```
DBMS_DATA_MINING.CREATE_MODEL (
    model_name              IN VARCHAR2,
    mining_function         IN VARCHAR2,
    data_table_name         IN VARCHAR2,
    case_id_column_name     IN VARCHAR2,
    target_column_name      IN VARCHAR2 DEFAULT NULL,
    settings_table_name     IN VARCHAR2 DEFAULT NULL,
    data_schema_name        IN VARCHAR2 DEFAULT NULL,
    settings_schema_name    IN VARCHAR2 DEFAULT NULL,
    xform_list              IN TRANSFORM_LIST DEFAULT NULL);
```

Parameter	Description
model_name	This is the name of the model you are creating. This is a meaningful name you want to give to the model.
mining_function	This parameter identifies the data mining function you want to use. The possible values are ASSOCIATION, ATTRIBUTE_IMPORTANCE, CLASSIFICATION, CLUSTERING, FEATURE_EXTRACTION, and REGRESSION.
data_table_name	This is the name of the table or view that contains the build data set.
case_id_column_name	This parameter sets the Case ID (PK) for the build data set.
target_column_name	This is the name of the target attribute in the build data set.
settings_table_name	This parameter specifies the name of the settings table.
data_schema_name	This is the schema where the build data set is located. This can be left NULL if the build data set is in the current schema.
settings_schema_name	This parameter identifies the schema where the settings table is located. This can be left NULL if the settings table is in the current schema.
xform_list	If you have a set of transformations you want to be embedded into the model, you can specify them here. These transformations can be instead of or in conjunction with the transformations performed by the ADP.

TABLE 15-4. *CREATE_MODEL Parameters*

In the following examples, a Decision Tree is created based on the same data set that was used in Chapter 8 for the Oracle Data Miner tool. This data set, MINING_DATA_BUILD_V, contains the previously generated cases and the new cases since the last model rebuild. One of the main differences between generating the data mining model using the CREATE_MODEL procedure and doing so using the Oracle Data Miner tool is that CREATE_MODEL does not separate the data set into one portion for building the model and another for testing the model. You need to use separate data sets for building a model and for testing a model. The CREATE_MODEL procedure takes all the cases in `MINING_DATA_BUILD_V` as inputs to create your model. In this example, the procedure creates a Decision Tree.

```
BEGIN
    DBMS_DATA_MINING.CREATE_MODEL(
        model_name            => 'DEMO_CLASS_DT_MODEL',
        mining_function       => dbms_data_mining.classification,
        data_table_name       => 'mining_data_build_v',
        case_id_column_name       => 'cust_id',
        target_column_name        => 'affinity_card',
        settings_table_name       => 'demo_class_dt_settings');
END;
/
```

If you want to create a number of classification models using the other classification algorithms, then you need to have a separate settings table for each of these models. You then have to execute the `CREATE_MODEL` command for each model. The command you use is the same as used in the preceding Decision Tree example except that you have a different settings table and a different model name. The following example illustrates the settings table and `CREATE_MODEL` command to generate a Support Vector Machine model for the same build data set:

```
-- create the settings table for a Support Vector Machine model
CREATE TABLE demo_class_svm_settings
( setting_name  VARCHAR2(30),
  setting_value VARCHAR2(4000));

-- insert the settings records for a Support Vector Machine.
-- Support Vector Machine algorithm. By default Naive Bayes is used for classification
-- ADP is turned on. By default ADP is turned off.
BEGIN
  INSERT INTO demo_class_svm_settings (setting_name, setting_value)
  VALUES (dbms_data_mining.algo_name, dbms_data_mining.algo_support_vector_machines);

  INSERT INTO demo_class_svm_settings (setting_name, setting_value)
  VALUES (dbms_data_mining.prep_auto,dbms_data_mining.prep_auto_on);
END;
/
BEGIN
    DBMS_DATA_MINING.CREATE_MODEL(
        model_name            => 'DEMO_CLASS_SVM_MODEL',
        mining_function       => dbms_data_mining.classification,
        data_table_name       => 'mining_data_build_v',
        case_id_column_name   => 'cust_id',
        target_column_name    => 'affinity_card',
        settings_table_name   => 'demo_class_svm_settings');
END;
/
```

The following code illustrates how to check that the classification models and the Support Vector Machine models have been built and what other classification models exist in your schema. You will see that the schema includes a number of other classification models. These were created when you used the Oracle Data Miner tool in Chapter 8. You also see a new Decision Tree model called `DEMO_CLASS_DT_MODEL` and a new Support Vector Machine called `DEMO_CLASS_SVM_MODEL`. These are highlighted in bold in the following listing.

```
SELECT  model_name,
        algorithm,
        build_duration,
        model_size
FROM    ALL_MINING_MODELS
WHERE   mining_function = 'CLASSIFICATION';
```

MODEL_NAME	ALGORITHM	BUILD_DURATION	MODEL_SIZE
CLAS_GLM_1_13	GENERALIZED_LINEAR_MODEL	13	.1611
CLAS_NB_1_13	NAIVE_BAYES	13	.061
CLAS_DT_1_13	DECISION_TREE	13	.0886
CLAS_SVM_1_13	SUPPORT_VECTOR_MACHINES	13	.0946
DEMO_CLASS_DT_MODEL	**DECISION_TREE**	**27**	**.0661**
DEMO_CLASS_SVM_MODEL	**SUPPORT_VECTOR_MACHINES**	**7**	**.1639**

NOTE
You may get slightly different numbers for `BUILD_DURATION` and `MODEL_SIZE`. These are dependent on the version of the database and database server you are using.

To see what settings were used to build the models, you need to query the `ALL_DATA_MINING_SETTINGS` view. This shows you the settings what were specified in the settings table and the other default settings for each algorithm.

```
SELECT  setting_name,
        setting_value,
        setting_type
FROM    all_mining_model_settings
WHERE   model_name = 'DEMO_CLASS_DT_MODEL';
```

SETTING_NAME	SETTING_VALUE	SETTING
TREE_TERM_MINREC_NODE	10	DEFAULT
TREE_TERM_MAX_DEPTH	7	DEFAULT
TREE_TERM_MINPCT_SPLIT	.1	DEFAULT
TREE_IMPURITY_METRIC	TREE_IMPURITY_GINI	DEFAULT
TREE_TERM_MINREC_SPLIT	20	DEFAULT
TREE_TERM_MINPCT_NODE	.05	DEFAULT
PREP_AUTO	ON	INPUT
ALGO_NAME	ALGO_DECISION_TREE	INPUT

Next you can have a look at what attributes were used to build the Decision Tree model. A data mining algorithm may not use all the attributes available, in the data source table or view, to build its model. The algorithm works out what attributes and the values of those attributes that contribute to the values in the target attribute.

To see what attributes were used in the model, you can query the ALL_MINING_ MODEL_ATTRIBUTES view:

```
SELECT  attribute_name,
        attribute_type,
        usage_type,
        target
FROM    all_mining_model_attributes
WHERE   model_name = 'DEMO_CLASS_DT_MODEL';


ATTRIBUTE_NAME                      ATTRIBUTE_T USAGE_TY TAR
----------------------------------- ----------- -------- ---
AFFINITY_CARD                       CATEGORICAL ACTIVE   YES
YRS_RESIDENCE                       NUMERICAL   ACTIVE   NO
OCCUPATION                          CATEGORICAL ACTIVE   NO
HOUSEHOLD_SIZE                      CATEGORICAL ACTIVE   NO
EDUCATION                           CATEGORICAL ACTIVE   NO
CUST_MARITAL_STATUS                 CATEGORICAL ACTIVE   NO
AGE                                 NUMERICAL   ACTIVE   NO
```

Evaluating the Classification Models

When you create a new model using the CREATE_MODEL procedure, it uses all the records from the data source to build the model. The algorithms do not divide the data into separate data sets for building and testing, as is done automatically when using the Oracle Data Miner tool. When you are using the PL/SQL package DBMS_DATA_MINING, the testing and evaluation are separate steps that you need to complete. If you are using the Oracle Data Mining tool, it completes these steps automatically for you. When using the DBMS_DATA_MINING package to create your models, you need to use a separate data source for testing your data. This separate data source can be a table or a view.

Preparing the Data

To prepare your data for testing and evaluating your models, you need to perform a number of steps to ensure that the data is ready.

First, the data set you want to use for testing and evaluation should have a similar structure as the data set (table or view) you used to build the model. All data preparation and transformation must be applied to the data to ensure that all the data is prepared and ready for input to the model.

When your testing data set is ready, you can then apply the model to the testing data set. You have two ways of doing this. The first is to use the APPLY procedure that is part of the DBMS_DATA_MINING package or to use the SQL functions of PREDICTION and PREDICTION_PROBABILITY. These are explained in more detail in later sections of this chapter. When you use the APPLY procedure a new table is created to store the results. If you do not want your schema to get filled up with tables, the alternative approach is to create a view in your schema. It is this latter approach that is illustrated in the following examples. In the following scenario, a view is created that contains the primary key of the table that contains the data, the predicted target value, and the prediction probability. The Case ID is needed so that you can link back to the testing data set to compare the actual target values with the predicted values. The sample data has a view defined called MINING_DATA_TEST_V that you will use for testing your Decision Tree model.

```
CREATE OR REPLACE VIEW demo_class_dt_test_results
AS
SELECT cust_id,
       prediction(DEMO_CLASS_DT_MODEL USING *)  predicted_value,
       prediction_probability(DEMO_CLASS_DT_MODEL USING *) probability
FROM   mining_data_test_v;

SELECT *
FROM demo_class_dt_test_results
WHERE rownum <=8;

    CUST_ID PREDICTED_VALUE PROBABILITY
---------- --------------- -----------
     103001               0 .952191235
     103002               0 .952191235
     103003               0 .859259259
     103004               0 .600609756
     103005               1 .736625514
     103006               0 .952191235
     103007               1 .736625514
     103008               0 .600609756
```

The following sections use the view DEMO_CLASS_DT_TEST_RESULTS and the MINING_DATA_BUILD_V to build the confusion matrix, calculate the lift, and calculate the Receiver Operating Characteristic (ROC). All the results from these operations are numbers, and the Oracle Data Miner tool graphs will not be available to help you understand the results.

Computing the Confusion Matrix

To calculate the confusion matrix for the model, you use the COMPUTE_CONFUSION_MATRIX procedure, which is part of the PL/SQL package DBMS_DATA_MINING.

The confusion matrix can be used to test your classification models by comparing the predicted target values, generated by the model, with the actual target values in the testing data set. The procedure requires two sets of inputs that consist of the predictions (Case ID as well as Prediction and Probabilities) and the actual target values from the testing data set (Case ID and target attribute). The syntax of the procedure is as follows:

```
DBMS_DATA_MINING.COMPUTE_CONFUSION_MATRIX (
    accuracy                          OUT NUMBER,
    apply_result_table_name           IN VARCHAR2,
    target_table_name                 IN VARCHAR2,
    case_id_column_name               IN VARCHAR2,
    target_column_name                IN VARCHAR2,
    confusion_matrix_table_name       IN VARCHAR2,
    score_column_name                 IN VARCHAR2 DEFAULT 'PREDICTION',
    score_criterion_column_name       IN VARCHAR2 DEFAULT 'PROBABILITY',
    cost_matrix_table_name            IN VARCHAR2 DEFAULT NULL,
    apply_result_schema_name          IN VARCHAR2 DEFAULT NULL,
    target_schema_name                IN VARCHAR2 DEFAULT NULL,
    cost_matrix_schema_name           IN VARCHAR2 DEFAULT NULL,
    score_criterion_type              IN VARCHAR2 DEFAULT 'PROBABILITY');
```

Using the Decision Tree model that was created earlier in the chapter, the following example shows how to create the confusion matrix for this model using the testing data set and the previously created view (DEMO_CLASS_DT_TEST_RESULTS). The confusion matrix results are stored in a new table called DEMO_CLASS_DT_CONFUSION_MATRIX.

```
set serveroutput on

DECLARE
    v_accuracy NUMBER;
BEGIN
    DBMS_DATA_MINING.COMPUTE_CONFUSION_MATRIX (
        accuracy                         => v_accuracy,
        apply_result_table_name          => 'demo_class_dt_test_results',
        target_table_name                => 'mining_data_test_v',
        case_id_column_name              => 'cust_id',
        target_column_name               => 'affinity_card',
        confusion_matrix_table_name      => 'demo_class_dt_confusion_matrix',
        score_column_name                => 'PREDICTED_VALUE',
        score_criterion_column_name      => 'PROBABILITY',
        cost_matrix_table_name           => null,
        apply_result_schema_name         => null,
        target_schema_name               => null,
        cost_matrix_schema_name          => null,
        score_criterion_type             => 'PROBABILITY');
    DBMS_OUTPUT.PUT_LINE('**** MODEL ACCURACY ****: ' ||
        ROUND(v_accuracy,4));
END;
/
**** MODEL ACCURACY ****: .8187
```

To view the confusion matrix, run the following:

```
SELECT *
FROM    demo_class_dt_confusion_matrix;
```

```
ACTUAL_TARGET_VALUE PREDICTED_TARGET_VALUE      VALUE
------------------- ----------------------  ----------
                  1                      0         192
                  0                      0        1074
                  1                      1         154
                  0                      1          80
```

Computing the Lift

The calculate the lift for the model, you use the COMPUTE_LIFT procedure that is part of the PL/SQL package DBMS_DATA_MINING. The lift is a measurement of the degree to which the predictions of the positive class, by the model, are an improvement over random chance. The lift is calculated based on the results from applying the model to the testing data set. These results are ranked by the probability and divided in quantiles. Each quantile has the score for the same number of cases.

The procedure requires two sets of inputs that consist of the predictions (Case ID as well as Prediction and Probabilities) and the actual target values from the testing data set (Case ID and target attribute). The syntax of the procedure is as follows:

```
DBMS_DATA_MINING.COMPUTE_LIFT (
    apply_result_table_name     IN VARCHAR2,
    target_table_name           IN VARCHAR2,
    case_id_column_name         IN VARCHAR2,
    target_column_name          IN VARCHAR2,
    lift_table_name             IN VARCHAR2,
    positive_target_value       IN VARCHAR2,
    score_column_name           IN VARCHAR2 DEFAULT 'PREDICTION',
    score_criterion_column_name IN VARCHAR2 DEFAULT 'PROBABILITY',
    num_quantiles               IN NUMBER DEFAULT 10,
    cost_matrix_table_name      IN VARCHAR2 DEFAULT NULL,
    apply_result_schema_name    IN VARCHAR2 DEFAULT NULL,
    target_schema_name          IN VARCHAR2 DEFAULT NULL,
    cost_matrix_schema_name     IN VARCHAR2 DEFAULT NULL
    score_criterion_type        IN VARCHAR2 DEFAULT 'PROBABILITY');
```

Using the Decision Tree model created earlier in this chapter, the following example shows how to create the lift for this model using the testing data set and the view DEMO_CLASS_DT_TEST_RESULTS created earlier that contains the results

from applying the model. The lift results are stored in a new table called DEMO_
CLASS_DT_LIFT.

```
BEGIN
    DBMS_DATA_MINING.COMPUTE_LIFT (
        apply_result_table_name       => 'demo_class_dt_test_results',
        target_table_name             => 'mining_data_test_v',
        case_id_column_name           => 'cust_id',
        target_column_name            => 'affinity_card',
        lift_table_name               => 'DEMO_CLASS_DT_LIFT',
        positive_target_value         => '1',
        score_column_name             => 'PREDICTED_VALUE',
        score_criterion_column_name   => 'PROBABILITY',
        num_quantiles                 => 10,
        cost_matrix_table_name        => null,
        apply_result_schema_name      => null,
        target_schema_name            => null,
        cost_matrix_schema_name       => null,
        score_criterion_type          => 'PROBABILITY');
END;
/
```

After you run the preceding code, the quantile lift results are stored in the
DEMO_CLASS_DT_LIFT table. This table has a number of attributes, and the core
set of these, illustrated in the following SQL, shows the main lift results.

```
SELECT  quantile_number,
        probability_threshold,
        gain_cumulative,
        quantile_total_count
FROM    demo_class_dt_lift;
```

QUANTILE_NUMBER	PROBABILITY_THRESHOLD	GAIN_CUMULATIVE	QUANTILE_TOTAL_COUNT
1	.736625514	.1025641	24
2	.736625514	.205128199	24
3	.736625514	.307692317	24
4	.736625514	.410256398	24
5	.736625514	.508547003	23
6	.736625514	.606837582	23
7	.736625514	.705128211	23
8	.736625514	.803418791	23
9	.736625514	.90170942	23
10	.736625514	1	23

Computing the ROC

To calculate the ROC for the model, you use the COMPUTE_ROC procedure that is
part of the PL/SQL package DBMS_DATA_MINING. The ROC is a measurement
of the false positive rate against the true positive rate. It can be used to assess the
impact of changes to the probability threshold for a model. The probability threshold
is the decision point used by the model for predictions. The ROC can be used to

determine an appropriate probability threshold. This can be achieved by examining the true positive fraction and the false positive fraction. The true positive fraction is the percentage of all positive cases in the test data set that were correctly predicted as positive. The false positive fraction is the percentage of negative cases in the test data set that were incorrectly predicted as positive.

The procedure requires two sets of inputs that consist of the predictions (Case ID as well as Prediction and Probabilities) and the actual target values from the testing data set (Case ID and the target attribute). The syntax of the procedure is as follows:

```
DBMS_DATA_MINING.COMPUTE_ROC (
    roc_area_under_curve            OUT NUMBER,
    apply_result_table_name         IN VARCHAR2,
    target_table_name               IN VARCHAR2,
    case_id_column_name             IN VARCHAR2,
    target_column_name              IN VARCHAR2,
    roc_table_name                  IN VARCHAR2,
    positive_target_value           IN VARCHAR2,
    score_column_name               IN VARCHAR2 DEFAULT 'PREDICTION',
    score_criterion_column_name     IN VARCHAR2 DEFAULT 'PROBABILITY',
    apply_result_schema_name        IN VARCHAR2 DEFAULT NULL,
    target_schema_name              IN VARCHAR2 DEFAULT NULL);
```

Using the Decision Tree model that was created earlier in the chapter, the following example shows how to create the ROC statistics for this model using the testing data set and the view created previously (DEMO_CLASS_DT_TEST_RESULTS) that contains the results from applying the model. The ROC results are stored in a new table called DEMO_CLASS_DT_ROC.

```
set serveroutput on

DECLARE
    v_area_under_curve NUMBER;
BEGIN
    DBMS_DATA_MINING.COMPUTE_ROC (
        roc_area_under_curve            => v_area_under_curve,
        apply_result_table_name         => 'demo_class_dt_test_results',
        target_table_name               => 'mining_data_test_v',
        case_id_column_name             => 'cust_id',
        target_column_name              => 'affinity_card',
        roc_table_name                  => 'DEMO_CLASS_DT_ROC',
        positive_target_value           => '1',
        score_column_name               => 'PREDICTED_VALUE',
        score_criterion_column_name     => 'PROBABILITY');
    DBMS_OUTPUT.PUT_LINE('**** AREA UNDER ROC CURVE ****: ' ||
        ROUND(v_area_under_curve,4));
END;
/
**** AREA UNDER ROC CURVE ****: .5
```

After you run the preceding code, the ROC results are stored in the DEMO_CLASS_DT_ROC table. This table has a number of attributes, and the core set of these, illustrated in the following SQL, shows the main ROC results.

```
SELECT probability,
       true_positive_fraction,
       false_positive_fraction
FROM   demo_class_dt_roc;
```

Applying the Model to New Data

This section shows you how to use the classification models produced in this chapter and the classification models that were produced using the Oracle Data Miner tool. Chapter 8 illustrated how you can apply a classification model to new data. This functionality is very simple to use, but at some point you may want to productionize your code. You need to embed the calling and scoring of new data in your applications as you are gathering the data or processing a record.

The Oracle Database offers two main ways of doing this. The first is to use the SQL functions PREDICTION and PREDICTION_PROBABILITY to score data as you are gathering it in your applications. The second way is to process a number of records in batch mode. This may be as part of an end-of-day process when you want to score your data and then perform another operation based on the outputs of this process. To do this, you use the APPLY procedure that is part of the DBMS_DATA_MINING package. The outputs of using this procedure are persisted as a table in the database.

Applying the Model in Real Time

With real-time data scoring, you can score the data as you are capturing it. This feature is particularly useful for applications where you need to score or label a data as it is being entered into an application. An example of this is when you are entering the details of a new customer. As you are entering the values in each field in the application, Oracle Data Mining can be used to determine whether this customer will be a high-value customer or a low-value customer, or whether you can make certain offers. Oracle has built this kind of functionality into a lot of its Fusion Applications.

There are two functions that you can use. The first is the PREDICTION function. This function returned the predicted value based on the input data and the Oracle Data Mining model. The second function is PREDICTION_PROBABILITY. This returns a value, in the range 0 to 1, that indicates how strong a prediction Oracle thinks it has made.

The PREDICTION function returns the best prediction for the given model and the data inputted. The syntax of the function is as follows:

```
PREDICTION ( model_name, USING attribute_list);
```

The attribute list can be a list of attributes from a table. The ODM model then processes the values in these attributes to make the prediction. This function processes one record at a time to make the prediction, and your query determines the number of records to process. The following example illustrates how the PREDICTION function can be used to score data that already exists in a table:

```
SELECT cust_id, PREDICTION(DEMO_CLASS_DT_MODEL USING *)
FROM   mining_data_apply_v
WHERE  rownum <= 8;

   CUST_ID PREDICTION(DEMO_CLASS_DT_MODELUSING*)
---------- ------------------------------------
    100001                                    0
    100002                                    0
    100003                                    0
    100004                                    0
    100005                                    1
    100006                                    0
    100007                                    0
    100008                                    0
```

The preceding example uses the Decision Tree model, DEMO_CLASS_DT_MODEL, that you created in the previous section. The USING * takes all the attributes and feeds their values into the Decision Tree model to make the prediction.

You can also use the PREDICTION function in the WHERE clause to restrict which records are returned from a query:

```
SELECT cust_id
FROM   mining_data_apply_v
WHERE  PREDICTION(DEMO_CLASS_DT_MODEL USING *) = 1
AND    rownum <= 8;

   CUST_ID
----------
    100005
    100009
    100012
    100026
    100029
    100034
    100035
    100036
```

The second function that you can use is PREDICTION_PROBABILITY. This function has the same syntax as the PREDICTION function. The syntax of the function is as follows:

```
PREDICTION_PROBABILITY ( model_name, USING attribute_list);
```

The PREDICTION_PROBABILITY function returns a value between 0 and 1 and is a measure of how strong a prediction ODM thinks it has made. You can use the function in the SELECT and the WHERE parts of a query, just as with the PREDICTION function:

```
SELECT cust_id,
       PREDICTION(DEMO_CLASS_DT_MODEL USING *) Predicted_Value,
       PREDICTION_PROBABILITY(DEMO_CLASS_DT_MODEL USING *) Prob
FROM   mining_data_apply_v
WHERE  rownum <= 8;

   CUST_ID PREDICTED_VALUE          PROB
---------- ---------------    ----------
    100001               0    .952191235
    100002               0    .952191235
    100003               0    .952191235
    100004               0    .952191235
    100005               1    .736625514
    100006               0    .952191235
    100007               0    .952191235
    100008               0    .952191235
```

These functions can also be used on data as it is being captured. In this type of scenario, the data is not in a table. Instead, you can feed the actual values being captured into the PREDICTION and PREDICTION_PROBABILITY functions:

```
SELECT prediction(DEMO_CLASS_DT_MODEL
            USING 'F' AS cust_gender,
                62 AS age,
            'Widowed' AS cust_marital_status,
                'Exec.' as occupation,
                2 as household_size,
                3 as yrs_residence)  Predicted_Value,
            prediction_probability(DEMO_CLASS_DT_MODEL, 0
                USING 'F' AS cust_gender,
                62 AS age,
            'Widowed' AS cust_marital_status,
                'Exec.' as occupation,
                2 as household_size,
                3 as yrs_residence) Predicted_Prob
FROM dual;

PREDICTED_VALUE PREDICTED_PROB
--------------- ---------------
              0       .935768262
```

As you capture more data or change some of the values, the functions return an updated value from the data mining model.

Applying the Model in Batch

Applying an ODM model in batch mode involves using the APPLY procedure in the PL/SQL package DBMS_DATA_MINING. The main difference with using this package and procedure is that the outputs are stored in a new table in your schema. This method is best suited to scenarios where you want to process a number of records in a batch or offline work. Table 15-5 describes the parameters of the APPLY procedure, and its syntax is as follows:

```
DBMS_DATA_MINING.APPLY (
     model_name              IN VARCHAR2,
     data_table_name         IN VARCHAR2,
     case_id_column_name     IN VARCHAR2,
     result_table_name       IN VARCHAR2,
     data_schema_name        IN VARCHAR2 DEFAULT NULL);
```

The table or view that contains the data to be scored (data_table_name) needs to be in the same format and have the same column names as the original data source used to create the ODM model. Any data processing that was performed separately from the data processing performed by the model also needs to be performed before you run the APPLY procedure.

The results from the APPLY procedure are stored in a new table (result_ table_name). The APPLY procedure creates this new table and determines which attributes this new table will contain. Table 15-6 describes the attributes that the results table contains for the classification models.

Parameter	Description
model_name	This is the name of the Oracle Data Mining model you want to use to score the data.
data_table_name	This parameter sets the name of the table or view that contains the data to be scored.
case_id_column_name	This is the Case ID attribute name.
result_table_name	This specifies the name of the table that will be created to store the results.
data_schema_name	This is the name of the schema that contains the data to be scored. If the table or view is in your schema, you can leave this parameter out or set it to NULL.

TABLE 15-5. *APPLY Function Parameters*

Columns	Description
Case ID	This is the Case ID attribute name from the data set to be scored.
PREDICTION	This attribute contains the predicted target attribute value.
PROBABILITY	This contains the prediction probability for the prediction.

TABLE 15-6. *Classification Model Attributes*

The results table (`result_table_name`) contains a record for each of the possible target variable values. In the case where you have two target variable values (0 or 1), you get two records in the results table for each record in the APPLY data set (`data_table_name`). For each of these records, the table gives the prediction probability of each prediction. You can then use this information to decide how you want to process the data.

Using the previously built Decision Tree model, the following example illustrates using the APPLY procedure to score the data in MINING_DATA_APPLY_V. The results table (DEMO_DT_DATA_SCORED) contains the output from the APPLY procedure.

```
BEGIN
    dbms_data_mining.APPLY(model_name         => 'DEMO_CLASS_DT_MODEL',
                           data_table_name    => 'MINING_DATA_APPLY_V',
                           case_id_column_name => 'CUST_ID',
                           result_table_name  => 'DEMO_DT_DATA_SCORED');
END;
/
SELECT *
FROM   demo_dt_data_scored
WHERE  rownum <= 10;

   CUST_ID PREDICTION PROBABILITY
---------- ---------- -----------
    100001          0 .952191235
    100001          1 .047808765
    100002          0 .952191235
    100002          1 .047808765
    100003          0 .952191235
    100003          1 .047808765
    100004          0 .952191235
    100004          1 .047808765
    100005          1 .736625514
    100005          0 .263374486
```

There are two possible target values in the DEMO_CLASS_DT_MODEL data mining model. MINING_DATA_APPLY_V has 1,500 records. The results table, DEMO_DT_ DATA_SCORED, has 3,000 records. A record is created for each of the target values and has the associated prediction probability for each possible target value.

Summary

Classification is a very powerful data mining technique and has many possible application areas. As your skills with data mining develop, you can use the many functions and procedures that are available in the database. Using these in-database functions and procedures, you can build data mining models and use a variety of methods to evaluate the models. Integrating the use of the data mining models into your organization's applications is a relatively simple task. Your Oracle developers can write some simple SQL code to use the data mining models in your database. This chapter included many examples that show how you can create data mining models, test them, evaluate them, and use these models to score new data.

CHAPTER
16

Clustering

C
lustering is one of the main types of data mining that you can use to discover patterns or groupings in your data. Clustering is an undirected data mining technique that discovers what records in your data set are related to each other. Chapter 9 looked at how you can build cluster models using the Oracle Data Miner tool and apply one of these models to new data. In this chapter, you learn how you can perform the same steps using the functions available in PL/SQL and SQL. By the end of this chapter, you should be able to use the PL/SQL and SQL functions to build and apply a cluster model and to investigate the properties of a cluster model.

Setting Up Your Data

For solving clustering problems, as with all data mining techniques in Oracle, you need a case table or view. The case table or view contains the data set you want to use to build your cluster data mining models. This case table should contain the following:

- One record per case

- One attribute as the primary key or the Case ID

Most of the work in preparing the case table or view can be completed using SQL and PL/SQL programs. These take data from various sources and merge the data together to form one record to represent a case. These programs then work out the value for the target variable.

In addition to writing programs to do this processing, you may also want to reformat the data in a variety of ways. The reformatting may include creating different bins for certain attributes, transforming values from one format to a different format, and so on.

Oracle has a feature called Automatic Data Preparation (ADP). This has a number of built-in data processing functions that are dependent on the data mining algorithm being processed. By default, ADP is turned on when you are using the Oracle Data Mining tool, but when you are using the PL/SQL functions to create a model, you need to turn it on explicitly.

Table 16-1 shows the ADP performed for the classification algorithms.

Algorithm	ADP Performed
K-Means	Numerical attributes are normalized with outlier-sensitive normalization.
O-Cluster	Numerical attributes are binned with a specialized form of equi-width binning, which computes the number of bins per attribute automatically. Numerical columns with all NULLs or a single value are removed.
Expectation Maximization	Non-nested single-column numerical columns that are modelled with Gaussian distributions are normalized with outlier-sensitive normalization. ADP has no effect on the other types of columns.

TABLE 16-1. *ADP Performed for Classification Algorithms*

Viewing Your Existing Cluster Models

Oracle Data Miner comes with a number of Data Dictionary views that allow you to see the details of what data mining models you have in your schema. The following example shows you how you can use the ALL_MINING_MODELS view to see what cluster models already exist in your schema. The models displayed are those that were created in Chapter 9.

```
column model_name format a22
column mining_function format a17
column algorithm format a20
SELECT model_name,
       mining_function,
       algorithm,
       build_duration,
       model_size
FROM ALL_MINING_MODELS
WHERE mining_function = 'CLUSTERING';


MODEL_NAME                   MINING_FUNCTION   ALGORITHM              BUILD_DURATION MODEL_SIZE
---------------------------- ----------------- ---------------------- -------------- ----------
CLUS_OC_1_19                 CLUSTERING        O_CLUSTER                          67     .9353
CLUS_KM_1_19                 CLUSTERING        KMEANS                             65     .3317
CLUS_KMEANS_5_CLUSTERS       CLUSTERING        KMEANS                             65     .3317
CLUS_EM_1_19                 CLUSTERING        EXPECTATION_MAXIMIZA               66     .3371
```

NOTE
You may have model names, settings, and values that differ from those shown in the examples in this chapter.

Using the `ALL_MINING_MODEL_SETTINGS` view, you can also look at the model settings that Oracle Data Miner produced for each cluster model. The following examples show the settings for the K-Means model produced in Chapter 9 when you created the cluster models using the Oracle Data Miner tool:

```
column setting_value format a20
SELECT setting_name,
       setting_value,
       setting_type
FROM   all_mining_model_settings
WHERE  model_name = 'CLUS_KM_1_19';


SETTING_NAME                     SETTING_VALUE        SETTING
-------------------------------- -------------------- -------
KMNS_BLOCK_GROWTH                2                    INPUT
CLUS_NUM_CLUSTERS                10                   INPUT
ALGO_NAME                        ALGO_KMEANS          INPUT
KMNS_NUM_BINS                    10                   INPUT
PREP_AUTO                        ON                   INPUT
KMNS_CONV_TOLERANCE              0.01                 INPUT
KMNS_MIN_PCT_ATTR_SUPPORT        0.1                  INPUT
KMNS_DISTANCE                    KMNS_EUCLIDEAN       INPUT
KMNS_SPLIT_CRITERION             KMNS_VARIANCE        INPUT
KMNS_ITERATIONS                  3                    INPUT
```

To see what attributes are used in the K-Means model, you can use the `ALL_MINING_MODEL_ATTRIBUTES` view:

```
column attribute_name format a25
SELECT attribute_name,
       attribute_type,
       usage_type,
       target
FROM   all_mining_model_attributes
WHERE  model_name = 'CLUS_KM_1_19';


ATTRIBUTE_NAME            ATTRIBUTE_T USAGE_TY TAR
------------------------- ----------- -------- ---
HAS_CHILDREN              CATEGORICAL ACTIVE   NO
LTV                       NUMERICAL   ACTIVE   NO
REGION                    CATEGORICAL ACTIVE   NO
SALARY                    NUMERICAL   ACTIVE   NO
AGE                       NUMERICAL   ACTIVE   NO
T_AMOUNT_AUTOM_PAYMENTS   NUMERICAL   ACTIVE   NO
CREDIT_BALANCE            NUMERICAL   ACTIVE   NO
N_TRANS_TELLER            NUMERICAL   ACTIVE   NO
CREDIT_CARD_LIMITS        NUMERICAL   ACTIVE   NO
HOUSE_OWNERSHIP           CATEGORICAL ACTIVE   NO
BUY_INSURANCE             CATEGORICAL ACTIVE   NO
...
```

Settings Table

To use the cluster data mining algorithms to build a model, you need to list the settings you want to use for each algorithm. To specify the settings, you need to create a table that contains one record for each setting. The settings table has two attributes:

- **setting_name** This contains the name of the setting parameter.

- **setting_value** This parameter contains the value of the setting parameter.

You can define the name of the settings table. As you may have a number of these settings tables in your schema, you need to ensure that each has a unique name and that the name is meaningful.

The settings table must have a minimum of two records in it. One of these records specifies the algorithm that you want to use when building the cluster model, and the second record specifies whether you want to use the ADP feature. ADP is turned on automatically when you are using the Oracle Data Miner tool, but when you are using the CREATE_MODEL PL/SQL function, ADP is turned off by default.

The following example gives the code to create a settings table and inserts three settings records. The first record tells you that a K-Means algorithm should be used to create the cluster model, the second record turns on the ADP, and the third record sets the number of clusters to build to 10:

```
-- create the settings table for a Decision Tree model
CREATE TABLE demo_clus_kmeans_settings
( setting_name   VARCHAR2(30),
  setting_value VARCHAR2(4000));

-- insert the settings records for a K-Means Cluster model
-- ADP is turned on. By default ADP is turned off.
-- Set the number of clusters to generate to 10
BEGIN
  INSERT INTO demo_clus_kmeans_settings (setting_name, setting_value)
  VALUES (dbms_data_mining.algo_name, dbms_data_mining.ALGO_KMEANS);

  INSERT INTO demo_clus_kmeans_settings (setting_name, setting_value)
  VALUES (dbms_data_mining.prep_auto, dbms_data_mining.PREP_AUTO_ON);

  INSERT INTO demo_clus_kmeans_settings (setting_name, setting_value)
  VALUES (dbms_data_mining.clus_num_clusters, 10);
END;
/
```

```
SELECT *
FROM    demo_clus_kmeans_settings;

SETTING_NAME                       SETTING_VALUE
------------------------------     --------------------
ALGO_NAME                          ALGO_KMEANS
PREP_AUTO                          ON
CLUS_NUM_CLUSTERS                  10
```

If you want to perform your own data preparation, then you can omit the second INSERT statement or you can change the setting value to PREP_AUTO_OFF.

You need to create a separate settings table for each algorithm you want to use. In this example, you are only specifying the settings for creating a K-Means model. If you want to create additional cluster models at the same time, then you need to create a separate settings table for each of the other algorithms.

Table 16-2 describes the algorithms available in Oracle.

Each algorithm has its own settings. Table 16-3 shows the settings for each classification algorithm and its default settings.

In addition to the settings specific to the various cluster algorithms, there is the CLUS_NUM_CLUSTERS setting that is common for all the cluster algorithms. The value for this setting should be a number greater or equal to 1. You can use this parameter setting to specify the number of leaf clusters that the clustering algorithm is to generate. For K-Means and O-Cluster algorithms, you get the exact number of clusters specified by CLUS_NUM_CLUSTERS. For the Expectation Maximization algorithm, you may get fewer clusters than CLUS_NUM_CLUSTERS specifies. The default value for CLUS_NUM_CLUSTERS is 10.

If you do not specify any of the preceding cluster algorithm settings, then Oracle uses the built-in default settings for the algorithm you are using.

Algorithm Name	Description
ALGO_KMEANS	K-Means (enhanced)
ALGO_OCLUSTER	O-Cluster
ALGO_EXPECTATION_MAXIMIZATION	Expectation Maximization

TABLE 16-2. *Oracle Algorithms*

Algorithm	Setting	Values and Default Value
K-Means	KMNS_BLOCK	This is the growth factor of the memory allocation to hold the cluster data. Data values are greater than 1 and less than or equal to 5. The default value is 2.
	KMNS_CONV_TOLERANCE	A smaller convergence tolerance means a greater likelihood of an optimal solution, but this can also increase the run time. This setting can have a value between 0 and 0.25. The default value is 0.01.
	KMNS_DISTANCE	This setting specifies the distance calculation to use. The allowed values are KMNS_COSINE, KMNS_EUCLIDEAN, and KMNS_FAST_COSINE. The default value is KMNS_EUCLIDEAN.
	KMNS_ITERATIONS	This is the number of iterations for the K-Means algorithm. Can have values between 1 and 20. The default is 3
	KMNS_MIN_PCT_ATTR_SUPPORT	This setting is used to determine whether an attribute should be included in the rule generated. The setting can have values between 0 and 1. The default value is 0.1.
	KMNS_MUM_BINS	This setting specifies the number of bins in the attribute histogram that is produced by k-Means. The binning method used is equi-width, and the bin boundaries for each attribute are set globally on the entire training data set. The setting can have any number greater than 0. The default number of bins is 10.

TABLE 16-3. *Oracle Algorithm Settings* (continued)

Algorithm	Setting	Values and Default Value
	KMNS_SPLIT_CRITERION	The split criterion controls when new clusters are created. When the split criterion is based on size, the new cluster is placed in the area where the largest current cluster is located. When the split criterion is based on variance, the new cluster is placed in the area of the most spreadout cluster. The allowed values are KMNS_SIZE and KMNS_VARIANCE. The default value is KMNS_VARIANCE.
O-Cluster	OCLT_MAX_BUFFER	This specifies the maximum size of the buffer for the O-Cluster algorithm. The value should be greater than 0. The default setting is 50,000.
	OCLT_SENSITIVITY	This setting's value specifies the peak density required for separating a new cluster. The value should be between 0 and 1. The default value is 0.5.
Expectation Maximization	EMCS_CLUSTER_COMPONENTS	This parameter enables or disables the grouping of components into high-level clusters. When the parameter is disabled, the components are treated as clusters. When it is enabled, the model scoring through the SQL CLUSTER function produces assignments to the higher-level clusters. The allowed values are EMCS_CLUSTER_COMP_ENABLE and EMCS_CLUSTER_COMP_DISABLE. The default value is EMCS_CLUSTER_COMP_ENABLE.

TABLE 16-3. *Oracle Algorithm Settings* (continued)

Algorithm	Setting	Values and Default Value
	EMCS_CLUSTER_THRESH	This is the dissimilarity threshold that controls the clustering components. When this measure is less than the threshold, the components are combined into a single cluster. The value should be greater than or equal to 1. The default value is 2.
	EMCS_LINKAGE_FUNCTION	This setting details a linkage function for the agglomerative clustering step. The possible values are EMCS_LINKAGE_SINGLE, EMCS_LINKAGE_AVERAGE, and EMCS_LINKAGE_COMPLETE. The default value is EMCS_LINKAGE_SINGLE.

TABLE 16-3. *Oracle Algorithm Settings*

You can specify the built-in default settings for each algorithm. The following example illustrates how to query the default setting for the K-Means algorithm:

```
column setting_value format a35
SELECT *
FROM    table(dbms_data_mining.get_default_settings)
WHERE   setting_name like 'KMNS%';


SETTING_NAME                      SETTING_VALUE
-------------------------------   ----------------------
KMNS_BLOCK_GROWTH                 2
KMNS_CONV_TOLERANCE               .01
KMNS_DISTANCE                     KMNS_EUCLIDEAN
KMNS_ITERATIONS                   3
KMNS_MIN_PCT_ATTR_SUPPORT         .1
KMNS_NUM_BINS                     10
KMNS_SPLIT_CRITERION              KMNS_VARIANCE
```

A similar query can be written to list the default setting for the O-Cluster algorithm (using 'OCLT%') and for the Expectation Maximization algorithm (using 'EMCS%').

Creating a Cluster Model

To create a new cluster model, you use the CREATE_MODEL procedure that is part of the DBMS_DATA_MINING package. The CREATE_MODEL procedure accepts the parameters described in Table 16-4.

Parameter	Description
`model_name`	This setting specifies a meaningful name that you want to give to the model you are creating.
`mining_function`	This is the data mining function you want to use. The possible values are `ASSOCIATION`, `ATTRIBUTE_IMPORTANCE`, `CLASSIFICATION`, `CLUSTERING`, `FEATURE_EXTRACTION`, and `REGRESSION`.
`data_table_name`	This setting specifies the name of the table or view that contains the build data set.
`case_id_column_name`	This is the Case ID (PK) for the build data set.
`target_column_name`	This setting enables you to set the name of the target attribute in the build data set.
`settings_table_name`	This specifies the name of the settings table.
`data_schema_name`	This parameter sets the schema where the build data set is located. This can be left `NULL` if the build data set is in the current schema.
`settings_schema_name`	This is the schema where the settings table is located. This can be left `NULL` if the settings table is in the current schema.
`xform_list`	If you have a set of transformations you want to embed into the model, you can specify them here. These transformations can be instead of or in conjunction with the transformations performed by the ADP.

TABLE 16-4. *CREATE_MODEL Procedure Parameters*

The syntax of the CREATE_MODEL procedure is as follows:

```
DBMS_DATA_MINING.CREATE_MODEL (
    model_name              IN VARCHAR2,
    mining_function         IN VARCHAR2,
    data_table_name         IN VARCHAR2,
    case_id_column_name     IN VARCHAR2,
    target_column_name      IN VARCHAR2 DEFAULT NULL,
    settings_table_name     IN VARCHAR2 DEFAULT NULL,
    data_schema_name        IN VARCHAR2 DEFAULT NULL,
    settings_schema_name    IN VARCHAR2 DEFAULT NULL,
    xform_list              IN TRANSFORM_LIST DEFAULT NULL);
```

The following examples show you how to create a K-Means cluster model using the same data set that was used in Chapter 9 to build some cluster models. You can update the following examples to use the other clustering algorithms, O-Cluster and Expectation Maximization.

In the following examples, you create a Decision Tree based on the same data set you used in Chapter 9. The table that contains the data set is called INSUR_CUST_LTV_ SAMPLE. You created this table when you created the DMUSER schema to access the ODM Repository and sample schemas in Chapter 3. The INSUR_CUST_LTV_SAMPLE table contains records for an example financial company. Each customer has one record and contains some personal, demographic, account, customer interaction, and life time value (LTV) information and indicates whether the customer has bought insurance in the past. The following examples build a clustering model that identifies groupings or clusters that exist in the data set.

To create the k-Means cluster model, you use the CREATE_MODEL function. The following example illustrates how this procedure can be used to create the K-Means model using the settings table that was illustrated in the section "Settings Table" earlier in this chapter:

```
BEGIN
    DBMS_DATA_MINING.CREATE_MODEL(
        model_name          => 'CLUSTER_KMEANS_MODEL',
        mining_function     => dbms_data_mining.CLUSTERING,
        data_table_name     => 'INSUR_CUST_LTV_SAMPLE',
        case_id_column_name => 'CUSTOMER_ID',
        target_column_name  => null,
        settings_table_name => 'DEMO_CLUS_KMEANS_SETTINGS');
END;
/
```

If you want to create a number of cluster models using the other cluster algorithms, or to create separate models using the same algorithm but using different settings, then you need to have a separate settings table for each of your models. You then need to execute the CREATE_MODEL command for each model. For example, if you want to create several K-Means cluster models using different settings, you can use the preceding example and then change the name of the model (MODEL_NAME) and the name of the settings table (SETTINGS_TABLE_NAME). The following example illustrates the settings table and CREATE_MODEL command to generate an O-Cluster model for the same data set.

CAUTION
Depending on the version of the Oracle documentation you are using, the documentation may say to use ALGO_O_CLUSTER. It should say to use ALGO_OCLUSTER.

```
-- create the settings table for an O-Cluster model
CREATE TABLE demo_clus_ocluster_settings
( setting_name  VARCHAR2(30),
  setting_value VARCHAR2(4000));

-- insert the settings records for an O-Cluster model
-- ADP is turned on. By default ADP is turned off.
-- Change the OCLT_SENSITIVITY setting to 0.3. The default value is 0.5
-- Set the number of clusters to generate to 6
BEGIN
  INSERT INTO demo_clus_ocluster_settings (setting_name, setting_value)
  VALUES (dbms_data_mining.algo_name, dbms_data_mining.ALGO_OCLUSTER);

  INSERT INTO demo_clus_ocluster_settings (setting_name, setting_value)
  VALUES (dbms_data_mining.prep_auto, dbms_data_mining.PREP_AUTO_ON);

  INSERT INTO demo_clus_ocluster_settings (setting_name, setting_value)
  VALUES (dbms_data_mining.oclt_sensitivity, 0.3);

  INSERT INTO demo_clus_ocluster_settings (setting_name, setting_value)
  VALUES (dbms_data_mining.clus_num_clusters, 6);
END;
/

BEGIN
    DBMS_DATA_MINING.CREATE_MODEL(
        model_name          => 'CLUSTER_OCLUSTER_MODEL',
        mining_function     => dbms_data_mining.CLUSTERING,
        data_table_name     => 'INSUR_CUST_LTV_SAMPLE',
        case_id_column_name => 'CUSTOMER_ID',
        target_column_name  => null,
        settings_table_name => 'DEMO_CLUS_OCLUSTER_SETTINGS');
END;
/
```

Examining the Cluster Model

After you have created some cluster models, you can look at what Oracle Data
Miner produces for each of these models. Some of these details include what
cluster models were produced, what their settings were, what attributes were used,
what clusters were produced, what the centroids were, and so on. In this section,
examples are given on how you can explore this kind of information about the
clusters in your schema. The examples build on and use the cluster models produced
in the previous sections.

Querying the Cluster Models in Your Schema

In a previous section, an example query was given to find out what cluster models existed in your schema. The following example is a version of this same query that looks at the details of the K-Means and O-Cluster models that were created in the previous section:

```
column model_name format a22
column mining_function format a15
column algorithm format a15
SELECT model_name,
       mining_function,
       algorithm,
       build_duration,
       model_size
FROM ALL_MINING_MODELS
WHERE model_name in ('CLUSTER_OCLUSTER_MODEL','CLUSTER_KMEANS_MODEL');


MODEL_NAME              MINING_FUNCTION ALGORITHM       BUILD_DURATION MODEL_SIZE
----------------------- --------------- --------------- -------------- ----------
CLUSTER_OCLUSTER_MODEL  CLUSTERING      O_CLUSTER                   62     1.8436
CLUSTER_KMEANS_MODEL    CLUSTERING      KMEANS                      19      .8543
```

NOTE
You need to change the names of the models used in this chapter to the names of the models you created in your schema.

To see the settings of each of these cluster models, you can use the following query:

```
break on model_name skip 1
column model_name format a22
column setting_name format a25
column setting_value format a20
SELECT model_name,
       setting_name,
       setting_value,
       setting_type
FROM   all_mining_model_settings
WHERE model_name in ('CLUSTER_OCLUSTER_MODEL','CLUSTER_KMEANS_MODEL')
ORDER BY model_name;


MODEL_NAME              SETTING_NAME              SETTING_VALUE         SETTING
----------------------- ------------------------- --------------------- -------
CLUSTER_KMEANS_MODEL    ALGO_NAME                 ALGO_KMEANS           INPUT
                        KMNS_SPLIT_CRITERION      KMNS_VARIANCE         DEFAULT
                        KMNS_DISTANCE             KMNS_EUCLIDEAN        DEFAULT
                        KMNS_MIN_PCT_ATTR_SUPPORT .1                    DEFAULT
                        KMNS_CONV_TOLERANCE       .01                   DEFAULT
                        KMNS_BLOCK_GROWTH         2                     DEFAULT
```

```
                            CLUS_NUM_CLUSTERS        10                    INPUT
                            KMNS_ITERATIONS          3                     DEFAULT
                            KMNS_NUM_BINS            10                    DEFAULT
                            PREP_AUTO                ON                    INPUT

CLUSTER_OCLUSTER_MODEL      OCLT_MAX_BUFFER          50000                 DEFAULT
                            PREP_AUTO                ON                    INPUT
                            ALGO_NAME                ALGO_O_CLUSTER        INPUT
                            CLUS_NUM_CLUSTERS        6                     INPUT
                            OCLT_SENSITIVITY         .3                    INPUT
```

The results returned from this query show the settings and the values used for each of your cluster models. The last column (setting_type) tells you whether the setting value was defined in a settings table and has a value of INPUT. If no setting existed in the settings table, then the default value for that setting, as defined in the database, is used and is indicated by the value DEFAULT in the setting_type column.

To see the attributes used by each cluster model, you can use the following query:

```
break on model_name skip 1
column model_name format a22
column attribute_name format a25
SELECT model_name,
       attribute_name
FROM   all_mining_model_attributes
WHERE  model_name in ('CLUSTER_OCLUSTER_MODEL','CLUSTER_KMEANS_MODEL')
ORDER BY model_name;
```

It is important to remember that not all attributes are used by a model. The algorithms determine what attributes are used, and different models may use different sets of attributes.

Examining the Cluster Details

To examine the internals of the cluster models, you can use one of the three PL/SQL procedures:

- GET_MODEL_DETAILS_KM

- GET_MODEL_DETAILS_OC

- GET_MODEL_DETAILS_EM

These procedures perform the same type of function, but each one is specific to each type of cluster algorithm and is part of the DBMS_DATA_MINING PL/SQL package.

The example SQL code and outputs are for the K-Means cluster model that was developed in the section "Creating a Cluster Model" and uses the GET_MODEL_DETAILS_KM procedure. You can use the other procedures to extract similar cluster details from an O-Cluster or Expectation Maximization models.

How to View the Clusters for a Model

To see what clusters were produced and their position within the hierarchy, you can convert the outputs of the GET_MODEL_DETAILS procedure into a table from which you can select the necessary information. You can use this information to draw your own cluster hierarchy diagram.

```
set pages 80
set lines 90
column child format a40
SELECT id,
       record_count,
       parent,
       tree_level,
       child
FROM   table(dbms_data_mining.get_model_details_km('CLUSTER_KMEANS_MODEL'));

    ID RECORD_COUNT     PARENT TREE_LEVEL CHILD(ID)
---------- ------------ ---------- ---------- ----------------------------------------
     1         1015                       1 DM_CHILDREN(DM_CHILD(2), DM_CHILD(3))
     2          606          1            2 DM_CHILDREN(DM_CHILD(4), DM_CHILD(5))
     3          409          1            2 DM_CHILDREN(DM_CHILD(NULL))
     4          269          2            3 DM_CHILDREN(DM_CHILD(NULL))
     5          337          2            3 DM_CHILDREN(DM_CHILD(6), DM_CHILD(7))
     6          169          5            4 DM_CHILDREN(DM_CHILD(8), DM_CHILD(9))
     7          168          5            4 DM_CHILDREN(DM_CHILD(NULL))
     8           20          6            5 DM_CHILDREN(DM_CHILD(10), DM_CHILD(11))
     9          149          6            5 DM_CHILDREN(DM_CHILD(12), DM_CHILD(13))
    10            1          8            6 DM_CHILDREN(DM_CHILD(NULL))
    11           19          8            6 DM_CHILDREN(DM_CHILD(NULL))
    12            3          9            6 DM_CHILDREN(DM_CHILD(14), DM_CHILD(15))
    13          146          9            6 DM_CHILDREN(DM_CHILD(16), DM_CHILD(17))
    14            1         12            7 DM_CHILDREN(DM_CHILD(NULL))
    15            2         12            7 DM_CHILDREN(DM_CHILD(NULL))
    16           78         13            7 DM_CHILDREN(DM_CHILD(18), DM_CHILD(19))
    17           68         13            7 DM_CHILDREN(DM_CHILD(NULL))
    18           24         16            8 DM_CHILDREN(DM_CHILD(NULL))
    19           54         16            8 DM_CHILDREN(DM_CHILD(NULL))
```

For each record displayed in the preceding example, you can see the Cluster node number or identifier, the number of records that were in each node, the parent node, the level the node is in the cluster hierarchy, and the details of the child or subcluster that a node has.

If a cluster is a terminating node, it has DM_CHILDREN(DM_CHILD(NULL)) under the CHILD(ID) column. You can see this in the preceding example for records having IDs of 3, 4, 7, 10, 11, 14, 15, 17, 18, and 19.

When examining the nodes produced by the Cluster model, you may notice that some clusters have a very small number or percentage of the records. One thing you need to investigate is how similar or dissimilar these records are in the cluster to the other records in the other cluster for the same parent. If there is no distinctive difference between these clusters, then you might consider these clusters the same. Later in this chapter, an example will show how you can treat these clusters as one merged cluster. Currently there is no functionality in Oracle Data Mining to allow you to do some post-pruning of the clusters. An example of this is with Clusters 10 and 11 in the preceding example listing. There is only one record in Cluster 10. After some investigation, you may decide to consider both of these clusters as one.

How to View the Centroids for a Cluster

To view the centroids, you can use the same PL/SQL procedure as before, but this time you can select the centroid-related features. The following example illustrates how to select the centroid information for Cluster 7 from the K-Means model (CLUSTER_KMEANS_MODEL):

```
column attribute_name format a25
column mode_value format a25
SELECT t.id,
       c.attribute_name,
       c.mean,
       c.mode_value,
       c.variance
FROM   table (dbms_data_mining.get_model_details_KM('CLUSTER_KMEANS_MODEL')) t,
       table(t.centroid) c
WHERE t.id = 7
ORDER BY c.attribute_name;
```

ID	ATTRIBUTE_NAME	MEAN	MODE_VALUE	VARIANCE
7	AGE	33.7202381		131.759588
7	BANK_FUNDS	2141.44048		9864620.43
7	BUY_INSURANCE		No	
7	CAR_OWNERSHIP	1		0
7	CHECKING_AMOUNT	786.309524		3801920.33
7	CREDIT_BALANCE	415.97619		7411722.84
7	CREDIT_CARD_LIMITS	1324.40476		755867.907
7	FIRST		SHIPLEY	
7	HAS_CHILDREN	.916666667		.076846307
7	HOUSE_OWNERSHIP	1.05357143		.06298118
7	LAST		LOGAN	
7	LTV	20066.9673		19535064.5
7	LTV_BIN		MEDIUM	
7	MARITAL_STATUS		MARRIED	
7	MONEY_MONTLY_OVERDRAWN	53.9120238		2.93359827
7	MONTHLY_CHECKS_WRITTEN	5.08928571		23.0039564
7	MORTGAGE_AMOUNT	2322.1369		2946427.16
7	N_MORTGAGES	1.05357143		.06298118
7	N_OF_DEPENDENTS	3.27380952		2.2958369

```
7  N_TRANS_ATM              3.4702381                              2.43024665
7  N_TRANS_KIOSK            1.99404762                             3.64667094
7  N_TRANS_TELLER           2.00595238                             1.51493442
7  N_TRANS_WEB_BANK         1433.30952                             1421010.05
7  PROFESSION                           IT Staff
7  REGION                               NorthEast
7  SALARY                   63459.4762                             37138136
7  SEX                                  M
7  STATE                                NY
7  TIME_AS_CUSTOMER         3.26190476                             1.69147419
7  T_AMOUNT_AUTOM_PAYMENTS  2156.96429                             15093150.5
```

The centroid details will include the attributes that were used to form the centroid and the values for each attribute.

The Cluster Rules

To view the centroid details, you can again use the GET_MODEL_DETAILS_KM procedure with a different set of attributes. In the following example, the cluster rules are extracted for Cluster 7.

```
column value format a20
SELECT t.id,
       a.attribute_name,
       a.conditional_operator,
       nvl(a.attribute_str_value, a.attribute_num_value)  value
FROM   TABLE(dbms_data_mining.get_model_details_km
           ('CLUSTER_KMEANS_MODEL'))  t,
       TABLE(t.rule.antecedent)  a
WHERE  t.id = 7
ORDER BY t.id, a.attribute_name, attribute_support, attribute_confidence
desc, value;
```

The following listing is a subset of results returned by the preceding query. It shows the rules that are applied to each attribute to determine whether a record belongs to a cluster or not. The rules consist of a series of value ranges or a listing of values for an attribute. For example, in Cluster 7 from the K-Means model, you can see that the age range is between 16.8 and 50.39.

```
    ID ATTRIBUTE_NAME               CO VALUE
---------- ------------------------ -- --------------------
     7 AGE                          >= 16.800000000000001
     7 AGE                          <= 50.399999999999999
     7 BANK_FUNDS                   >= 0
     7 BANK_FUNDS                   <= 7199.9999999999955
     7 BUY_INSURANCE                IN No
     7 BUY_INSURANCE                IN Yes
     7 CAR_OWNERSHIP                >= .90000000000000002
     7 CAR_OWNERSHIP                <= 1
```

```
7 CHECKING_AMOUNT          <= 2370.0999999999995
7 CHECKING_AMOUNT          >= 25
7 CREDIT_BALANCE           >= 0
7 CREDIT_BALANCE           <= 17049.799999999999
7 CREDIT_CARD_LIMITS       <= 1850
7 CREDIT_CARD_LIMITS       >= 500
7 FIRST                    IN ALVARADO
7 FIRST                    IN ARELLANO
...
```

For a new record, all clusters are evaluated to see which cluster the record should belong to. In the next section of this chapter, examples are given of how to apply a cluster model to new data.

Applying the Cluster Model to New Data

This section is divided into two main sections. The first of these sections looks at what SQL functions are available. These functions allow you to discover what cluster a new record belongs to and other details associated with the cluster. The second section looks at how you can label a set of records, in batch mode, with their corresponding cluster values. An example is given of how to use a PL/SQL procedure to apply a cluster model in batch mode.

Applying the Cluster Model in Real Time

With real-time labeling of data, you can apply a cluster model to a single record or as the data is being captured in your applications. An example of this is when you are entering the details of a new customer and want to use the cluster model to determine what segmentation or cluster they belong to. As you are entering the values in each field in the application, Oracle Data Mining can be used to determine whether this customer is a high-value or low-value customer.

Oracle Data Miner has a number of SQL functions that can be used to extract cluster information about new data. Table 16-5 describes each SQL function.

The attribute list can be a list of attributes from a table or a set of data values. The ODM model then processes the values in these attributes to make the cluster prediction. The following examples illustrate how you can use each of these SQL functions and what type of data each function returns.

The following SQL query shows an example of using the CLUSTER_ID, CLUSTER_PROBABILITY, and CLUSTER_DISTANCE functions for three of the records in the INSUR_CUST_LTV_SAMPLE table. The cluster model that is being used in this SQL is one of the K-Means cluster models that was developed using the

SQL Function	Description
CLUSTER_ID	This returns the Cluster ID or label of the predicted cluster. CLUSTER_ID (MODEL_NAME USING *attribute_list*)
CLUSTER_PROBABILITY	Gives the probability of the data/record being part of the given cluster. CLUSTER_PROBABILITY (MODEL_NAME, CLUSTER_ID *attribute_list*)
CLUSTER_DETAILS	Gives detailed information about the predicted cluster. CLUSTER_DETAILS (MODEL_NAME, CLUSTER_ID *attribute_list*)
CLUSTER_DISTANCE	Gives the distance, for the given data/record, from the centroid to the predicted cluster. CLUSTER_DISTANCE (MODEL_NAME, CLUSTER_ID *attribute_list*)
CLUSTER_SET	Returns the list of possible clusters that the given data/record can belong to and the associated probability for each predicted cluster. CLUSTER_SET (MODEL_NAME attribute_list)

TABLE 16-5. *ODM SQL Functions for Extracting Clusters*

Oracle Data Miner tool in SQL Developer (see Chapter 9). For that cluster model, labels were assigned to some of the clusters to give them a meaningful name.

```
column customer_id format a15
column cluster_id format a25
column cluster_prob format 999.999
column cluster_distance format 999.999
SELECT customer_id,
       cluster_id(clus_km_1_19 USING *) as Cluster_Id,
       cluster_probability(clus_km_1_19 USING *) as cluster_Prob,
       cluster_distance(clus_km_1_19 USING *) as cluster_Distance
FROM   insur_cust_ltv_sample
WHERE  customer_id in ('CU13386', 'CU6607', 'CU100');


CUSTOMER_ID     CLUSTER_ID               CLUSTER_PROB CLUSTER_DISTANCE
--------------- ------------------------ ------------ ----------------
CU13386         14                               .996          232.731
CU6607          Long Term Value Customers        .998          230.665
CU100           Short Term Value Customer        .850          227.469
```

If you want to see all the possible clusters that a set of data or a record can belong to, you can use the CLUSTER_SET function. The following example illustrates how you can use this function in a query and shows the corresponding output:

```
column customer_id format a15
column cluster_id format a25
column probability format 9.999999
SELECT t.customer_id, s.cluster_id, s.probability
FROM    (SELECT customer_id, cluster_set(clus_km_1_19 USING *)
    AS Cluster_Set
        FROM    insur_cust_ltv_sample
        WHERE   customer_id in ('CU13386', 'CU100')) T,
            TABLE(T.cluster_set) S
ORDER BY t.customer_id, s.probability desc;
```

CUSTOMER_ID	CLUSTER_ID	PROBABILITY
CU100	Short Term Value Customer	.850116
CU100	14	.088546
CU100	Long Term Value Customers	.061005
CU100	19	.000224
CU100	18	.000103
CU100	12	.000004
CU100	15	.000003
CU100	16	.000000
CU100	13	.000000
CU100	10	.000000
CU13386	14	.996251
CU13386	Short Term Value Customer	.002626
CU13386	Long Term Value Customers	.001118
CU13386	15	.000003
CU13386	19	.000002
CU13386	12	.000000
CU13386	18	.000000
CU13386	16	.000000
CU13386	13	.000000
CU13386	10	.000000

You can see from the preceding output that by using CLUSTER_SET, you get a record for each of the clusters that exist in the model. The cluster model used was set up to generate ten clusters. When you use the CLUSTER_SET function, it generates a record of each cluster and determines the probability that the record belongs to a cluster. When you use the CLUSTER_ID function, only one record is returned: the record for the cluster that the record has the highest probability of belonging to.

To see what attributes were involved in determining the cluster for a record, you can use the CLUSTER_DETAILS function. This function outputs in XML format the attributes, the values used, the weighting applied, and the rank of the attributes.

The following query outputs these details for Customer CU13386, using Cluster 14 in the Cluster model `CLUS_KM_1_19`:

```
column cluster_details format a50
SELECT cluster_details(clus_km_1_19, 14 USING *) as Cluster_Details
FROM    insur_cust_ltv_sample
WHERE   customer_id = 'CU13386';
```

CAUTION
If you run this query in SQL*Plus, it may not display all of the output. If you run the same query in SQL Developer, you need to select the output and then select the pencil icon to view the outputs, or you can copy and paste the output.

When this query is run in SQL Developer, you get the results shown in Figure 16-1. These functions can also be used on data as it is being captured. In this type of scenario, you do not have the data in a table. Instead, you can feed the actual values being captured into the functions, and the cluster details can be updated in real time on your application screens. The following examples illustrate how these data values can be passed to the `CLUSTER_ID` and `CLUSTER_PROBABILITY` functions:

```
SELECT cluster_id(clus_km_1_19
            USING 3 time_as_customer,
                  0 has_children,
                  3 n_of_dependents,
                  'OK' state,
                  1 n_trans_teller )  CLUSTER_ID,
        cluster_probability(clus_km_1_19
            USING 3 time_as_customer,
                  0 has_children,
                  3 n_of_dependents,
                  'OK' state,
                  1 n_trans_teller )  Cluster_Prob
FROM dual;

CLUSTER_ID               CLUSTER_PROB
------------------------ ------------
14                               .999
```

As you capture more data or change some of the values, the functions can be rerun and will return an updated value based on the cluster data mining model.

Applying the Cluster Model in Batch Mode

Applying a cluster model in batch mode involves using the `APPLY` procedure in the PL/SQL package `DBMS_DATA_MINING`. When you use this procedure to label a data set, the outputs are stored in a new table in your schema. This method is best suited

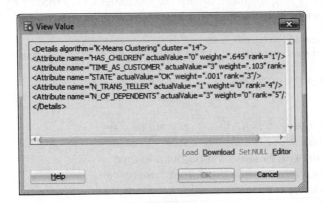

FIGURE 16-1. *Output from the* `CLUSTER_DETAILS` *function when viewed in SQL Developer*

to scenarios where you want to process a number of records in a batch or offline work. The syntax of the `APPLY` procedure is as follows:

```
DBMS_DATA_MINING.APPLY (
    model_name          IN VARCHAR2,
    data_table_name     IN VARCHAR2,
    case_id_column_name  IN VARCHAR2,
    result_table_name   IN VARCHAR2,
    data_schema_name    IN VARCHAR2 DEFAULT NULL);
```

Table 16-6 describes the parameters of the `APPLY` procedure.

Parameter	Description
`model_name`	This is the name of the Oracle Data Mining model you want to use to score the data.
`data_table_name`	This parameter sets the name of the table or view that contains the data to be scored.
`case_id_column_name`	This is the Case ID attribute name.
`result_table_name`	This setting specifies the name of the table that will be created to store the results.
`data_schema_name`	This is the name of the schema that contains the data to be scored. If the table or view is in your schema, you can leave this parameter out or set it to `NULL`.

TABLE 16-6. `APPLY` *Procedure Parameters*

Columns	Description
CASE_ID	This is the Case ID attribute name from the data set to be labeled.
CLUSTER_ID	This column contains the predicted cluster ID.
PROBABILITY	This contains the cluster probability.

TABLE 16-7. *Results Table Contents for Classification Models*

The table or view that contains the data to be labeled (data_table_name) needs to be in the same format and have the same column names as the original data source used to create the cluster model. Any data processing that was performed separately to the data before building the cluster model also needs to be performed before you run the APPLY procedure.

The results from the APPLY procedure are stored in a new table (result_table_ name). The procedure creates this new table and determines what attributes this new table will contain. Table 16-7 describes what attributes the results table contains for the classification models.

The results table (result_table_name) contains a record for each of the possible clusters in the model. If your cluster model contains ten clusters, then you get ten records per original case records (in data_table_name). You can then use this information to decide how you want to process the data.

Using the previously built K-Means cluster model, the following example illustrates using the APPLY procedure to label the data in the INSUR_CUST_LTV_ SAMPLE table. The results table (DEMO_KMEANS_DATA) contains the output from the APPLY procedure.

```
BEGIN
    dbms_data_mining.APPLY(model_name          => 'CLUS_KM_1_19',
                           data_table_name     => 'INSUR_CUST_LTV_SAMPLE',
                           case_id_column_name => 'CUSTOMER_ID',
                           result_table_name   => 'DEMO_KMEANS_DATA');
END;
/

column customer_id format a20
column cluster_id  format a25
column probability format 999.999
SELECT *
FROM   demo_kmeans_data
WHERE  rownum <= 40
ORDER BY customer_id, probability desc;
```

CUSTOMER_ID	CLUSTER_ID	PROBABILITY
CU13386	14	.996
CU13386	Short Term Value Customer	.003
CU13386	Long Term Value Customers	.001
CU13386	15	.000
CU13386	19	.000
...		
CU13388	15	.899
CU13388	18	.101
CU13388	16	.000
CU13388	14	.000
CU13388	Long Term Value Customers	.000
...		
CU6607	Long Term Value Customers	.998
CU6607	14	.002
CU6607	Short Term Value Customer	.000
CU6607	19	.000
CU6607	18	.000
...		
CU7331	15	.940
CU7331	18	.059
CU7331	14	.001
CU7331	16	.000
CU7331	Short Term Value Customer	.000
...		

NOTE
*Only a subset of the output from the DEMO_KMEANS_
DATA is shown in the output listing. Each customer
would have had ten records that correspond to the
ten clusters that exist in the CLUS_KM_1_19 cluster
model.*

Combining Clusters

When processing a case record or recording data in your application, you can use
the preceding SQL and PL/SQL code to determine what cluster it belongs to. After
building your cluster model, you analyze it to work out what each cluster actually
means. As part of this post-processing, you may discover that two or more of the
clusters are very similar and could be merged into one cluster. At this point, there is
no facility to merge clusters into a new cluster. To overcome this, you can use some
code like an IF, DECODE, or CASE statement to perform this step.

For example, if you have discovered that Clusters 10 and 11 in the CLUSTER_ KMEANS_MODEL contain the same type of data, then you can consider them to be one cluster and use an IF statement in your PL/SQL code to determine what should happen next:

```
IF cluster_id in ('10', '11') THEN
...
END IF;
```

Summary

Clustering is one of the main types of data mining that you can use to discover patterns or groupings in your data. Clustering is an undirected data mining technique that discovers what records in your data set are related to each other. This chapter looked at the steps required to set up, build, and apply a cluster model to your data. In this chapter, examples were given on how to perform these steps using the functions available in PL/SQL and SQL.

CHAPTER
17

Regression

egression is a technique that models the relationship between dependent variables and a target variable. It is used to determine or predict what the possible value will be of the target variable. In Chapter 10, examples were given showing you how to build and apply regression models using the Oracle Data Miner tool. In this chapter, you learn how you can perform the same steps using the SQL and PL/SQL procedures and functions.

Examining the Existing Regression Model(s)

Oracle Data Miner comes with a number of Data Dictionary views that allow you to see the details of what data mining models you have in your schema. The following example shows you how you can use the ALL_MINING_MODELS view to see what regression models already exist in your schema. The regression models were built using a version of the Generalized Linear Model (GLM) and the Support Vector Machine (SVM) using the Oracle Data Miner tool. To retrieve the list of regression models that already exist, you can select where the MINING_FUNCTION is equal to REGRESSION:

```
column model_name format a20
column mining_function format a15
column algorithm format a25
SELECT model_name,
       mining_function,
       algorithm,
       build_duration,
       model_size
FROM   ALL_MINING_MODELS
WHERE mining_function = 'REGRESSION';
```

MODEL_NAME	MINING_FUNCTION	ALGORITHM	BUILD_DURATION	MODEL_SIZE
REGR_GLM_1_25	REGRESSION	GENERALIZED_LINEAR_MODEL	12	.0925
REGR_SVM_1_25	REGRESSION	SUPPORT_VECTOR_MACHINES	7	.2524

The results from this query lists the regression models that were created by the workflow in Chapter 10.

To view the details of the SVM regression model, you can query the
`ALL_MINING_MODEL_SETTINGS` table:

```
column setting_value format a30
SELECT setting_name,
       setting_value,
       setting_type
FROM  all_mining_model_settings
WHERE model_name = 'REGR_SVM_1_25';
```

SETTING_NAME	SETTING_VALUE	SETTING
ALGO_NAME	ALGO_SUPPORT_VECTOR_MACHINES	INPUT
PREP_AUTO	ON	INPUT
SVMS_COMPLEXITY_FACTOR	0.450764	DEFAULT
SVMS_KERNEL_CACHE_SIZE	50000000	DEFAULT
SVMS_EPSILON	0.006248	DEFAULT
SVMS_KERNEL_FUNCTION	SVMS_GAUSSIAN	INPUT
SVMS_ACTIVE_LEARNING	SVMS_AL_ENABLE	INPUT
SVMS_STD_DEV	2.971519	DEFAULT
SVMS_CONV_TOLERANCE	0.001	INPUT

You can run a similar query to see what the model settings were for the GLM
regression model by changing the WHERE clause to use the GLM regression model
name.

To see what attributes were used in the regression model, you can use the
following query. The results from this query list the input attributes that were used to
build the regression model. In addition to viewing these attributes, you can also see
what attribute was used as the target. In this case, you see the last record in the
results has the ATTRIBUTE_NAME of LTV and the target column set to YES. You can
also see that the non-target attribute lists NO for each attribute, as illustrated in the
following example:

```
column attribute_name format a25
column target format a6
SELECT attribute_name,
       attribute_type,
       usage_type,
       target
FROM  all_mining_model_attributes
WHERE  model_name = 'REGR_SVM_1_25';
```

ATTRIBUTE_NAME	ATTRIBUTE_T	USAGE_TY	TARGET
HAS_CHILDREN	CATEGORICAL	ACTIVE	NO
REGION	CATEGORICAL	ACTIVE	NO
SALARY	NUMERICAL	ACTIVE	NO
AGE	NUMERICAL	ACTIVE	NO
T_AMOUNT_AUTOM_PAYMENTS	NUMERICAL	ACTIVE	NO

```
CREDIT_BALANCE             NUMERICAL    ACTIVE    NO
N_TRANS_TELLER             NUMERICAL    ACTIVE    NO
CREDIT_CARD_LIMITS         NUMERICAL    ACTIVE    NO
HOUSE_OWNERSHIP            CATEGORICAL  ACTIVE    NO
BUY_INSURANCE             CATEGORICAL  ACTIVE    NO
PROFESSION                CATEGORICAL  ACTIVE    NO
MORTGAGE_AMOUNT           NUMERICAL    ACTIVE    NO
N_OF_DEPENDENTS           NUMERICAL    ACTIVE    NO
CAR_OWNERSHIP             CATEGORICAL  ACTIVE    NO
N_TRANS_KIOSK             NUMERICAL    ACTIVE    NO
TIME_AS_CUSTOMER          CATEGORICAL  ACTIVE    NO
BANK_FUNDS               NUMERICAL    ACTIVE    NO
N_TRANS_WEB_BANK          NUMERICAL    ACTIVE    NO
STATE                    CATEGORICAL  ACTIVE    NO
MONTHLY_CHECKS_WRITTEN    NUMERICAL    ACTIVE    NO
SEX                      CATEGORICAL  ACTIVE    NO
CHECKING_AMOUNT          NUMERICAL    ACTIVE    NO
N_TRANS_ATM              NUMERICAL    ACTIVE    NO
MARITAL_STATUS           CATEGORICAL  ACTIVE    NO
N_MORTGAGES              CATEGORICAL  ACTIVE    NO
MONEY_MONTLY_OVERDRAWN    NUMERICAL    ACTIVE    NO
LTV                      NUMERICAL    ACTIVE    YES
```

Settings Table for Regression

To use a data mining algorithm to build a model, you need to list what settings you want to use for the algorithm. To specify the settings, you must create a table that contains one record for each setting. The settings table has two attributes:

- **setting_name** This contains the name of the setting parameter.

- **setting_value** This attribute contains the value of the setting parameter.

Typically the settings table has two records in it. One of these records specifies the algorithm that you want to use when building the model. For regression, this algorithm is Generalized Linear Model or Support Vector Machine. The second record specifies whether you want to use the Automatic Data Processing (ADP) feature. ADP is turned on automatically when you are using the Oracle Data Miner tool, but when you use the CREATE_MODEL PL/SQL function ADP is turned off by default.

The following example gives the code to create a settings table and insert three settings records. These records specify the use of the Support Vector Machine algorithm and the linear kernel function. This is similar to one of the regression models that was created using the Oracle Data Miner tool in Chapter 10.

```
-- create the settings table for a Regression model
CREATE TABLE demo_regression_settings
( setting_name   VARCHAR2(30),
  setting_value  VARCHAR2(4000));

-- insert the settings records for Regression
-- Support Vector Machine algorithm using the Linear kernel
-- ADP is turned on. By default ADP is turned off.
BEGIN
  INSERT INTO demo_regression_settings (setting_name, setting_value)
  VALUES (dbms_data_mining.algo_name, dbms_data_mining
    .algo_support_vector_machines);

  INSERT INTO demo_regression_settings (setting_name, setting_value)
  VALUES (dbms_data_mining.svms_kernel_function, dbms_data_mining
    .svms_linear);

  INSERT INTO demo_regression_settings (setting_name, setting_value)
  VALUES (dbms_data_mining.prep_auto,dbms_data_mining.prep_auto_on);
END;
/
column setting_name format a30
column setting_value format a30

SELECT *
FROM    demo_regression_settings;

SETTING_NAME                         SETTING_VALUE
------------------------------       ------------------------------
ALGO_NAME                            ALGO_SUPPORT_VECTOR_MACHINES
SVMS_KERNEL_FUNCTION                 SVMS_LINEAR
PREP_AUTO                            ON
```

NOTE
For regression, SVM is the default algorithm. You need not include the first INSERT statement in the preceding code to populate the settings table. But it is good practice to state explicitly the algorithm you want to use. There is no guarantee that the SVM will be the default algorithm in later releases of the Oracle Database.

If you want to perform your own data preparation, then you can omit the third INSERT statement or you can change the setting value to PREP_AUTO_OFF.

Table 17-1 shows the settings available for the Support Vector Machine algorithm and their default values.

The default algorithm for regression is the Support Vector Machine algorithm. Table 17-2 shows the regression algorithm names to use in the settings tables.

Algorithm	Setting	Values and Default Value
Support Vector Machine	SVMS_ACTIVE_ LEARNING	This specifies whether active learning is enabled or disabled.
		SVMS_AL_DISABLE
		SVMS_AL_ENABLE (default)
	SVMS_COMPLEXITY_ FACTOR	This setting establishes the value of the complexity factor.
		Values > 0
		Default value is estimated by the algorithm.
	SVMS_CONV_ TOLERANCE	This is the convergence tolerance for the algorithm.
		Values > 0
		0.001 (default)
	SVMS_EPSILON	This setting specifies the value of the epsilon factor.
		Values > 0
		Default value is estimated by the algorithm.
	SVMS_KERNEL_ CACHE_SIZE	This is the value of the kernel cache size and is for Gaussian kernels only.
		Values > 0
		50MB (default)
	SVMS_KERNEL_ FUNCTION	This setting establishes the kernel used by the algorithm.
		svms_gaussian
		svms_linear
		Default is determined by the algorithm.
	SVMS_STD_DEV	This is the value of standard deviation for the algorithm using the Gaussian kernel.
		Values > 0
		Default is estimated by the algorithm.
Generalized Linear Model	GLMS_CONF_LEVEL	This value sets the confidence level for the intervals.
		Values > 0 and < 1
		0.95 (default)

TABLE 17-1. *Settings for the Support Vector Machine Algorithm* (continued)

Algorithm	Setting	Values and Default Value
	GLMS_DIAGNOSTICS_ TABLE_NAME	This is the name of the table that contains row-level diagnostic information, which is created during the model build. Default is determined by the algorithm.
	GLMS_REFERENCE_ CLASS_NAME	This setting specifies the target value to be used as the reference value in a logistic regression model. Default is determined by the algorithm.
	GLMS_RIDGE_ REGRESSION	This specifies whether ridge regression is enabled. GLMS_RIDGE_REG_ENABLE GLMS_RIDGE_REG_DISABLE Default is determined by the algorithm.
	GLMS_RIDGE_VALUE	The value of the ridge parameter is used by the algorithm and should be set only when ridge regression is enabled. Values > 0 Default is determined by the algorithm if the value is set automatically; otherwise, a value must be provided.
	GLMS_VIF_FOR_ RIDGE	This specifies whether Variance Inflation Factor statistics are created when ridge is used. GLMS_VIF_RIDGE_ENABLE GLMS_VIF_EIDGE_DISABLE (default)

TABLE 17-1. *Settings for the Support Vector Machine Algorithm*

Regression Algorithm	Setting Name
Support Vector Machine	ALGO_SUPPORT_VECTOR_MACHINES
Generalized Linear Model	AwwLGO_GENERALIZED_LINEAR_MODEL

TABLE 17-2. *Regression Algorithm Names for Settings Tables*

Creating a Regression Model

To create a new regression model, you use the CREATE_MODEL procedure that is part of the DBMS_DATA_MINING package. The CREATE_MODEL procedure accepts the parameters described in Table 17-3.

Parameter	Description
model_name	This is a meaningful name that you want to give to the model you are creating.
mining_function	This parameter specifies the data mining function you want to use. The possible values are ASSOCIATION, ATTRIBUTE_IMPORTANCE, CLASSIFICATION, CLUSTERING, FEATURE_EXTRACTION, and REGRESSION.
data_table_name	This is the name of the table or view that contains the build data set.
case_id_column_name	This parameter identifies the Case ID (PK) for the build data set.
target_column_name	This is the name of the attribute that you want the regression algorithm to predict.
settings_table_name	This parameter specifies the name of the settings table.
data_schema_name	This is the schema where the build data set is located. This can be left NULL if the build data set is in the current schema.
settings_schema_name	This parameter sets the schema where the settings table is located. This can be left NULL if the settings table is in the current schema.
xform_list	If you have a set of transformations you want to embed into the model, then you can specify them here. These transformations can be instead of or in conjunction with the transformations performed by the ADP.

TABLE 17-3. *CREATE_MODEL Procedure Parameters*

The syntax of the `CREATE_MODEL` procedure is as follows:

```
DBMS_DATA_MINING.CREATE_MODEL (
    model_name                IN VARCHAR2,
    mining_function           IN VARCHAR2,
    data_table_name           IN VARCHAR2,
    case_id_column_name       IN VARCHAR2,
    target_column_name        IN VARCHAR2 DEFAULT NULL,
    settings_table_name       IN VARCHAR2 DEFAULT NULL,
    data_schema_name          IN VARCHAR2 DEFAULT NULL,
    settings_schema_name      IN VARCHAR2 DEFAULT NULL,
    xform_list                IN TRANSFORM_LIST DEFAULT NULL);
```

The following example illustrates the creation of a regression model using the same data set that was used when creating the regression model using the Oracle Data Miner tool, as described in Chapter 10. This data set is called `INSUR_CUST_LTV_SAMPLE` and contains a sample of some customer-related information. The target attribute is `LTV` and contains the life time value for the customer. The attribute `LTV_BIN` must be removed as an input to the model build process. During the data investigation stage in Chapter 10, it was discovered that the `LTV_BIN` attribute was directly correlated with the target attribute `LTV`. The simplest way to do this is to create a view that does not include this attribute. The view can also be used to remove any other attributes that should not be used as input to the model build process.

In addition to removing attributes, you can use the view to define any new attributes that should be included. Such attributes might come from other tables or be created as part of the data preparation stage.

The following view is created on the `INSUR_CUST_LTV_SAMPLE` table and includes only the attributes that are needed as inputs to the model build process:

```
CREATE or REPLACE VIEW   INSUR_CUST_LTV_SAMPLE_V
as SELECT CUSTOMER_ID,
        LAST,
        FIRST,
        STATE,
        REGION,
        SEX,
        PROFESSION,
        BUY_INSURANCE,
        AGE,
        HAS_CHILDREN,
        SALARY,
        N_OF_DEPENDENTS,
        CAR_OWNERSHIP,
        HOUSE_OWNERSHIP,
        TIME_AS_CUSTOMER,
        MARITAL_STATUS,
```

```
       CREDIT_BALANCE,
       BANK_FUNDS,
       CHECKING_AMOUNT,
       MONEY_MONTLY_OVERDRAWN,
       T_AMOUNT_AUTOM_PAYMENTS,
       MONTHLY_CHECKS_WRITTEN,
       MORTGAGE_AMOUNT,
       N_TRANS_ATM,
       N_MORTGAGES,
       N_TRANS_TELLER,
       CREDIT_CARD_LIMITS,
       N_TRANS_KIOSK,
       N_TRANS_WEB_BANK,
       LTV
FROM INSUR_CUST_LTV_SAMPLE;
```

When you have finished preparing all your data for input to the regression algorithm, the new step is to prepare the CREATE_MODEL statement to create the regression model. The following example illustrates the creation of a regression model using the SVM algorithm, using the settings table that was created in the section "Settings Table for Regression" earlier in this chapter and the INSUR_CUST_LTV_SAMPLE_V view that was created in the preceding example:

```
BEGIN
    DBMS_DATA_MINING.CREATE_MODEL(
        model_name            => 'DEMO_REGRESSION_MODEL',
        mining_function       => dbms_data_mining.regression,
        data_table_name       => 'INSUR_CUST_LTV_SAMPLE_V',
        case_id_column_name   => 'CUSTOMER_ID',
        target_column_name    => 'LTV',
        settings_table_name   => 'demo_regression_settings');
END;
/
```

When the preceding CREATE_MODEL code has completed, your regression model has been created. You can view the details of the regression model using the following query, which is similar to the query given earlier in this chapter. The following query retrieves the results for the newly created regression model called DEMO_REGRESSION_MODEL:

```
column model_name format a25
column setting_name format a22
column setting_value format a28
SELECT model_name,
       setting_name,
       setting_value,
       setting_type
FROM  all_mining_model_settings
WHERE model_name in ('DEMO_REGRESSION_MODEL');
```

MODEL_NAME	SETTING_NAME	SETTING_VALUE	SETTING
DEMO_REGRESSION_MODEL	ALGO_NAME	ALGO_SUPPORT_VECTOR_MACHINES	INPUT
DEMO_REGRESSION_MODEL	PREP_AUTO	ON	INPUT
DEMO_REGRESSION_MODEL	SVMS_COMPLEXITY_FACTOR	0.457947	DEFAULT
DEMO_REGRESSION_MODE	SVMS_EPSILON	0.005209	DEFAULT
DEMO_REGRESSION_MODEL	SVMS_KERNEL_FUNCTION	SVMS_LINEAR	INPUT
DEMO_REGRESSION_MODEL	SVMS_ACTIVE_LEARNING	SVMS_AL_ENABLE	DEFAULT
DEMO_REGRESSION_MODEL	SVMS_CONV_TOLERANCE	.001	DEFAULT

In the query results displayed in the preceding listing, you see listed under the last column (SETTING) the algorithm settings specified using the settings table. These algorithm settings are listed with the SETTING value of INPUT. The other algorithm settings are listed with the SETTING value of DEFAULT. These are the default settings that are defined in the database. If you would like to use a different value for the algorithm setting, then you can define the new value in the settings table. For example, if you want to use a smaller kernel cache size, you can add a new statement to the settings table. The following example shows the settings table that was created earlier in this chapter in the section "Settings Table for Regression" and now includes the new algorithm setting for the kernel cache size. You can do this with all of the other algorithm settings.

```
-- insert the settings records for Regression
-- Support Vector Machine algorithm using the Linear kernel
-- ADP is turned on. By default ADP is turned off.
-- Kernel Cache Size is set to 10,000,000
DELETE FROM demo_regression_settings;
BEGIN
  INSERT INTO demo_regression_settings (setting_name, setting_value)
  VALUES (dbms_data_mining.algo_name, dbms_data_mining.algo_support_vector_machines);

  INSERT INTO demo_regression_settings (setting_name, setting_value)
  VALUES (dbms_data_mining.svms_kernel_function, dbms_data_mining.svms_gaussian);

  INSERT INTO demo_regression_settings (setting_name, setting_value)
  VALUES (dbms_data_mining.prep_auto, dbms_data_mining.prep_auto_on);

  INSERT INTO demo_regression_settings (setting_name, setting_value)
  VALUES (dbms_data_mining.SVMS_KERNEL_CACHE_SIZE, 10000000);
END;
/
```

If you now drop the `DEMO_REGRESSION_MODEL`, use the preceding `CREATE_MODEL` code to re-create the regression model, and query the model settings, you will see that the kernel cache size is now set as being an `INPUT`.

Examining and Evaluating the Regression Models

After you have created your regression models, you want to examine them to see what statistical information has been created about their performance. In this section of the chapter, examples are given on how you can extract statistical information for the different regression models. The statistical information consists of some global statistics and the details of the coefficients produced by the different regression algorithms. The final section gives example code that you can use to calculate the residual value along with some additional statistics.

Global Statistics for a GLM Regression Model

For each of the Generalized Linear Models produced, a set of statistical information is produced for the model. These sets are referred to as global statistics for the model. To generate the global statistics for your regression model, you use the `GET_MODEL_DETAILS_GLOBAL` procedure that is part of the `DBMS_DATA_MINING` PL/SQL package. In the following example, this procedure is used to list the global statistics that were produced for the GLM regression model that was created in Chapter 10 using the Oracle Data Miner tool.

NOTE
You need to rename the regression model in the following code to match the name of your GLM regression model.

```
SELECT *
FROM TABLE(DBMS_DATA_MINING.GET_MODEL_DETAILS_GLOBAL('REGR_GLM_1_25'));

GLOBAL_DETAIL_NAME                GLOBAL_DETAIL_VALUE
-------------------------------   -------------------
ADJUSTED_R_SQUARE                          .880371328
AIC                                        9767.07435
COEFF_VAR                                  9.89335454
CORRECTED_TOTAL_DF                                624
CORRECTED_TOT_SS                            2.6171E+10
DEPENDENT_MEAN                             22640.7936
```

```
ERROR_DF                                      481
ERROR_MEAN_SQUARE                       5017304.24
ERROR_SUM_SQUARES                       2413323340
F_VALUE                                  32.498929
GMSEP                                   6522462.07
HOCKING_SP                              10452.7172
J_P                                     6173291.14
MODEL_CONVERGED                                  1
MODEL_DF                                       143
MODEL_F_P_VALUE                                  0
MODEL_MEAN_SQUARE                        163057015
MODEL_SUM_SQUARES                       2.3317E+10
NUM_PARAMS                                     144
NUM_ROWS                                       625
ROOT_MEAN_SQ                            2239.93398
R_SQ                                     .907786232
SBIC                                    10406.1106
VALID_COVARIANCE_MATRIX                          0
```

GET_MODEL_DETAILS_GLOBAL generates a set of global statistics for models produced using the GLM Linear Regression, GLM Logistic Regression, Association Rules, Singular Value Decomposition, and Expectation Maximization algorithms.

CAUTION
No global statistics are produced for SVM regression models.

Table 17-4 briefly describes the global statistics that are produced for a GLM regression model.

GLM Regression Model Details

When a model is created, it is very useful to be able to see some of the details of what was used to create it. In particular, it is useful to see the attributes and the values of these attributes that were used to model the values in the target attribute. For the GLM regression model, you can use the GET_MODEL_DETAILS_GLM procedure that is part of the DBMS_DATA_MINING PL/SQL package.

The GET_MODEL_DETAILS_GLM procedure returns the results as a DM_GLM_COEFF_SET record. Table 17-5 describes the columns that are part of the record.

As the results are retuned as a pipelined set of rows, you need to convert this into a table so that you can select the individual columns that you require from the results. The following code example shows you how you can retrieve the details

Global Detail Name	Description
ADJUSTED_R_SQUARE	Adjusted R Squared
AIC	Akaike's information criterion
COEFF_VAR	Coefficient of variation
CORRECTED_TOTAL_DF	Corrected total degrees of freedom
CORRECTED_TOT_SS	Corrected total sum of squares
DEPENDENT_MEAN	Dependent mean
ERROR_DF	Error degrees of freedom
ERROR_MEAN_SQUARE	Error mean square
ERROR_SUM_SQUARES	Error sum of squares
F_VALUE	Model F value statistic
GMSEP	Estimated mean square error of the prediction, assuming multivariate normality
HOCKING_SP	Hocking Sp statistic
J_P	JP statistic (the final prediction error)
MODEL_CONVERGED	Whether or not the model converged. Value is 1 if it converged, or 0 if it did not converge.
MODEL_DF	Model degrees of freedom
MODEL_F_P_VALUE	Model F value probability
MODEL_MEAN_SQUARE	Model mean square
MODEL_SUM_SQUARES	Model sum of squares
NUM_PARAMS	Number of parameters (the number of coefficients, including the intercept)
NUM_ROWS	Number of rows
ROOT_MEAN_SQ	Root mean square error
R_SQ	R-Square
SBIC	Schwarz's Bayesian information criterion
VALID_COVARIANCE_MATRIX	Valid covariance matrix. Value is 1 if the covariance matrix was computed, or 0 if it was not computed.

TABLE 17-4.   *GLM Regression Model Global Statistics*

Column Name	Description
class	For linear regression, class is NULL. This column shows the nonreference target class for logistic regression. The model is built to predict the probability of this class.
attribute_name	This is the name of the column in the case table that is the source for this attribute.
attribute_subname	This column presents the name of an attribute in a nested table. The full name of a nested attribute has the following form: attribute_name.attribute_subname
attribute_value	This is the value of the attribute (categorical attribute only). For numerical attributes, attribute_value is NULL.
feature_expression	This column shows the feature name constructed by the algorithm when feature selection is enabled. If feature selection is not enabled, the feature name is simply the fully qualified attribute name.
coefficient	This is the linear coefficient estimate.
std_error	This column shows the standard error of the coefficient estimate.
test_statistic	For linear regression, this column shows the t-value of the coefficient estimate. For logistic regression, it presents the Wald chi-square value of the coefficient estimate.
p-value	This is the probability of the test_statistic.
VIF	This column shows the Variance Inflation Factor.
std_coefficient	This is the standardized estimate of the coefficient.
lower_coeff_limit	This column shows the lower confidence bound of the coefficient.
upper_coeff_limit	This is the upper confidence bound of the coefficient.
exp_lower_coeff_limit	This column presents the exponentiated coefficient for logistic regression. For linear regression, exp_coefficient is NULL.
exp_upper_coeff_limit	This is the exponentiated coefficient for the lower confidence bound of the coefficient for logistic regression. For linear regression, exp_lower_coeff_limit is NULL.

TABLE 17-5. *DM_GLM_COEFF_SET Record Columns*

using the `GET_MODEL_DETAILS_GLM` procedure and converts the returned record
set into a table:

```
column a_name format a25
column a_value format a20
SELECT attribute_name   a_name,
       attribute_value  a_value,
       coefficient
FROM   TABLE(DBMS_DATA_MINING.GET_MODEL_DETAILS_GLM('REGR_GLM_1_25'))
ORDER BY attribute_name;
```

```
A_NAME                        A_VALUE                COEFFICIENT
------------------------      --------------------   -----------
AGE                                                  203.533322
BANK_FUNDS                                           -.03323057
BUY_INSURANCE                 Yes                     226.284958
CAR_OWNERSHIP                 0                       540.361199
CHECKING_AMOUNT                                       .004345663
CREDIT_BALANCE                                        .036816482
CREDIT_CARD_LIMITS                                   -.21786797
HAS_CHILDREN                  0                       4437.61057
HOUSE_OWNERSHIP               0                      -5064.0571
HOUSE_OWNERSHIP               2                       5046.55705
MARITAL_STATUS                DIVORCED               -270.17779
MARITAL_STATUS                MARRIED                -108.98981
MARITAL_STATUS                WIDOWED                -1024.3533
MARITAL_STATUS                OTHER                   -1448.456
MONEY_MONTLY_OVERDRAWN                                37.9941179
MONTHLY_CHECKS_WRITTEN                               -4.9701817
MORTGAGE_AMOUNT                                       .11054341
N_MORTGAGES                   0                      -5064.0571
N_MORTGAGES                   2                       5046.55705
N_OF_DEPENDENTS                                      -1790.3756
N_TRANS_ATM                                           67.5936553
N_TRANS_KIOSK                                        -21.433238
...
```

SVM Regression Model Details

For your SVM regression models that were developed using a linear kernel, you can
use the `GET_MODEL_DETAILS_SVM` to produce the details of the attributes and the
coefficient values. The syntax of the `GET_MODEL_DETAILS_SVM` procedure is as
follows:

```
DBMS_DATA_MINING.GET_MODEL_DETAILS_SVM (
         model_name          VARCHAR2,
         reverse_coef        NUMBER DEFAULT 0)
RETURN DM_SVM_LINEAR_COEFF_SET PIPELINED;
```

The main difference between this procedure and the equivalent one for the GLM model is that there is an extra parameter for the procedure. If you do not provide a value for the second parameter, the procedure uses the default value of 0. The REVERSE_COEF parameter tells the procedure whether it should transform the attribute coefficients using the original attribute transformations, if any were applied. The default value (0) returns the coefficients directly from the model without applying transformations. The alternative value is 1, which transforms the coefficients and bias by applying the normalization shifts and scales that were generated using Automatic Data Preparation.

The following code illustrates how GET_MODEL_DETAILS_SVM can be used with the regression model DEMO_REGRESSION_MODEL created earlier in this chapter in the section "Creating a Regression Model":

```
column class format a15
column a_name a15
column a_value a20
SELECT b.attribute_name    a_name,
       b.attribute_value   a_value,
       b.coefficient
FROM   TABLE(DBMS_DATA_MINING
          .GET_MODEL_DETAILS_SVM('DEMO_REGRESSION_MODEL')) a,
       TABLE(a.attribute_set) b
ORDER BY attribute_name;
```

```
A_NAME                    A_VALUE                COEFFICIENT
------------------------- ---------------------- -----------
AGE                                               .370096093
BANK_FUNDS                                        -.01677132
BUY_INSURANCE             No                      -.00340701
BUY_INSURANCE             Yes                     .003407006
CAR_OWNERSHIP                                     -.01627262
CHECKING_AMOUNT                                   -.02204768
CREDIT_BALANCE                                    -.01261996
CREDIT_CARD_LIMITS                                .011360529
FIRST                     GARRETT                 .025560527
FIRST                     GARCIA                  .019473246
FIRST                     GANT                    -.00394772
FIRST                     GANN                    .008764073
FIRST                     GALLEGOS                .017398125
FIRST                     GALINDO                 .003894159
FIRST                     GAGNE                   -.01165459
FIRST                     GAGE                    -.04762246
FIRST                     FULTON                  .002868996
FIRST                     FRY                     -.00794215
```

The records returned by GET_MODEL_DETAILS_SVM contain a nested table, which is why a set TABLE is required in the preceding query.

Column Name	Description
class	For SVM regression models, class is NULL. For classification, it contains the target attribute.
attribute_set	This column contains a nested table of type DM_SVM_ATTRIBUTE_SET.

TABLE 17-6. *DM_SVM_LINEAR_COEFF_SET Record Columns*

The GET_MODEL_DETAILS_SVM procedure returns the results as a DM_SVM_LINEAR_COEFF_SET record that contains a nested table of type DM_SVM_ATTRIBUTE_SET. Table 17-6 describes the columns that are part of the record.

Table 17-7 describes the columns that are part of the nested table of type DM_SVM_ATTRIBUTE_SET.

CAUTION
GET_MODEL_DETAILS_SVM returns the model details for SVM models with a linear kernel. If the model was developed using the Gaussian kernel, an error message is displayed. This problem may be resolved in later releases of the Oracle Database.

Column Name	Description
attribute_name	This is the name of the column in the case table that is the source for this attribute.
attribute_subname	This column shows the name of an attribute in a nested table. The full name of a nested attribute has the following form: attribute_name.attribute_subname
attribute_value	This is the value of the attribute (categorical attribute only). For numerical attributes, attribute_value is NULL.
coefficient	This column presents the coefficient estimate.

TABLE 17-7. *DM_SVM_ATTRIBUTE_SET Columns*

Residual Statistics

The residual is a measure of the difference between the expected or actual values and the predicted value of the target attribute. The larger the value of the residual, the less accurate the model is; the smaller the residual, the more accurate the model is. Figure 17-1 shows a graphical representation of the residuals produced by the REGR_GLM_1_25 model that was produced in Chapter 10 using the Oracle Data Miner tool.

In SQL, you can calculate the residual values and compare them with the actual values, but without the graphical representation that is shown in Figure 17-1. In Chapter 10, a portion of the data set was used to build the regression model, whereas a separate portion was kept to test the regression model. The testing consisted of applying the regression model against this separated data set. The model was used to predict a value for the target attribute. The testing data set already contained the values for the target attribute. The residual graph in Figure 17-1 shows the predicted value versus the residual value.

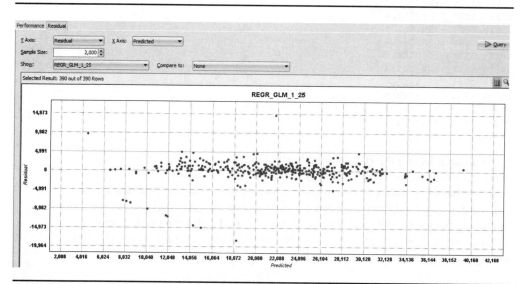

FIGURE 17-1. *Residual graph of the GLM regression model produced by the Oracle Data Miner tool*

The following SQL code calculates the residual values for the training data set `CUST_INSUR_LTV_SAMPLE`. The code creates a view that returns the predicted value for the LTV as determined by the regression model. It also returns the residual value, which is the difference between the actual value and the predicted value. The code shows these values being calculated and retrieved using a database view.

```
create or replace view demo_regression_residual
as
SELECT PREDICTION(regr_glm_1_25 using *)  prediction,
       (LTV - PREDICTION(regr_glm_1_25 using *)) residual
FROM   insur_cust_ltv_sample;

SELECT * FROM demo_regression_residual;

PREDICTION   RESIDUAL
----------   ----------
18781.0169  -1160.0169
22413.8775  -230.87746
19027.2418  -221.99182
21448.8259  1125.92411
15853.0091   1364.2409
  16605.09  -464.33997
23368.1799  1523.07014
20028.7027  -790.45267
17501.6189  3096.13106
20243.8024   -690.8024
34090.4592  -904.70916
23504.0044  706.495564
23524.8744  2.12559855
30179.9768  25.0231699
26003.7435  -3043.2435
8439.27387  -679.77387
```

You can now use the database view given in the preceding code example to generate a residual graph using the Graph node that is part of the Oracle Data Miner tool. In Chapter 5, examples were given showing how you can produce various graphs of your data. Using the steps outlined in that chapter, you can create a scatter plot using the view DEMO_REGRESSION_RESIDUAL to plot the prediction value against the residual. Figure 17-2 shows the residual graph based on the database view generated by the preceding code.

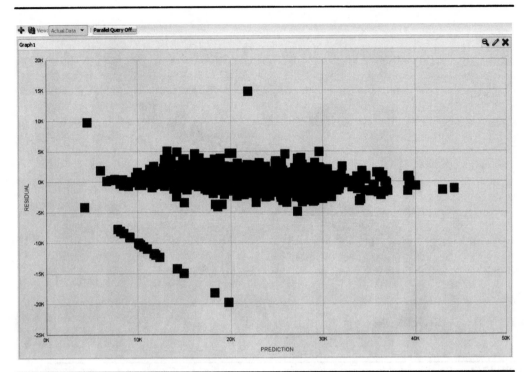

FIGURE 17-2. *Residual scatter plot using the Graph node in the Oracle Data Miner tool*

Figure 17-3 shows the graph of the predicted value versus the actual value. This graph was created using the Graph node in the Oracle Data Miner tool. The graph is very similar to the one shown in Figure 10-16 of Chapter 10.

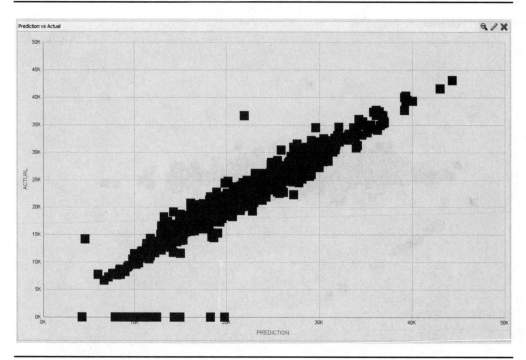

FIGURE 17-3. *Predicted value versus the actual value, using the Graph node in the Oracle Data Miner tool*

Applying Regression Model to Your Data

In this section, examples are given showing you how to use the regression model produced in this chapter and Chapter 10 using the Oracle Data Miner tool. In Chapter 10, it was illustrated how you can apply a regression model to your data set. In this chapter, examples are given to illustrate how you can use these models in a real-time mode using the PREDICTION SQL function. In addition, an example is given on how you can apply the regression model in batch mode. This is useful when you have data that is delivered to your organization at certain points during the day.

Using the Regression Model in Real Time

There are two distinct ways of using the regression model in real time. The first of these is the examining of the data that already exists in your database. The PREDICTION function can be used to return the predicted value based on the input data and the Oracle data mining model.

The following example illustrates the use of the PREDICTION function using ten records from the INSUR_CUST_LTV_SAMPLE data set. This query returns some of the details of the records and the predicted LTV value. The regression model produced earlier in this chapter in the section "Creating a Regression Model" is used to predict the LTV.

```
column customer_id format a15
SELECT customer_id,
       prediction(demo_regression_model USING *) LTV_Prediction
FROM   insur_cust_ltv_sample
WHERE  rownum <= 10;


CUSTOMER_ID     LTV_PREDICTION
--------------- ---------------
CU13388             17872.0492
CU13386              22411.216
CU6607              18570.1446
CU7331              22361.2987
CU2624               17001.589
CU6389              15915.5384
CU100               24657.4547
CU8653              19034.9674
CU2639              20367.0652
CU1330              19764.5298
```

Although the data set contains a lot of attributes, by defining the model to use USING *, it tells the PREDICTION function to use only the attributes that have been defined in the model.

Another scenario where you might want to use your regression model in real time in your applications is when capturing your data so you can make a regression prediction. In this type of scenario, the data is not in a table, so you need to input these attributes and the values to the model. The following example illustrates how you can calculate the LTV of a customer as the data is being recorded in the application. As you capture more data, you can update the prediction value by rerunning the query with additional inputs.

```
SELECT prediction(DEMO_REGRESSION_MODEL
            USING 'MI' AS STATE,
                  'M' AS SEX,
                  '70' AS AGE,
                  '2' AS N_OF_DEPENDENTS,
                  '0' AS MORTGAGE_AMOUNT)  LTV_Prediction
FROM dual;
LTV_PREDICTION
--------------
    29447.6679
```

Using the Regression Model in Batch Mode

Applying an ODM model in batch mode involves using the APPLY procedure in the PL/SQL package DBMS_DATA_MINING. The main difference with using this package and procedure is that the output is stored in a new table in your schema. This method is best suited to scenarios where you want to process a number of records in batch mode or offline work. There have been examples of the syntax and structure of the APPLY procedure in previous chapters.

The APPLY procedure creates the results in a new table. The structure of this new table contains two attributes. The first of these is the CASE ID that is specified as a parameter to the APPLY procedure. This attribute allows you to link the records generated by the APPLY procedure back to the original data. The second attribute that is created is called PREDICTION, which contains the predicted value of the target attribute.

In the following example, the INSUR_CUST_LTV_SAMPLE data set has the regression model that was created earlier in this chapter in the section "Creating a Regression Model" applied to it using the APPLY procedure. The APPLY procedure creates a new table in your schema that contain the results. In this example, the new table is called DEMO_LTV_PREDICTION.

```
BEGIN
    dbms_data_mining.APPLY(model_name          => 'DEMO_REGRESSION_MODEL',
                           data_table_name     => 'INSUR_CUST_LTV_SAMPLE',
                           case_id_column_name => 'CUSTOMER_ID',
                           result_table_name   => 'DEMO_LTV_PREDICTION');
END;
/

column customer_id format a15
SELECT *
FROM   demo_ltv_prediction
WHERE  rownum <=10;

CUSTOMER_ID       PREDICTION
---------------   ----------
CU13388           17872.0492
CU13386            22411.216
CU6607            18570.1446
CU7331            22361.2987
CU2624             17001.589
CU6389            15915.5384
CU100             24657.4547
CU8653            19034.9674
CU2639            20367.0652
CU1330            19764.5298
...
```

The sample output from the DEMO_LTV_PREDICTION table shows that only one record is created by the APPLY procedure for each case record. This is different from the other scenarios of using the APPLY procedure illustrated in this book. For the other data mining models, the APPLY procedure typically creates two records for each case record.

Summary

Regression can be used in a variety of ways, from identifying the values of missing data to predicting important numerical values of attributes in your data. In this chapter, an example was given showing how you can build a regression model to predict the life time value of a customer. The regression model took into account the other attributes that were part of the data set and determined how they contribute toward predicting the required attribute. Regression is another data mining technique that is available for you to use either individually or in conjunction with the data mining techniques.

CHAPTER
18

Anomaly Detection

A nomaly detection is a useful technique to apply to your data to discover whether your data includes any anomalous case records. These anomalous case records could represent fraudulent activity or activity that warrants further investigation. In Chapter 11, examples were given showing you how to build and apply an anomaly detection model to your data using the Oracle Data Miner tool. In this chapter, you learn how you can perform the same steps using the functions available in PL/SQL and SQL. The CLAIMS data set used in this chapter is the same as was used in Chapter 11.

Examining the Existing Anomaly Detection Model(s)

Oracle Data Miner comes with a number of Data Dictionary views that allow you to see the details of what data mining models you have in your schema. The following example shows how you can use the ALL_MINING_MODELS view to see what anomaly detection models already exist in your schema. The anomaly detection models are built using a version of the Support Vector Machine (SVM) that is used for classification. So when you are looking for your anomaly detection models, if you just search for the models created using the SVM algorithm, then you find a lot of classification models listed. To narrow the list down to just anomaly detection models, you need to look for one of the settings that is only used for anomaly detection. This setting is called SVMS_OUTLIER_RATE. This is the anomaly detection percentage setting and has a default value of 0.1, or 10 percent. The following query looks for models that were built using an SVM and the anomaly detection percentage setting:

```
column model_name format a22
column mining_function format a17
column algorithm format a23
SELECT  a.model_name,
        a.mining_function,
        a.algorithm,
        a.build_duration,
        a.model_size
FROM    ALL_MINING_MODELS          A,
        ALL_MINING_MODEL_SETTINGS  B
WHERE   a.model_name = b.model_name
AND     a.algorithm = 'SUPPORT_VECTOR_MACHINES'
AND     b.setting_name = 'SVMS_OUTLIER_RATE';
```

MODEL_NAME	MINING_FUNCTION	ALGORITHM	BUILD_DURATION	MODEL_SIZE
ANOM_SVM_1_19	CLASSIFICATION	SUPPORT_VECTOR_MACHINES	6	.0808

The results from this query list the anomaly detection model that was created by the workflow in Chapter 11.

To view the details of the anomaly detection model, you can query the `ALL_MINING_MODEL_SETTINGS` table, as follows:

```
column setting_value format a30
SELECT  setting_name,
        setting_value,
        setting_type
FROM   all_mining_model_settings
WHERE  model_name = 'ANOM_SVM_1_19';
```

SETTING_NAME	SETTING_VALUE	SETTING
ALGO_NAME	ALGO_SUPPORT_VECTOR_MACHINES	INPUT
SVMS_OUTLIER_RATE	0.1	INPUT
PREP_AUTO	ON	INPUT
SVMS_KERNEL_FUNCTION	SVMS_LINEAR	INPUT
SVMS_ACTIVE_LEARNING	SVMS_AL_ENABLE	INPUT
SVMS_CONV_TOLERANCE	0.001	INPUT

To see what attributes were used in the model, you can use the following query. Notice that the target attribute lists NO for each attribute. One of the key differences between using the SVM for typical classification scenarios versus using the SVM for anomaly detection is that there is no target attribute for anomaly detection. This is illustrated in the following example, where the attributes used by the existing anomaly detection model do not include an attribute indicated as the target under the TAR column.

```
SELECT  attribute_name,
        attribute_type,
        usage_type,
        target
FROM   all_mining_model_attributes
WHERE  model_name = 'ANOM_SVM_1_19';
```

ATTRIBUTE_NAME	ATTRIBUTE_T	USAGE_TY	TAR
DEDUCTIBLE	CATEGORICAL	ACTIVE	NO
AGEOFVEHICLE	CATEGORICAL	ACTIVE	NO
DAYS:POLICY-ACCIDENT	CATEGORICAL	ACTIVE	NO
DAYS:POLICY-CLAIM	CATEGORICAL	ACTIVE	NO
AGEOFPOLICYHOLDER	CATEGORICAL	ACTIVE	NO
WEEKOFMONTHCLAIMED	CATEGORICAL	ACTIVE	NO

```
BASEPOLICY              CATEGORICAL ACTIVE   NO
MARITALSTATUS           CATEGORICAL ACTIVE   NO
DRIVERRATING            CATEGORICAL ACTIVE   NO
POLICEREPORTFILED       CATEGORICAL ACTIVE   NO
PASTNUMBEROFCLAIMS      CATEGORICAL ACTIVE   NO
WEEKOFMONTH             CATEGORICAL ACTIVE   NO
WITNESSPRESENT          CATEGORICAL ACTIVE   NO
DAYOFWEEKCLAIMED        CATEGORICAL ACTIVE   NO
FRAUDFOUND              CATEGORICAL ACTIVE   NO
MONTHCLAIMED            CATEGORICAL ACTIVE   NO
MAKE                    CATEGORICAL ACTIVE   NO
REPNUMBER               NUMERICAL   ACTIVE   NO
NUMBEROFCARS            CATEGORICAL ACTIVE   NO
FAULT                   CATEGORICAL ACTIVE   NO
NUMBEROFSUPPLEMENTS     CATEGORICAL ACTIVE   NO
ADDRESSCHANGE-CLAIM     CATEGORICAL ACTIVE   NO
SEX                     CATEGORICAL ACTIVE   NO
ACCIDENTAREA            CATEGORICAL ACTIVE   NO
VEHICLEPRICE            CATEGORICAL ACTIVE   NO
VEHICLECATEGORY         CATEGORICAL ACTIVE   NO
AGENTTYPE               CATEGORICAL ACTIVE   NO
DAYOFWEEK               CATEGORICAL ACTIVE   NO
```

Settings Table

To use a data mining algorithm to build a model, you need to list the settings you want to use for the algorithm. To specify the settings, you must create a table that contains one record for each setting. The settings table has two attributes:

- **setting_name**   This contains the name of the setting parameter.

- **setting_value**   This contains the value of the setting parameter.

Typically the settings table has two records in it. One of these records specifies the algorithm that you want to use when building the model (for anomaly detection models, this algorithm is always Support Vector Machine), whereas the second record specifies whether you want to use the Automatic Data Processing (ADP) feature. ADP is turned on automatically when you are using the Oracle Data Miner tool, but when you are using the CREATE_MODEL PL/SQL function, ADP is turned off by default.

TIP
For anomaly detection models, you may want to provide a third setting value. This value is for the outlier rate. If you do not specify a value for this rate in the settings table, then the default value of 0.1, or 10 percent, is used. This value is perhaps on the high side, and you typically will want to set it to a much lower value.

The following example gives the code to create a settings table and inserts three settings records. These records specify to use the Support Vector Machine algorithm, turn on the ADP, and set the outlier rate to 0.05, or 5 percent.

```
-- create the settings table for an Anomaly Detection model
CREATE TABLE demo_anomaly_settings
  (setting_name   VARCHAR2(30),
   setting_value VARCHAR2(4000));

-- insert the settings records for Anomaly Detection
-- Support Vector Machine algorithm.
-- ADP is turned on. By default ADP is turned off.
-- Outlier Rate is set to 0.05. By default the outlier rate is 0.1 or 10%
BEGIN
   INSERT INTO demo_anomaly_settings (setting_name, setting_value)
   VALUES (dbms_data_mining.algo_name, dbms_data_mining.algo_support_vector_machines);

   INSERT INTO demo_anomaly_settings (setting_name, setting_value)
   VALUES (dbms_data_mining.prep_auto,dbms_data_mining.prep_auto_on);

   INSERT INTO demo_anomaly_settings (setting_name, setting_value)
   VALUES (dbms_data_mining.svms_outlier_rate, 0.05);
END;
/
column setting_name format a30
column setting_value format a30
SELECT *
FROM   demo_anomaly_settings;

SETTING_NAME                      SETTING_VALUE
------------------------------    ------------------------------
ALGO_NAME                         ALGO_SUPPORT_VECTOR_MACHINES
PREP_AUTO                         ON
SVMS_OUTLIER_RATE                 .05
```

If you want to perform your own data preparation, then you need not include the second INSERT statement, or you can change the SETTING_VALUE to PREP_AUTO_OFF.

Table 18-1 shows the settings available for the Support Vector Machine algorithm and their default values.

Algorithm	Setting	Values and Default Value
Support Vector Machine	SVMS_ACTIVE_LEARNING	This determines whether active learning is enabled or disabled. SVMS_AL_DISABLE SVMS_AL_ENABLE (default)
	SVMS_COMPLEXITY_FACTOR	This setting specifies the value of the complexity factor. Values > 0 Default value is estimated by the algorithm.
	SVMS_CONV_TOLERANCE	This is the convergence tolerance for the algorithm. Values > 0 0.001 (default)
	SVMS_EPSILON	This setting determines the value of the epsilon factor. Values > 0 Default value is estimated by the algorithm.
	SVMS_KERNEL_CACHE_SIZE	This setting is the value of the kernel cache size and is for Gaussian kernels only. Values > 0 50Mb (default)
	SVMS_KERNEL_FUNCTION	This specifies the kernel used by the algorithm. svms_gaussian svms_linear Default is determined by the algorithm.
	SVMS_OUTLIER_RATE	This is the rate of outliers in the training data for one-class models. Values > 0 and < 1 1 (default)
	SVMS_STD_DEV	This setting specifies the value of standard deviation for the algorithm using the Gaussian kernel. Values > 0 Default is estimated by the algorithm.

TABLE 18-1. *Settings and Default Values for the Support Vector Machine Algorithm*

Creating an Anomaly Detection Model

To create a new Oracle Data Mining model, you use the CREATE_MODEL procedure that is part of the DBMS_DATA_MINING package. The CREATE_MODEL procedure accepts the parameters described in Table 18-2.

Parameter	Description
model_name	This is a meaningful name that you want to give to the model you are creating.
mining_function	This parameter specifies the data mining function you want to use. The possible values are ASSOCIATION, ATTRIBUTE_IMPORTANCE, CLASSIFICATION, CLUSTERING, FEATURE_EXTRACTION, and REGRESSION.
data_table_name	This is the name of the table or view that contains the build data set.
case_id_column_name	This sets the Case ID (PK) for the build data set.
target_column_name	For anomaly detection, there is no target attribute. This parameter should be set to NULL.
settings_table_name	This is the name of the settings table.
data_schema_name	This parameter determines the schema where the build data set is located. This can be left NULL if the build data set is in the current schema.
settings_schema_name	This is the schema where the settings table is located. This can be left NULL if the settings table is in the current schema.
xform_list	If you have a set of transformations you want to embed into the model, you can specify them here. These transformations can be instead of or in conjunction with the transformations performed by the ADP.

TABLE 18-2. *CREATE_MODEL Procedure Parameters*

The syntax of the `CREATE_MODEL` procedure is as follows:

```
DBMS_DATA_MINING.CREATE_MODEL (
    model_name              IN VARCHAR2,
    mining_function         IN VARCHAR2,
    data_table_name         IN VARCHAR2,
    case_id_column_name     IN VARCHAR2,
    target_column_name      IN VARCHAR2 DEFAULT NULL,
    settings_table_name     IN VARCHAR2 DEFAULT NULL,
    data_schema_name        IN VARCHAR2 DEFAULT NULL,
    settings_schema_name    IN VARCHAR2 DEFAULT NULL,
    xform_list              IN TRANSFORM_LIST DEFAULT NULL);
```

The following example illustrates the creation of an anomaly detection model using the same data set that was used when an anomaly detection model was created in Chapter 11 using the Oracle Data Miner tool. This data set is called `CLAIMS` and contains the details of car insurance claims. All the data in the `CLAIMS` data set is used to create the anomaly detection model. As a target column is not included in anomaly detection, the `TARGET_COLUMN_NAME` parameter must be set to `NULL`. All the other parameter settings are defined in the `DEMO_ANOMALY_SETTINGS` table.

```
BEGIN
    DBMS_DATA_MINING.CREATE_MODEL(
        model_name              => 'DEMO_ANOMALY_MODEL',
        mining_function         => dbms_data_mining.classification,
        data_table_name         => 'CLAIMS',
        case_id_column_name     => 'POLICYNUMBER',
        target_column_name      => NULL,
        settings_table_name     => 'demo_anomaly_settings');
END;
/
```

Using the queries that were given earlier in this chapter, you can query the database to see that `DEMO_ANOMALY_MODEL` was generated and the settings that were used. You should see the same list of attributes that are used for both models and a similar set of model settings. The only difference that you see is that the value setting for the outlier rate is different. In Chapter 11, the default outlier rate of 0.1, or

10 percent, was used. In the anomaly detection model created in this chapter, an outlier rate of 0.05, or 5 percent, is used, as shown in the following listing:

```
break on model_name
column model_name format a25
column setting_value format a28
SELECT model_name,
       setting_name,
       setting_value,
       setting_type
FROM   all_mining_model_settings
WHERE model_name in ('ANOM_SVM_1_19', 'DEMO_ANOMALY_MODEL');
```

MODEL_NAME	SETTING_NAME	SETTING_VALUE	SETTING
DEMO_ANOMALY_MODEL	ALGO_NAME	ALGO_SUPPORT_VECTOR_MACHINES	INPUT
	SVMS_OUTLIER_RATE	**.05**	**INPUT**
	PREP_AUTO	ON	INPUT
	SVMS_KERNEL_FUNCTION	SVMS_LINEAR	DEFAULT
	SVMS_ACTIVE_LEARNING	SVMS_AL_ENABLE	DEFAULT
	SVMS_CONV_TOLERANCE	.001	DEFAULT
ANOM_SVM_1_19	ALGO_NAME	ALGO_SUPPORT_VECTOR_MACHINES	INPUT
	SVMS_OUTLIER_RATE	**0.1**	**INPUT**
	PREP_AUTO	ON	INPUT
	SVMS_KERNEL_FUNCTION	SVMS_LINEAR	INPUT
	SVMS_ACTIVE_LEARNING	SVMS_AL_ENABLE	INPUT
	SVMS_CONV_TOLERANCE	0.001	INPUT

You can examine the coefficients produced by the anomaly detection model by examining the model details using the GET_MODEL_DETAILS_SVM procedure. This procedure is part of the DBMS_DATA_MINING package. This is the same procedure you would use to see the model details and coefficients when Support Vector Machine is used for a classification problem. With anomaly detection, you are using the Support Vector Machine with a single class. You can use the following query to see the coefficients produced by the anomaly detection model that was produced in Chapter 11. You can change the model name in this query to see the coefficients produced by the DEMO_ANOMALY_MODEL that was produced in this chapter.

```
column class format a5
column aname format a20
column aval format a30
SELECT class, attribute_name aname, attribute_value aval, coefficient coeff
FROM   TABLE(DBMS_DATA_MINING.GET_MODEL_DETAILS_SVM('ANOM_SVM_1_19'))  a,
       TABLE(a.attribute_set) b
ORDER BY coefficient desc;
```

CLASS	ANAME	AVAL	COEFF
1	WITNESSPRESENT	No	.807348183
1	AGENTTYPE	External	.780644403
1	DAYS:POLICY-CLAIM	morethan30	.779793849

```
1    DAYS:POLICY-ACCIDENT  morethan30              .760813036
1    POLICEREPORTFILED     No                      .755215858
1    DEDUCTIBLE            400                      .611335474
1    SEX                   Male                    .607877936
1    ACCIDENTAREA          Urban                   .602086148
1    NUMBEROFCARS          1vehicle                .570162437
1    FAULT                 PolicyHolder            .56566381
1    ADDRESSCHANGE-CLAIM   nochange                .484904225
1    VEHICLECATEGORY       Sedan                   .482719026
1    MARITALSTATUS         Married                 .478962722
1    FRAUDFOUND            No                      .416386641
1    FRAUDFOUND            Yes                     .408129937
1    REPNUMBER                                     .357238264
1    NUMBEROFSUPPLEMENTS   none                    .343652331
1    MARITALSTATUS         Single                  .324544499
...
```

These are the same results that are displayed in Figure 11-6 in Chapter 11. There may be some very minor differences in the values displayed above compared to Figure 11-6. ODM displays the coefficient value to eight decimal places and the listing above displays to nine decimal places.

Unlike a classification problem, in anomaly detection there is no separation of data into training and testing data sets. The entire data set is used to train the model. After creating your anomaly detection model, you next apply the model to your data set to identify the homogeneous and anomalous case records.

Applying the Anomaly Detection Model to Your Data

This section shows how you can use the anomaly detection model produced in this chapter and Chapter 11. In Chapter 11, it was illustrated how you can apply an anomaly detection model to your data set. In this chapter, examples are given to illustrate how you can use these models in a real-time mode using the PREDICTION and PREDICTION_PROBABILITY SQL functions that exist in the database. In addition, an example is given that demonstrates how you can apply the anomaly detection model in batch mode. This is useful when you have data that is delivered to your organization at certain points during the day.

Using the Anomaly Detection Model in Real Time

With real-time anomaly detection, you examine your current data to see whether it is anomalous or not. There are two distinct types of real-time anomaly detection. The first of these is the examining of the data that already exists in your database. There are two functions that you can use. The first is the PREDICTION function. This function returns the predicted value (0 for an anomalous case) based on the input

data and the Oracle data mining model. The second function is PREDICTION_
PROBABILITY, which returns a value, in the range 0 to 1, that indicates how strong
of a prediction Oracle thinks it has made. Previous chapters have presented several
examples of the use of these functions.

The following example illustrates the use of these functions on five records from
the CLAIMS data set. This query returns the details of the top ten anomalous policy
records that exist in the CLAIMS table, using the anomaly detection model that was
produced in Chapter 11.

```
column prob format 9.9999
SELECT POLICYNUMBER,
       PROB
FROM (
   SELECT POLICYNUMBER,
          prediction_probability(ANOM_SVM_1_19, 0 using *) prob
   FROM    CLAIMS
   ORDER BY prediction_probability(ANOM_SVM_1_19, 0 using *) DESC, 1)
WHERE rownum <= 10;


POLICYNUMBER     PROB
------------  -------
       14485   .6374
           1   .6252
       11677   .6116
         654   .6095
       11068   .6091
       11119   .5969
       11489   .5792
        1588   .5791
        1599   .5773
       10415   .5758
```

The prediction_probability(ANOM_SVM_1_19, 0 using *) command
can be divided into three parts. The first part is the Oracle data mining model that
you want to use (ANOM_SVM_1_19). The second part is the class that you want the
model to focus on or make a prediction about. In this example, this is set to 0, as
you want to focus on the anomalous records. The third part allows you to specify
what attributes you want to use as input to the data mining model. In this example,
you want the data mining model to use all the attributes, and this is specified by
USING *.

Another scenario where you might want to use your anomaly detection model in
real time is in your applications, so that as you are capturing your data you can
make an anomaly prediction. In this type of scenario, the data is not in a table, so
you need to input these attributes and their values to the model. The following
example illustrates how you can calculate how anomalous a customer is as the data

is being recorded in the application. As you capture more data, you can require that the anomaly detection model makes an updated prediction.

```
column predicted_prob format 9.9999
SELECT prediction(DEMO_ANOMALY_MODEL
           USING 'FORD' AS MAKE,
                 '5YEARS' AS AGEOFVEHICLE,
                 'more than 69_000' AS VEHICLEPRICE,
                 '26to30' AS AGEOFPOLICYHOLDER,
                 'Sport' AS VECHICLECATEGORY)  Predicted_Value,
       prediction_probability(DEMO_ANOMALY_MODEL
           USING 'FORD' AS MAKE,
                 '5YEARS' AS AGEOFVEHICLE,
                 'more than 69_000' AS VEHICLEPRICE,
                 '26to30' AS AGEOFPOLICYHOLDER,
                 'Sport' AS VECHICLECATEGORY) Predicted_Prob
FROM dual;

PREDICTED_VALUE PREDICTED_PROB
--------------- --------------
              1         .5521
```

You can see based on this query and the data used that the customer is more likely to be normal and does not warrant further investigation. The data used in this example is a subset of the columns from the CLAIMS data set for POLICYHOLDER = 1. If you look at the previous examples in this chapter and in Chapter 11, this policy has been identified as a possible anomalous case. The reason for the difference might be due to only a small subset of the attributes being used in the preceding example. In the previous examples, all the columns were used to determine how anomalous a case is. So the more data you can input into the models, when used this way, the more accurate the predictions will be.

Using the Anomaly Detection Model in Batch Mode

Applying an ODM model in batch mode involves using the APPLY procedure in the PL/SQL package DBMS_DATA_MINING. The main difference with using this package and procedure is that the output is stored in a new table in your schema. This method is best suited to scenarios where you want to process a number of records in batch mode or offline work. Previous chapters, such as Chapter 15, have presented examples of the syntax and structure of the APPLY procedure.

In the following example, the CLAIMS data has the anomaly detection model that was produced earlier in this chapter in the section "Creating an Anomaly

Detection Model" applied to it using the APPLY procedure. The APPLY procedure creates a new table in your schema that contains the results. In this example, the new table is called DEMO_CLAIMS_SCORED. This new table created by the APPLY procedure contains three attributes. The first of these attributes is the primary key of the CLAIMS table, and this attribute is a parameter of the APPLY procedure. The other two attributes contain the prediction and the probability values. In a manner similar to when you use the APPLY procedure for your classification problems, the APPLY procedure creates two records in the new table (DEMO_CLAIMS_SCORED) for each record in the original data set (CLAIMS). One record is created that contains the probability for each case record being normal and has a prediction value of 1. A second record is created that contains the anomalous prediction probability (prediction = 0).

```
BEGIN
    dbms_data_mining.APPLY(model_name            => 'DEMO_ANOMALY_MODEL',
                           data_table_name       => 'CLAIMS',
                           case_id_column_name => 'POLICYNUMBER',
                           result_table_name     => 'DEMO_CLAIMS_SCORED');
END;
/

SELECT *
FROM    demo_claims_scored
WHERE   rownum <=10;

POLICYNUMBER PREDICTION PROBABILITY
------------ ---------- -----------
           1          0       .5791
           1          1       .4209
          29          1       .5338
          29          0       .4662
          53          1       .5000
          53          0       .5000
          54          1       .5679
          54          0       .4321
          80          1       .5315
          80          0       .4685
```

The sample output from the DEMO_CLAIMS_SCORED table shows the two records created for each policy that was in the CLAIMS table. You can use this information to filter the anomalous records to those you might want to concentrate on first.

Summary

Anomaly detection is an important data mining technique that can help you identify possible anomalous records in your data sets. These anomalous case records could represent fraudulent activity or activity that warrants further investigation. In this chapter, a number of examples were given to show how you can use the in-database SQL and PL/SQL functions to create an anomaly detection model and how you can apply this model to your data in real time or in batch mode.

PART
IV

Migration and Implementations

CHAPTER
19

How to Migrate
Your ODM Models

When developing your Oracle Data Miner workflows and data mining models, you may create them on a development server. At some point, you will want to deploy your data mining models in another schema or in another database. This chapter looks at what is involved in productionalizing your models. This includes the generation of scripts to run your Oracle Data Miner workflows, as well as the exporting and importing of your data mining models in another schema or database.

Oracle Data Miner Script Generation

When you have developed your Oracle Data Miner workflows, at some point you might want to automate the execution of the workflow on a regular basis. Having to open Oracle Data Miner and to rerun the workflow might seem like a tedious task. Instead of you having to do this, Oracle Data Miner can produce a number of SQL scripts that perform these tasks for you.

Oracle Data Miner can generate scripts that allow you to re-create all the necessary objects, run the scripts to build a model, collect the model performance statistics, and apply the model to new data. These SQL scripts enable you to replicate the full behavior of your workflow.

To generate the SQL scripts, you can select a node from the completed workflow, right-click on this node, then select Deploy from the pop-up menu. An example of this is shown in Figure 19-1, using the workflow that was generated in Chapter 8 with Oracle Data Miner.

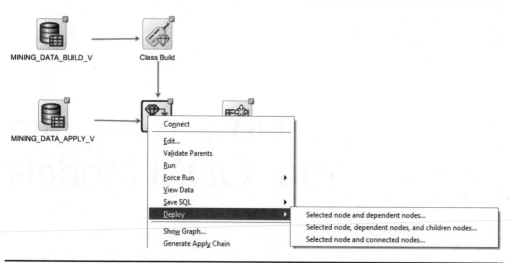

FIGURE 19-1. *Selecting the Deploy option from the menu*

From the Deploy menu, select the option that best describes what you want produced. As your workflow may contain a large number of nodes that were part of your data investigation stages, you may not want these to be part of the regularly scheduled (for example, nightly) run of the workflow.

Select either the Selected Node and Dependent Nodes or the Selected Node and Connected Nodes option. When one of these options is selected, a window opens asking for the Target Database version and the location where the SQL scripts will be placed. There is a drop-down list for the Target Database. As you probably will be running the SQL scripts in your current schema or another schema in your current database, you can leave this with the default value, which is your current database version. When finished, Oracle Data Miner creates a directory with the name of the workflow in the location you have specified.

A number of scripts are created for the workflow. These consist of scripts for each of the data nodes, the transformation nodes, the build model node, the apply mode node, and any output nodes. In addition to these scripts, the scripts directory also contains an image of the workflow called `<workflow_name>`.png, where `workflow_name` is the name of your workflow. The main set of SQL scripts consists of a master run script (called `<workflow_name>`_Run.sql) that controls all the other scripts, and a cleanup script (called `<workflow_name>`_Drop.sql>) removes any hidden or visible objects that were created during the running of the workflow that are used to store intermediary results during the workflow. A script called `<node_name>`.sql is created for each of the nodes in the workflow.

Table 19-1 describes the node scripts that can be created for a workflow.

Running the ODM Workflow Scripts

You can pass these SQL scripts on to your DBA to schedule them to run on a regular basis, or, if you are skilled enough and have the necessary privileges, you can do this yourself.

The Master script (`<workflow_name>`_Run.sql) is responsible for invoking all the underlying node-level scripts in the correct order. The master script contains all variable definitions that are used in all the node-related scripts. You may need to alter some of these variables to conform to your environment and to avoid any possible conflicts in the naming of the objects. The following variables are supported:

- Variables that allow you to change the name of the object names that are input to the node-level scripts, such as tables/views and models. By default, these names are the original table/view and model names.

- Variables that allow you to change the name of the control table (described later in this section). By default, this name is the workflow name.

- Variables that indicate whether named objects should be deleted before they are generated by the script.

Node Type	Script Description and Functionality
Data Source, Transformation, Aggregate, Join, Filter, Sample, Model Details, Apply, Apply Text	These nodes create a view reflecting the output of the node.
Filter Columns	This creates a view reflecting the output of the Filter Columns node. If the Attribute Importance setting is used, a table is generated containing the results.
Build Text	For each Text Transformation it will create a Feature Table Name and Oracle Text Policy objects. It also creates a view reflecting the output of the Build Text node.
Classification Build	A model is created for each algorithm selected in the node. A master test result table is generated to store the list of test result tables that are generated for each model. These include Performance, Performance Matrix, ROC, Lift, and Profit.
Regression Build	A model is created for each algorithm selected in the node. A master test result table is generated to store the list of test results generated for each model.
Cluster Build, Anomaly Detection, Feature Extraction, Association Build	A model is created for each model listed in the node.
Test Node for Classification	A master test result table is generated to store the list of test results generated for each model. These include Performance, Performance Matrix, ROC, Lift, and Profit.
Test Node for Regression	A master test result table is generated to store the list of test results generated for each model.
Model and Text Reference	No scripts are generated. These nodes are reference nodes to metadata in the database.

TABLE 19-1. *Node Scripts*

When the master script is run, it first creates a control table using the name specified in the control table name variable and defaults to the name of the workflow. The purpose of the control table is to store details of which objects are generated, such as views, models, and text specifications. The node scripts in the workflow can look up their input objects and register their output objects in the control table. The cleanup script uses the control table to determine what objects need to be dropped. For advanced users, the control table provides the internal name of objects that are not readily accessible.

Before the workflow scripts can be run, they should be edited to contain the directory location where they are located. The directory path can be added to the master script where each of the node scripts is called.

When all the scripts are ready, you can schedule the execution of the master script by using Enterprise Manager, by using the Schedule option under your schema in SQL Developer, or by using the DBMS_SCHEDULER PL/SQL package. The scheduling of a script type job is supported only in Oracle 12c (or greater) Database.

PL/SQL Procedures for ODM Model Migration

As your skills with Oracle Data Miner evolve and with the increased usage of the models produced by Oracle Data Miner in your organization, you need to be able to refresh and update your Oracle Data Mining models. Typically you perform the updating of your models on your analytics development server, although you could do this on your production server as long as the data volumes are low and there is no impact on the performance of the server. When you have identified the new updated model that you want to deploy in your production environment, you can use a number of procedures that are part of the DBMS_DATA_MINING package to help you manage this task.

To migrate a model from one environment to another, you need to ensure that you have completed the following steps:

1. Install the Oracle Data Miner Repository in the destination database if you are going to use the Oracle Data Miner tool. If you are only using the SQL and PL/SQL functions then you can skip this step.

2. Set up in the destination database schema the objects that contain the new data that will be labeled by the Oracle Data Mining model.

3. Copy to the destination database schema all data preprocessing scripts that perform all the necessary data gathering, integration, transformations, and so on. These are in addition to the data transformations that have been defined using the DBMS_DATA_MINING_TRANSFORM package and have been added

to the Oracle Data Mining model using the DBMS_DATA_MINING
.APPLY procedure or have been defined in the Oracle Data Miner workflow.
Any transformations that are embedded into the model are automatically
included in the export of the model.

4. Export the new Oracle Data Mining model, from your analytics server,
   using the EXPORT_MODEL procedure that is part of the DBMS_DATA_MINING
   package.

5. Import the new model to the relevant schema on the production database
   server, using the IMPORT_MODEL procedure.

6. Drop or rename the existing Oracle Data Mining model being using in
   production. A model can be dropped using the DROP_MODEL procedure.

7. Rename the imported model to the model name to be used in production,
   using the RENAME_MODEL procedure.

System Privileges Needed
for Exporting and Importing ODM Models

The CREATE ANY DIRECTORY system privilege must be granted to the schemas that
are exporting and importing the Oracle Data Mining models. The directory should
point to the directory on the file system that contains the dumped/exported Oracle
Data Mining model files.

Ask your DBA to grant the CREATE ANY DIRECTORY system privilege.
Alternatively, if you know the password for SYS, then you can run the following
command:

```
GRANT CREATE ANY DIRECTORY TO DMUSER;
```

When the CREATE ANY DIRECTORY system privilege has been granted to your
ODM schema, you then need to connect to the ODM schema and create the
directory object in the database. The following example illustrates the CREATE
DIRECTORY command:

```
CREATE OR REPLACE DIRECTORY DataMiningDir AS '/u01/app/Data_Mining_Exports';
```

This command creates an object in the database that points to the '/u01/app/
Data_Mining_Exports' directory. The command does not verify that the directory
exists. This happens only when the directory object is used.

CAUTION
*The directory on the file system must be created as
a separate step rather than as part of the preceding
command.*

Exporting an ODM Model

To export your Oracle Data Mining model from your schema, you need to use the `EXPORT_MODEL` procedure that is part of the `DBMS_DATA_MINING` package. This export procedure is based on Oracle Data Pump and requires that the necessary system privileges are set up, as shown in the previous section.

The `EXPORT_MODEL` procedure exports one or more of the Oracle Data Mining models in a schemas and their associated transformations. This procedure has the following syntax:

```
DBMS_DATA_MINING.EXPORT_MODEL (
        filename        IN VARCHAR2,
        directory       IN VARCHAR2,
        model_filter    IN VARCHAR2 DEFAULT NULL,
        filesize        IN VARCHAR2 DEFAULT NULL,
        operation       IN VARCHAR2 DEFAULT NULL,
        remote_link     IN VARCHAR2 DEFAULT NULL,
        jobname         IN VARCHAR2 DEFAULT NULL);
```

Table 19-2 explains each of the parameters of the `IMPORT_MODEL` procedure and their default values.

The following examples illustrate some of the different ways of executing the `EXPORT_MODEL` procedure. These examples use the `DataMiningDir` directory that

Parameter	Required	Description
filename	Mandatory	This is the name of the file to be created on the file system. All the specified models are exported to this file. The `EXPORT_MODEL` procedure uses the Oracle Data Pump utility to export the models. All files produced have a number attached to the end of the filename. This number is incremented when the default file size is reached, and another file will be created with the same filename but with a different sequence number at the end, as in `filename01.dmp`, `filename02.dmp`, and so on.
directory	Mandatory	This parameter specifies the system parameter name that was created to store the directory where the export files will be saved.

TABLE 19-2. *IMPORT_MODEL Procedure Parameters and Default Values (continued)*

Parameter	Required	Description
model_filter	Optional	This allows you to specify the list of models you want to export. If you do not specify a value for model_filter, all models in the schema are exported. You can also specify NULL (the default) or 'ALL' to export all models.
		Examples of different ways to specify the models you want to export include the following:

		`'DEMO_CLASS_DT_MODEL'`
		    Exports a single model
		`'name= ''CLASS_DT_MODEL'''`
		    Exports a single model
		`'name IN (''CLASS_DT_MODEL'', ''CLASS_SVM_`
		        `MODEL'')'`
		    Exports the listed models
		`'ALGORITHM_NAME = ''DECISION_TREE''`
		    Exports models for a particular
		        algorithm
		`'FUNCTION_NAME = ''CLASSIFICATION'''`
		    Exports models of a particular type

filesize	Optional	Specifies the maximum size of the dump/export file. The default size is 50MB. If the total size of the model being exported exceeds 50MB, then an additional dump/export file is created.
operation	Optional	The default value for this parameter is 'EXPORT'. This tells the procedure to export the model. The other allowed value, 'ESTIMATE', is used to estimate the size of the exporting models.
remote_link	Optional	This specifies the database link to be used to export the model from a remote system. The default value is NULL.
jobname	Optional	This parameter specifies the name of the export job. By default, the name has the form *username*_exp_*NUM*, where *NUM* is a number. For example, a job name in the SCOTT schema might be BRENDAN_exp_134. If you specify a job name, it must be unique within the schema. The maximum length of the job name is 30 characters. A log file for the export job, named *jobname.log*, is created in the same directory as the dump file set.

TABLE 19-2. *IMPORT_MODEL Procedure Parameters and Default Values*

was created in the previous section. The first example illustrates how all the Oracle Data Mining models can be exported from the DMUSER schema:

```
BEGIN
    DBMS_DATA_MINING.EXPORT_MODEL('Exported_DM_Models', 'DataMiningDir');
END;
/
```

When executed, the preceding command produces two files in the specified directory. One is EXPORTED_DM_MODELS01.DMP. This is the file that contains the exported Oracle Data Mining models. Notice the 01 at the end of the filename. The other file is a log file produced during the export procedure (which uses Data Pump).

The following example illustrates the EXPORT_MODEL procedure that exports all the classification models in your schema:

```
BEGIN
    DBMS_DATA_MINING.EXPORT_MODEL('Exported_CLASS_Models', 'DataMiningDir',
        'FUNCTION_NAME = ''CLASSIFICATION''');
END;
/
```

This command produces the exported models in the file EXPORTED_CLASS_MODELS01.DMP and a log file.

To export one specific model, you can just list its name in the filter list:

```
BEGIN
    DBMS_DATA_MINING.EXPORT_MODEL('Exported_DEMO_CLASS_Models', 'DataMiningDir',
        'name= ''DEMO_CLASS_DT_MODEL''');
END;
/
```

To export more than one specified model, you can list each of the model names. In this example, the command exports a classification and a cluster model:

```
BEGIN
    DBMS_DATA_MINING.EXPORT_MODEL('Exported_DEMO_Models', 'DataMiningDir',
        'name IN (''DEMO_CLASS_DT_MODEL'', ''CLUSTER_KMEANS_MODEL'')');
END;
/
```

Importing and the ODM Model

You can use the IMPORT_MODEL procedure to import an Oracle Data Mining model into your schema. This import procedure is based on Oracle Data Pump and requires the CREATE ANY DIRECTORY system privilege granted to the import schema.

The IMPORT_MODEL procedure imports one or more of the Oracle Data Mining models into a schema along with their associated transformations that were exported using the EXPORT_MODEL procedure.

NOTE
When Oracle Data Pump is used directly to export or import an entire schema or database, the mining models in the schema or database are included. EXPORT_MODEL and IMPORT_MODEL export and import mining models only.

The IMPORT_MODEL procedure has the following syntax:

```
DBMS_DATA_MINING.IMPORT_MODEL (
    filename          IN  VARCHAR2,
    directory         IN  VARCHAR2,
    model_filter      IN  VARCHAR2 DEFAULT NULL,
    operation         IN  VARCHAR2 DEFAULT NULL,
    remote_link       IN  VARCHAR2 DEFAULT NULL,
    jobname           IN  VARCHAR2 DEFAULT NULL,
    schema_remap      IN  VARCHAR2 DEFAULT NULL,
    tablespace_remap  IN  VARCHAR2 DEFAULT NULL);
```

Table 19-3 explains each of the parameters of the IMPORT_MODEL procedure and their default values.

Parameter	Required	Description
filename	Mandatory	This is the name of the file that contains the Oracle Data Mining models that you want to import. This file should have been created using the EXPORT_MODEL procedure.
directory	Mandatory	This parameter is the name of the DIRECTORY object defined in the schema that points to the directory on the server that contains the dump file.

TABLE 19-3. *IMPORT_MODEL Procedure Parameters and Default Values* (continued)

Parameter	Required	Description

`model_filter`	Optional	This allows you to specify the list of models you want to import. If you do not specify a value for `model_filter`, all models are imported into the schema. You can also specify `NULL` (the default) or specify `'ALL'`, which imports all models.
		
		Examples of different ways of specifying what models you want exported include the following:
		
		`'DEMO_CLASS_DT_MODEL'`
		      `Imports a single model`
		`'name= ''CLASS_DT_MODEL'''`
		      `Imports a single model`
		`'name IN (''CLASS_DT_MODEL'', ''CLASS_`
		            `SVM_MODEL'')'`
		      `Imports the listed models`

`operation`	Optional	The default value is `'IMPORT'`. The other value for this parameter is `'SQL_FILE'`, which writes to a text file the SQL Data Definition Language (DDL) for creating the models. The text file is created in the dump directory.
`remote_link`	Optional	The default value is `NULL`. If a database link exists, you can use this parameter to import the required models. The `IMP_FULL_DATABASE` role is required for importing the remote models.
`jobname`	Optional	A default job name is assigned to the import process. Alternatively, you can assign a job name.
`schema_remap`	Optional	By default, the import procedure assumes that the same schema name is used for the exporting and importing of the models. If this is not the case, then you need to specify the `Export_Schema:Import_Schema` names. An example is `DMUSER:DMUSER2`, where `DMUSER` is the export schema name, and `DMUSER2` is the import schema name.
`tablespace_remap`	Optional	By default, the import process loads the models into the same tablespace from which they were exported. If these are different, then you need to specify the `Export_Tablespace:Import_Tablespace` name.

TABLE 19-3. *IMPORT_MODEL Procedure Parameters and Default Values*

TIP
*Use the same tablespace name in your
development/testing databases and production
databases for your Oracle Data Mining models.
For example, the tablespace could be called
DATAMINING.*

The following examples illustrate some of the different ways of executing the
IMPORT_MODEL procedure to import the models into the schema DMUSER2. The
DMUSER2 schema was created in Chapter 3. You need to grant CREATE ANY
DIRECTORY privileges to the DMUSER2 schema and then create the DataMiningDir
directory for DMUSER2 to point to the directory that contains the dump files. The first
example illustrates how all the Oracle Data Mining models can be imported from
the DMUSER2 schema:

```
BEGIN
    DBMS_DATA_MINING.IMPORT_MODEL(
        'Exported_DM_Models01.DMP',
        'DataMiningDir',
        null,
        'IMPORT',
        null,
        null,
        'DMUSER:DMUSER2',
        null);
END;
/
```

The following is an alternative way of writing this IMPORT_MODEL procedure
that excludes all the NULLs and specifies only the parameters with inputs:

```
BEGIN
    DBMS_DATA_MINING.IMPORT_MODEL(
        filename =>'Exported_DM_Models01.DMP',
        directory => 'DataMiningDir',
        schema_remap => 'DMUSER:DMUSER2');
END;
/
```

To import one specific model, you can just list its name in the filter list:

```
BEGIN
    DBMS_DATA_MINING.IMPORT_MODEL(
        filename =>'Exported_DM_Models01.DMP',
        directory => 'DataMiningDir',
        model_filter => 'DEMO_CLASS_DT_MODEL',
        schema_remap => 'DMUSER:DMUSER2');
END;
/
```

To import more than one specific model, you can list each of the model names. In this example, a classification and a cluster model are imported:

```
BEGIN
    DBMS_DATA_MINING.IMPORT_MODEL(
        filename =>'Exported_DM_Models01.DMP',
        directory => 'DataMiningDir',
        model_filter => 'name in (''DEMO_CLASS_DT_MODEL'', ''CLUSTER_KMEANS_MODEL'')',
        schema_remap => 'DMUSER:DMUSER2');
END;
/
```

Dropping an ODM Model

The DROP_MODEL procedure can be used to drop or remove an Oracle Data Mining model from your schema. To drop a model, you need to be the owner of the model or have been granted the DROP MINING MODEL system privilege.

The syntax of the DROP_MODEL procedure is as follows:

```
DBMS_DATA_MINING.DROP_MODEL (model_name IN VARCHAR2,
                             force      IN BOOLEAN DEFAULT FALSE);
```

Table 19-4 explains each of the parameters of the DROP_MODEL procedure and their default values.

Parameter	Required	Description
model_name	Mandatory	This is the full name of the ODM model you want to drop and remove from your schema. If the model exists in another schema and you have the DROP MINING MODEL privilege for that model, then you need to add the schema name to the model name, as in the following example: DMUSER.DEMO_CLASS_DT_MODEL.
force	Optional	The default value is FALSE. This forces the mining model to be dropped even if it is invalid. A mining model may be invalid if a serious system error interrupted the model build process. In most cases, you can use the default of FALSE. Otherwise, you can use TRUE if the DROP_MODEL procedure did not work when using FALSE.

TABLE 19-4. *DROP_MODEL Procedure Parameters and Default Values*

The following example illustrates how you can use the DROP_MODEL procedure to drop one ODM model:

```
BEGIN
    DBMS_DATA_MINING.DROP_MODEL('DEMO_CLASS_DT_MODEL');
END;
/
```

The following example illustrates how you can drop all the models of a particular data mining type, such as clustering:

```
set serveroutput on
DECLARE
    CURSOR odm_drop IS SELECT model_name
                       FROM user_mining_models
                       WHERE mining_function = 'CLUSTERING';
BEGIN
    FOR r_drop IN odm_drop LOOP
        dbms_output.put_line('Dropping model : '||r_drop.model_name);
        DBMS_DATA_MINING.DROP_MODEL(r_drop.model_name);
    END LOOP;
END;
/
```

CAUTION
Be careful when you drop a model, particularly if it is in production. Pick a time when the model is not in use; otherwise, indeterminate results can be produced and impact the application that is using the model.

Renaming an ODM Model

The RENAME_MODEL procedure can be used to rename an existing model. To rename a model, you need to be the owner of the model or have been granted the CREATE MINING MODEL system privilege.

The syntax of the RENAME_MODEL procedure is as follows:

```
DBMS_DATA_MINING.RENAME_MODEL (
    model_name          IN VARCHAR2,
    new_model_name      IN VARCHAR2);
```

Table 19-5 explains each of the parameters of the RENAME_MODEL procedure and their default values.

Parameter	Required	Description
model_name	Mandatory	This is the name of the model you want to rename.
new_model_name	Mandatory	This is the new name of the model.

TABLE 19-5. *RENAME_MODEL Procedure Parameters and Default Values*

TIP
The Oracle Data Mining model name you use in production should remain consistent. This ensures that no code changes are necessary when you have an updated model you want to drop in production. You can use the RENAME_MODEL procedure to change the imported model to the production model name.

CAUTION
Be careful when you rename a model, particularly if it is in production. Pick a time when the model name is not in use; otherwise, indeterminate results can be produced and impact the application that is using the model.

The following example illustrates how you can rename an Oracle Data Mining model to a new name. DEMO_CLASS_DT_MODEL was generated in the DMUSER schema, exported using EXPORT_MODEL, and imported in the DMUSER2 schema using the IMPORT_MODEL procedure. Here the imported model (DEMO_CLASS_DT_MODEL) is renamed CHURN_MODEL:

```
BEGIN
    DBMS_DATA_MINING.RENAME_MODEL('DEMO_CLASS_DT_MODEL', 'CHURN_MODEL');
END;
/
```

TIP
Perform the DROP_MODEL and RENAME_MODEL procedures in one PL/SQL block.

The following code example illustrates how you can import a new model, drop an existing model, and rename the imported model to use the required production model name:

```
BEGIN
    -- Import the new ODM Model
    DBMS_DATA_MINING.IMPORT_MODEL(
        filename =>'Exported_DM_Models01.DMP',
        directory => 'DataMiningDir',
        model_filter => 'DEMO_CLASS_DT_MODEL',
        schema_remap => 'DMUSER:DMUSER2');

    -- Drop the existing production model
    DBMS_DATA_MINING.DROP_MODEL('CHURN_MODEL');
    -- Rename the imported model to the production name
    DBMS_DATA_MINING.RENAME_MODEL('DEMO_CLASS_DT_MODEL', 'CHURN_MODEL');
END;
```

Summary

Being able to move your models between schemas or databases is a very important feature that allows you to incorporate all your data analytics work in the one database server, thus eliminating the need to move the data. This way, you are moving the data mining models to the data instead of moving the data to the models. In addition to the moving of the models, if you have developed complex workflows, you can now schedule the generated scripts to run in your Oracle 12c Database.

CHAPTER
20

Implementation-Related Topics

I n the previous chapters, examples were given for how you can apply your Oracle Data Mining models to new data. When you are implementing your Oracle Data Mining models, you may do so in a number of different ways. Some implementations may involve including your models in your Oracle Fusion Middleware applications, adding them in your dashboards, or simply seeking improvement of the performance of your models when you are running them in parallel against many millions of records. This chapter explores these topics, presenting examples of how to perform these tasks.

How to Add Your ODM Models to Your OBI Dashboards

Most organizations have a way of delivering their reports via some form of dashboard or end-user reporting. One such solution is the dashboards that are available as part of the Oracle Business Intelligence (OBI) Suite. You can incorporate your Oracle Data Mining models as part of your dashboards to allow you to analyze your data in a variety of ways. The remainder of this section illustrates the steps needed to include an Oracle Data Mining model in your dashboards.

Importing the ODM Model

If your development database for your Oracle Data Mining models is different from the database being used for the OBI dashboards, the first step is to migrate the ODM model. Chapter 19 showed examples of how to export and import the models. You need to perform the steps described in that chapter. In addition, you must ensure that the data you want to input to the ODM models is in the same format and has all the sample transformation and data cleanup steps applied to them. Again, examples of the different ways to do this have been given in the previous chapters. The aim is to get together in the one environment all the ODM models and any other code that needs to be applied to the data. When you have this all together in one place, you can look at how it can all be integrated. The simplest way to do this is to use a view, as described in the next section.

The examples given in the following sections are for a student churn prediction system that was built for universities in the United Kingdom.

Creating a View to Include the ODM Model

You can create a view that uses the PREDICTION and PREDICTION_PROBABILITY functions to apply the imported ODM model to your data. For example, the view created in this section is used to apply the imported ODM model to the data that is stored in HE_STUDENT_DATA. The ODM model is a student churn model for first-year students. This is similar to the classification models that were shown in previous

ST_PK	WITHDRAW_PREDICTION	WITHDRAW_PROBABILITY
45084.0	N	83.2142857142857
45087.0	N	66.8668407310705
45115.0	N	94.495412844 0367
45222.0	N	73.7106918238994
45302.0	N	66.8668407310705
45313.0	N	94.495412844 0367
45326.0	N	66.8668407310705
45357.0	N	73.7106918238994

FIGURE 20-1.   *Sample output from the* HE_FIRST_YEAR_PREDICTION *view*

chapters. The view gives the scored data that consists of the student ID, the predicted churn value, and a probability value that indicates how strong of a prediction the model has made. The code for the view is as follows:

```
CREATE or REPLACE VIEW  HE_FIRST_YEAR_PREDICTION as
SELECT st_pk,
       prediction(clas_decision_tree using *) WITHDRAW_PREDICTION,
       prediction_probability(clas_decision_tree using *) WITHDRAW_PROBABILITY
FROM   HE_STUDENT_DATA
WHERE  ACAD_YEAR = 1;
```

Figure 20-1 shows an example of the output generated by this view.

Importing the View to the Physical Layer of the BI Repository (RPD)

You can now move on to setting up the OBI environment to include the HE_FIRST_YEAR_PREDICTION view. The view can be imported into the physical layer of the BI Repository (RPD) (see Figure 20-2), where it can be joined on the primary key to the

▦ HE_FIRST_YEAR_APPLY				
Columns ⟋	Types	Length	Nullable	▲
STUDENT_AGE	DOUBLE	15	True	
ST_PK	DOUBLE	15	True	
TITLE	VARCHAR	1,130	True	
WITHDRAW_FLAG	CHAR	1	True	▼

▦ HE_FIRST_YEAR_PREDICTI.				
Columns ⟋	Types	Length	Nullable	
ST_PK	DOUBLE	15	True	
WITHDRAW_PREDIC...	VARCHAR	1	True	
WITHDRAW_PROBAB...	DOUBLE	0	True	

FIGURE 20-2.   *Including the* HE_FIRST_YEAR_PREDICTION *view in the RPD*

other student tables. The view contains one record per student. With the tables and view being joined, you can use the prediction and the probability columns to filter the student data. For example, you may want to have a filter for all the customers who are likely to churn, called `WITHDRAW_PREDICTION = 'Y'`.

Adding New Columns to the Business Model Layer

The new prediction columns can then mapped into the Business Model and Mapping layer (see Figure 20-3), where they can be incorporated into various relevant calculations, such as the percentage of withdrawals predicted, and then subsequently be presented to the end-users for reporting.

Adding to the OBI Dashboards

The student churn withdraw prediction columns can then be published on the OBI dashboards, where they can be used to filter the data content. In the example shown in Figure 20-4, the user has chosen to show data for only those students who are predicted to withdraw with a probability rating of > 70 percent.

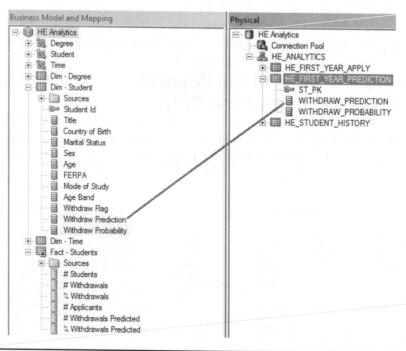

FIGURE 20-3. *Including churn attributes into the Business Model and Mapping layer*

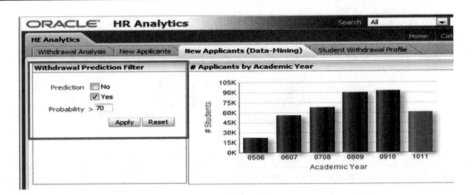

FIGURE 20-4. *ODM Prediction and Probability fields used for filtering on an OBI dashboard*

How to Build and Apply ODM Models in Parallel

As your data volumes increase, particularly as you evolve into the Big Data world, you will begin to see that your Oracle data mining workflows and scoring functions start to take longer and longer. This section illustrates how you can use the Parallel option to improve the performance of your workflows in the tool and how you can run the in-database Oracle data mining SQL and PL/SQL procedures in parallel.

How to Run Your ODM Workflows and ODM Models in Parallel

A new feature was added in SQL Developer version 4 that allows you to add Parallel Query to the various nodes of your workflow. By default, the Parallel Query option is disabled or turned off for your workflow, as shown in Figure 20-5. This is indicated on the top right-hand corner of your worksheet. You should only use the Parallel Query option if you have the license to use it for your database.

Setting Parallel Query for Workflow Nodes

To enable the Parallel Query option for your workflow, you need to click on the Parallel Query link as shown in Figure 20-5. When you click on this link, a window opens that allows you to set whether you want to use the Parallel Query option for each node of the workflow and what the degree of parallelism should be. You need

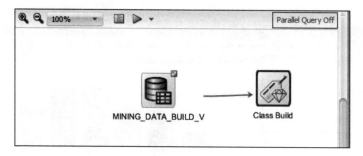

FIGURE 20-5. *Parallel Query option for your workflows*

not set all nodes to use the Parallel Query option, only the nodes that require it. You will see a noticeable improvement in performance.

You can select the nodes that you want to use the Parallel Query option with by clicking on the check boxes. If you want all nodes to use the Parallel Query option, then you can click on the All button (shown in Figure 20-6).

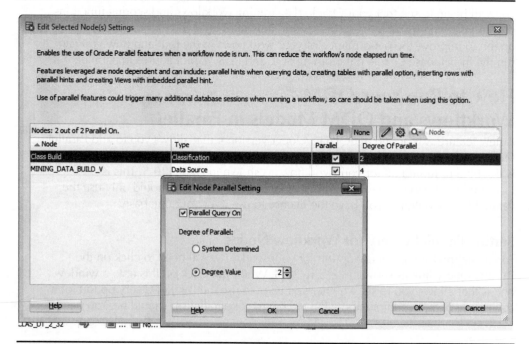

FIGURE 20-6. *Setting the degree of parallelism*

You then set the degree of parallelism to use for each node. To customize the degree of parallelism, click on the row that describes the node, then click on the Edit Parallel Settings (the pencil icon). You can now specify the degree of parallelism that you want to use for that node.

NOTE
You can change the default settings to have a specific degree of parallelism for each of the node types. See the next section for details on how to change these settings.

NOTE
Not all algorithms can be run in parallel. In Oracle 12.1c Database, the algorithms that support parallel build include Decision Trees, Naïve Bayes, Apriori, MDL, and Expectation Maximization. With later releases of the database, more algorithms will be enabled to allow model build in parallel.

Changing the Default Setting for Parallel Query

You can set the Parallel Query option and degree of parallelism for each type of node by changing the default settings. These settings are used by default when you turn on the Parallel Query option on your ODM Workflow Worksheet.

You can find the default settings by selecting Tools | Preferences. You need to scroll down the list of preferences until you come to the preferences section for Oracle Data Miner. When you expand the list of preferences for Oracle Data Miner and then the Node Settings, you see Parallel Query listed. Click on Parallel Query and the list of nodes available for use with the Parallel Query option will be displayed, as shown in Figure 20-7. You can choose to enable all of the nodes to use parallel query or just specific nodes. You can also set a default degree of parallelism to use for all nodes or you can customize the degree of parallelism for each node type.

The default degree of parallelism is 1.

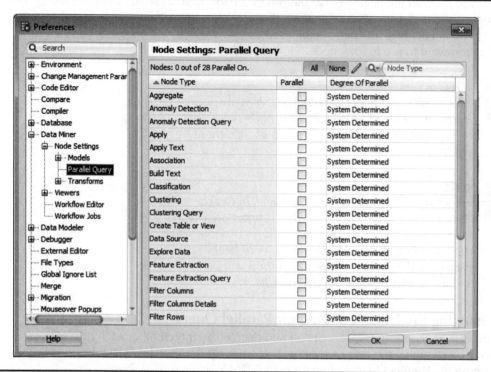

FIGURE 20-7. *Default settings for the Parallel Query option*

How to Run Your ODM Model in Real Time Using Parallel Query

When you want to use your Oracle Data Mining model in real time on one record or a set of records, you use the PREDICTION and PREDICTION_PROBABILITY function. The following example shows how a classification model (which was built in Chapter 15) is being applied to some data in a view called MINING_DATA_APPLY_V:

```
column prob format 99.99999
SELECT cust_id,
       PREDICTION(DEMO_CLASS_DT_MODEL USING *)  Pred,
       PREDICTION_PROBABILITY(DEMO_CLASS_DT_MODEL USING *) Prob
FROM   mining_data_apply_v
WHERE  rownum <= 18
/
```

```
    CUST_ID        PRED      PROB
---------- ---------- ---------
    100574         0    .63415
    100577         1    .73663
    100586         0    .95219
    100593         0    .60061
    100598         0    .95219
    100599         0    .95219
    100601         1    .73663
    100603         0    .95219
    100612         1    .73663
    100619         0    .95219
    100621         1    .73663
    100626         1    .73663
    100627         0    .95219
    100628         0    .95219
    100633         1    .73663
    100640         0    .95219
    100648         1    .73663
    100650         0    .60061
```

If the volume of data warrants the use of the Parallel Query option, then you can add the necessary hint to the preceding query, as illustrated in the following example:

```
SELECT /*+ PARALLEL(mining_data_apply_v, 4) */
       cust_id,
       PREDICTION(DEMO_CLASS_DT_MODEL USING *)  Pred,
       PREDICTION_PROBABILITY(DEMO_CLASS_DT_MODEL USING *) Prob
FROM   mining_data_apply_v
WHERE  rownum <= 18
/
```

If you turn on autotrace, you see that Parallel Query was used. Because of this, you should now be able to use your Oracle Data Mining models to work on a very large number of records, and by adjusting the degree of parallelism, you can see varying degrees of improvement.

How to Run Your ODM Model in Batch Mode Using Parallel Query

When you want to perform some batch scoring of your data using your Oracle Data Mining model, you need to use the APPLY procedure that is part of the DBMS_DATA_MINING package. But the problem with using a procedure or function is that you cannot give it a hint to tell it to use the Parallel Query option. So unless you have the tables(s) set up with Parallel Query and/or set up the session to use Parallel Query, you cannot run your Oracle Data Mining model with Parallel Query using the APPLY procedure.

To run a function or a procedure in parallel you must use the DBMS_PARALLEL_
EXECUTE package. The following steps walk you through what you need to do to use
the DMBS_PARALLEL_EXECUTE package to run your Oracle Data Mining models
in parallel.

The first step required is for you to put the DBMS_DATA_MINING.APPLY code
into a stored procedure. The following code shows how DEMO_CLASS_DT_MODEL
can be used by the APPLY procedure and how all of this can be incorporated into a
stored procedure called SCORE_DATA:

```
CREATE or REPLACE PROCEDURE score_data
is
BEGIN

    dbms_data_mining.apply(
    model_name              => 'DEMO_CLASS_DT_MODEL',
    data_table_name         => 'NEW_DATA_TO_SCORE',
    case_id_column_name     => 'CUST_ID',
    result_table_name       => 'NEW_DATA_SCORED');
END;
/
```

Next you need to create a parallel task for the DBMS_PARALLEL_EXECUTE
package. In the following example, this task is called ODM_SCORE_DATA:

```
BEGIN
  -- Create the TASK
  DBMS_PARALLEL_EXECUTE.CREATE_TASK ('ODM_SCORE_DATA');
END;
/
```

Next you need to define the parallel workload chunk details, as shown in the
following code:

```
BEGIN
    -- Chunk the table by ROWID
    DBMS_PARALLEL_EXECUTE.CREATE_CHUNKS_BY_ROWID('ODM_SCORE_DATA',
        'DMUSER', 'NEW_DATA_TO_SCORE', true, 100);
END;
/
```

The scheduled jobs process an unassigned workload chunk and then move on to
the next unassigned chunk.

Now you are ready to execute the stored procedure for your Oracle Data Mining model with a degree of parallelism of 10:

```
DECLARE
    l_sql_stmt    varchar2(200);
BEGIN
    -- Execute the DML in parallel
    l_sql_stmt := 'begin score_data(); end;';

    DBMS_PARALLEL_EXECUTE.RUN_TASK('ODM_SCORE_DATA', l_sql_stmt,
                                    DBMS_SQL.NATIVE,
                                    parallel_level => 10);
END;
/
```

When everything is finished, you can then clean up and remove the task using the following code:

```
BEGIN
    dbms_parallel_execute.drop_task('ODM_SCORE_DATA');
END;
/
```

NOTE
The schema that runs the preceding code must have the necessary privileges to run DBMS_SCHEDULER, as in the following example:
`grant create job to dmuser;`

Predictive Queries

Predictive Queries is a new feature that came with the Oracle 12c Database. When using the Oracle Data Miner tool in SQL Developer, the Predictive Queries nodes become visible only if SQL Developer detects that it is running against an Oracle 12c Database.

Predictive Queries (PQ) allows you to build a query that incorporates the dynamic building and scoring of data. A PQ builds a model based on the data that exists and then uses this model to score or label the same data set. The data mining model produced and all associated objects in the database do not exist after the query has been run.

TIP
You may not find the term "Predictive Queries" in the Oracle 12c documentation. Instead, the documentation may refer to the feature as "Dynamic Scoring." The documentation will be updated at some stage to reflect the new name.

Using Predictive Queries is very similar to using the PREDICT procedure in the DMBS_PREDICTIVE_ANALYTICS PL/SQL package, except that instead of using PL/SQL, Predictive Queries uses SQL.

Predictive Queries enable you to build and score data quickly using the in-database data mining algorithms, without the complexity of needing to understand the required settings and fine-tuning of the models. Another advantage of using Predictive Queries is that you can partition the data so that the models built can be specific to each partition. The use of partitions also allows you to use the Parallel Query option in your Predictive Queries to speed up the process of scoring the data.

Scoring using Predictive Queries nodes, however, has limitations. The transient models created during predictive query execution are not available for inspection or fine-tuning. If it is necessary to inspect the model, correlate scoring results with the model, specify special algorithm settings, or execute multiple scoring queries that use the same model, you must create a predefined model.

There are two ways you can go about creating your predictive queries. The first option is to write a SQL statement to prompt the database to use the in-database data mining algorithms. The second (and much easier) option is to use the Predictive Queries nodes in the Oracle Data Miner tool.

The following example illustrates the use of Predictive Queries to build a model using a data source and then to score the data source. The data source being used is MINING_DATA_BUILD_V. The target attribute that you want the predictive query to make a prediction about is the AFFINITY_CARD attribute. The sample code that follows displays a subset of the results that shows the actual value of AFFINITY_CARD and the predicted value using Predictive Queries.

The sample code has a PARTITION BY clause that is used to indicate how many predictive queries should be generated. In this example code, the PARTITION BY is the CUST_GENDER attribute. The database then generates a separate data mining model for each value that this attribute contains and then applies this separate data mining model to the records that match the PARTITION BY condition.

```
SELECT cust_id, affinity_card, pred_affinity_card
FROM (SELECT cust_id,
             affinity_card,
             PREDICTION(FOR to_char(affinity_card) USING *)
                OVER (PARTITION BY "CUST_GENDER") pred_affinity_card
             FROM mining_data_build_v)
WHERE rownum <= 15;

   CUST_ID AFFINITY_CARD PRED_AFFINITY_CARD
---------- ------------- ------------------
    102610             0 0
    102621             0 0
    102627             0 0
    102638             0 0
    102640             0 0
    102649             0 0
```

```
101864              0 1
101885              1 1
101912              1 1
101924              1 1
101925              0 0
101934              0 0
101944              0 0
101946              1 1
101949              0 0
```

As this is a sample of the possible output; if you run the same query against the same data set, your results might return a slightly different set of records. If you run the query a second time, then you might get a different set of records, and so on.

If you choose not to use the PARTITION BY clause and allow the predictive query to generate one data mining model for all the data, then you could leave the OVER section of the statement blank, as illustrated in the following code:

```
SELECT cust_id, affinity_card, pred_affinity_card
FROM   (SELECT cust_id,
               affinity_card,
               PREDICTION(FOR to_char(affinity_card) USING *) OVER ()
                 pred_affinity_card
        FROM   mining_data_build_v)
WHERE rownum <= 15;
```

TIP
For a classification type of problem where you have an attribute that indicates a particular outcome, such as whether or not the customer takes up the offer, and you define this attribute as a number, you need to use TO_CHAR with this attribute to convert it into a categorical value. Predictive Queries then treats your problem as a typical classification problem. If you don't use TO_CHAR with the number attribute, then Predictive Queries treats the data as a regression data mining problem.

To create Predictive Queries in the Oracle Data Miner tool, you need to create or open an existing Oracle Data Miner worksheet. The Oracle Data Miner tool checks to see what database version you are using. If it detects an Oracle 12c Database, the Predictive Queries section appears as part of the Components Workflow Editor, as shown in Figure 20-8. There are four template Predictive Queries nodes that allow you to perform queries for classification, regression (both can be done using the Prediction Queries node), anomaly detection, clustering, and feature extraction.

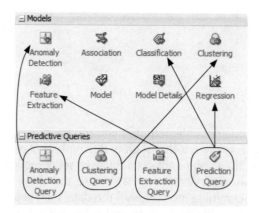

FIGURE 20-8. *Predictive Queries in the Oracle Data Miner tool*

The Predictive Queries node allows you to create a classification or a regression model for your predictive query. The reminder of this section walks you through the steps of setting up a predictive query that performs the same as the SQL code version that was given earlier in this section.

The first step is to define your data source. To do this, select the Data Source node from the Data section of the Components Workflow Editor. Then click on your new or existing worksheet. A node is created where you can select `MINING_DATA_BUILD_V` from the list of available tables and views. To create the Predictive Queries node on your worksheet, select this node from the Predictive Queries section of the Components Workflow Editor, then click again on the worksheet near the Data Source node. You now need to define the connection or link between these two nodes by right-clicking on the Data Source node, then selecting Connect from the menu. Then move your mouse over to the Predictive Queries node and click again. An arrow connection line appears on your worksheet. You are now ready to define the Predictive Queries properties.

To edit the Predictive Queries properties and to define what type of predictive query to perform, you will need to double-click on the Predictive Queries node. The Edit Prediction Query Node window opens. This window contains four tabs, which are explained in the following paragraphs.

The Predictions tab allows you to define the Case ID if one exists for your data set, and the target attributes that you want the predictive query to be based on and to predict. Using the sample predictive query given previously in SQL, you want to set the `CASE_ID` to `CUST_ID`. To define the attribute or attributes you want to predict, click on the green plus sign above the Targets section of the window. A window opens that lists the attributes for the data source. Select the attribute or attributes you want to predict. For this example, you can select the AFFINITY_CARD attribute, then click on the OK button to close the window. The AFFINITY_CARD attribute now appears in the Targets section of the window. To tell Oracle what type of data mining to perform, you may need to change the mining type for the Target attribute. For this example, you want classification to be performed. To ensure that this happens, you need to change the Mining Type to Categorical (and click OK for the warning message). If the mining type was left as numerical, then a regression model is created.

The next step you need to perform is to define what predictions you want created for this target attribute. By default, Prediction, Prediction Details, and Prediction Probabilities attributes are created. To match the output from the SQL Predictive Queries example, you can select the Prediction Details and Prediction Probabilities (in the Prediction Outputs section of the window), and then click on the red *X* to remove them. Figure 20-9 shows the setting of the Predictions tab.

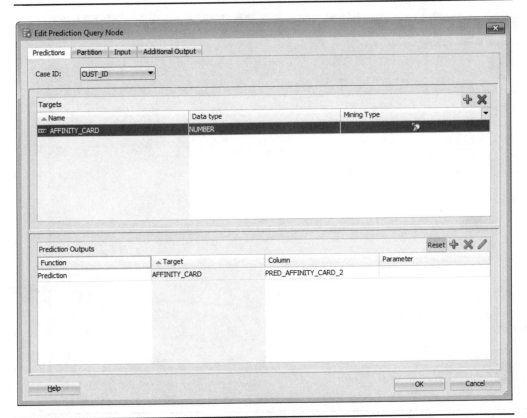

FIGURE 20-9. *Predictions tab for the Predictive Queries node*

The Partition tab allows you to define what partitions you want applied to the model build and scoring processes. If a partition is applied, then the Oracle Database creates a separate model for each value of the partition attribute(s). These separate models are then applied to the data set to score it based on the values of the partition. In the SQL example, a partition was created based on the customer gender (CUST_GENDER). To create this partition, click on the green plus sign on the Partition tab. Select the CUST_GENDER attribute from the list, then click on the OK button to finish. The Partition tab is updated to contain this attribute, as illustrated in Figure 2-10.

The Input tab allows you to define what attributes you want the data mining algorithm to use to build the data mining model. By default, all the attributes are selected as inputs to building the data mining model. If there are any attributes you think should be removed as inputs, you can remove them by deselecting the

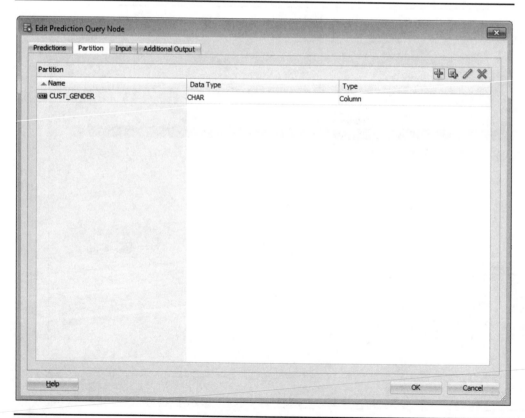

FIGURE 20-10. *Partition tab for the Predictive Queries node*

Determine Input Automatically check box. You can then click on an attribute and remove it from the list.

The Additional Output tab allows you to define what attributes will be displayed by the predictive query. By default, the attribute set as the CASE_ID, the defined target attribute, and any partition attributes are included in the output. In addition to these, the predicted attributes that were defined in the Predictions tab are also outputted.

When you have defined all the Predictive Queries properties, you can close the window. To run the Predictive Queries node, you can right-click on the node, then select Run from the menu. When the Predictive Queries node is finished, a small green tick mark appears at the top right-hand corner of the node. To view the results that were generated by the node, you can right-click the Predictive Queries node, then select View Data from the menu. A new window opens that displays the results, as illustrated in Figure 20-11.

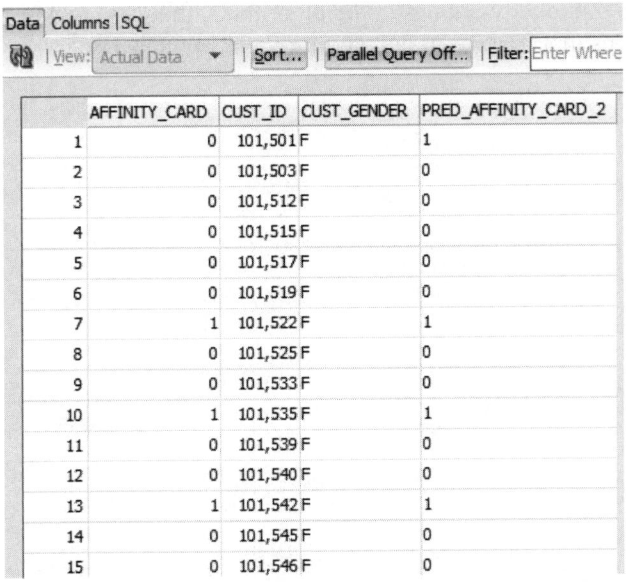

	AFFINITY_CARD	CUST_ID	CUST_GENDER	PRED_AFFINITY_CARD_2
1	0	101,501	F	1
2	0	101,503	F	0
3	0	101,512	F	0
4	0	101,515	F	0
5	0	101,517	F	0
6	0	101,519	F	0
7	1	101,522	F	1
8	0	101,525	F	0
9	0	101,533	F	0
10	1	101,535	F	1
11	0	101,539	F	0
12	0	101,540	F	0
13	1	101,542	F	1
14	0	101,545	F	0
15	0	101,546	F	0

FIGURE 20-11. *Results from running the Predictive Queries node*

Summary

The Oracle Data Mining models that you create are objects in the database. This allows you to use them similarly to how you use most of the other functions that exist in the database. Examples were given in previous chapters of how to use these data mining models to apply to new data in batch and real-time modes. In this chapter, examples were given of how you can include your ODM models in OBI dashboards. This approach could be used to include the models in other front-end applications. As the volume of your data increases, you may need to look to use the Parallel Query option for the Oracle Database. Examples were given of how you can use the parallel database features in the Oracle Data Miner tool using the SQL and PL/SQL functions. Although not all the Oracle data mining algorithms support the Parallel Query option, you will find over time that more algorithms will be enabled for this. The final part of this chapter looked at Predictive Queries. This feature allows you to build models on the fly, using them to score your data. All the data mining models and associated objects exist only during the execution of the predictive query. Predictive Queries are a simple approach to data mining. When you want to delve into the inner workings of the algorithms, then you will need to use the ODM algorithms that have been detailed throughout the book.

Index

A

Q

Join the Largest Tech Community in the World

 Download the latest software, tools, and developer templates

 Get exclusive access to hands-on trainings and workshops

 Grow your professional network through the Oracle ACE Program

 Publish your technical articles – and get paid to share your expertise

Join the Oracle Technology Network
Membership is free. Visit oracle.com/technetwork

🐦 @OracleOTN f facebook.com/OracleTechnologyNetwork

Reach More than 700,000 Oracle Customers with Oracle Publishing Group

Connect with the Audience that Matters Most to Your Business

Oracle Magazine
The Largest IT Publication in the World
Circulation: 550,000
Audience: IT Managers, DBAs, Programmers, and Developers

Profit
Business Insight for Enterprise-Class Business Leaders to Help Them Build a Better Business Using Oracle Technology
Circulation: 100,000
Audience: Top Executives and Line of Business Managers

Java Magazine
The Essential Source on Java Technology, the Java Programming Language, and Java-Based Applications
Circulation: 125,000 and Growing Steady
Audience: Corporate and Independent Java Developers, Programmers, and Architects

For more information or to sign up for a FREE subscription:
Scan the QR code to visit Oracle Publishing online.